VICTIMOLOGY

VICTIMOLOGY

A CLOSER LOOK AT CRIME VICTIMIZATION

First Edition

Edited by Aida Y. Hass-Wisecup, Ph.D.

Missouri State University

cognella®

SAN DIEGO

Bassim Hamadeh, CEO and Publisher
Angela Schultz, Senior Field Acquisitions Editor
Alisa Munoz, Project Editor
Abbey Hastings, Production Editor
Abbie Goveia, Graphic Design Assistant
Greg Isales, Licensing Associate
Natalie Piccotti, Director of Marketing
Kassie Graves, Vice President of Editorial
Jamie Giganti, Director of Academic Publishing

Cover image copyright © 2012 Depositphotos/jamesgroup.

Printed in the United States of America.

3970 Sorrento Valley Blvd., Ste. 500, San Diego, CA 92121

CONTENTS

INTRODUCTION

This reader is designed to give students a more comprehensive overview of the study of crime victimization within the context of justice, law, and society. The readings provided will allow you to explore the historical development of the field of victimology; emerging trends in criminal justice response to crime victimization; as well as the various issues and dilemmas involved in the study of the relationships among crime, criminal offending, and victimization. We will use specific case profiles as well as provide examples of principles and theories of crime victimization from multiple perspectives. Our goal will be to approach the field of victimology from a critical perspective, paying particular attention to the social, economic, and political context in which crime takes place and how these contexts influence the responses to crime victimization and the variety of victims of crime.

Historical Overview of Victimology

Introduction

The term "victim" conjures up many images in our society, most of which focus on an action that is perpetrated by an individual that results in a harm against another. Within the context of criminal justice, the role of victim has come to incorporate all individuals who experience an injury, loss, or hardship that is the result of the illegal actions of another. Throughout the years, the field of victimology has emerged to embrace a comprehensive, scientific understanding of the relationship between victims, offenders, agents of criminal justice, and society in general. The context of crime, the legal definition of criminal actions, as well as the sociocultural context are all components of influence that shape our understanding of victimization and its connection to the larger structure of society. The relevance and timeliness of this discipline is connected to its impact on the discipline of criminology as a whole, shaping our course of inquiry into the causes of crime, philosophical approaches and attitudes toward punishment, and the development of programmatic methods of intervention and prevention.

The selection presented in this chapter examines the development of the various typologies of crime victims that have emerged to sculpt our definition and understanding of victims of crime. The role of a multidisciplinary approach to the understanding of victimization is examined, as well as the legal impact of emerging trends in the perception and definition of victims of crime. This reading expands our understanding of the field of victimology by outlining various victim typologies and the role that is played by historical experiences, social problems, and political climate in impacting the study of crime victimization.

Guiding Questions

As you read, consider the following questions:

1   What do you see as the most integral component in developing a typology of crime victims?

2   If you were a lobbyist advocating for the development of programs addressing the needs of crime victims, what arguments would you make?

3   How is the study of crime victims relevant to the field of criminology?

4   Is there such a thing as mutual victimization? How does this concept affect the perception of victims of crime?

Key Terms

mutual victimization   Victimization that occurs when both the victim and the offender share in the experience through consent and participation in the crime.

primary victimization   The direct harm that is experienced by a victim of a crime.

secondary victimization   When the harm of a crime extends to other individuals or organizations that are not the direct victims of the crime.

tertiary victimization   The wrong experienced by society in general or a community as a whole from the crime.

typology   Classification developed by taking a set of existing subjects who fit the characteristics of a phenomenon, and further arranging them into subcategories.

The Concept of Victim in Crime Studies

Marilyn D. McShane and Traqina Q. Emeka

Introduction

Who Gets to Be a Victim?

A young woman in Texas is charged with second-degree murder in a case where two gangs were fighting in a park. In a startling ruling, the judge accepted a motion from her defense and agreed that the murdered youth who died as a result of a wound she inflicted, would not be referred to as a "victim" in the trial. Many seasoned lawyers were taken aback by the decision. Historically, the dead person got to be the victim. Perhaps the lack of a "victim" in this murder case, or the fact that the deceased was a gang member influenced the final outcome, a hung jury at trial and a subsequent plea agreement to a two-year term of probation for aggravated assault with a deadly weapon (Rogers, 2009). In another case, the founder of an Islamic-oriented television station in Buffalo, New York defended his actions in beheading his wife by claiming that she had abused him for years. The district attorney refuted the idea that the 45-year-old suspect was a victim and simply stated "He chopped her head off. That's all I have to say about Mr. Hassan's apparent defense that he was a battered spouse." (*Associated Press*, January 23, 2010)

Today, we can argue that the concept of victim has been expanded to include all types of civil and criminal wrongs from birth to death that can give a person the status of victim. As social values and attitudes about crime change, as we develop more new crimes and crime areas, the range of victims appears to continue to grow. Some even argue that we have too many victims. Based on an assumption of limited resources and the negative effects of having too large a pool of "victims" on our social conscience, should we restrict our consideration of who is truly a victim and who is perhaps less "deserving" of victim status? Should we prioritize victims by some hierarchy of blamelessness? Who are the most popular victims and why? Are there any types of victims who should be excluded? Is there too much competition for victim status in our country today?

Concerns about the potential boundaries of victimology leads us to ask several questions about the limits of what can be considered. For example, can a corpse be a victim? An animal? A town square? The answer would depend on your definition of what is a victim. Is there really any such thing as a victimless crime? What determines whether there is a victim—the law? When a Birmingham, Alabama funeral director is charged with felony abuse of a corpse, the implication seems to be that there is a victim of the abuse (Reeves, 2009) the same way there might be with a person charged with harassing wildlife, or desecrating a sacred space.

In order to determine answers to these questions we might want to know more about whether there is suffering, who is harmed, and how we go about assessing that harm. Can victimization be self-assessed? Frequently an individual will say "I am not a victim, I do not want to be considered a victim." Or, in the reverse, someone makes a claim to be a victim. They might say, despite the opinions of others, "I am the victim here." Can someone decide whether or not he or she is the victim? In the case of a person charged with desecrating a corpse, for example, who is the victim? A person who is dead cannot feel pain or experience harm and the law has been fairly consistent in its determination that a person cannot be raped if they are already deceased. Is it instead the family of the deceased who is suffering from the idea that their loved one has been violated? Is it society, who must somehow have faith in those who are entrusted with the care of our departed loved ones? In these cases, does the state represent the victim of the whole and prosecute the case in the name of the greater good of society? Perhaps by the end of this book, you will have a better idea of how we could best address these questions. One way to begin is by looking at the field of victimology in general.

The Legal and Scientific Study of Victims

As Burgess and Roberts (2010) point out, the term victim is not, by itself, a legal or scientific concept. Recognition of the role of the victim in society dates back as far as ancient civilizations. Historically, folklore and literature chronicle the complex relationships between offenders and victims and even those that occur within families such as Cain who slew his brother Able. Often these interactions symbolize the good victim triumphing over the evil offender as in David and Goliath as well as Cinderella and Snow White and their wicked archenemies.

Victims probably had the most input and influence on justice outcomes prior to the emergence of systems of law. Victims and their relatives controlled the extent of retribution and, consequently, the extent of their satisfaction with the punishment meted out to the offender. Ironically, this "most satisfied" version also yielded one of the greatest problems for those societies. Retribution created a disturbing threat of blood feuds which, ultimately, called for a more formal society intervention. Law, or the creation of a third-party interest, began the process of restricting the role of the victim. With the advent of such concepts as "the King's peace," the actual victim was no longer a principle figure in the criminal process and, in a move calculated to reinforce central authority, the state came to represent the aggrieved party in judicial proceedings. True, individual victims appeared to testify at trial or give information to the authorities in a variety of ways, but they were no longer the accusers nor did they have to bear the expense of prosecuting the accused. That role was assumed by the "official" prosecutor.

The state's historically-increasing indifference to the victim is reflected in the changing criminal justice role it assigns to them. One reflection of this indifference is found in the modification of the victim's role from a person who has been harmed in some way to the person who provides emotional credibility to the prosecution. In this fashion, the state ignores the actual harm and instead focuses on the social harm. The symbolic value of punishing the offender, exacting the price for transgressing the legal codes is the basis of retribution and deterrence. Such a process, where the victim is concerned, may lack satisfaction and reduces him or her to a secondary role. Real harm has thus been subordinated to theoretical conceptions of legal harm and the definition of a victim becomes an artificial one. Therefore, the traditional (system-oriented) definition of victim used in victimology is entirely created by law and the legal process.

While the victim is often a prominent feature in cultural identities and moral instruction, the scientific study of victims is a product of twentieth-century positivism, empiricism and the accumulation of data necessary for meaningful analysis. Until we began to collect information about victimization, we could not test theories or develop insights into this critical component of the criminal justice system. While most contemporary criminal justice programs offer a course in victimology it is also found in the fields of sociology and criminology although some theorists have argued that the substantial body of theory and research within the study area warrants its consideration as a separate discipline.

Victim Typologies

A typology is one of the more primitive forms of theory and thus is frequently used in early forms of scientific analysis. Positivistic inquiry relies on identifying and categorizing subjects into groups according to traits they share with others. A typology is an ordered and systematic classification of phenomena that best describes the characteristics of its members. A typology organizes information about a group according to some theory or rational explanation.

A typology is developed by taking a set of existing subjects, who all fit the definition of a particular phenomenon and further arranging them into subsets. For the purposes of our discussion, we are looking at theorists who said (hypothetically), "after studying all types of victims, I find that they can be sorted and labeled according to the following scheme." The premise is that if all victims can be further subdivided into a range of types, this will help us to improve methods of identifying and servicing victims. It also promises to clarify how we might prevent victimization by recognizing early patterns of behaviors and the need for potential intervention.

What you can discern from the discussion of victim typologies that follows is that the categories of victims seem to evolve over time with changes resulting from new ways of viewing social problems and new events to which individuals are exposed. Categories also seem to reflect the influence of new academic disciplines for example, psychology or forensics.

Hans von Hentig

When Hans von Hentig published his famous study *The Criminal and His Victim* in 1948, *Time* magazine even published a story about it. In the book von Hentig argued that the factors shaping the development of both criminals and victims are varied and complex, including the possibility of physical impairments and disabilities, things that may cause one to be bitter or ostracized and teased by others. In discussing victimization, von Hentig noted, much like earlier cartographers and demographers, that particular times of the day or year may produce a higher likelihood of offenses. He noted that "... *crimes of violence and sex reach their peak in late Spring; most women are murdered between 6 and 8 p.m.*" Like our contemporary social-disorganization theories, von Hentig explained that *"Some types of criminals are attracted to slum areas; so are their victims."* And, perhaps being influenced by the writings of Italian physician and early criminologist Cesare Lombroso, he attempted to classify his victims and offenders by their common traits. As the article in *Time* relates:

> Feeblemindedness, common among some types of criminals, is also common among their victims ... certain characteristics of law-abiding citizens arouse a counterreaction in the criminal. The inexperienced businessman, for example, invites embezzlement; the nagging wife is flirting with murder; the alcoholic is a natural for robbery. Thus the victim becomes the "tempter." Since society does not yet recognize the close relationship between criminal and victim ... the whole machinery of prisons, parole boards and probation is drastically out of date. Until a new theory of crime prevention is adopted, victims will go on being a self-perpetuating group, as dangerous to society as criminals (*Science*, 1948).

In his work, von Hentig discussed a typology that appears primarily sociological and seems to focus on weaknesses or demographics that might make someone more vulnerable or easily preyed upon. He divided victims into:

1   The Young
2   The Old
3   The Mentally Defective/Deranged

4   The Intoxicated

5   The Immigrant

6   Minority Group Members

7   Those with Low Intelligence

Over the years, data have consistently supported the idea that victims, as well as offenders, are disproportionately young. Though those who are older are generally more fearful of crime than their lower rates of victimization seem to justify, that fear may be linked to the seriousness of injuries, when involved in some type of physical altercation, sustained by those who are frail. In the news today, we still see evidence of the logic of von Hentig's classifications. As Barrow (2008, p. 47) explains:

> Von Hentig claims that the vulnerability of the immigrant is less a function of linguistic differences and more a result of the isolation and unfamiliarity with social norms and rules. With respect to minorities, he claims that such individuals do not enjoy the same protections from the law as do the dominant class members, thereby making it easier to victimize them. And finally, a person identified as 'dull' is seen as a perfect victim. They fall, intellectually, outside of the immunity extended to very old and very young by 'honorable thieves' (Sutherland, 1937) and are, generally, not smart enough to know they are being victimized.

Looking at von Hentig's categories, it is obvious that in some events, victims may be represented in multiple categories. A young coed partying on spring break in the islands disappears with some new-found "friends" and is murdered. In the classic Chicago School work (Shaw, 1930), the delinquent, Stanley, and his young friends prey upon old drunks in the alleys, stealing what they can with little risk of physical confrontation, an offense nicknamed "jackrolling" (thus the title of the book, *The Jackroller*).

Von Hentig also created a typology of victims that centers on psychological traits that also may be associated with criminal events. They include:

- The Depressed/Apathetic

- The Acquisitive or Greedy (eagerly enter into schemes or illegal investments)

- The Wanton or Sensual (includes prostitutes or one who uses sex as a weapon)

- The Lonesome and Heartbroken (who today may be victimized through the internet)

- The Tormentor (an abusive person is later killed or rendered unable to inflict harm)

- The Blocked (in a no-win situation, defeated and unable to escape. A good example of this is the battered woman who feels she cannot get away or be helped.)

Overall, von Hentig was instrumental in developing interest in the view of victim as a potential provocateur, someone responsible for their involvement in a crime. At the least, his work called attention to the need for legal and social–psychological analysis of the relationship between victims and offenders. If von Hentig was responsible for the creation of a penal couple (a victim and offender tied in some type of relationship), then our next contributor, Benjamin Mendelsohn would be viewed as advocating the "divorce" of the penal couple (Schafer, 1968) and a more separate view of the culpability or role of each in a criminal event.

Benjamin Mendelsohn

Mendelsohn was an attorney who surveyed his clients to develop a database about crime incidents (Schafer, 1968). Mendelsohn is often called the father of victimology, as he coined the term emphasizing it as the "reverse" of criminology. He developed a typology of six victim types. Unlike von Hentig, Mendelsohn (1956) focused primarily on the idea of blameworthiness in formulating the categories described below.

- Completely innocent victim (victim of traditional crime, no provocation or facilitation)
- Victims with minor guilt or victim due to ignorance (such as venturing into a high crime area or believing what others might consider a transparent scam)
- Victim as guilty as the offender (drug buyers and sellers who pull guns and shoot each other, suicide)
- Victim more guilty than the offender by provoking or abusing (in cases where a neighbor witnesses a burglary and shoots the suspect and public outcry condemns the dead burglar and praises the shooter)
- Most-guilty victim (causes one to use self-defense, home-invasion robber killed by home owner)
- Simulating or imaginary victim (pretends to have or falsely claims victim status)

While these categories seem to be of some "legal" consequence, they do not seem to tell us much about what motivated the behavior or what the underlying causes of a person's victimization might be.

Stephen Schafer

Twenty years after von Hentig wrote his noted work, Stephen Schafer (1968) wrote his classic rebuttal in *The Victim and His Criminal*. The shift in the title reflects a change in focus to perhaps herald the new age of the study of the victim. By putting the victim first, Schafer foreshadows the influence that a more-conservative public perspective on social justice will have on the field of criminal justice. It also reflects the prominent role that the victim will have in shaping criminal law in the next half century.

Schafer's typology included varying levels of victim responsebility:

- Unrelated victims (stranger-activated crimes, with no victim responsibility)
- Provocative victims (victim's behavior is responsible to some degree for the offender's reaction)
- Precipitative victims (make themselves vulnerable particularly by being in certain places at certain high-risk times)
- Biologically weak victims (have no responsibility in the offense such as a youth who is raped in jail)
- Socially-weak victims (like powerless minorities and immigrants who bear no fault)
- Self-victimizing victims (these are fully responsible because of their direct involvements in high-risk activities like vice, prostitution, drugs)
- Political victims (bear no responsibility as they are created by shifts in power)

Typology of Victimization

According to Decker, Shichor and O'Brien (1982), another way to approach the issue of typologies is by classifying the event of victimization itself. An example of this is found in the work of Thorsten Sellin and Marvin Wolfgang (1964) when they assessed the context of an incident by considering the role of the victim. They used *primary victimization* to refer to any direct personal harm such as a person being robbed at an ATM or assaulted by a spouse. *Secondary victimization* was used to designate a non-human victim such as an organization or business, as when a Red Cross worker steals from the organization, a cable company experiences theft from people who rewire connections to obtain free service, or riders enter a subway without purchasing tokens. In this case, consumers suffer, needy citizens may go without support and public services may be restricted by diminished revenues. *Tertiary victimization* refers to a general social harm or a wrong against society as a whole, as when a public official embezzles from the state, vandals destroy a public monument or a terrorist act undermines the feelings of safety within a nation. *Mutual victimization* involves the sharing of the offender/victim experience where there is mutual consent and participation, as in vice activities or conspiracies that backfire on one or more of the participants. This is also the case when someone dies when involved in an illegal drag race, sideswiped by a co-offender. Fifth and finally, Sellin and Wolfgang recognized the potential for an event to be resolved by the determination that *no victimization* had occurred. This is a probable outcome when it cannot be determined that anyone was victimized.

Typologies Within Specific Crimes

More recently, typologies have been developed to help organize the study of certain types of victimization. It may be that legislation, policy, programming, and services need to be more specifically focused within these broader categories of crimes in order to be more effective.

For example, Levin and McDevitt (1993) divided hate crime offenders into groups that might help us predict who victims are and to create interventions that might reduce the risk of victimization. They saw three types of motivations behind hate crime: "thrill seeking," which is usually a characteristic of teen perpetrators; "reactive hate crimes," where offenders are somehow threatened by the differences they see between themselves and the victims such as gays and lesbians; and "mission-oriented" offenders, who are more likely to be psychotic on a crusade against individuals who may be singled out for attack such as seniors in a Jewish community center.

Sapp, Holden and Wiggins (1993) also constructed a typology of hate crime on the basis of ideology. To these researchers, hate crimes are rooted in either Christian conservatism which would include the abortion doctor who was slain by a remorseless offender who testified to his belief in his actions as he was sentenced to life in prison for first degree murder; white racial supremacists such as the offenders in Jasper, Texas, who dragged James Byrd to his death behind their pickup truck; and incidents motivated by an aggressive and exaggerated sense of patriotism or survivalism. By acknowledging that hate crimes can be sponsored by a variety of circumstances, theorists can address the differences more accurately and not attempt to derive a "one-size-fits-all" type of approach. The specificity of research may lead to more practical and effective responses from the criminal justice system.

In the early 1990s, several theorists offered typologies of stalkers, a type of offender who was receiving attention from law enforcement and policymakers as a result of a number of high-profile murders. Gavin de Becker (1994) profiled four types of stalkers. First there was the mentally-ill stalker who pursued a famous person with whom there was no prior relationship. The second was a pursuit of a public figure by someone who is not otherwise identified as mentally ill and with whom the public figure has no prior relationship. The third category is the stalking of a regular citizen with whom the stalker has no prior relationship. The fourth and final category is the stalking of a regular citizen by someone with whom that person has had a prior relationship, such as a former girlfriend or roommate.

In another, somewhat more clinical, typology McAnaney, Curliss and Abeyta-Price (1993) classify four types of stalkers. There are those who display (1) erotomania and de Clerambault's syndrome or (2) borderline erotomania; (3) those who are former intimates and (4) sociopathic stalkers. Erotomania is the psychotic delusion someone may have that a famous or distinguished person, particularly someone of high status or influence, is in love with them, even from afar. The term "de Clerambault's syndrome" refers to a similar affliction, except that in this case the subject believes that the object of his or her affection actually initiated the relationship. The syndrome was named after Gaetan de Clerambault, a French psychiatrist of the early 1900s who worked with the insane and wrote one of the first papers on this subject. Today, many refer to these subjects as "obsessed fans" such as Margaret Ray who has been ar-rested many times for stalking David Letterman, often appearing at his home and claiming to be his wife. John Hinkley is frequently cited as another good example of erotomania. In 1981 Hinkley shot President Reagan and White House Press Secretary James Brady as a gesture to actress Jodie Foster, with whom he believed he was in a relationship and who wanted a sign of his devotion. Because the diagnosis is three times more common in women than in men, the psychiatric literature often refers to it as "Old Maid's Insanity." The difference appears to be, however, that men are more likely to be represented in criminal or forensic samples than women (Kelly, 2005).

Studying Victims

As the field of victimology grows its research base becomes broader, what we refer to as the "literature of the field." Many studies are specifically funded by legislation targeting victim needs, such as services for domestic-violence victims and victims of rape. Others are mandated as evaluations of criminal-justice-system policy changes such as the benefits of mandatory arrest or the use of victim-impact statements. Some look at direct effects of victimization while others study less obvious, secondary, or indirect effects such as a child witnessing violence between his or her parents at home.

How victims respond to their experiences with crime varies considerably from person to person. Research has indicated that differences in perceived levels of support from family and friends has an effect on recovery from crimes, as do different levels of involvement in the criminal justice system, particularly the prosecution. Variations in demographics may also influence whether or not victims suffer post-traumatic stress or depression subsequent to an offense or benefit from counseling and therapy. In the past, studies of particular types of victims have relied on such small sample sizes that one could not derive any meaningful generalizations from them. Only recently have larger surveys and databases made it possible to get more accurate estimates of the frequency of various types of victimization and, as a result, we have improved our ability to predict those most likely to be victimized.

For example, in a series of studies of juvenile victimization, Finkelhor and colleagues have identified a phenomenon they refer to as "poly-victims" whereby roughly one-third of all youth victims go on to be subsequently victimized within a relatively short period of time. His survey indicated that 71% of children experienced at least one victimization in the last year, and that crimes against youth are three to four times more frequent than reported to police. Older youth and males are most likely to be poly-victims (Finkelhor, 2007). Finkelhor also suggests that a more specific inquiry into what he calls "developmental victimology," or the study of issues associated with childhood exposure to certain types of risks and crimes, would be helpful in prevention and treatment efforts.

References

Associated Press (2010, January 23). Man accused of beheading wife claims abuse. *Houston Chronicle,* A18.

Barrow, L. (2008). *Criminal victimization of the deaf.* New York: LFB Scholarly.

Becker, de, G. (1994, June 29). Intervention decisions: The value of flexibility. Paper presented at the 4th Annual Threat Management Conference, Anaheim, CA.

Burgess, A. W., & Roberts, A. R. (2010) Crime and victimology. In A. W. Burgess, C. Regehr, A. R. Roberts (Eds.), *Victimology: Theories and Applications* (pp. 1–30). Boston: Jones and Bartlett.

Decker, D., Shichor, D., & Obrien, R. M. (1982). *Urban structure and victimization.* New York: Lexington Books.

Finkelhor, D. (2007). Developmental victimology. In R. Davis, A. Lurigio, & S. Herman (Eds.). *Victims of crime,* 3rd *Ed.* (pp. 9–34). Thousand Oaks, CA: Sage.

Kelly, B. (2005). Erotomania: Epidemology and management. *CNS Drugs, 19,* 8, 657–669.

Levin, J., & McDevitt, J. (1993). *The rising tide of bigotry and bloodshed.* New York: Plenum.

McAnaney, K. G., Curliss, L. A., & Abeyta-Price, C. E. (1993). From imprudence to crime: Anti-stalking laws. *Notre Dame Law Review, 68,* 819–909.

Mendelsohn, B. (1956). The victimology (in French). *Etudes Internationales de Psycho-Sociologie Criminelle, 3,* 25–26.

Reeves, J. (2009, February 26). Man allegedly let body rot in hearse. *Associated Press.*

Rogers, B. (2009, September 18). Probation cut short in fatal gang knifing. *Houston Chronicle,* B1.

Sapp, A., Holden, R., & Wiggins, M. (1993). Value and belief systems of right-wing extremists" In R. J. Kelly (Ed.), *Bias crimes: American law enforcement and legal responses.* Berkshire, UK: Office of the International Criminal Justice Administration.

Schafer. S. (1968). *The victim and his criminal: A study in functional responsibility.* New York: Random House.

Science, Go ahead, hit me. (1948, September 20). Retrieved from http://www.time.com/time/magazine/article/0,9171,799202,00.html#ixzz0cLBEggNs.

Sellin, T., & Wolfgang, M. (1964). *The measurement of delinquency.* New York: Wiley.

Shaw, C. (1930). *The jackroller.* Chicago: University of Chicago Press.

Von Hentig, H. (1948). *The criminal and his victim: Studies in the sociobiology of crime.* New Haven, CT: Yale University Press.

Chapter 1: Concluding Remarks

As we reflect on the study of victims of crime, we see the importance of victimology as a discipline in gaining a complete picture of crime through the lens of typologies that help us form a scientific understanding of the relationships among offenders, victims, and the larger framework of social structure. The role of the victim in historical context has changed over the years within the criminal justice system. This change has been due to the nature of social definition as it applies to the dynamic interplay between perception and reaction to crime victimization and the relational interconnection between offenders and their victims. Attempts to identify various characteristics of victims have played an integral role in addressing the needs of victims of crime by the criminal justice system, evaluating the role of social services in meeting those needs, and raising awareness for the rights of individuals impacted by criminal behavior.

Challenges Facing the Study of Crime Victimization

Introduction

A comprehensive presentation of the field of victimology would not be complete without consideration of the global nature and complexity of crime victimization from an international perspective. From an academic standpoint, this encompasses an analysis of the many facets of victimology as an international discipline that explores the diverse nature of victim-related issues in a comparative context. This focus can serve to address the challenges in policy application presented by the variable definition of "crime victimization"; the philosophical, cultural, and legal definition of crime victims; as well as the practical and theoretical mechanisms of intervention, treatment, and restoration of victims of crime.

The reading in this chapter provides us with an overview of the field of victimology in global perspective. The author explains the study of crime victimization as a discipline that has become of international interest in recent years, with research on the subject generating worldwide attention with regard to the various components of crime victimization, including the definition of "victim," the treatment of victims in court proceedings, the expansion of victim rights and services, as well as the development of uniform protocols for addressing victim needs. A focus and emphasis on national- and comparative-level research is suggested in order to better advocate for a victim-centered approach in addressing criminal behavior and meeting the needs of victims of crime through a proactive application of principles and practices of restorative justice as a dynamic intervention within criminal justice systems around the world.

Guiding Questions

As you read, consider the following questions:

1   How has victimology become an international discipline?

2   Why is there a need to explore crime victimization from a global perspective?

3   What is the role of criminal justice research in advancing protocols dealing with the victimization of crime?

4   Can international cooperation among governments and criminal justice agencies help address the various issues involving crime victims?

Key Terms

comparative victimology   The analysis of issues pertaining to victims of crime, including victim rights and services, victim advocacy, victim behavior patterns, and victim treatment by courts, from a global standpoint to include variations in cultures and societies.

International Criminal Court   Located in the Netherlands, this court has international jurisdiction through its intergovernmental organization and international tribunal to prosecute cases involving international crimes such as war crimes, genocide, and crimes against humanity.

Office for Victims of Crime   A U.S. Department of Justice agency established in 1988 as part of the Victims of Crime Act to assist crime victims by providing national research support, leadership in victim advocacy, and funding to victims of crime.

World Society of Victimology   An international agency affiliated with the United Nations and the Council of Europe that coordinates international service providers for victims of crime, global research on the topic of victimization, government-sponsored support, and international representation from multiple disciplines and areas of expertise in the advancement of victim support rights and services.

Future Challenges of International Victimology

Michaela Lehner-Zimmerer

I. Introduction

Victimology Has Become an International Discipline

In terms of the sheer amount and geographic scope of the victimological research that has been produced over recent years, it would readily appear that victimology has become truly international. Appearances, however, can be deceiving. Progress has been made, but far more comparative work is needed. In the brief span of less than three decades, victimology has evolved from a subject studied by a few scattered researchers to one that generates world-wide interest. The work of the World Society of victimology (WSV), beginning with the first years under the presidency of Hans Joachim Schneider, serves as a clear indicator of this expansion. The first symposia organized by the WSV brought together vicitimologists from a very few countries.

The most recent symposium in Amsterdam (1997) was attended by over 600 victimologists from 67 countries, both record numbers. At earlier national and international conferences, the "hard science" of victimology appeared to consist of empirical research on victims of crime, and in particular on differential victimization, on victim-offender interaction and on the impact of victimization. The victimologists discussing this research came almost invariably from Western Europe, North America, Australia, New Zealand and Japan. When victimologists from developing countries or countries in transition attended such conferences, their papers usually dealt with theory, pure description, or abuse of power and sometimes all trees. Today, this no longer appears to be case.

The best illustration of the spread of the "hard science" of victimology is the international crime victim survey, which by 1997 covers almost 60 countries, including most recently Albania, Belarus, Bolivia, Botswana, Bulgaria, China, Croatia, the Federal Republic of Yugoslavia, the Former Yogoslaw Republic of Macedonia, Kyrgystan, Latvia, Lithania, Mongolia, Paraguay, Romania, Ukraine and Zimbabwe (Van Dijk, Jan J.M, Pat Mayhew, Experiences in Crime across the World, 1990). This push towards developing victimology on the international level can also be seen in literature. At the beginning of the 1990s, the Max Planck Institute of Foreign und International Criminal Law produced four thick volumes from studies around the world. The international coverage of victimology has fostered the creation of national societies of victimology in both developing and developed countries. The United Nations General Assembly, in its 1985 resolution adopted the "Declaration" of Basic Principles of Justice for Victims of Crime and Abuse of Power", recommended that collaborative research be conducted at the interregional and regional levels on ways in which victimization can be reduced and victims aided, and that the exchange of information be promoted as an effective means of so doing.

Despite the efforts of a few scholars, and with the notable exception of the support that the Dutch Government and the United Nations have provided to the second and third sweeps of the international victimization survey (which specifically brought in a number of developing countries and countries in transition), it would seem that this call for international cooperation in research has met with little interest. While the changes in law and practice as a result, victimological research elsewhere is only slowly emerging, and examples of international cooperation remain few and far between (Elias (1993), (Critical Criminology) argues on the basis on the experience in the United States that these changes have to a large extent remained cosmetic. It is true that little evaluative research has been done on the reforms. However, it would seem that at least in Europe, for example the work of victim support groups in a number of countries, guidelines issued to police and prosecutors, and State compensation schemas—even if they have not necessarily always been implemented as originally envisaged—have benefitted a great number of victims.

II. International Protocols

1. International Protocols, with Special Reference to the European Union Framework Decision on the Standing of Victims in Criminal Proceedings

The victim is the forgotten party in the criminal justice system. It would be factually wrong if this type of criticism would still be maintained today. It is generally known that criminal justice systems around the world feature vast differences. They vary from strictly adversarial systems in Anglo-Saxon countries to more inquisitorial jurisdictions on the mainland of the European

Union. No matter the incompatibilities between the various systems, nowadays they have one thing in common—they all share the ambition of reform on behalf of victims of crime. The roots of these reformist efforts can be traced to the final quarter of the 20th century.

In 1985, virtually simultaneously, to powerful documents were issued urging the international community to enhance the status of victims. The first one of these was the United Nations Declaration of basic Principles of Justice for Victims of Crime and Abuse of Power (A/res/40/34, adopted by the General Assembly in 1985). The second one was the council of Europe's Recommendation on the Position of the Victim in the Framework of Criminal Law and Procedure (R (85)11, also adopted in 1985). Although differences in language and in details cannot be overlooked, the contents of the Declaration and the Recommendation are to a large extent overlapping and have subsequently been echoed and expanded on in other international protocols of a similar nature (e.g. Statement of Victims' Rights in the Process of Criminal Justice, issued by the European Forum for Victim Services in 1996). The European Forum for Victim Services (EFVS) is an umbrella organization comprising as members the existing national (voluntary) victim support organizations throughout Europe.

It follows that statutory organizations with similar objectives are not eligible for full membership, and ultimately the European Union Framework Decision on the Standing of Victims in Criminal Proceedings Council Framework Decision of 15 march 2001. It is impossible—as it is unnecessary—to give a detailed account of all the articles (with the inevitably attached specifications, conditions and exceptions) contained on these main or general bill of rights for victims).

2. Conclusion and Evaluation

This conclusion is, however, as robust as it is fair. The preceding paragraphs have made it abundantly clear that similar remarks apply equally to the other member states of the European Union. The lessons to be drawn from this episode are the need to re-examine the basic conditions or requirements for effective implementation of (inter)national protocols on victim's rights. Self-evident as it may seen, as a preliminary we need accurate information. Even though this precondition borders on the obvious, it is a sad truth that reliable data is more often than not completely absent. It is here that the academic discipline of victimology has an important role to play in the future. Victimology could and should greatly enhance the relevance of international protocols and victim's rights.

Lawmakers and those responsible for shaping and executing policy can only hope to achieve real progress when their actions are closely monitored by independent and critical researchers. This type of evaluation should be organized on a systematic basis, which will usually have to include in-depth studies stretched over a long period of time. One-shot questionnaires are, as a rule, insufficient to yield the kind of knowledge required for the present purposes. This was made painfully clear by the virtual absence of critical follow-up research in the aftermath of the 1985 United Nations Declaration; yet similar deficiencies are now visible in the European Union in connection with the Framework Decision.

Admittedly there are several projects in place and running, but not all of these appear to be well designed and methodologically sound (Studies like Wergens (1999) are based on information supplied by people unknown to the researcher. The reliability and validity of the data can thus not be checked by the researcher, and hence these projects produce inadequate tools for policy formation or adjustment). The community of victimologists should take up this challenge and fill the gaps in existing sets of available data. They can build on results of previously published, evidence-based research. Existing studies have releaved that effective reform can only be achieved if there is comprehensive strategy which provides coherence to the various specific measures to be taken. From those perspectives, several critical variables for success or failure have been identified. Without attempting to be exhaustive, a number of prominent ones will the highlighted.

a) Probably more important than the content of the legal rules is the attitude of the officials who come into contact with the victims. This may be particularly relevant for the police (Wemmers, 1996:112, in Victims of Crime in 22 European Criminal Justice Systems). Considering the very high attrition rate in every jurisdiction, most victims will never get beyond the stage of reporting the crime. For this majority, the satisfaction with the criminal justice system will largely depend on the way they have been treated by the police. Police performance in this respect can only be acceptable if the officers radiate a spirit of empathy or then they execute their job on the basis of the conviction that decent treatment of victim's crime and catching criminals.

b) No matter how important the attitude factor may be, it has to be recognised that good intentions alone do not suffice. The right mindset has been backed up by basic knowledge on victims' issues. This requires training of police, prosecutors and judges. Many countries have been able to secure mandatory training modules for police officials and prosecutors.

Experience has shown that is much more difficult in persuade the judiciary to accept compulsory courses in this area. Quite often representatives of the courts have invoked their right to independence as an argument to refuse this type of training. Victim support organizations have frequently countered this argument by stating that the right to independence does not include the right to ignorance or the right to arrogance. Of course when this kind of language is exchanged, the debate is not likely to be productive. It is much more useful to look at examples of best practice. In the United Kingdom a project started on "judicial studies". This new label proved to be helpful in bypassing the initial reluctance to engage in mandatory "training". Another example is the "Judicial Education Project", organized by the Office for Victims of Crime in the United States. The goal of this project is to develop a curriculum to provide judges and court personnel with initial and continuing education about the laws concerning victims' rights, the impact on victims and their families, and how the judiciary can comply with victims' rights laws without infringing on defendants' rights.

- Taking care of legitimate victims' rights and interests is an additional responsibility for the authoritites. Since the agencies operating the criminal justice system have never been over funded or overstaffed, it is obvious that this relatively new obligation can only be executed properly when adequate resources are provided. Simply stated, this basic condition turns out to be hard to meet. Even in the most affluent societies, it is increasingly difficult to earnmark funds for this purpose. In the long run, this might jeopardize the viability of any reform project on behalf of victims of crime (According to the Phare Report (2002:59) "The accession states guarantee the viability of properly accredited victim service organizations by apportioning 1% of their criminal justice budgets to the third sector, having regard for the need for a comprehensive pattern of service delivery". This author doubts whether this level of funding is available in more than a tiny fraction of even the first world countries).

    c) Effective implantation of (inter)national protocols requires close cooperation between all the stakeholders. Government agencies from different departments (justice, public health) the police, the prosecution service, the judiciary, probation, victim support and welfare agencies should all be represented as partners in a network. The network should serve as a platform to exchange information and to smooth out problems.

    d) On top of that, strong leadership is essential for success. Two elements may be highlighted here. One is hat in every country, designated senior officials in the relevant ministries and criminal justice agencies should be charged with the express responsibility of identifying and promoting policies and programmes for victims of crime (Phare Report, 2002:57). The second is that the service-providing organizations should act as "problem owners" by permanently appealing to the government when discrepancies between law in the books and the law in action have been discovered.

3. New Horizons in Victimology—Reflections on International Development

The exposition on international protocols has uncovered some good news and some bad news. The bad news is that reforme measures on behalf of victims of crime cannot be taken at these measures do not always aspire to actual improvements of their legal system. Sometimes exposing hidden agendas of national representatives charged with negotiation the international agreements can prove this. In other instances this is evidenced by the fact that national governments are satisfied by the mere existence of legal provisions, without bothering to check whether or not these rules have any significant practical impact.

Finally, there is the danger that promoting victim's rights is just a fashion of the day. The topic is so popular that no politician or other segment of society could credibly oppose it. This very fact, however, also contains a twofold risk, namely that victims could be replaced by another target group which is suddenly embraced as the next "sexy" issue and, since everybody is (superficially) in favour of expanding victim's rights, it may be hard to sustain a sense of problem ownership and genuine commitment in the ranks of the powerful decision makers. There is also lots of good news.

There is no way of denying that the international protocols have sensitised national communities that something had be done to emancipate victims of crime. Consequently, many jurisdictions have brought about more improvements in this area during the last 25 years than during the preeceding century. The standards contained in the protocols show progressive insight into the nature of criminal victimisation and how to reduce the resulting adverse effects. Article of the European Union Framework Decicion reads "Every Member States shall support the progressive creation, in respect of proceedings in general, and in particular in venues where criminal proceedings may be initiated, of the necessary conditions for attempting to prevent secondary victimization and avoiding placing victims under unnecessary pressure (Helen Reeves CBE (vice-president of the word society of Victimology and chief executive of the World Society of Victimology and chief executive of Victim Support United Kingdom). This is the first time in history that a legally binding document expressly acknowledges that criminal procedures can actually lead to secondary victimization.

The existence of international protocols has further led to one specific obligation with a particularly positive symbolic value, namely the inclusion in national codes of criminal procedure of separate chapters listing victims' rights. This kind of legislative technique reflects the statutory recognition of the victim as one of the main "participant" is carefully used in this context; it indicates that the victim is involved in the procedure to an extent like few others, without necessarily the capacity of a party.

Experience with international protocols has also furnished domestic authorities with knowledge on the do's and don'ts for effective implementation. A government which takes victims' rights seriously must be aware that it needs a comprehense strategy to achieve its ends. Part of that strategy must be to appoint senior officials in the relevant ministries charged with express responsibility for policies and programmes for the implementation of victims' rights. South Africa and the international experience taught us that it is extremely difficult to be successful in this area when victim care is regarded as an issue of public health and/or welfare. Victims' rights and victim care are basically issues of administering justice. Consequently, the justice department should accept primary responsibility for this policy area, or face the risk of jeopardizing the entire enterprise.

The observation of international protocols is directly related to the main trends and developments. The relationship between restorative justice and the traditional criminal system cannot be envisaged how restorative justice could survive as a genuine alternative paradigm; the real question shall turn out to be how to institutionalize restorative justice elements in the currently existing systems. Evidence-based knowledge on implementation issues will then be valuable to the point to being indispensable. As far as the threat of terrorism is concerned, experience with international protocols has shown that quick legislative responses, inspired by the spur of the moment, are usually not the cleverest ones. Two big dangers are then likely to materialize. One is that the new statutory provisions raise hopes and expectations, which will be dashed shortly after. This is a well-known cause of secondary victimization.

The other hazard is that the incident-driven measures may have unforeseen negative side effect, which can even outweigh their potential benefits. The International Criminal Court and the other international tribunals have been presented as examples of best practice in the historical development of victim care. The link with the subject matter of the section on international protocols is obvious. National governments would be wise to study the provisions in the International Criminal Court Statute and appended Rules of Evidence and Procedure and actually consider them as inspirational standards, as benchmarks, which should be taken into account as if they were included in international agreements binding on national jurisdictions. The problems emanating from the multicultural composition of modern-day societies shall never completely resolve.

In an era of massive migration they ought to attract increasing attention from researchers in the field of victimology. In the light of the developments outlined above, it is clear that victimology is not an ideology, it is an academic discipline. Yet the objectives of this branch can only be fully achieved if research is conducted with conviction, compassion, commitment and courage. It is exciting to be a victimologist in the first quarter of the 21st century (Young 1992).

4. Legislative Initiatives and Best Practice in Europe

Based on the number of legislative initiatives Belgium, England and Wales, France, Ireland, the Netherlands and Sweden reach the highest scores. England and Wales, the Netherlands, Sweden followed closely by Zurich, achieved the best practice followed by England and Wales, Norway and Belgium. We need to reflect on the current position of victims within the criminal justice system. The question of procedural justice for victims is still as it was 15 years ago, when the Council of Europe adopted Recommendation. The research shows without a doubt that victims are still frequently confronted with a criminal justice system that largely neglects their rights and interests. Many victims are deprived of information, though it is a right and a service that does not conflict with the rights to the offender in any way.

Criminal courts order or award compensation to the victim had in far fewer cases than possible under national law. However it is an elementary requirement of justice that the offender compensates the victim for his losses and injuries suffered as a result of crime.

Furthermore, many victims are not assisted in the enforcement of compensation. State compensation schemes are available in 16 jurisdictions; however, they differ greatly with respect to who can claim compensation, the period of limitation and the amount awarded for comparable offences. In addition, victims are not necessarily aware of the schemas they qualify for. Regarding the questioning of vulnerable victims, in particular children, significant efforts are being made. The protection of victims against intimidation or retaliation and from publicity is still by and large inadequate (Victims of Crime in 22 European Criminal Justice Systems, Brienen/Hoegen, P. 1162).

5. General Recommendations for Europe

In Recommendation the Council of Europe advises its member states to conduct comparative research on the practical consequences of victim-oriented reforms, and on the solutions that exist in the different legal system. The underlying research is essentially an analytic and comparative study that draws up an inventory of the ways in which the Recommendation is implemented in the 22 jurisdictions. Where relevant national criminal justice statistics (empirical) studies were available we incorporated them in this study. However, in many jurisdictions such data are missing. Furthermore, the criminal justice statistics are generally for comparison (Victims of Crime in 22 European Criminal Justice Systems, Brienen/Hoegen, P. 1169). Statistics, for example, do not always include the same points of reference: some only contain data on felonies, other include data on both felonies and misdemeanors.

More importantly, however, no accurate data are kept on essential data that would allow for a detailed comparative analysis. Only if statistics are kept on a standardized basis can they be compared and definite conclusions are drawn. We, therefore, strongly recommend that national empirical studies are carried out, and criminal justice statistics are standardized in all member states of the Council of Europe to allow for further, more detailed, studies on the position of the victim in criminal law and procedure.

The criminal justice authorities should record the number of victims who reported a crime and who wished to be informed of their rights and opportunities. In addition, the number of victims who were provided with basic information, referred to victim or social services, and notified of relevant developments during the proceedings should be recorded. These data need to be registered in the same way as data on the number of the reports, prosecutions and penal sanctions imposed on offenders. The authorities should also monitor the treatment and protection of victims.

It would be advisable to include all these data in the criminal justice statistics. Statistics must also include data on the frequency in which victims act as private prosecutors, civil claimants, compensation order beneficiaries and/or auxiliary prosecutors; the number of victims who have suffered losses and injuries as a result of crime; the number of victims who want to be compensated; the number of victims who inform the courts of their need for compensation; the amount of money claimed or needed to cover the losses; the number of victims who are the beneficiaries of a court decision on compensation; the amount of compensation ordered or awarded by the courts; the number of victims who receive payments from the offender, whether they are compensated in full or in part, and within what period of time the received the money; and frequency in which protective measures are used by the authorities.

Research should be undertaken on a national and comparative level to allow policy to propose victim-oriented reforms and to evaluate any such reforms or policies in order to effectively remedy any shortcomings. Also, implementation by the criminal justice authorities of new reforms should be monitored. Phenomena that are taken for granted and seldom questioned should be studied. Member states should undertake studies to measure, inter alia, the need for, and effectiveness of, private prosecution in all member states of the Council of Europe (Victims of Crime in 22 European Criminal Justice Systems (Brienen/Hoegen), p. 1170; to evaluate the (dis)advantages of different legal systems and compensation models for victims; to study potential benefits of other systems; and to carry out in-depth examinations of the reasons why the prosecuting authorities and the judiciary are generally so unwilling to deal with victims and their need for compensation within criminal proceedings.

In addition, research should be carried out to study indicators that influence the functioning of the criminal justice system and the determination how is funded. As far as funding is concerned, clearly, the criminal justice authorities should have adequate resources and the allocation of resources should no longer be exclusively related to offender-related activities. Many questions remain to be resolved. What is the rationale behind the allocation of funding for the police forces, prosecution services, the courts and criminal justice partners? Which decisive factors cause reallocation of funding towards victim-oriented duties? What is the amount of resources needed to improve the position of victims in the criminal justice systems, compared to the actual funding?

These and other questions need to be addressed in national and comparative studies. Concerning the functioning of the criminal justice system, officials should promote the creation of criminal justice steering groups composed of representatives of the criminal justice and partners. Steering groups that meet on a regular (monthly) basis are essential to the provision of key-services to victims, cooperation between the agents and job demarcation. The state, in cooperation with the criminal justice authorities and partners, should promote the creation of a national victim support organization where lacking. These organizations not only improve the provision of free and easily accessible assistance to victims, but they are also important partners for the criminal justice authorities in providing information, legal assistance, and practical help to victims. Furthermore, the criminal justice authorities should set up systematic referral systems to victim support and social services. The attitudes of all officials involved, in particular the criminal justice authorities, should be supportive of victim-oriented reforms and measures. Judges and lawyers should inspire the law with life (Victims of Crime in 22 European Criminal Justice Systems (Brienen/Hoegen), p. 1171).

III. The Future of Victimology

In 2003, Xth International Symposium on Victimology was organized in Stellenbosch, South Africa. The overarching conference theme was "New horizons in victimology". Under this heading, attention was focused on the issues of victim's right's, victim services and transnational victimisation. These themes were well chosen because they clearly underline that victimology as an academic discipline has matured, as it has by now acquired an undisputable international dimension.

When victimologists from around the globe gather to discuss the issues mentioned, it is clear that the presentation of their research findings and their insights will be relevant for colleagues from all continents. Hence contemporary reflections on fundamental questions in this area are of equal importance to colleagues from South Africa and from Europe. The present contribution proceeds from the same assumption. There are some prominent international protocols concerning the rights of victims of crime and abuse of power.

Given the universal nature of the values and objectives underlying these documents, the European Union Framework Decision on the Standing of Victims in Criminal Proceedings will be used as a special example to elucidate some points, which also apply in the South Africa context. The subsequent section covers some of the main trends in recent victimology.

Victimology is rapidly moving forward and it has attracted many academics and practitioners from different backgrounds and with widely diverging interests. The resulting avalanche of publications in this field plainly asks for some analysis. What are the most important issues which are likely to dominate victimological debate in the next decade? This contribution is geared to the future. An overview of the past is presented by Schneider (2001). Which fundamental choices need to be made when we want to preserve (or to establish?) some coherence in victimology as a respectable academic discipline? Some inferences will be drawn from the content of the preceding parts of the present contribution.

IV. Victimology in South Africa: The Way Forward

Internationally and also in South Africa, every attempt possible is being made to expand the rights of victims and their participation in the formal legal system and to encourage the use of restorative justice principles. Despite the major milestones for victims of crime in terms of legislations, policies, administrative changes to improve their participation in the criminal justice system and victim empowerment in general, wants to bring closure to the above discussion for victimologists in South Africa (Karmen 1990).

> a) Victimology has been been many faces, reflecting victimologist's fields
> of interest. It is, however, true that a significant percentage of these fields
> of interest is guided by crimes that they are very prominent and that

often receive great media attention. Although any form of victimization or injustice warrants research, care should be taken not to neglect crimes with a low profile that are often more difficult to control and research. Postgraduate students and other researches in the field of victimology should be encouraged to put these issues on their research agenda.

b) Victimology in South Africa still needs to make a shift from theory and policy to practice. It is a dynamic tension between theory and practice that produces change and without change, there is stagnation (Friday P., 1992 the faces of victimology: general report—part 1. In David, S & Kirchhoff, G International faces of victimology, Monchengladbach; World Society of Victimology Publishing). Research needs to underpin legislation and policy. A good example of the major challenges in this regard is the limited research done on human trafficking that skews the information that should inform legislation, policy and practice. Researchers and practitioners should also collaborate more and the objective knowledge provided by researchers should be coupled with the passion and compassion of the direct service professional (Gaboury M.T. 2003 Role and current status of higher education and research in victim services. Paper sented at the XIth International Symposium on Victimology, 13.–18 July). Despite the tension between "formal" and "informal" victimologists and the risk of transforming victimology work into an activist rather than a scientific discipline will truly be able to assist victims in more and better ways.

c) From a policy perspective, care should be taken not to use victims of crime for political purposes and as a vehicle that serves only the interests of opportunistic politicians (as can be seen by the banners focusing on the reduction of crime during the 2004 election). The real objectives of government policies on victims and victim empowerment are often questioned. The minimum Standards on Services for Victims of Crime that were developed to strengthened victims' rights, as contained in the South African Victims' Charter of Rights, and to make these rights a reality is a major milestone for crime victims in South Africa. The document of the Department of Justice and Constitutional Development not only outlines the basic rights and principles but also supplies detailed information that enables victims to exercise their rights and service providers to uphold these rights.

The integrated Victim Empowerment Policy issued by the Department of Social Development (that's the policy that informs, guides, regulates and coordinates services for victims of crime and violence) is another attempt by government to illustrate its commitment, to the plight of crime victims in the country (Department of Social Development 2004 Preamble), Integrated victim empowerment policy (4th draft). A giant step forward to ensure that victim's' rights in South Africa do not remain paper rights and that policies and legislation supporting victims' rights do not succeed only in providing "window dressing for criminal justice reform", or largely serve as a mere symbolic function in the overall attempt to reform criminal justice practice, will be the establishment of a Statutory Victim's Office that will, once established, oversee the implementation of Victim's Charter and other measures that seek to empower victims (Artz & Moult 2004).

As a final remark on the scope of victimology, it is ultimately not productive to put too much weight to the exact meaning of words. The real problems of the people who have been victimized should direct the focus of our attention. Crime and violence in South Africa is often accepted as a normal way of life. Public tolerance of violence that supports, justifies and legitimizes victimization should rather be challenged. Public education is very much needed in this regard and consciousness should be raised that violence begets violence. Since violence is embedded in our history and has become woven in the emotional make-up of many South Africans, its causes, effect and remediation and, even more importantly, it's impact on victims of crime must continue to be the subject of research. Every attempt should be also be made to break the cycle of violence and to change the conditions, the attitudes, the practices and the behaviours that are the origin of violence or that contribute to it. The victim movement is maturing and efforts to improve the plight of victims have gained momentum.

Although our discipline is growing at a tremendous rate and the philosophical debates on the scope and challenges for victimologists are keeping the discipline vibrant, it is clear that victimology has yet much to learn "It is our responsible to review and evaluate past work in this field and to develop a future agenda that will spur, guide and support future research and policy interventions". (Viano, E.C. 2000, Victimology today: major issues in research and public policy. In Tobolowsky PM. Understanding victimology, selected readings, Cincinnati, OH: Andersson 9–22). "There could be no better time to analyze evolution, take stock of past achievements and prepare for the problems, the hurdles and the challenges than the present time"(Fattah, E.A. 1997 Criminology past, present and future, a critical overview). It is hoped that the contributions, all for whom are passionate about the plight of the victims in South Africa, did exactly this.

V. The Need for International Cooperation

International cooperation can benefit victimology in both developed and developing countries. Encouraging such cooperation requires us to overcome the two difficulties already noted the lack of resources and the egocentricity of victimologists, or for that matter, the egocentricity of governments (Joutsen 1996, Managing International Technical Assistance Projects in Criminal Justice, HEUNI papers no. 8, Helsinki). In respect of resources, the main problem is that governments in developing countries are swamped with priorities.

A variety of economic, social and political problems has to be addressed: unemployment, poverty, infant mortality, disease, inequality, and the need to develop a sound economic base and democratic institutions. Victim services and initiatives, and more generally crime prevention and criminal justice often tend to be looked at as peripheral issues, and not as integral parts of plans for national development. Although Governments understand the need to "do something about crime", it would appear that the preferred Government response (in the East as in the West, in the North as in the South) is to increase the repressiveness of the system, rather than to see whether the repressiveness itself may have been—and may well continue to be—part of the problem (Hatchard John (1991) Victims of Crime an Abuse of Power in Africa: An Overview, in: Günther Kaiser, Helmut Kury and Hans-Jörg Albrecht (1991), Victims and Criminal Justice, Max Planck Institute for Foreign and International Criminal Law publications nos. 52/2, Freiburg i. Breisgau, pp 689–732).

In line with the United Nations Victim Declaration, Governments should allocate funds to the training of researchers and to research itself responding to this problem. Governments should also provide a greater priority to the compiling of adequate criminal and victimological data. For example, national and local victimization surveys should be instituted as a regular part of policy information. The Government of the Netherlands deserves considerable praise for its support of the international contacts between the developed countries and other parts of the world. The sad fact is that, for most of Africa, Latin America, Asia and Central and Eastern Europe, the riches of Western victimological research and experience are out of reach, due to practical problems of finance and in knowing how to access the data. Initiatives such as the World Criminal Justice Library Network and the use of Internet to disseminate data should be strengthened. International research projects should be carried out by multinational teams representing a diversity of views. Monocultural teams may also be more subject to the risk of cultural misunderstandings. Bringing together practitioners from more than one culture can help in identifying and overcoming these dangers.

Finally, victimologists should consider how they could contribute to the development and evaluation of victim policy. Much has been learned in Western industrialized countries over the past years about what works and what does not work in victim policy, but considerably more evaluative research is needed. What is also needed is research that could help in identifying promising practices that could be replicated in other jurisdictions, after sufficient cultural tailoring to the specific economic, legal, political and social circumstances. The United Nations is currently preparing a guide to implementation of the United Nations Victim Declaration, which could serve as a basis for new research projects. Such research would go a long way towards assisting practitioners and policy makers in developing countries and in countries in transition in re-evaluating their criminal justice system, and in developing suitable responses. Ultimately, this could help in achieving a major reduction in the amount of victimization, and considerable progress in securing international justice for the victim.

The corruption charge alleges that Chief Selebi received money from a convicted drug trafficker who was then on trial for murder (McGreal 2008). In exchange for the money it is alleged that Selebi protected drug shipments and passed on confidential information on both the murder trial and current drug operations (McGreal 2008). In addition to being the police chief in South Africa, Jackie Selebi was also president of Interpol, the international police organization. Interpol acts as a clearinghouse for information on crime and maintains a database of fingerprints, mug shots, and more (Naim 2001). He resigned this position at the same time as his position as chief of police (McGreal 2008). Selebi was elected president of the Interpol General Assembly in 2004, becoming the first African elected to the position (Interpol 2004).

References

Artz, L., & Moult, L. (2004). A critical-realist analysis of South African victimology theories. Unpublished electronic document received on 3 May, 2011.

Brewer, J. D. (1994). *Black and blue: Policing in South Africa*. Oxford: Claredon Press.

Brienen M. E. I., & Hoegen E. H. (2000). *Victims of crime in 22 European criminal justice systems*. Nijmegen: WLP.

Brogden, M. (1994). Reforming police power in South Africa. *Police Studies, 17*(1), 25–43.

Brogden, M. (1996). The indigenisation of policing in South Africa. In O. Marenin (Ed.), *Policing change, changing police: International perspectives* (pp. 223–250). New York: Garland Publishing.

Cawthra, G. (1993). *Policing South Africa: The South African police and the transition from Apartheid*. London: Zed Books Ltd.

Clark, N. L., & Worger, W. H. (2004). *South Africa: The rise and fall of Apartheid*. New York: Pearson Longman.

Department of Social Development (2004). Integrated victim empowerment policy (4th draft). Pretoria, South Africa.

Doerner, W. G. & Lab, S. P. (2003). *Victimology* (3rd ed). Cincinnati: Anderson Publishing Company.

Elias, R. (1993). *Victims still: The political manipulation of crime victims*. London: SAGE Publications.

Fattah, E. A. (2000). Prologue: On some visible and hidden dangers of victim movements. In P. M. Tobolowksy (Ed.), *Understanding victimology, Selected readings* (pp. 23–34). Cincinnati: Anderson Publishing Company.

Friday P. (1992). The faces of victimology: General report–part 1. In S. David & G. Kirchhoff (Eds.), *International faces of victimology*. Monchengladbach: World Society of Victimology Publishing.

Gaboury, M. T. (2003). Role and current status of higher education and research in victim services. Paper presented at the XIth International Symposium on Victimology, Stellenbosch, South Africa, 13–18 July.

Hatchard, J. (1991). Victims of crime and abuse of power in Africa: An overview. In: G. Kaiserk, H. Kury, & H. Albrecht (Eds.), *Victims and criminal justice* (pp. 689–732). Max Planck Institute for Foreign and International Criminal Law publication nos. 52/2, Freiburg im Breisgau, Germany.

Joutsen, M. (1996). Managing international technical assistance projects in criminal justice. HEUNI papers no. 8, Helsinki.

Joutsen, M. (1998). The internalization of victimology. In H. Schwind, E. Kube, & H. Kühne (Eds.) *Essay in honor of Hans-Joachim Schneider: Criminology on the threshold of the 21st century.* Berlin: De Gruyter.

Karmen, A. (1990). *Crime Victims: an introduction to victimology.* Pacific Grove, CA: Brooks/Cole.

Schneider, H. J. (2001). Victimological developments in the world during the past three decades: A study of comparative victimology—Part 2. *International Journal of Offender Therapy and Comparative Criminology, 45*(5), 539–555.

Snyman, R., & Davis, L. (2005). *Victimology in South Africa.* Pretoria: Van Schaik Publishers.

Tonry, M. (1993). Sentencing commissions and their guidelines. In M. Tonry (Ed.) *Crime and justice: A review of research, vol. 17.* Chicago: The University of Chicago Press.

Van Dijk, J. J. M., Mayhew, P., & Kilias, M. (1990). *Experiences of crime across the world: Key findings from the 1989 International Crime Survey.* Boston: Kluwer Law International.

Viano, E. C. (2000). Victimology today: major issues in research and public policy. In P. M. Tobolowksy (Ed.), *Understanding victimology, Selected readings* (pp. 9–22). Cincinnati: Anderson Publishing Company.

Chapter 2: Concluding Remarks

This reading selection has provided us with a glimpse of the challenges of studying crime victimization from a global perspective. Here, we see the need for oversight in the implementation of policies and practices that address victim rights and needs across nations in order to ensure the fair and equitable distribution of funds and services that provide compensation and care for victims. This challenge is not only imperative to address, but also of utmost important for the field of victimology to properly focus attention on crime victimization from a comparative approach that accounts for variations in legal principles, moral and social definitions, and cultural concerns in different countries and governments throughout the world. It is up to criminologists, researchers, and legal scholars to continue the growth and expansion of this field to incorporate research endeavors that advance this knowledge and understanding to the scientific community, policy makers, and legal advocates for victims of crime.

CHAPTER 3

Micro- and Macro-Level Considerations in Explaining Victimization

Introduction

The role of individual-level traits as well as the contextual elements of the social environment in mediating crime and victimization have been the subject of debate for many years. A myriad of research suggests that predatory criminal activity can be directly correlated with a victim's personal lifestyle, routine activity, and cognitive functioning. Likewise, some studies have found a significant connection between crime victimization and structural variables within neighborhoods and social contexts that increase the risk of becoming the victim of crime. These micro- and macro-level considerations in explaining crime victimization have become the focus of study for criminologists seeking to integrate the various theoretical literature to develop a more comprehensive approach to understanding the relationship between criminal offenders and their victims. This link between micro and macro dimensions of criminal behavior and crime victimization has taken on a pivotal role in developing a multilevel approach when addressing the various needs of individuals impacted by crime as well as advocating for changes that can reduce the risk of criminal offending and victimization.

This chapter contains two reading selections that illustrate the importance of incorporating micro- and macro-level considerations in studying crime victimization. The first reading focuses on a study of bullying behavior and the association of emotional difficulties, social skills, and executive functioning in relation to the roles of bully, victim, and defender. The authors here stress the value of addressing the social, emotional, and cognitive factors associated with bullying in order to fully understand this type of behavior, its impact on victims, as well as its amenability to prevention. The second reading directs attention to the study of various forms of violence and their relationship to larger structures of power and inequality. Here, we see the connection between family structure and function and the role this plays in the dynamics of intimate partner violence as well as child abuse.

Guiding Questions

As you read, consider the following questions:

1   How are micro- and macro-level considerations in the study of victimization different?

2   What do you see as the most effective approach to understanding the relationship between criminal offending and crime victimization?

3   Do policy makers benefit from research studies that focus on individual-level explanations of victimization?

4   Are there benefits to the study of crime victimization using a broader structural level of analysis?

5   Can behaviors such as bullying, intimate partner violence, and child abuse be explained from multiple levels of understanding that include both individual traits and environmental context?

Key Terms

Bully Behavior Participant Questionnaire (BBPQ)   A 50-item self-report questionnaire that assesses an individual's participation in bullying situations across various roles.

dyadic research   Combined research that explores relationships, allowing for comparisons, cross-referencing, and triangulation.

polyvictimization   When victims of crime experience four or more victimizations within a given year.

Social, Emotional, and Cognitive Factors Associated with Bullying

Lyndsay N. Jenkins, Michelle K. Demaray, and Jaclyn Tennant

The goal of the current study was to examine social, emotional, and cognitive predictors of bullying, victimization, and defending among sixth- through eighth-grade students. The social competence and emotional health of individuals directly (bullies, victims) and indirectly (defenders, outsiders) involved in bullying have been the topic of investigations over the past few decades. Many studies have attempted to explain the behavior of individuals who demonstrate aggressive and prosocial behavior or experience victimization, and most of these studies have included social (e.g., social skills), emotional (e.g., internalizing problems), and cognitive (e.g., social information processing, executive functioning) variables as either predictors or outcomes associated with different bullying role behaviors. However, no known study has examined these characteristics with three types of bullying role behaviors in a single investigation.

Research on bullying has attempted to elucidate the social and emotional competence of individuals in specific bullying roles. For example, the social skills deficit model (Crick & Dodge, 1994) suggested that aggressive participants of bullying (bullies and assistants) have impaired social skills; however, Sutton, Smith, and Swettenham (1999a, 1999b) argued that impaired cognitive processes are related to aggression, not social skills deficits. Executive functioning skills, including emotional regulation, flexible thinking, planning, and goal setting, are socially oriented cognitive processes used to process information in social situations (Camodeca & Goossens, 2005; Crick & Dodge, 1994; Riggs, Jahromi, Razza, Dillworth-Bart, & Mueller, 2006) and may help to explain why individuals engage in or experience bullying, victimization, and defending. Though social and cognitive skills are related to emotional difficulties, the exact association of these three characteristics in relation to aggressive, victim, and pro-social behaviors has not been investigated. Both observable social skills and less observable, underlying cognitive processes should be considered in order to more fully understand bullying role behavior.

Emotional difficulties, social skills, and executive functioning skills are intertwined, and their development is interdependent. For example, social skills develop when children have opportunities to interact with other peers and adults; however, opportunities for practice are not the only requirement. Executive functioning skills are necessary in order for children to process social information processing properly (Camodeca & Goossens, 2005; Crick & Dodge, 1994), so executive functioning is partially a prerequisite for engaging in productive social interactions. Without proper executive functioning skills, children are less likely to have opportunities to interact with others (Beck, 2011). In addition, a hallmark of emotional difficulties is that these symptoms can interfere with everyday functioning, such as social interactions. Being withdrawn or anxious may reduce the number of opportunities to interact; thus, there are fewer opportunities for social skill use and development (Beck, 2011).

The current study focuses on the association of emotional difficulties, social skills, and executive functioning skills in relation to three bullying roles: bully, victim, and defender. Though there are other roles (e.g., outsiders, assistants, and reinforcers), these three are the most commonly studied and most prevalent (Salmivalli, Lagerspetz, Björkqvist, Österman, & Kaukiainen, 1996). A bully is an individual who perpetrates aggressive (i.e., verbal, physical, or relational) acts on peers, while a victim is the recipient of that aggression. A defender is a prosocial individual who intervenes either by stopping bullying or reporting bullying to an adult or by trying to help a victim by becoming the victim's friend, including the victim, or otherwise consoling the victim after bullying has occurred (Salmivalli et al., 1996).

Emotional Difficulties and Bullying Role Behavior

Emotional health is critical to appropriate social and emotional competence. Individuals in various bullying roles tend to have differing levels of emotional difficulties. One of the most commonly studied negative outcomes of bullying is emotional difficulties, such as anxiousness, depressive symptoms, and school avoidance (Swearer-Napolitano, 2011). In fact, one reason that bullying is so frequently studied is arguably because of the negative social and emotional outcomes of both bullies and their victims. Although exact results vary from study to study, there is overwhelming support that both perpetrators and recipients of peer aggression have emotional difficulties to some degree (Card, Stucky, Sawalani, & Little, 2008; Nakamoto & Schwartz, 2010). Card et al. (2008) noted that some studies show bullies have no internalizing problems but others do find evidence of internalizing problems. In their meta-analysis, Card et al. found that indirect aggression (i.e., relational aggression) had a greater association with emotional difficulties compared to direct aggression (i.e., physical and verbal aggression). Victims tend to show high levels of emotional difficulties, such as depression, anxiety, loneliness, and difficulties with self-esteem, when compared to other students (Hawker & Boulton, 2000; Nakamoto & Schwartz, 2010). On the other hand, very few studies have investigated the emotional difficulties of students who engage in defending, but early studies suggest that defenders are less likely than victims to have emotional difficulties (Janosz et al., 2008). Though emotional difficulties (or the lack of emotional difficulties) of bullying participants have received much attention in the literature, there are other variables, including social skills and executive functioning skills, that are also related to different bullying role participants.

Social Skills and Bullying Role Behavior

Social skills (Gresham & Elliott, 2008) and executive functioning skills (Riggs et al., 2006) are two individual characteristics that are vital to appropriate social and emotional development and are also related to each other. Social skills are observable behaviors often used to determine if someone has social competence, such as empathy, assertiveness, cooperation, and responsibility (Gresham & Elliott, 2008).

Some theories postulate that bullies do not have social skills deficits; instead, they use sophisticated social skills to manipulate others in social situations (Sutton, Smith, & Swettenham, 1999a, 1999b). Nonaggressive youth with strong social and perspective-taking skills may be more likely to engage in prosocial behavior, such as defending. Individuals with high levels of bullying and defending behavior may have similar levels of social skills but use them in very different ways. In fact, Gasser and Keller (2009) found bullies and prosocial children received similar scores on measures of social competence but bullies had significantly lower scores on measures of moral competence. This is supported by a line of research by Hawley et al. that focuses on the influence and uses of power in childhood (Hawley, 2003, 2007; Hawley, Little, & Pasupathi, 2002; Hawley, Shorey, & Alderman, 2009; Hawley & Williford, 2015). This work examined bullying from a social psychological perspective and postulated that high social power among children and adolescents can be used in a positive way (i.e., defending) or negative way (e.g., bullying). Those with high power often have well-developed social competence as well but can wield their power in beneficial or destructive ways.

Generally, studies have found that victimized students tend to have low social skills and that bullies and defenders have high levels of some social skills (assertiveness for both bullies and defenders, empathy and self-control for defenders) but lower levels of other social skills (cooperation and self-control for bullies; Jenkins, Demaray, Fredrick, & Summers, 2014). More specifically, when investigating social skills of 800 middle school students in relation to bullying role behaviors, Jenkins et al. (2014) found that victimization was negatively associated with cooperation, assertion, empathy, and self-control. Other studies have found similar results (e.g.,

Champion, Vernberg, & Shipman, 2003; Egan & Perry, 1998; Kokkinos & Kipritsi, 2012). Jenkins et al. found bullying behavior to be negatively associated with cooperation and self-control but positively associated with assertion, which is supported by other studies as well (e.g., Chui & Chan, 2013; Perren & Alsaker, 2006; Unnever & Cornell, 2003). Finally, they found a positive association between defending behavior and assertion, empathy, and self-control, which corroborates findings from other studies on defending (e.g., Gini, Albiero, Benelli, & Altoe, 2007; Nickerson, Mele, & Princiotta, 2008; Thornberg & Jungert, 2014).

Executive Functioning and Bullying Role Behavior

Executive functioning encompasses a set of self-regulatory processes responsible for problem solving and the management of goal-oriented behavior (Séguin & Zelazo, 2005). Executive functioning is a somewhat malleable construct that could be targeted through intervention to improve social–emotional function of children and adolescents in an effort to reduce occurrences and negative outcomes of victimization. However, to date, interventions focused on promoting social–emotional well-being have largely ignored executive functioning skills (Riggs et al., 2006). Deficits in executive functioning have been associated with difficulties in the social domain. Working memory, attention control, and inhibition are some executive functioning skills that have implications for social–emotional well-being and social competence (Riggs et al., 2006). Deficiencies in these skills may impair an individual's ability to take others' perspectives, shift attention, or recognize and consider the potential consequences of behavior.

The social information processing theory links executive functioning to social competence (Camodeca & Goossens, 2005; Crick & Dodge, 1994). The social information processing theory explains how individuals perceive and react to social stimuli though five cyclical mental steps and an ultimate sixth step during which they enact their plan. The first five steps involve encoding and interpreting social cues (Steps 1 and 2), clarifying goals (Step 3), searching for response options (Step 4), and selecting a response (Step 5). Executive functioning skills are used throughout this model. Executive functioning ability and emotions affect social information processing. For example, individuals who are high in negative emotionality and are easily emotionally aroused may have their executive functioning resources flooded during stressful social interactions such that they cannot cope effectively and they consequently engage in maladaptive social information processing (Ferrier, Bassatt, & Denham, 2014). On the basis of this evidence, impaired executive functioning may account for poor social competence through interfering with social information processing. Using this theory, Camodeca and Goossens (2005) found victims and bullies to engage in more hostile interpretation, anger, retaliation, and aggression than their peers. Conversely, defenders of victims demonstrated more adaptive social information processing with significantly fewer interpretation errors and lower likelihood of engaging in retaliation.

Several studies have been conducted that provide corroborating evidence that differences in executive functioning underlie the likelihood of engaging in aggressive behavior. When examining the association between bullying role behavior and executive control among a sample of early elementary students, Verlinden et al. (2013) found that domains of executive functioning predicted risk for bullying and victimization. Specifically, inhibition problems, working memory deficits, and global executive functioning were predictive of being a bully, while inhibition problems and low intelligence were predictive of being a victim. The authors did not explore prosocial behavior. Other studies with preschoolers have also found impaired executive functioning and theory of mind among aggressors (Monks, Smith, & Swettenham, 2005). Defenders in this study performed the best on theory of mind, deception, planning, and inhibition, while aggressors demonstrated the lowest performance. These results suggest that executive functioning supports prosocial behavior and deficits in executive function-ing promote aggression. Preschoolers tend to engage in direct aggression more often than indirect aggression, and the latter type likely requires better theory of mind and planning. Therefore, these results may not generalize to older age groups whose members engage in more indirect aggression.

Among middle school students, bullying behavior was significantly correlated with impairments in three areas of executive functioning: metacognition, social judgments, and decision making (Coolidge, DenBoer, & Segal, 2003). Toblin, Schwartz, Gorman, and Abou-Ezzeddine (2005) compared the behavioral characteristics of bullies, aggressive victims, passive victims, and peers. Similar to Verlinden et al. (2013), they also found evidence for executive functioning impairments among victims, with aggressive victims demonstrating significantly greater emotion dysregulation than all other groups. Mahady-Wilton, Craig, and Pepler (2000) also found evidence that bullies and victims demonstrated unique patterns of emotional displays and emotion dysregulation. Specifically, bullies demonstrated high levels of anger and contempt, which presumably motivated them to engage in aggression to achieve personal desires. Both passive and aggressive victims most frequently engaged in maladaptive displays of emotion and emotion regulation. Fox and Boulton (2005) also found that victims demonstrated poor emotion regulation and concluded that this may be a result of high negative emotionality and emotional reactivity that impaired coping through the use of executive functioning. Poor peer relationships have also been associ-ated with impaired cognitive flexibility. Alternatively, prosocial behavior, observed among defenders, is associated with strong regulation ability, low emotionality, and constructive problem solving (Eisenberg, Carlo, Murphy, & Van Court, 1995). Executive functioning skills and deficits appear to predict bullying roles. Specifically, response inhibition and working memory problems predict proactive aggression (bullying); planning deficits, inhibition problems, cognitive inflexibility, and emotion dysregulation predict reactive aggression and victimization; and cognitive flexibility, emotion regulation, and planning skills predict defending behaviors.

Gender Differences in Study Variables

There are notable gender differences in many of the variables in this study, so relations among emotional difficulties, social skills, executive functioning, and bullying role behavior were explored separately for boys and girls. Studies suggest boys and girls have a tendency to display different types of bullying behaviors. Although boys are more likely to physically victimize, recent meta-analyses indicate that girls are not more likely to display relational aggression, as widely thought (Card et al., 2008). Girls are more likely to take on the role of the outsider or the defender, whereas boys are more likely to take on the role of the assistant or reinforcer (Salmivalli et al., 1996). In addition, boys are more likely to be traditional bullies, victims, and bully-victims than girls (Espelage & Holt, 2007).

There are also notable gender differences in emotional difficulties and social skills. Boys are more often identified with behavioral at-risk screening tools (such as the Behavior Assessment System for Children, Second Edition [BASC-2] Behavioral and Emotional Screening System [BESS] measure used in the current study) than girls (Dowdy, Doane, Eklund, & Dever, 2011). However, girls often have higher levels of internalizing problems (Verhulst & Ende, 1992). Furthermore, bullying has been found to have a stronger association with internalizing problems for girls than boys (Ledwell & King, 2015). Gender differences in social skills have also been found. For example, girls have been found to score higher than boys on responsiveness, empathy, and emotional regulation (Anme et al., 2010). Girls also tend to be rated higher than boys in social skills (e.g., cooperative, assertive, responsible, and self-control) by teachers and parents (Abdi, 2010). Finally, inconsistent gender effects have been found on executive functioning skills; some studies have found that girls outperform boys on executive functioning measures of verbal skill and inhibitory control (Berlin & Bohlin, 2002; Carlson & Moses, 2001; Levin et al., 1991; Reader, Harris, Schuerholz, & Denckla, 1994), but others have found no gender effects (Welsh, Pennington, & Groisser, 1991). Therefore, executive functioning was also explored separately for boys and girls.

Current Study

Previous research has found that bullying, victimization, and defending have unique associations with social skills, emotional difficulties, and cognitive processes, but these characteristics have not been examined simultaneously as predictors of bullying role behaviors (e.g., in a single model where social, emotional, and cognitive predictors predict victimization). There is evidence that social skills, lack of emotional difficulties, and executive functioning are all indicators of healthy social and emotional development and the ability to interact appropriately with others in social situations; thus, including all these variables as predictors is important in order to determine which is most strongly related to bullying role behaviors.

By examining the relative strength of the association of these variables in a single model, the importance of these individual variables can be elucidated. Determining which of these predictors may be most important would inform prevention and intervention programs that are currently being developed or already implemented in schools. To this end, the current study tested three separate models using structural equation modeling. See Figure 3.1 for an example of the theoretical model. Each model was tested separately for boys and girls because of gender differences in the experience of and outcomes of emotional problems (Card et al., 2008), social skills (Gresham & Elliott, 2008), and bullying

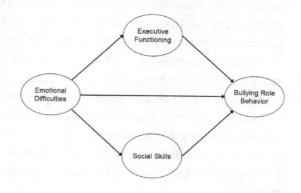

Figure 3.1   Theoretical Model

role behaviors (Salmivalli et al., 1996). In each model, social skills, emotional difficulties, and executive functioning served as predictors of bullying role behavior. The model was tested three times with bullying behaviors, defending behaviors, and victimization serving as three separate dependent variables (see Figure 3.1).

On the basis of previous studies investigating individual characteristics and bullying role behaviors, it was hypothesized that (a) bullying behavior would be negatively associated with social skills and executive functioning skills (Chui & Chan, 2013; Coolidge et al., 2003; Jenkins et al., 2014; Mahady-Wilton et al., 2000; Monks et al., 2005; Perren & Alsaker, 2006; Unnever & Cornell, 2003; Verlinden et al., 2013); (b) victimization would be negatively related to social skills and executive functioning skills but positively related to emotional difficulties (Champion et al., 2003; Egan & Perry, 1998; Fox & Boulton, 2005; Jenkins et al., 2014; Kokkinos & Kipritsi, 2012; Mahady-Wilton et al., 2000; Toblin et al., 2005; Verlinden et al., 2013); and (c) defending behaviors would be positively associated with social skills and executive functioning skills (Eisenberg et al., 1995; Gini et al., 2007; Jenkins et al., 2014; Monks et al., 2005; Nickerson et al., 2008; Thornberg & Jungert, 2014).

Method

Student participants completed three rating scales (Bully Participant Behavior Questionnaire [BPBQ], Social Skills Improvement System Rating Scale, and BESS, described below) as part of a school-wide universal screening evaluation. Teacher participants completed one rating scale, Comprehensive Executive Functioning Index.

Participants

There were 246 participants in sixth through eighth grade, including 136 boys (55.3%) and 110 girls (44.7%). There were 90 sixth graders (36.6%), 83 seventh graders (33.7%), and 73 eighth graders (29.7%). Thirty-one of the students were in special education (12.6%), but additional information regarding eligibility or type of program was not available. Approximately 72% of the school completed the survey. According to Illinois Interactive Report Card, of the 343 students enrolled in the school, 14.9% received special education services and 53.1% were low income, and the ethnic makeup of the school was 97% White and 3% two or more races. Ratings by teachers occurred approximately one month after the students completed their survey, as described in the Procedures section below. Fourteen teachers provided ratings for students, and the number of students they rated ranged from 12 to 22. In order to provide ratings, teacher participants had to have the student in at least one academic class and to have known the student for at least 6 weeks.

Procedures

Students completed their rating scales in large groups during their physical education class. To reduce the chance of missing data, teachers checked for skipped items as students turned in rating scales. Items were read aloud to students receiving special education services for reading. Teachers completed their ratings within 1 month of the student data collection. Students and teachers both used school-issued identification numbers so that data would remain anonymous to researchers but the rating scales could be connected later for research purposes. Active consent from teacher participants was collected as part of the original institutional review board. Later, institutional review board approval was given for access to the extant student survey data, and the two datasets were combined using identification numbers.

Measures

Student participants completed three self-report rating scales and teacher participants completed one rating scale. Each scale is described below.

Bully Participant Behavior Questionnaire

The BPBQ (Summers & Demaray, 2008) is a 50-item self-report questionnaire that assesses participation in bullying situations across several roles. The measure has five subscales: Bully, Assistant, Victim, Defender, and Outsider. Only the Bully, Victim, and Defender subscales were used in the current study, for example, "I have pushed, punched, or slapped another student" (Bully); "People have tried to make others dislike me" (Victim); and "I defended someone by telling people that a rumor is not true" (Defender). For each item, participants are asked how often they have performed or experienced the behavior over the past 30 days and respond using a Likert scale ranging from 1 (never) to 5 (seven or more times). Higher scores indicate more frequent engagement in or experience of behavior associated with that role.

Psychometric support for the BPBQ is strong. This measure has demonstrated high internal consistency with coefficients of 0.88 for the Bully subscale, 0.93 for the Victim subscale, and .94 for the Defender subscale (Demaray, Summers, Jenkins, & Becker, 2014). In the current study, α coefficients were 0.84, 0.93, and 0.94 for the Bully, Victim, and Defender subscales, respectively. According to Demaray et al. (2014), subscale–to–total correlations for the total sample were all moderate to high and significant, $p. < 01$. Item–subscale correlations ranged from $r. = 51$ to .80 for the Bully subscale, from $r. = 73$ to .84 for the Victim subscale, and from $r = .76$ to .85 for the Defender subscale. The factor structure was supported via exploratory and confirmatory factor analysis. Alpha coefficients for each subscale ranged from 0.88 to 0.94. See Demaray et al. (2014) for additional evidence of reliability and validity.

Student Version of Social Skills Improvement System Rating Scale

The student version of the Social Skills Improvement System Rating Scale (SSIS; Gresham & Elliott, 2008) consists of 76 items designed to measure social skill performance and engagement in problem behavior. For each item, participants decide how true it is for them and respond using a four-point Likert scale (*not true* to *very true*). Only the social skills items were used in the current study. The social skills items represent acquired behaviors that positively benefit social interactions and address communication, cooperation, assertion, responsibility, empathy, engagement, and self-control. Psychometric evidence for the SSIS student version is strong. According to the manual (Gresham & Elliott, 2008), internal consistency estimates for both scales and all subscales range from 0.72 to 0.95. In the current study, α coefficients were 0.81, 0.73, 0.82, and 0.79 for the Empathy, Assertion, Cooperation, and Responsibility subscales, respectively. For more detailed information on scoring and the psychometric support for the SSIS, see the manual (Gresham & Elliott, 2008).

BASC-2 Behavioral and Emotional Screening System

The student version of the BASC-2 BESS (Kamphaus & Reynolds, 2007) is designed for students in Grades 3 through 12 and consists of 30 items designed to measure students' behavioral and emotional strengths and weaknesses. For each item, participants decide how often a statement is true for them and respond using a four-point Likert scale (*never* to *always*). Items assess a range of positive behaviors and behavioral problems, including internalizing problems, externalizing problems, school problems, and adaptive skills. Psychometric evidence for the BESS Student Form is strong. Internal consistency estimates are excellent and range from 0.90 to 0.93 across norm types and age groups according to the manual (Kamphaus & Reynolds, 2007). For more detailed information on scoring and the psychometric support for the BESS, see the manual (Kamphaus & Reynolds, 2007).

Although the BESS is intended to be used as a screening tool to estimate a student's general risk for experiencing social and emotional difficulties, Dowdy, Twyford, et al. (2011) performed a factor analysis of the scale and found evidence of four discrete subscales: Personal Adjustment

(9 items), Inattention–Hyperactivity (5 items), Internalizing Problems (10 items), and School Problems (6 items). The current study used the Internalizing Problems, Personal Adjustment, and School Problems frequency scores in the analyses. The Inattention–Hyperactivity items were not used. Though externalizing problems are common among children who engage in bullying, inattention is not commonly associated with bullying, victimization, or defender behavior. Internalizing Problems reflect possible depressed thoughts, high amounts of worry or fear, and self-blame and criticism (e.g., "I feel like my life is getting worse and worse"). Finally, Personal Adjustment reflects how comfortable students feel around others and how well they fit in with peers (e.g., "I feel out of place around people"). School Problems represents a student's positive or negative perceptions about school and feelings toward teachers and classmates (e.g., "School is boring"). Scores for Internalizing Problems can range from 10 to 40; Personal Adjustment, 8 to 32; and School Problems, 4 to 16. In the current study, coefficients were .85, .87, and .83 for the Personal Adjustment, Internalizing Problems, and School Problems subscales, respectively.

Comprehensive Executive Functioning Index

The teacher version of the Comprehensive Executive Functioning Index (CEFI; Naglieri & Goldstein, 2012) was used to assess executive functioning. The CEFI is a 100-item rating scale intended to measure behaviors associated with the executive functioning of children and adolescents age 5 to 18 years. It includes items addressing strengths and weaknesses in attention, emotion regulation, flexibility, inhibitory control, initiation, organization, planning, self-monitoring, and working memory, resulting in a full-scale score and nine subscale scores. Two additional scales assess positive and negative impressions. The teacher is asked to report how often specific behaviors have been observed during the past 4 weeks. For each item, the teacher responds using a six-point Likert scale ranging from *never* to *always*. For the purposes of the current study, only the Emotion Regulation, Flexibility, Inhibitory Control, and Self-Monitoring subscales were used. An example item from the Emotion Regulation subscale is, "During the past 4 weeks, how often did the child wait patiently?" An exemplar item from the Flexibility subscale is, "During the past 4 weeks, how often did the child solve a problem in different ways?" An example Inhibitory Control item is, "During the past 4 weeks, how often did the child have trouble waiting his/her turn?" Finally, an example item from the Self-Monitoring subscale is, "During the past 4 weeks, how often did the child make careless errors?" Scores are based on a normative sample consisting of 1,400 students age 5 to 18 years. The normative sample was stratified in terms of race–ethnicity, geographic region, and parent education level and was equally composed of male and female students.

Psychometric evidence for the CEFI Teacher Form version is excellent. Internal consistency estimates for both the full scale and all subscales range from 0.90 to 0.99 according to the manual (Naglieri & Gold-stein, 2012). In the current study, α coefficients were .74, .93, .89, and .92 for the Self-Monitoring, Inhibitory Control, Flexibility, and Emotion Regulation subscales, respectively. The manual reported that test–retest reliability was high across subscales (adjusted $r = .82$ to .91). Interrater reliability for the Teacher Form was moderate (adjusted $r = .54$ to .68). Validity of the CEFI Teacher Form was supported by moderate and directionally appropriate subscale intercorrelations. For more detailed information on scoring and the psychometric support for the CEFI, see the manual (Naglieri & Goldstein, 2012).

Plan of Analysis

A multigroup structural equation modeling method was used to determine if the direct and indirect effects of social skills, emotional difficulties, and executive functioning on bullying role behaviors (i.e., bullying, victim, defender) varied by gender. To achieve adequate power (0.8), it was estimated that a minimum of 290 participants would be required to detect an effect, and the recommended sample size to infer a strong model structure was 956 (Cohen, 1988; Soper, 2015; Westland, 2010). The current study included only 246 participants, but paths were tested using bootstrapping (Preacher & Hayes, 2008; Shrout & Bolger, 2002), which allows researchers to have more robust estimates, even with a small sample (i.e., as small as 20–80 cases; Shrout & Bolger, 2002), and is viewed as a superior method for testing direct effects compared to the causal steps (i.e., Baron & Kenny, 1986) approach (Hayes, 2009). The direct effect of each predictor (executive functioning, emotional difficulties, and social skills) on each bullying role behavior was estimated, in addition to the direct effect of emotional difficulties on executive functioning, social skills, and bullying role behavior (see Figure 3.1).

Separate models were tested with each type of bullying role behavior serving as the outcome variable. For each model, one for each bullying role behavior, there were three predictors, or latent variables: executive functioning, emotional difficulties, and social skills. There were four indicators for the executive functioning latent variable: emotion regulation, self-monitoring, flexibility, and initiation. There were three indicators for emotional difficulties: personal adjustment, internalizing problems, and school problems. There were four indicators for the social skill latent variable: responsibility, empathy, assertion, and cooperation. Indicators for the bullying role behavior variable were individual items from the BPBQ that were associated with each respective subscale. Model fit was evaluated based on five measures of fit based on recommendations by Hooper, Coughlan, and Mullen (2008): χ^2, comparative fit index (CFI), standardized root mean residual (SRMR), root mean square error of approximation (RM-SEA), and parsimonious normed fit index (PNFI). It is desirable to have a nonsignificant χ^2 value (Barrett, 2007); however, there are some cautions when interpreting model fit using χ^2; thus, other fit indices were also considered. Models may be considered to have adequate fit with CFI values above .90 (Browne & Cudeck, 1989) or .95 (Schermelleh-Engel, Moosbrugger, & Müller, 2003), SRMR values below .08 (Hu & Bentler, 1999), RMSEA values below .06 (Hu & Bentler, 1999), and PNFI values greater than .50 (Mulaik et al., 1989). To test for significant differences in the strength of the direct effects for boys and girls, critical ratios were calculated. To test for differences between path coefficients, critical ratios employ a z test; thus, absolute values exceeding 1.96 indicate a significant difference in the path coefficients.

Results

Means, standard deviations, and analysis-of-variance F and p values comparing mean scores for boys and girls are presented in Table 3.1. Comparison of mean values of bullying, victimization, and defending across gender indicated that girls reported significantly higher levels of defending than boys, but there were no gender differences for bullying and victimization. Gender comparisons also indicated that girls had significantly higher empathy, cooperation, and responsibility scores and significantly lower school problems scores compared to boys.

Bivariate correlations among all study variables by gender are reported in Table 3.2. For girls and boys, bullying and victimization were significantly and negatively related to all four social skills, except correlations between victimization and empathy and between victimization and assertion were not significant for girls. Defending was significantly and positively related to all social skills for girls but only significantly related to empathy for boys. For girls, bullying was significantly and negatively related to personal adjustment and positively related to internalizing problems and school problems, but it was significantly and positively related to personal adjustment, internalizing problems, and school problems for boys. The same pattern emerged for victimization. For girls, defending was significantly and positively related to personal adjustment and school problems, but none of these correlations were significant for boys. For girls and boys, bullying and victimization were significantly and negatively related to all executive functioning variables, with the exception of the correlation between bullying and self-monitoring. Correlations between the defending and executive functioning variables were not significant for boys or girls.

Bullying Role Behavior

Model 1 tested the direct effect of executive functioning, emotional difficulties, and social skills on bullying behavior, as well as the direct effect of emotional difficulties on executive functioning and social skills, which then affects bullying behavior. Table 3.3 contains the standardized and unstandardized coefficients, standard errors, and p values for the measurement and structural models, and Figure 3.2 presents a diagram of all standardized path coefficients. The χ^2 value was significant, χ^2 (366) = 581.11, $p < .001$, but because other fit indices indicated acceptable fit, CFI = .93, SRMR = .07, RMSEA = .05, 95% confidence interval (CI) [.04,.06], PNFI = .73, the structural components of the model were interpreted. All path coefficients for both boys and girls were significant and in the expected direction, except for the paths between executive functioning and bullying behavior, as well as emotional difficulties and bullying, which were not significant. The critical-ratio z test was significant for the path between social skills and bullying (stronger association for boys). There was not a significant difference between girls and boys for the other path coefficients.

Table 3.1 Main Study Variables and MANOVA Results

	M	SD	MINIMUM	MAXIMUM	F	p
Empathy						
Boys	12.64	3.43	1.00	18.00	22.73	**.001**
Girls	14.65	3.09	3.00	18.00		
Assertion						
Boys	13.80	3.38	3.00	21.00	1.14	.287
Girls	14.29	3.80	3.00	21.00		
Cooperation						
Boys	15.44	3.55	4.00	21.00	7.95	**.005**
Girls	16.74	3.62	6.00	21.00		
Responsibility						
Boys	15.60	3.54	4.00	21.00	3.93	**.049**
Girls	16.49	3.44	4.00	21.00		
Personal adjustment						
Boys	5.85	4.63	0.00	22.00	0.45	.502
Girls	6.27	5.32	0.00	22.00		
Internalizing problems						
Boys	6.59	5.33	0.00	24.00	3.68	.056
Girls	8.05	6.58	0.00	29.00		
School problems						
Boys	3.70	3.10	0.00	12.00	8.27	**.004**
Girls	2.66	2.39	0.00	10.00		
Self-monitoring						
Boys	26.60	7.20	13.00	41.00	1.04	.308
Girls	27.46	5.70	15.00	41.00		
Inhibitory control						
Boys	33.50	10.96	3.00	50.00	1.39	.240
Girls	34.98	8.16	8.00	50.00		
Flexibility						
Boys	18.60	7.30	3.00	35.00	0.03	.861
Girls	18.75	6.03	6.00	35.00		
Emotion regulation						
Boys	31.90	9.10	4.00	45.00	0.02	.880
Girls	32.06	7.94	3.00	45.00		
Bullying						
Boys	3.21	4.25	0.00	25.00	1.39	.240
Girls	2.61	3.56	0.00	22.00		
Victimization						
Boys	6.63	7.34	0.00	40.00	3.42	.066
Girls	8.59	9.29	0.00	39.00		
Defending						
Boys	9.62	8.03	0.00	36.00	6.23	**.013**
Girls	12.57	10.53	0.00	40.00		

Note. Differences between boys and girls on the main study variables were assessed using MANOVA. Corresponding F and p values are listed. Significant analyses are in boldface. MANOVA multivariate analysis of variance.

Table 3.2 Intercorrelations Among Main Study Variables

	1	2	3	4	5	6	7	8	9	10	11	12	13	14
1. Empathy		.72**	.68**	.75**	−.40**	−.35**	−.46**	.28**	.39**	.28**	.39**	−.46**	−.33**	.22**
2. Assertion	.54**		.66**	.69**	−.40**	−.34**	−.33**	.27**	.35**	.21*	.37**	−.50**	−.29**	.14
3. Cooperation	.67**	.58**		.78**	−.49**	−.41**	−.54**	.34**	.46**	.35**	.44**	−.54**	−.34**	.08
4. Responsibility	.78**	.58**	.81**		−.47**	−.42**	−.43**	.35**	.42**	.34**	.45**	−.51**	−.34**	.13
5. Personal adjustment	−.41**	−.42**	−.44**	−.56**		.68**	.48**	−.36**	−.42**	−.38**	−.41**	.31**	.49**	.02
6. Internal problems	−.27**	−.27**	−.31**	−.42**	.77**		.50**	−.45**	−.51**	−.46**	−.50**	.22**	.55**	.05
7. School problems	−.37**	−.39**	−.47*	−.48**	.51**	.47**		−.28**	−.36**	−.32**	−.32**	.43**	.40**	−.14
8. Self-monitoring	.17	.13	.15	.21*	−.20*	−.29**	−.14		.86**	.92**	.79**	−.12	−.31**	−.14
9. Inhibitory control	.19*	.11	.29**	.30**	−.28**	−.34**	−.25**	.72**		.84**	.93**	−.29**	−.43**	−.14
10. Flexibility	.15	.11	.22*	.22*	−.22*	−.29**	−.22*	.82**	.68**		.77**	−.13	−.34**	−.12
11. Emotion regulation	.13	.04	.26**	.25**	−.22*	−.28**	−.14	.51**	.86**	.50**		−.31**	−.43**	−.11
12. Bullying	−.38**	−.30**	−.44**	−.42**	.25**	.19*	.34**	−.09	−.27**	−.24*	−.24*		.42**	−.07
13. Victimization	−.16	−.17	−.23*	−.29**	.56**	.67**	.40**	−.30**	−.31**	−.33**	−.17	.36**		.23**
14. Defending	.41**	.37*	.31**	.32**	.01	.20*	−.07	−.08	−.09	−.15	−.05	−.09	.32**	

Note. Correlations above the diagonal are for boys; those below the diagonal are for girls.
*p < .05. **p < .01.

Victim Role Behavior

Model 2 tested the direct effect of executive functioning, emotional difficulties, and social skills on victim behavior, as well as the direct effect of emotional difficulties on executive functioning and social skills. Table 3.4 contains the standardized and unstandardized coefficients, standard errors, and p values for the measurement and structural models, and Figure 3.3 presents a diagram of all standardized path coefficients. All path coefficients for both boys and girls were significant and in the expected direction, except for the paths between social skills and victimization, as well as executive functioning and victimization, which were not significant for either boys or girls. The χ^2 value was significant, $\chi^2(364) = 696.20$, $p < .001$, but because other fit indices indicated acceptable fit, CFI = .93, SRMR = .05, RMSEA = .06, 95% CI [.05,.07], PNFI = .73, the structural components of the model were interpreted. The critical-ratio z test was significant for the path between executive functioning and emotional difficulties (stronger association for boys). There was not a significant difference between girls and boys for the other path coefficients.

Table 3.3 Standardized and Unstandardized Coefficients for Model 1 (Bullying)

	BOYS				90% CI		GIRLS				90% CI	
	B	SE	P	β	LL	UL	B	SE	P	β	LL	UL
SS												
Empathy	0.90	.07	***	.83	.75	.89	0.76	.06	***	.81	.72	.88
Assertion	0.85	.07	***	.79	.72	.85	0.74	.09	***	.63	.50	.74
Cooperation	0.97	.07	***	.86	.80	.91	0.95	.07	***	.85	.78	.91
Responsibility	1.00			.89	.85	.93	1.00			.95	.91	.99
Emo diff												
Personal adjustment	1.86	.26	***	.80	.69	.88	3.51	.55	***	.92	.85	.99
Internalizing problems	2.18	.30	***	.81	.70	.89	3.91	.62	***	.83	.74	.89
School problems	1.00			.64	.51	.75	1.00			.58	.40	.73
EF												
Self-monitoring	0.73	.04	***	.86	.83	.89	0.60	.07	***	.72	.64	.79
Inhibitory control	1.28	.04	***	1.00	1.00	1.00	1.19	.07	***	.99	.99	.99
Flexibility	0.72	.05	***	.84	.81	.88	0.60	.07	***	.68	.59	.76
Emotion regulation	1.00			.93	.91	.95	1.00			.86	.81	.90
Bullying behavior												
Bad names	1.00			.91	.84	.96	1.00			.85	.64	.97
Made fun of	0.83	.06	***	.83	.72	.90	0.52	.08	***	.63	.45	.81
Left out	0.62	.06	***	.77	.64	.86	0.31	.06	***	.51	.28	.70
Push, punch, slap	0.54	.05	***	.72	.55	.84	0.42	.07	***	.58	.24	.82
Told lies	0.22	.05	***	.41	.17	.58	0.38	.06	***	.57	.28	.80
Make people dislike	0.11	.03	***	.32	.11	.53	0.31	.06	***	.47	.04	.78
Stolen things	0.04	.02	*	.21	.03	.43	0.10	.03	***	.36	.07	.69
Thrown things	0.35	.05	***	.55	.33	.72	0.16	.05	**	.30	.08	.52
Said bad things	0.24	.05	***	.39	.12	.60	0.82	.09	***	.79	.55	.89
Talked behind back	0.31	.06	***	.42	.20	.62	0.90	.11	***	.74	.50	.84
Structural model												
Emo diff → EF	−2.58	.45	***	−.60	−.71	−.47	−1.74	.54	**	−.35	−.51	−.17
Emo diff → SS	−1.05	.18	***	−.66	−.78	−.54	−1.43	.29	***	−.61	−.75	−.43
Emo diff → bullying	0.02	.07	.77	.04	−.22	.33	−0.01	.07	.91	−.02	−.31	.27
EF → bullying	−0.01	.01	.61	−.05	−.22	.13	−0.02	.01	.13	−.15	−.39	.05
SS → bullying	−0.17	.04	***	−.58	−.78	−.32	−0.09	.03	***	−.44	−.73	−.12

Note. The table presents standardized and unstandardized coefficients, 90% CIs, standard errors, and *p* values for Model 1 (bullying). CI = confidence interval; EF = executive functioning; Emo diff = emotional difficulties; *LL* = lower limit; SS = social skills; *UL* = upper limit.
*$p < .05$. **$p < .01$. ***$p < .001$.

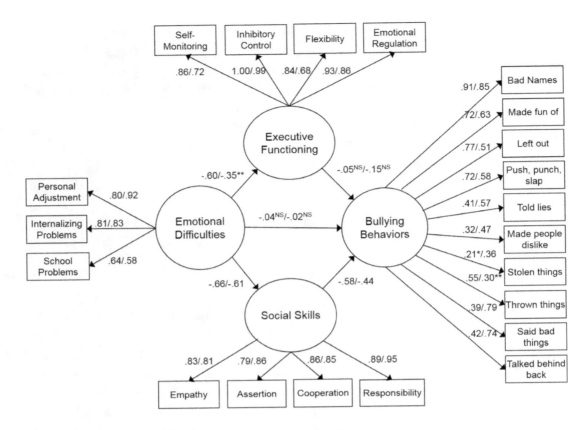

Figure 3.2   Structural Equation Model for Model 1 (Bullying)

Note. The structural equation model shows standardized path coefficients for boys/girls, with *p* < .001 unless otherwise noted. ** *p* < .01, NS = not significant.

Defender Role Behavior

Model 3 tested the direct effect of executive functioning, emotional difficulties, and social skills on defender behavior, as well as the direct effect of emotional difficulties on executive functioning and social skills. Table 3.5 contains the standardized and unstandardized coefficients, standard errors, and *p* values for the measurement and structural models, and Figure 3.4 presents a diagram of all standardized path coefficients. All path coefficients for both boys and girls were significant and in the expected direction, except for the paths between executive functioning and defending for girls, as well as between emotional difficulties and defending for boys, which were not significant. The χ^2 value was significant, $\chi^2(368) = 621.30, p < .001$, but because other fit indices indicated acceptable fit, CFI = .95, SRMR = .07, RMSEA = .05, 95% CI [.05,.06], PNFI = .75, the structural components of the model were interpreted. The critical-ratio *z* test was significant for the path between emotional difficulties and defending (with a stronger association for girls

Table 3.4 Standardized and Unstandardized Coefficients for Model 2 (Victimization).

	BOYS				90% CI		GIRLS				90% CI	
	B	SE	p	β	LL	UL	B	SE	p	β	LL	UL
SS												
Empathy	0.90	.07	***	.83	.76	.88	0.76	.06	***	.81	.71	.87
Assertion	0.84	.07	***	.79	.71	.85	0.72	.09	***	.63	.50	.74
Cooperation	0.96	.07	***	.86	.79	.90	0.93	.07	***	.85	.77	.90
Responsibility	1.00			.90	.85	.94	1.00			.96	.91	1.00
Emo diff												
Personal adjustment	1.86	.26	***	.79	.69	.87	3.28	.50	***	.87	.79	.94
Internalizing problems	2.25	.31	***	.83	.73	.91	4.03	.62	***	.87	.78	.92
School problems	1.00			.63	.50	.73	1.00			.59	.41	.72
EF												
Self-monitoring	0.74	.04	***	.88	.84	.91	0.60	.07	***	.71	.60	.80
Inhibitory control	1.26	.05	***	.98	.96	1.00	1.22	.08	***	1.01	.97	1.05
Flexibility	0.74	.04	***	.87	.82	.90	0.59	.07	***	.66	.55	.76
Emotional regulation	1.00			.94	.91	.96	1.00			.85	.80	.89
Victimization behavior												
Mean names	1.00			.85	.78	.88	1.00			.91	.86	.94
Made fun of	0.91	.08	***	.84	.75	.90	0.99	.06	***	.93	.89	.96
Purposely left out	0.83	.07	***	.83	.69	.90	0.82	.07	***	.82	.73	.87
Ignored	0.79	.08	***	.73	.58	.84	0.93	.07	***	.86	.81	.90
Punched or slapped	0.42	.08	***	.47	.28	.64	0.74	.06	***	.81	.71	.87
Pushed or shoved	0.48	.07	***	.56	.37	.72	0.71	.07	***	.74	.60	.83
Told lies about me	0.79	.07	***	.78	.66	.86	0.86	.07	***	.81	.68	.89
Others dislike me	0.86	.08	***	.81	.68	.88	0.73	.08	***	.69	.52	.80
Threatened	0.38	.07	***	.47	.29	.65	0.47	.06	***	.66	.51	.77
Things taken	0.37	.07	***	.44	.23	.61	0.44	.07	***	.53	.37	.69
Structural model												
Emo diff → EF	−2.66	.46	***	−.61	−.71	−.46	−1.75	.53	***	−.37	−.52	−.20
Emo diff → SS	−1.06	.18	***	−.65	−.76	−.52	−1.39	.28	***	−.60	−.74	−.38
Emo diff → victim	0.36	.09	***	.42	.98	.32	0.63	.13	***	.77	.48	.98
EF → victim	−0.01	.01	.32	−.10	−.27	.08	−0.01	.01	.34	−.08	−.23	.06
SS → victim	0.03	.04	.42	−.09	−.10	.32	0.07	.04	.08	.19	−.05	.43

Note. The table presents standardized and unstandardized coefficients, 90% CIs, standard errors, and *p* values for Model 2 (victimization). CI = confidence interval; EF = executive functioning; Emo diff = emotional difficulties; *LL* = lower limit; SS = social skills; *UL* = upper limit.

***p < .001.

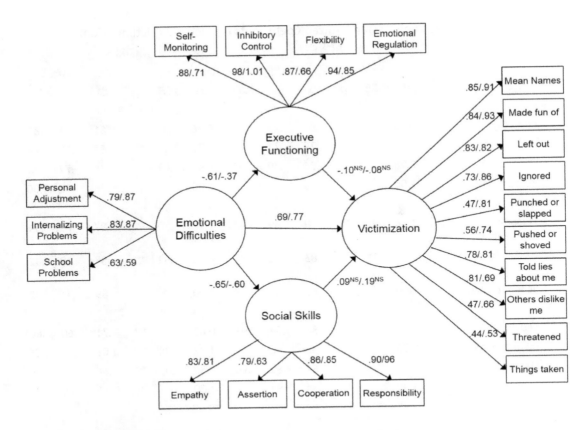

Figure 3.3 Structural Equation Model for Model 2 (Victimization).

Note. The structural equation model shows standardized path coefficients for boys/girls, with $p < .001$ unless otherwise noted. [NS] = not significant.

but it was not significant for boys). There was not a significant difference between girls and boys for the other path coefficients.

Discussion

The goal of the current study was to understand the associations among bullying experiences (i.e., bullying, victimization, and defending) and social skills (i.e., empathy, assertion, cooperation, responsibility), emotional difficulties (i.e., personal adjustment, internalizing problems, school problems), and executive functioning skills (i.e., self-monitoring, inhibitory control, flexibility, emotional regulation). Learning more about social skills, emotional difficulties, and executive functioning skills of students in relation to bullying experiences may help inform intervention efforts. Data were collected in a sample of 246 sixth- through eighth-grade students via

Table 3.5 Standardized and Unstandardized Coefficients for Model 3 (Defending).

	BOYS				90% CI		GIRLS				90% CI	
	B	SE	p	β	LL	UL	B	SE	p	β	LL	UL
SS												
Empathy	0.91	.07	***	.84	.77	.89	0.77	.06	***	.82	.72	.88
Assertion	0.84	.07	***	.79	.71	.85	0.76	.09	***	.65	.52	.75
Cooperation	0.96	.07	***	.86	.78	.90	0.95	.07	***	.85	.77	.90
Responsibility	1.00			.90	.85	.93	1.00			.95	.90	.98
Emo diff												
Personal adjustment	1.89	.27	***	.80	.70	.88	3.42	.53	***	.90	.82	.97
Internalizing problems	2.22	.31	***	.82	.71	.90	3.96	.62	***	.84	.75	.90
School problems	1.00			.63	.50	.74	1.00			.59	.40	.73
EF												
Self-monitoring	0.73	.04	***	.86	.83	.89	0.60	.07	***	.72	.63	.79
Inhibitory control	1.28	.04	***	1.00	1.00	1.00	1.19	.07	***	.99	.99	.99
Flexibility	0.72	.05	***	.84	.80	.87	0.60	.07	***	.68	.59	.75
Emotional regulation	1.00			.93	.91	.95	1.00			.86	.81	.90
Defending behavior												
Become friends	1.00			.71	.60	.81	1.00			.69	.56	.79
Encouraged to tell	1.03	.13	***	.71	.60	.80	1.53	.18	***	.85	.79	.90
Defend if pushed	0.89	.12	***	.67	.51	.79	1.64	.19	***	.88	.82	.92
Defend things taken	0.75	.11	***	.62	.43	.77	1.40	.17	***	.83	.75	.88
Defend called names	1.08	.12	***	.78	.69	.85	1.46	.19	***	.80	.71	.87
Include	1.03	.12	***	.74	.64	.82	1.29	.17	***	.75	.65	.82
Help books knock out	1.21	.14	***	.78	.66	.87	1.48	.19	***	.78	.66	.84
Help purposely tripped	1.25	.13	***	.83	.74	.90	1.58	.18	***	.89	.84	.93
Told an adult	1.03	.12	***	.76	.64	.85	1.52	.18	***	.84	.76	.90
Defend if tricked	1.07	.12	***	.83	.75	.89	1.54	.19	***	.84	.72	.90
Structural model												
Emo diff → EF	−2.61	.46	***	−.60	−.70	−.45	−1.77	.54	***	−.36	−.52	−.18
Emo diff → SS	−1.06	.18	***	−.66	−.77	−.52	−1.40	.28	***	−.61	−.75	−.41
Emo diff → defending	0.03	.06	.63	.08	−.19	.35	0.23	.08	**	.44	.19	.69
EF → defending	−0.02	.01	*	−.27	−.45	−.08	−0.02	.01	.12	−.15	−.31	.02
SS → defending	0.08	.03	**	.35	.07	.58	.015	.03	***	.69	.51	.89

Note. The table presents standardized and unstandardized coefficients, 90% CIs, standard errors, and p values for Model 3 (defending). CI = confidence interval; EF = executive functioning; Emo diff = emotional difficulties; LL = lower limit; SS = social skills; UL = upper limit.
*p < .05. **p < .01. ***p < .001.

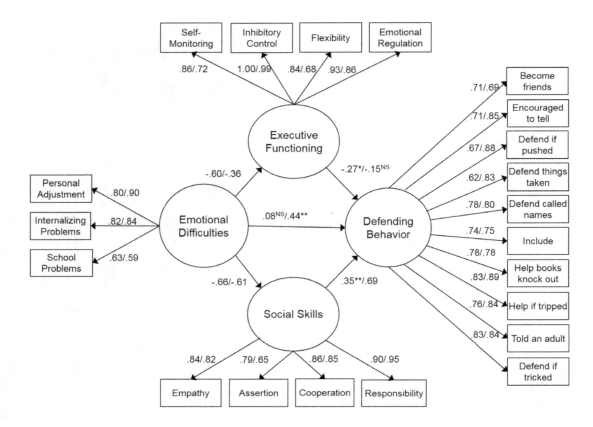

Figure 3.4 Structural Equation Model for Model 3 (Defending).

Note. The structural equation model shows standardized path coefficients for boys/girls, with $p < .001$ unless otherwise noted. ** $p < .01$, NS = not significant.

self-report (i.e., bullying behaviors, social skills, emotional difficulties) and teacher report (i.e., executive functioning skills). On the basis of previous studies investigating individual characteristics and bullying role behaviors, it was hypothesized that (a) bullying behavior would be negatively associated with social skills and executive functioning skills (Chui & Chan, 2013; Coolidge et al., 2003; Jenkins et al., 2014; Mahady-Wilton et al., 2000; Monks et al., 2005; Perren & Alsaker, 2006; Unnever & Cornell, 2003; Verlinden et al., 2013); (b) victimization would be negatively related to social skills and executive functioning skills, but positively related to emotional difficulties (Champion et al., 2003; Egan & Perry, 1998; Fox & Boulton, 2005; Jenkins et al., 2014; Kokkinos & Kipritsi, 2012; Mahady-Wilton et al., 2000; Toblin et al., 2005; Verlinden et al., 2013); and (c) defending behaviors would be positively associated with social skills and executive functioning skills (Eisenberg et al., 1995; Gini et al., 2007; Jenkins et al., 2014; Monks et al., 2005; Nickerson et al., 2008; Thornberg & Jungert, 2014).

For all three models (i.e., bullying, victimization, and defending), emotional difficulties were significantly and negatively associated with executive functioning skills and social skills for both boys and girls. Greater emotional problems were related to lower social skills and more difficulties with executive functioning. Emotional difficulties were not significantly related to bullying behaviors but were significantly and positively associated with victimization for both girls and boys. Thus, more emotional problems were associated with more victimization. This finding supported the prediction that emotional difficulties would be significantly and positively related to victimization and is consistent with prior research findings. Research has consistently demonstrated that victims tend to have high levels of emotional problems, such as depression, anxiety, and low self-esteem (Hawker & Boulton, 2000; Nakamoto & Schwartz, 2010).

In addition, emotional difficulties were significantly and positively associated with defending behaviors for girls but not for boys. Thus, more defending behaviors, for girls, were associated with more emotional problems. This finding was not predicted and is somewhat surprising. It may be that girls with more emotional difficulties witness more bullying in their peer group and, thus, have more opportunities to defend. Alternatively, defending peers in bullying situations may be stressful and may be associated with more emotional difficulties. Moreover, victims are likely to play a secondary role as a defender (Salmivalli et al., 1996). The emotional difficulties could be an artifact of being victimized. The present study did not examine outcomes for students who were both victims and defenders. Moreover, there are gender differences in the type of victimization that girls and boys experience (Card et al., 2008), so female defenders may experience more emotional problems because if they are defending another girl, then they may be witnessing or be indirectly involved in relational aggression. More research needs to be done on the emotional health of girls who defend victims of bullying.

Executive functioning was not significantly related to bullying and victimization for boys and girls. We predicted that executive functioning would be negatively related to both bullying and victimization because other studies have found that skills in executive functioning are related to bullying and victimization (Monks et al., 2005; Verlinden et al., 2013). Prior research investigated specific areas of executive functioning deficits and found significant associations with bullying role behaviors. For example, bullying behavior has been associated with inhibition problems, working memory deficits, and global executive functioning (Verlinden et al., 2013), as well as problems with metacognition, social judgments, and decision making (Coolidge et al., 2003). Victimization has been associated with inhibition and low intelligence (Verlinden et al., 2013). Aggressive victims have been found to have problems with emotional dysregulation (Toblin et al., 2005). For both victims and bullies, unique patterns of emotions and emotion dysregulation have been found (Mahady-Wilton et al., 2000). Specifically, bullying has been associated with high levels of anger and contempt. Both passive and aggressive victims engage in maladaptive displays of emotion and emotion regulation. The current study included four areas of executive functioning: self-monitoring, inhibitory control, flexibility, and emotional regulation. Prior research has investigated some of these areas of executive functioning but also other areas. One reason for the lack of findings in the current study may be different constructs assessed across studies.

Executive functioning was significantly and negatively associated with defending for boys only (the relation was not significant for girls). For boys, higher executive functioning (e.g., higher levels of self-monitoring, emotional regulation, and inhibition) was associated with lower levels of defending behavior, which does not support the hypotheses. Prior research has found a positive association between executive functioning tasks and defending. For example, in a study by Monks et al. (2005), defenders demonstrated strong theory of mind, deception, planning, and inhibition. Eisenberg et al. (1995) found that defending was associated with strong regulation ability, low emotionality, and constructive problem solving.

Youth who engage in defending are taking a "social risk." Defenders run the risk of becoming a target themselves or being perceived as a tattletale if reporting to an adult, or if being friendly toward victimized peers, they may be viewed as having a lower social status. Individuals with high executive functioning tend to be socially aware and likely know their social standing (Monks et al., 2005). So, social self-efficacy, one's sense of control over one's social status, may moderate defending behavior. Boys who are aware of their social standing, and perhaps concerned about damaging their status, may choose not to defend. It may be that boys who are less inhibited, have less emotional regulation, and less self-monitoring (reflected in lower executive functioning scores) are more likely to defend victims because they are less aware of, or concerned about, their social standing.

Social skills were not significantly related to victimization for boys and girls, counter to hypotheses. Other research has found significant, negative associations among victimization and various social skills. For example, cooperation, assertion, empathy, and self-control were significantly and negatively related to victimization in a recent study (Jenkins et al., 2014); however, the current study included other variables: executive functioning and emotional difficulties. Including all three of these variables allows the model to statistically account for interrelationships among the variables. Although other research has found that social skills are negatively related to victimization, the connections between social skills, executive functioning, and emotional difficulties may account for that finding.

As predicted, bullying was significantly and negatively related to social skills. Finally, social skills were significantly and positively related to defending behavior for both boys and girls. This finding supported the prediction in the current study and replicated prior research findings (Gini et al., 2007; Nickerson et al., 2008; Thornberg & Jungert, 2014). For example, Jenkins et al. (2014) found a positive association between defending behavior in middle school students and the social skills of assertion, empathy, and self-control.

Social, emotional, and cognitive skills are all important factors to consider in relation to bullying behaviors, including defending and victimization. It is important to understand the specific skills and characteristics that are associated with engaging in bullying, being victimized, or defending victims from bullying. Our findings highlight the importance of including social, emotional, and cognitive skills in studies on bullying behaviors as each of these constructs was significantly related to at least one of the bully role behaviors.

Limitations and Future Research

The current sample was homogeneous, and consequently, the results may not generalize to all populations. Ethnicity, setting (e.g., urban), and age can differentially affect bullying and victimization rates and experiences (Swearer-Napolitano, 2011). The relationship between executive functioning skills and bullying roles should be examined with diverse populations to determine if the relationship differs across demographics since participants in the current study were from a single school. The sample size is another limitation of the current study. Although some significant results were found, overall the results may not capture all potential effects. Similar studies should be conducted with larger and more diverse samples. Also, the current study did not address the potential association between executive functioning skills and social skills, and future research may want to include this association in the analyses to further our understanding of relations among the variables studied.

The present study relied mainly on student self-report measures in the analyses. When self-report data are being collected, there is always the possibility that students are responding in a biased or dishonest way. Fourteen teachers also provided ratings; this averages to over 17 ratings per teacher. Teachers completed 40 items of the CEFI, which would take approximately 10 minutes to complete. Teachers may have experienced fatigue while completing this many long surveys, and that fatigue may have resulted in response bias. Conclusions drawn from this study would be strengthened by corroborating evidence from more objective forms of data collection such as observation or behavioral experiments. Moreover, longitudinal research is necessary to determine if these individual variables are related to bullying role behaviors over time, in addition to in a cross-sectional manner.

Finally, prior studies have included other types of executive functioning skills. The latent variable of executive functioning created for this study may not correspond exactly to conceptualizations of executive functioning from other studies. Results should be compared judiciously across studies.

In order to gain a better understanding of the roles that social skills, emotional difficulties, and executive functioning play in bullying situations, observational data and reports from other sources (e.g., teachers, peers, parents) should be collected for these variables. Furthermore, intervention programs that target the executive functioning of those involved in bullying should be developed and validated. Currently, social–emotional interventions used for students involved in bullying involve social skills lessons but are not designed to promote executive functioning or emotion regulation.

Conclusions

The current study investigated the relations among bullying behaviors, social skills, emotional difficulties, and executive functioning skills for boys and girls in middle school. Results indicated that (a) emotional difficulties were significantly and positively associated with victimization for boys and girls, (b) emotional difficulties were significantly and positively associated with defending for girls, (c) executive functioning was significantly and negatively associated with defending for boys, and (d) social skills were significantly and positively related to defending behavior for boys and girls. These results may provide direction for future intervention ideas. For example, given that social skills were significantly and positively related to defending behavior, interventions could be targeted at increasing specific social skills in the school-wide population to give students the tools they need to engage in defending behaviors. More work may be needed to understand why boys with high executive functioning were not engaging in defending. There may be specific executive functioning skills that are the true mechanism (versus a global executive functioning score) that need to be developed. The study highlights the importance of addressing associated emotional difficulties in schools for both boys and girls who are victims and for girls who are defending others. These different associations demonstrate the importance of considering different skills and characteristics of boys and girls in relation to engaging in or receiving bullying behaviors.

References

Abdi, B. (2010). Gender differences in social skills, problem behaviours and academic competence of Iranian Preschool children based on their parent and teacher ratings. *Procedia-Social and Behavioral Sciences, 5*, 1175–1179. doi:10.1016/j.sbspro.2010.07.256

Anme, T., Shinohara, R., Sugisawa, Y., Tong, L., Tanaka, E., Watanabe, T., & Japan Children's Study Group. (2010). Gender differences of children's social skills and parenting using Interaction Rating Scale (IRS). *Procedia-Social and Behavioral Sciences, 2*, 260–268. doi:10.1016/j.sbspro.2010.03.008

Baron, R. M., & Kenny, D. A. (1986). The moderator-mediator variable distinction in social psychological research: Conceptual, strategic, and statistical considerations. *Journal of Personality and Social Psychology, 51*, 1173–1182. doi:10.1037/0022-3514.51.6.1173

Barrett, P. (2007). Structural equation modeling: Adjudging model fit. *Personality and Individual Differences, 42*(5), 815–824. doi:10.1016/j.paid.2006.09.018

Beck, J. S. (2011). *Cognitive therapy: Basics and beyond* (2nd ed.). New York, NY: Guilford Press.

Berlin, L., & Bohlin, G. (2002). Response inhibition, hyperactivity, and conduct problems among preschool children. *Journal of Clinical Child and Adolescent Psychology, 31*, 242–251. doi:10.1207/S15374424JCCP3102_09

Browne, M. W., & Cudeck, R. (1989). Single sample cross-validation indices for covariance structures. *Multivariate Behavioral Research, 24*, 445–455. doi:10.1207/s15327906mbr2404_4

Camodeca, M., & Goossens, F. A. (2005). Aggression, social cognitions, anger and sadness in bullies and victims. *Journal of Child Psychology and Psychiatry, 46*, 186–197. doi:10.1111/j.1469-7610.2004.00347.x

Card, N. A., Stucky, B. D., Sawalani, G. M., & Little, T. D. (2008). Direct and indirect aggression during childhood and adolescence: A meta-analytic review of gender differences, intercorrelations, and relations to maladjustment. *Child Development, 79*, 1185–1229. doi:10.1111/j.1467-8624.2008.01184.x

Carlson, S. M., & Moses, L. J. (2001). Individual differences in inhibitory control and children's theory of mind. *Child Development, 72*, 1032–1053. doi:10.1111/1467-8624.00333

Champion, K., Vernberg, E., & Shipman, K. (2003). Non-bullying victims of bullies: Aggression, social skills, and friendship characteristics. *Applied Developmental Psychology, 24*, 535–551. doi:10.1016/j.appdev.2003.08.003

Chui, W. H., & Chan, H. C. O. (2013). Association between self-control and school bullying behaviors among Macanese adolescents. *Child Abuse & Neglect, 37*, 237–242. doi:10.1016/j.chiabu.2012.012.003

Cohen, J. (1988). *Statistical power analysis for the behavioral sciences* (2nd ed.). Hillsdale, NJ: Lawrence Erlbaum Associates.

Coolidge, F. L., DenBoer, J. W., & Segal, D. L. (2003). Personality and neuropsychological correlates of bullying behavior. *Personality and Individual Differences, 36*, 1559–1569. doi:10.1016/j.paid.2003.06.005

Crick, N. R., & Dodge, K. A. (1994). A review and reformulation of social information-processing mechanisms in children's social adjustment. *Psychological Bulletin, 115*, 74–101. doi:10.1037/0033-2909.115.1.74

Demaray, M. K., Summers, K. H., Jenkins, L. N., & Becker, L. (2014). The Bully Participant Behavior Questionnaire (BPBQ): Establishing a reliable and valid measure. *Journal of School Violence, 15*, 158–188. doi:10.1080/15388220.2014.964801

Dowdy, E., Doane, K., Eklund, K., & Dever, B. V. (2011). A comparison of teacher nomination and screening to identify behavioral and emotional risk within a sample of underrepresented students. *Journal of Emotional and Behavioral Disorders, 21*, 127–137. doi:10.1177/1063426611417627

Dowdy, E., Twyford, J. M., Chin, J. K., DiStefano, C. A., Kamphaus, R. W., & Mays, K. L. (2011). Factor structure of the BASC-2 Behavioral and Emotional Screening System Student Form. *Psychological Assessment, 23*, 379–387. doi:10.1037/a0021843

Egan, S. K., & Perry, D. G. (1998). Does low self-regard invite victimization? *Developmental Psychology, 34*, 299–309. doi:10.1037/0012-1649.34.2.299

Eisenberg, N., Carlo, G., Murphy, B., & Van Court, P. (1995). Prosocial development in late adolescence: A longitudinal study. *Child Development, 66*, 1179–1197. 10.2307/1131806

Espelage, D. L., & Holt, M. K. (2007). Dating violence & sexual harassment across the bully-victim continuum among middle and high school students. *Journal of Youth and Adolescence, 36*, 799–811. doi:10.1007/s10964-006-9109-7

Ferrier, D. E., Bassatt, H. H., & Denham, S. A. (2014). Relations between executive functioning and emotionality in preschoolers: Exploring a transitive cognition-emotion linkage. *Frontiers in Psychology, 27*, 1–12. doi:10.3389/fpsyg.2014.00487

Fox, C. L., & Boulton, M. J. (2005). The social skills problems of victims of bullying: Self, peer, and teacher perceptions. *British Journal of Educational Psychology, 75*, 313–328. doi:10.1348/000709905X25517

Gasser, L., & Keller, M. (2009). Are the competent the morally good? Perspective taking and moral motivation of children involved in bullying. *Social Development, 18*, 798–816. doi:10.1111/j.1467-9507.2008.00516.x

Gini, G., Albiero, P., Benelli, B., & Altoe, G. (2007). Does empathy predict adolescents' bullying and defending behavior? *Aggressive Behavior, 33*, 467–476. doi:10.1002/ab.20204

Gresham, F. M., & Elliott, S. N. (2008). *Social skills improvement system: Rating scales manual*. Minneapolis, MN: Pearson Assessments.

Hawker, D. S., & Boulton, M. J. (2000). Twenty years' research on peer victimization and psychosocial maladjustment: A meta-analytic review of cross-sectional studies. *Journal of Child Psychology and Psychiatry, 41*, 441–455. doi:10.1111/1469-7610.00629

Hawley, P. H. (2003). Prosocial and coercive configurations of resource control in early adolescence: A case for the well-adapted Machiavellian. *Merrill-Palmer Quarterly, 49*, 279–309. doi:10.1353/mpq.2003.0013

Hawley, P. H. (2007). Social dominance in childhood and adolescence: Why social competence and aggression may go hand in hand. In P. H. Hawley, T. D. Little, & P. Rodkin (Eds.), *Aggression and adaptation: The bright side to bad behavior* (pp. 1–29). Hillsdale, NJ: Lawrence Erlbaum Associates.

Hawley, P. H., Little, T. D., & Pasupathi, M. (2002). Winning friends and influencing peers: Strategies of peer influence in late childhood. *International Journal of Behavioral Development, 26*, 466–473. doi:10.1080/01650250143000427

Hawley, P. H., Shorey, H. S., & Alderman, P. M. (2009). Attachment correlates of resource control strategies: Possible origins of social dominance and interpersonal power differentials. *Journal of Social and Personal Relationships, 26*, 1097–1118. doi:10.1177/0265407509347939

Hawley, P. H., & Williford, A. (2015). Articulating the theory of bullying intervention programs: Views from social psychology, social work, and organizational science. *Journal of Applied Developmental Psychology, 37*, 3–15. doi:10.1016/j.appdev.2014.11.006

Hayes, A. F. (2009). Beyond Baron and Kenny: Statistical mediation analysis in the new millennium. *Communication Monographs, 76*(4), 408–420. doi:10.1080/03637750903310360

Hooper, D., Coughlan, J., & Mullen, M. (2008). Structural equation modelling: Guidelines for determining model fit. *Electronic Journal of Business Research Methods, 6*, 53–60.

Hu, L. T., & Bentler, P. M. (1999). Cutoff criteria for fit indexes in covariance structure analysis: Conventional criteria versus new alternatives. *Structural Equation Modeling, 6*, 1–55. doi:10.1080/10705519909540118

Janosz, M., Archambault, I., Pagani, L. S., Pascal, S., Morin, A. J., & Bowen, F. (2008). Are there detrimental effects of witnessing school violence in early adolescence? *Journal of Adolescent Health, 43*, 600–608. doi:10.1016/j.jadohealth.2008.04.011

Jenkins, L. N., Demaray, M. K., Fredrick, S. S., & Summers, K. H. (2014). Associations among middle school students' bullying roles and social skills. *Journal of School Violence, 15*, 259–278. doi:10.1080/15388220.2014.986675

Kamphaus, R. W., & Reynolds, C. R. (2007). *BASC-2 Behavioral and Emotional Screening System (BESS) manual.* Circle Pines, MN: Pearson.

Ledwell, M., & King, V. (2015). Bullying and internalizing problems gender differences and the buffering role of parental communication. *Journal of Family Issues, 36*, 543–566. doi:10.1177/0192513X13491410

Levin, H. S., Culhane, K. A., Hartmann, J., Evankovich, K., Mattson, A. J., Harward, H., … Fletcher, J. M. (1991). Developmental changes in performance on tests of purported frontal lobe functioning. *Developmental Neuropsychology, 7*, 377–395. doi:10.1080/87565649109540499

Kokkinos, C. M., & Kipritsi, E. (2012). The relationship between bullying, victimization, trait emotion intelligence, self-efficacy and empathy among preadolescents. *Social Psychology of Education, 15*, 41–58. doi:10.1007/s11218-011-9168-9

Mahady-Wilton, M., Craig, W. M., & Pepler, D. J. (2000). Emotional regulation and display in classroom bullying: Characteristic expressions of affect, coping styles and relevant contextual factors. *Social Development, 9*, 226–245. doi:10.1111/1467-9507.00121

Monks, C. P., Smith, P. K., & Swettenham, J. (2005). Psychological correlates of peer victimization in preschool: Social cognitive skills, executive functioning and attachment profiles. *Aggressive Behavior, 31*, 571–588. doi:10.1002/ab.20099

Mulaik, S. A., James, L. R., Van Alstine, J., Bennet, N., Lind, S., & Stilwell, C. D. (1989). Evaluation of goodness-of-fit indices for structural equation models. *Psychological Bulletin, 105*, 430–445. doi:10.1037/0033-2909.105.3.430

Naglieri, J. A., & Goldstein, S. (2012). *Comprehensive executive functioning index.* North Tonawanda, NY: Multi Health Systems.

Nakamoto, J., & Schwartz, D. (2010). Is peer victimization associated with academic achievement? A meta-analytic review. *Social Development, 19,* 221–242. doi:10.1111/j.1467-9507.2009.00539.x

Nickerson, A. B., Mele, D., & Princiotta, D. (2008). Attachment and empathy as predictors of roles as defenders or outsiders in bullying interactions. *Journal of School Psychology, 46,* 687–703. doi:10.1016/j.jsp.2008.06.002

Perren, S., & Alsaker, F. D. (2006). Social behavior and peer relationships of victims, bully-victims, and bullies in kindergarten. *Journal of Child Psychology and Psychiatry, 47,* 45–57. doi:10.1111/j.1469-7610.2005.01445.x

Preacher, K. J., & Hayes, A. F. (2008). Asymptotic and resampling strategies for assessing and comparing indirect effects in multiple mediator models. *Behavior Research Methods, 40,* 879–891. doi:10.3758/BRM.40.3.879

Reader, M. J., Harris, E. L., Schuerholz, L. J., & Denckla, M. B. (1994). Attention deficit hyperactivity disorder and executive dysfunction. *Developmental Neuropsychology, 10,* 493–512. doi:10.1080/87565649409540598

Riggs, N. R., Jahromi, L. B., Razza, R. P., Dillworth-Bart, J. E., & Mueller, U. (2006). Executive functioning and the promotion of social-emotional competence. *Journal of Applied Developmental Psychology, 26,* 300–309. doi:10.1016/j.appdev.2006.04.002

Salmivalli, C., Lagerspetz, K., Björkqvist, K., Österman, K., & Kaukiainen, A. (1996). Bullying as a group process: Participant roles and their relations to social status within the group. *Aggressive Behavior, 22,* 1–15. doi:10.1002/(SICI)1098-2337(1996)22:1 1::AID-AB1 3.0.CO;2-T.

Schermelleh-Engel, K., Moosbrugger, H., & Müller, H. (2003). Evaluating the fit of structural equation models: Test of significance and descriptive goodness-of-fit measures. *Methods of Psychological Research-Online, 8*(2), 23–74.

Séguin, J., & Zelazo, P. (2005). Executive functioning in early physical aggression. In R. E. Tremblay, W. H. Willard, & J. Archer (Eds.), *Developmental origins of aggression* (pp. 307–329). New York, NY: Guilford Press.

Shrout, P. E., & Bolger, N. (2002). Mediation in experimental and nonexperimental studies: New procedures and recommendations. *Psychological Methods, 7,* 422–445. doi:10.1037/1082-989X.7.4.422

Soper, D. S. (2015). A-priori sample size calculator for structural equation models [Software]. Retrieved from http://www.danielsoper.com/statcalc

Summers, K. H., & Demaray, M. K. (2008). *Bully participant behavior questionnaire.* DeKalb, IL: Northern Illinois University.

Sutton, J., Smith, P. K., & Swettenham, J. (1999a). Bullying and "theory of mind": A critique of the "social skills deficit" view of anti-social behaviour. *Social Development, 8,* 117–134. doi:10.1111/1467-9507.00083

Sutton, J., Smith, P. K., & Swettenham, J. (1999b). Socially undesirable needs not be incompetent: A response to Crick and Dodge. *Social Development, 8,* 132–134. doi:10.1111/1467-9507.00085

Swearer-Napolitano, S. M. (2011). Risk factors for and outcomes of bullying and victimization (Paper 132). In *Educational Psychology Papers and Publications.* Retrieved from http://digitalcommons.unl.edu/edpsychpapers/132

Thornberg, R., & Jungert, T. (2014). School bullying and the mechanisms of moral disengagement. *Aggressive Behavior, 40,* 99–108. doi:10.1002/ab.21509

Toblin, R. L., Schwartz, D., Gorman, A. H., & Abou-Ezzeddine, T. (2005). Social cognitive and behavioural attributes of aggressive victims of bullying. *Applied Development Psychology, 26,* 329–346. doi:10.1016/j.appdev.2005.02.004

Unnever, J. D., & Cornell, D. G. (2003). Bullying, self-control, and ADHD. *Journal of Interpersonal Violence, 18,* 129–147. doi:10.1177/0886260502238731

Verhulst, F. C., & Ende, J. (1992). Agreement between parents' reports and adolescents' self-reports of problem behavior. *Journal of Child Psychology and Psychiatry, 33,* 1011–1023. doi:10.1111/j.1469-7610.1992.tb00922.x

Verlinden, M., Veenstra, R., Ringoot, A. P., Jansen, P. W., Raat, H., Hofman, A., … Tiemeier, H. (2013). Detecting bullying in early elementary school with a computerized peer-nomination instrument. *Psychological Assessment, 42,* 953–966. doi:10.1007/s10802-013-9832-y

Welsh, M. C., Pennington, B. F., & Groisser, D. B. (1991). A normative-developmental study of executive functioning: A window on prefrontal function in children. *Developmental Neuropsychology, 7,* 131–149. doi:10.1080/87565649109540483

Westland, J. C. (2010). Lower bounds on sample size in structural equation modeling. *Electronic Commerce Research and Applications, 9,* 476–487. doi:10.1016/j.elerap.2010.07.003

Conflict, Power, and Violence in Families

Kristin L. Anderson

Research on conflict, power, and violence in families in the 2000s developed a promising focus on the interconnections between types of violence and between the experience of violence and locations in larger structures of power and inequality. I examine research on poly-victimization, typologies of violence, dyadic research, and links between violence and inequalities of gender, race, class, and sexual orientation. Additionally, this review evaluates research on the connections between violence in families and other arenas of family study, including teen pregnancy, marriage formation, cohabitation, and divorce. The review concludes with a discussion of studies showing declines in rates of abuse within families in the 2000s.

As it developed, the field of family violence research divided into subareas focusing on distinct types of violence. Separate research literatures on sexual, physical, emotional, and neglect/economic abuse emerged. Different researchers specialized in the study of child maltreatment, adult intimate partner violence (IPV), parent abuse, sibling violence, and elder abuse. Specialized journals were created to publish research in these distinct areas. In this review, I argue that although this process of differentiation was perhaps necessary in a field of study that is comparatively young, it has hampered our understanding of the larger problem of violence within families. Research on conflict, power, and violence in families conducted during the past decade has engendered a new and promising focus on the interconnections between types of violence and between the experience of violence and locations in larger structures of power and inequality. Additionally, researchers have begun to connect the problem of violence in families to other arenas of family study, including teen pregnancy, marriage formation, cohabitation, and divorce. I argue that this focus on the *connections* between types of violence and between violence and other family and structural processes has helped to resolve old disputes in the study of family violence. Additionally, this focus on connections suggests important new areas of inquiry for research conducted in the next decade.

In the first part of the review, I describe four developments in the research of the past decade that extend our understanding of the causes and consequences of violence in families. First, new research on poly-victimization among child abuse and adult intimate partner violence victims suggests that specific combinations of types of violence victimization are associated with more negative outcomes for victims. Additionally, research in this area indicates that variation in the consequences of victimization depends on both the life course stage in which people experience violence and the particular types of victimization they experience. Second, a growing body of research on typologies of violence suggests that there may be different patterns of risk factors and consequences for different types of adult IPV. Third, researchers have begun to apply structural theories of gender, race, and class to the study of child abuse and adult IPV and this theoretical innovation has extended our understanding of the connections between power and family violence. Fourth, researchers have begun to study how the combined characteristics of victims of perpetrators may create a dynamic that facilitates or discourages conflict and violence. In the final section, I examine new research on how violence influences teen pregnancy, marriage formation, cohabitation, divorce, and economic well-being. This research uses violence as the independent rather than dependent variable and it suggests that many areas of family studies will be enhanced by considering how violence may be a precursor of family formation and dissolution. The review concludes with a discussion of recent studies showing declining rates of intimate partner homicides and child physical and sexual abuse.

Connecting Types of Violence

Poly-Victimization: Connecting Physical, Sexual, and Emotional Abuse

Family violence researchers have long recognized emotional, physical, sexual, and economic abuse as distinct types that often co-occur in the lives of victims, but the majority of studies consider one type of violence in isolation from the others. In the past decade, new research on poly-victimization documented the extent of this co-occurrence and its importance for understanding the effects of abuse on victims. There was substantial evidence that different types of violence co-occurred in victims' lives (Finkelhor, Olmrod, & Turner, 2007; Smith, White, & Holland, 2003; Williams, 2003). In their meta-analysis of 85 studies of risk factors for adult IPV, Stith, Smith, Penn, Ward, and Tritt (2004) found large effect sizes between men's physical abuse perpetration and emotional and sexual abuse. Using a nationally representative sample of children ages 2–17, Finkelhor et al. (2007) found that 22% of the sample experienced "poly-victimization," defined as experiencing four or more different types of violence within a single year. Poly-victims suffered greater trauma than victims who suffered multiple incidents of a single type of violence. Romito and Grassi (2007) studied the links between five types of violence victimization—by family members, witnessed family violence, peers/school violence, IPV, and sexual violence—and negative mental health outcomes in a college student sample. They found that the negative effects of violence on mental health increased gradually among students who experienced zero to three types of abuse and dramatically among those who experienced four or five types of violence. Similarly, M. A. Dutton, Kaltman, Goodman, Weinfurt, and Vankos (2005) used cluster analysis to identify three patterns of IPV victimization among women using shelters and requesting civil protection orders. They found the highest levels of depressive and post-traumatic stress disorder symptoms among victims of Pattern 3, which was defined by high levels of concurrent physical, psychological, and sexual abuse. These results suggest that studies on single types of abuse may not effectively explain variation in abuse outcomes because poly-victimization compounds to increase negative consequences for victims (Cherlin, Burton, Hurt, & Purvin, 2004; Finkelhor et al.; Richmond, Elliot, Pierce, Aspelmeir, & Alexander, 2009).

Another limitation of studies of single types of abuse is that they may overestimate the consequences of single types because they fail to control for other types of victimization. Preliminary findings suggested that the cooccurrence of physical and sexual abuse was especially predictive of negative outcomes suffered by victims and that sexual abuse victims were particularly likely to be polyvictims (Finkelhor et al., 2007). This has important implications for research on the correlates and consequences of single types of violence. For example, if research on the correlates or consequences of physical abuse victimization fails to control for sexual abuse, then the research might misidentify the causes of variation in predictors or outcomes of physical abuse (Finkelhor et al.). It is highly plausible that sexual abuse victimization is correlated with a number of standard predictors of physical abuse victimization and with the negative consequences of abuse, yet the vast majority of published studies on the negative consequences of physical abuse victimization failed to control for sexual abuse.

Connecting Child, Partner, Elder, Parent, and Sibling Abuse

A second connection documented in research over the past decade was between abuse perpetrated and suffered concurrently by different members of the same families. Research on the connections between the different forms of violence in families, particularly child maltreatment and adult IPV, consistently documented that the risk of child abuse was greater in families with adult IPV (Appel & Holden, 1998; Daro, Edleson, & Pinderhughes, 2004; Edleson, 1999; Edleson, Mbilinyi, Beeman, & Hagemeister, 2003; Slep & O'Leary, 2001). Few studies have focused on the causal connections between child abuse and IPV or on a theoretical integration of these distinct research areas. On the basis of a review of studies on the correlates of mother's child abuse perpetration and of men's IPV against female partners, Slep and O'Leary identified substantial overlap between IPV and child abuse for sociodemographic predictors and the psychological characteristics of perpetrators. Moreover, they suggested that the role-specific theories developed in child abuse research may apply to adult IPV. For example, child abuse research indicates that abusive mothers have unrealistic expectations for child behavior and that they attribute negative intentions to children's behavior. Although these predictors have not been studied in the adult IPV research, "it seems reasonable to hypothesize that parallel unrealistic or rigid expectations of and low levels of positive interactions with partners might relate to partner abuse, and that their current absence in the partner violence literature reflects a gap rather than processes that are unique to child abuse" (Slep & O'Leary, p. 100). Similarly, theories of adult IPV such as status inconsistency/gendered resource theory (Atkinson, Greenstein, & Lang, 2005; Kaukinen, 2004; Melzer, 2002) may apply to child abuse. It is possible that men who engage in violence against wives and partners when they are threatened by the gendered meanings of being out-earned by their partners are also more likely to perpetrate child abuse.

Studies of the connections between child, partner, sibling, parent, and elder abuse were much rarer, although the existing research indicated that these forms of family violence were linked. Children's violence against parents was the most understudied form of family violence, and the handful of studies to date revealed contradictory information about characteristics of perpetrators and victims (Walsh & Krienert, 2007). Parental abuse was linked to child abuse and to witnessing adult IPV in several studies (McCloskey & Lichter, 2003; Ulman & Straus, 2003) and sibling violence was associated with subsequent dating violence perpetration and victimization in a college student sample (Simonelli, Mullis, Elliot, & Pierce, 2002). Yan and Tang (2003) found that abuse in the family of origin was the strongest predictor of reported proclivity to perpetrate elder abuse in a community sample of Chinese residents of Hong Kong. Although social learning theory predicts strong connections between these types of abuse, the empirical research on sibling and elder abuse has been largely disconnected from work on child abuse and IPV.

Additionally, these types of violence may be causally connected. Victims of adult IPV may be less able to respond effectively to child misbehavior because of the stress and psychological impact of IPV victimization, increasing their risk of perpetrating child abuse (Slep & O'Leary, 2001). Adult victims of IPV may become abusive toward a child in an effort to avoid having child misbehavior anger the abusive partner. Alternatively, if parents disagree about disciplinary methods, child abuse may cause partner abuse if one parent intervenes to stop abuse against children (Slep & O'Leary). Hoffman and Edwards (2004) proposed that sibling violence may cause dating violence and adult IPV by socializing young people into violence; siblings practice aggressive responses to conflict and learn to justify abusive behavior in the context of their relationships with brothers and sisters.

Research into these connections may help to address unanswered questions in family violence research. For example, previous findings of great variation in the resiliency of child abuse victims may reflect variation in the co-occurrence of types of violence exposure; reduced resiliency may be because of exposure to multiple types of violence in the family of origin (Finkelhor et al., 2007). Heyman and Slep (2002) found that the risk of intergenerational transmission of violence was higher among women who were exposed to both interparental violence and child abuse as compared to those who experienced only one type. Efforts to study the connections between types of violence and the effects of co-occurrence demonstrated the importance of considering how the experience of one type of violence changes depending on the perpetrators' or victims' experience with other types of violence.

Connecting Conflict, Power, and Violence to the Life Course

An important trend over the past decade was the application of a life course perspective to the study of violence in families (Williams, 2003). Several studies demonstrated that age was an important predictor of victimization risk, with the highest rates of sexual and physical abuse victimization occurring in adolescence (Macmillan, 2001; Smith et al., 2003). Research on the trajectories of victimization experiences over time indicated that the time period of violence exposure influenced future victimization and other negative consequences of victimization (Cherlin et al, 2004; Kaukinen & DeMaris, 2005; Smith et al.). Longitudinal studies found that childhood victimization was a predictor of revictimization in adolescence and adulthood and that this effect occurred in part because of the positive relationship between childhood maltreatment and victims' conduct and substance abuse disorders during adolescence (Ehrensaft et al., 2003). Using a longitudinal panel study of college women, Smith and colleagues found that the risk of physical and sexual assault victimization in college was greater among respondents who reported experiencing both childhood abuse and physical abuse victimization in adolescence. Moreover, they found that childhood abuse did not predict victimization in college for respondents who did not experience dating violence in adolescence. Findings from these studies suggest the need for additional research on the connections between child abuse, dating violence, and adult IPV from a life course perspective (White, 2009).

Connecting Victim and Perpetrator Characteristics: Dyadic Research

Attention to connections requires that we consider how interactions between partners, parents and children, and siblings are linked to family violence. A number of scholars studied the connections between IPV and the combined characteristics of victims and perpetrators, or relationship dyads. Couple-level relationship patterns such as insecure attachment, demand-withdraw, and emotional reactivity were consistently linked to IPV (Allison, Bartholomew, Mayseless, & Dutton, 2008; Bookwala, 2002; Henderson, Bartholomew, Trinke, & Kwong, 2005). Another body of dyadic research demonstrated that the combined characteristics of partners' depression, antisocial behaviors, and conduct disorders were linked to IPV (Kim & Capaldi, 2004; Woodward, Fergusson, & Horwood, 2002). Kim, Laurent, Capaldi, and Feingold (2008) found that depressive symptoms and antisocial behavior of both partners influenced men's physical and psychological aggression toward female partners over time. Moreover, a few studies identified a pattern of assortative partnering in which one partner's IPV risk factors were positively linked to their choice of a high-risk partner (Kim & Capaldi).

Connecting Violence, Control, and Personality Disorders: Domestic Violence Typologies

In their 2000 decade-in-review article, Johnson and Ferraro (2000) argued for the importance of making distinctions between types of adult IPV. Johnson's (2008) four-category typology of intimate terrorism (IT), situational couple violence (SCV), violent resistance (VR), and mutual violence control (MVC) and Holzworth-Munroe and Stuart's (1994) threefold typology of generally violent/antisocial, dysphoric/borderline, and family-only batterers made distinctions on the basis of motivations for violence, personality disorders, frequency/severity of violence, and the co-occurrence of violence within and outside of the family context. At first glance, the growing body of research on domestic violence typologies seems to further the differentiation of the literature by breaking down physical violence in intimate adult relationships into new categories or subtypes. Yet, taken another way, the typology research has furthered our understanding of the causes and consequences of violence by asking researchers to consider how family violence is and is not connected to controlling behaviors, psychopathology, and other forms of violent behavior.

Johnson (2008) recently proposed an integration of his typology and the typology developed by Holzworth-Munroe and Stuart (1994). Johnson argued that intimate terrorism, or the type of violence characterized by high levels of controlling behavior enacted by the perpetrators, may include the generally violent/antisocial and dysphoric/borderline categories. Johnson's situational couple violence type shares many characteristics with the family-only batterers identified in the Holzworth-Munroe and Stuart typology. If this claim can be empirically demonstrated, it will be an important connection between the most influential sociological and psychological typologies of adult IPV.

Typology research in the 2000s established that the negative effects of IPV were much greater for some types of violence than others. Multiple studies showed that violence that occurred in the context of personality disorders or high levels of controlling behaviors had greater negative effects for victims, including fear, injury, depressive and post-traumatic stress disorder symptoms, and substance abuse (Anderson, 2008; Delsol, Margolin, & John, 2003; Holzworth-Munroe & Meehan, 2004; Johnson, 2008; Johnson & Leone, 2005). Additionally, studies found that SCV or family-only violence was less likely to escalate over time than violence perpetrated in the context of high control or the perpetrators' personality disorders (Holzworth-Munroe & Meehan; Johnson). These studies supported Johnson and Ferraro's (2000) claim that researchers should make distinctions between types of adult IPV to understand variation in the consequences of abuse for victims.

Additionally, preliminary studies using Johnson's typology provided findings that may, if replicated, resolve some long-standing debates within the domestic violence literature. One of the biggest puzzles has been the contradictory findings about the effects of experiencing childhood abuse on adult perpetration of intimate partner violence, or the intergenerational transmission of abuse. Studies in the past decade found that witnessing IPV or experiencing abuse as a child, or both, had a modest positive effect on adult IPV perpetration and victimization (Delsol & Margolin, 2004; Heyman & Slep, 2002; Kwong, Bartholomew, Henderson, & Trinke, 2003; Stith et al., 2000). Johnson (2008) proposed that the contradictory findings of strong effects in some samples and weak effects in others may reflect a failure to distinguish types of abuse. His reanalysis of data from a clinical and community sample of women in Pittsburgh found a high rate of intergenerational transmission among IT perpetrators and a very weak effect among SCV perpetrators. This argument was supported by results from Stith et al.'s meta-analysis, which found that studies using identified samples that should contain higher levels of IT had stronger intergenerational transmission effects than studies using community samples that should contain higher levels of SCV. The transmission of child abuse to perpetration of adult IPV was mediated by adolescent problem behaviors, conduct disorder, psychopathology or personality disorders, and hostility (Delsol & Margolin, 2004; Ehrensaft et al., 2003; Swinford, DeMaris, Cernkovich, & Giordano, 2000), further suggesting that the intergenerational transmission of abuse may be stronger among IT, generally violent/antisocial, or dysphoric/borderline types of abusers than among SCV or family-only perpetrators.

Although research in the past decade demonstrated the utility of making distinctions for understanding negative outcomes of violence, researchers also raised important practical and theoretical questions about typologies. First, findings about whether variation in the negative consequences of adult IPV was better explained by typological differences or dimensional differences in levels of control, violence severity, and personality disorders were inconclusive. Two studies to date compared the effectiveness of dimensional versus typological approaches to explain variation in negative effects of IPV, and both found that dimensional and typological approaches were equally effective (Anderson, 2008; Holzworth-Munroe & Meehan, 2004). Studies conducted over the past decade did not use a consistent strategy to classifying domestic violence perpetrators into types, raising questions about what level of control or personality disorder is required to classify a perpetrator as IT or generally violent/antisocial versus other categories (Holzworth-Munroe & Meehan). Other researchers suggested that the distinction between instrumental controlling aggression (IT) and situational hostile aggression (SCV) was difficult to apply to actual cases of violence. Capaldi and Kim (2007) proposed that the same motives can drive both instrumental and hostile/situational aggression, that multiple motives can drive the same types of violence, and that many actual acts of violence seem to combine instrumental and hostile motives.

Additional concerns were raised about the stability of the typological categories across different types of samples and over time within the same samples. Typologies developed with clinical samples that distinguished groups based on personality disorder or psychopathology did not replicate to community samples (Delsol et al., 2003; Waltz, Babcock, Jacobsen, & Gottman, 2000). In the only study to date to examine the stability of typologies within a sample over time, Holzworth-Munroe and Meehan (2004) found that 58% of their sample of batterers was classified into the same type at a 3-year follow-up. A number of researchers suggested that the clinical utility of these typologies is limited because of these concerns (Capaldi & Kim, 2007; Delsol et al.: Langhinrichsen-Rohling, Huss, & Ramsey, 2000).

Connecting Violence to Structural Inequality

Research on the connections between intimate violence and gender, race, class, and sexuality in the past decade benefited from theoretical work that extended our understanding of these categories beyond the level of individual characteristics or identities. Race, class, gender, and sexuality were reconceptualized to include social structure and social interaction in addition to individual-level characteristics (Baca-Zinn & Thornton-Dill, 1996; Bonilla-Silva, 1997; Lewin, 2004; Risman, 1998). The concept of *social location* can be used to represent gender, race, class, and sexuality as multilevel, intersecting forms of inequality. People's locations within structures of inequality influence their individual level identities and behaviors and the ways in which they perform or negotiate their identities in microlevel social interaction. This shift led researchers to consider how the differential positioning of women and men, gays and straights, and Blacks and Whites within social structures influenced their risk of domestic violence perpetration and victimization.

Gender and Sexual Orientation

The longest running controversy in domestic violence scholarship is the explanation for the contradictory findings about gender symmetry in IPV. Studies of community samples of heterosexual couples found that women and men reported IPV victimization and perpetration at similar rates (Archer, 2000; Fergusson, Horwood, & Ridder, 2005; Straus, 2008). These findings were used to justify the position that IPV be studied using family or crime/violence theoretical frameworks rather than feminist frameworks (D. G. Dutton, 2006; Felson, 2002; Mills, 2003; Straus, 2007). Feminist theorists disagreed, arguing that the gender symmetry findings were based on flawed data and interpretation (Anderson, 2005; Dasgupta, 2002; DeKeseredy & Dragiewicz, 2007; Kimmel, 2002). Studies that used criminal justice or clinical samples found that men perpetrated violence against women at much higher rates than women perpetrated violence against men (Saltzman, Mahendra, Ikeda, & Ingram, 2005).

Johnson (1995, 2006) proposed that contradictory findings about gender symmetry in IPV could be explained by the use of typologies (see also Stark, 2007). He proposed that men and women were equally likely to perpetrate SCV, whereas men were more likely to perpetrate IT. Yet the empirical evidence for the claim that the gender symmetry findings were due to women's less extensive perpetration of IT was limited. Some studies showed that women and men were equally likely to perpetrate control-driven violence in nonshelter samples (Felson, 2002; Felson & Outlaw, 2007; Graham-Kevan & Archer, 2003; Straus, 2008). In a test of Johnson's IT/

SCV typology with four British samples, Graham-Kevan and Archer found that women perpetrated IT as often as men among student and male prisoner samples. Alternatively, Johnson (2008) found that 89% of IT perpetrators were husbands in his reanalysis of data collected from a shelter, court, and community sample of women. Evidence to support Johnson's theory that the IT/SCV distinction explains the contradictory findings about gender-symmetry is currently inconclusive.

Researchers in the past decade raised theoretical concerns about Johnson's (1995, 2008) claim that making a distinction between IT and SCV will resolve the debate about gender symmetry in adult IPV. By proposing that some types of violence were more gendered than others (Johnson, 1995; Stark, 2007), typology researchers undertheorized gender by treating it solely as an individual characteristic that predicts violence perpetration or victimization (Anderson, 2005). A theoretical development of the past decade was the application of structural theories of gender, race, and class to the problem of adult IPV (Anderson, 2005, 2007; Benson, Fox, DeMaris, & VanWyck, 2003; Brush, 2001; Schuck, 2005). Structural theories of gender propose that men and women are differentially located in the social world because of gender inequality and thus they experience IPV differently. From this theoretical perspective, it is not that the frequency or severity of acts of control and violence differ by gender, as Johnson (2006, 2008) proposes, but rather that the location of the perpetrators and victims who experience the acts is gendered (Anderson, 2005).

The argument for viewing gender as a social location was elaborated by Risman (1998), who suggested that gender is a social structure that operates to influence lives at multiple levels. At the individual level, gender is an identity and a set of beliefs or attitudes. Individuals self-identify (or are categorized by others) as masculine or feminine or they resist this classification and adopt a transgender identity. At the level of social interaction, gender is a performance. Men and women "do gender" in order to conform to social expectations, and violence is one means by which men can perform masculinity (Anderson & Umberson, 2001; J. Miller & White, 2003). At the level of social structure, gender is the basis for dividing resources and responsibilities. As a social structure, gender organizes women and men into different occupations and roles and provides differential rewards and resources to women and men as groups.

Comparative studies of the past decade demonstrated that the interactive and structural levels of gender explained why men's violence led to more negative outcomes for victims than women's violence and why SCV was a gendered phenomenon even if men and women were equally likely to perpetrate this type of violence. J. Miller and White's (2003) qualitative study of dating violence in a disadvantaged sample of African American youth found that women's violence was perceived as irrational and ineffectual by both male victims and the wider peer group, whereas men's violence was perceived as justified and powerful (see also Anderson & Umberson, 2001). Although men's violence against women was culturally denigrated as weak and cowardly, specific incidents of men's violence against girlfriends were interpreted as necessary or justified within the context of the situation. Moreover, Miller and White found that although young women attempted to use violence to gain control over a dating partner, they did not succeed because of gendered cultural expectations for behavior.

These findings were replicated by a survey of 502 Italian university students in which students identified their responses to acts of dating violence (Romito & Grassi, 2007). Women were significantly more likely than men to report feeling fear, pain, humiliation, and anger, whereas men were more likely to react with laughter. Felson and Pare (2005) found that men victimized by female partners were less likely than women victimized by male partners to report IPV to the police, supporting the argument that interpretations of abuse seriousness are gendered. These studies suggested that victims, perpetrators, and the peer group created gender inequality by interpreting IPV through a gendered lens. The result was that men's violence was an effective strategy for control over women whereas women's violence did not result in the desired outcome of controlling men's behavior.

Additional support for the theory that violence is gendered at the level of social interaction emerged in multiple studies finding that the risk of men's physical and emotional abuse was greater when female partners had higher income or occupational status than their male partners (Atkinson et al., 2005; Kaukinen, 2004; Melzer, 2002). These findings supported the theoretical argument that violence is a means by which men perform or demonstrate masculinity, as men's IPV perpetration was higher in contexts in which masculine identity was threatened. Atkinson et al. demonstrated an interaction between gender ideology and women's higher share of couples' earnings: The higher risk of men's IPV when women earned the greater share of the couples' income occurred only among men with traditional gender ideologies in their sample.

Very few studies examined links between gender and violence using a structuralist perspective and most of these conceptualized gender as macrolevel structural inequality, measured by levels of women's empowerment or equality across regions, states, or nations. Archer's (2006) study of cross-cultural differences in gender symmetry demonstrated the benefits of theorizing gender from a structuralist perspective. On the basis of a comparison of the gender difference in IPV perpetration rates across nations that vary in levels of women's empowerment, Archer found that women's violence against men increased in contexts of women's greater political and economic empowerment. In a multilevel study of IPV and contextual variation in women's empowerment across regions in rural Bangladesh, Koenig, Ahmed, Hossain, and Khorshed Alam Mozumder (2003) determined that women's higher levels of individual education and mobility were positively associated with IPV victimization in a conservative region in which women were generally disempowered, but these status variables were not associated with women's victimization in a region with higher overall empowerment for women. Additional evidence suggested that structural gender inequality influenced the resources held by individual women and men in intimate relationships. Anderson (2007) found that women victimized by asymmetrical or injurious partner violence were significantly more likely than similarly victimized men to be economically dependent on a partner. Additionally, women's but not men's ability to leave an abusive relationship was constrained by economic dependency. On the basis of their longitudinal ethnographic study of women's victimization experiences in the context of welfare reform, Scott, London, and Myers (2002) proposed that the welfare reform's goals of self-sufficiency pushed poor women into dependency on abusive men. In the context of these findings, studies showing that women and men reported using similar rates and types of violence and control against a partner did not contradict findings about more severe consequences from men's violence. These findings indicated instead that although violence and control may not be gendered at the level of individual motives or behavior, they were highly gendered at the levels of social structure and interaction.

Although this argument for viewing gender as social location is similar to feminist critiques of gender symmetry findings that contend that the context of violence must be taken into account (Dasgupta, 2002; Kimmel, 2002), it varies in two important respects. First, the structuralist gender perspective suggests that we need to consider the context of gender, or gender as a context, rather than the context of violence. Second, the argument for studying gender as a social location implies that gender must be studied using a comparative lens to test hypotheses about whether, when, and how gender matters in the experience of domestic violence. The vast majority of studies on gender and IPV were not comparative. Most studies on gender and violence analyzed only men's violence against women, even where comparative data on women's violence against men were available, because of the assumption that men's violence against women was more prevalent and damaging. Although there was an explosion of studies focused on women's use of violence in intimate relationships in the 2000s, few of these studies were comparative by gender (Brush, 2005; Frieze, 2005; McHugh, Livingston, & Ford, 2005; Swan & Snow, 2002). Of 27 studies on IPV published in the *Journal of Marriage and Family* since 2000, only 9 (33%) compared women and men as perpetrators or victims. Comparative data are needed to assess theoretically driven hypotheses about whether, why, and how violence is connected to gender.

Sexual orientation can also be theorized as a social location that influences violence in families. To date, the research on violence in same-sex relationships was not guided by theoretical work on sexual orientation as a structure of inequality. Researchers claimed that risk factors and rates of violence were similar in same-sex and heterosexual relationships (Felson, 2002; Freedner, Freed, Yang, & Austin, 2002; Greenwood et al., 2002), but these claims were based on findings from separate studies rather than theoretically informed comparative studies of abuse in same-sex and heterosexual relationships. Studies of dating violence or IPV in lesbian, gay, bisexual, or transgender (LGBT) relationships used small, unrepresentative samples (Balsam, Rothblum, & Beauchaine, 2005; Freedner et al.). Moreover, research on violence in LGBT families did not apply a structuralist theoretical framework that recognizes sexual orientation as a location within a structure of inequality: "Rarely do researchers consider the real institutional differences, that affect, for example, homosexual and heterosexual couples differently; nor do they question the strategy of directly comparing gay and straight couples without regard for their distinct circumstances" (Lewin, 2004, p. 5).

Race and Class

A structuralist theoretical approach was used in studies of the links between child abuse, IPV, and social class and racial/ethnic inequalities through the application of social disorganization and neighborhood theories (Brush, 2001; Browning, 2002; Hampton, Oliver, & Magarian, 2003; Lau, Takeuchi, & Alegria, 2006; Lauritsen & Schaum, 2004). These theories, like structuralist or systemic theories of racism (Bonilla-Silva, 1997), recognize that economic and racial inequalities organize society, impacting the opportunities and experiences of those who are differentially located by race and class. Researchers applied social disorganization and ecological theories to assess whether neighborhood characteristics such as concentrated poverty and unemployment or the concentration of liquor stores and number of drug-offense arrests affected rates of violence even when individual risk factors for violence among neighborhood residents were controlled (Friesthler, Merritt, & LaScala, 2006; Lauritsen & Schaum). A few studies showed that, when individual risk factors and neighborhood demographic characteristics were controlled for, a higher concentration of bars and higher rate of drug offense arrests was associated with increased risk for child maltreatment in neighborhoods (Friesthler et al., 2006; Friesthler, Needell, & Gruenewald, 2005).

A key methodological innovation of research on family violence over the past decade was the application of multilevel models that allowed researchers to examine the influence of context on individual-level outcomes (Teachman & Crowder, 2002). Two studies conducted by Benson and colleagues used multilevel models to apply structural theories of race and class to the study of IPV. Benson et al. (2003) examined the link between social class and IPV by theorizing class as both an individual characteristic (employment instability, subjective financial distress) and a contextual variable (neighborhood-level concentrated disadvantage). Their results indicated that concentrated neighborhood disadvantage was associated with greater odds of men's IPV against women even when they controlled for individual-level risk factors. Importantly, they found that some individual risk factors, including substance abuse, income, and race, were not significantly associated with the odds of IPV when concentrated disadvantage was controlled. In a follow-up study, Benson, Wooldredge, Thistlewaite, and Fox (2004) reported that the racial difference in domestic violence between Blacks and Whites was diminished when neighborhood concentrated disadvantage was controlled, suggesting that "the dramatic differences in domestic violence so often observed between Whites and African Americans are in part a function of their location in different ecological contexts" (p. 337).

Structuralist theories suggest that the important questions are not whether IPV perpetration is more common among heterosexual women or men, Blacks or Whites, or gay men or lesbians, but rather how inequalities of gender, race, citizenship status, and sexual orientation position people differently such that they experience different demands, opportunities, and constraints and such that violence has different meanings and consequences for their lives. The application of multilevel models and structural theories of race and class to IPV and child abuse was an important innovation of the past decade because it encouraged researchers to think beyond race, gender, class, and sexual orientation as individual characteristics to consider how these inequalities locate people within society. Research in the 2000s demonstrated that social location in hierarchies of gender, race/ethnicity, and class is important to consider in violence research for two reasons. First, social location shapes the stressors, resources, opportunities, and constraints that people experience, and this affects violent behavior. Second, social location influences the attributions of violence that victims, perpetrators, and bystanders make, resulting in variable outcomes for similar acts across contexts.

Connecting Poly-Victimization, Typologies, and Structural Inequalities

Although connections between types of violence and structural inequality were not a research focus of the past decade, preliminary evidence suggested that the risk of co-occurrence of multiple types of family violence, polyvictimization, IT, and Holzworth-Munroe's categories of generally violent-antisocial and borderline/dysphoric batterers was greater among people who were structurally disadvantaged. Several studies found that the co-occurrence of IPV and child abuse was greater in the context of higher financial stress or lower income (Cox, Kotch, & Everson, 2004; Edleson et al., 2003; Margolin & Gordis, 2003). M. A. Dutton et al. (2005) found that the co-occurrence of specific types of women's adult IPV victimization varied by social class locations. Victims who reported high levels of concurrent physical, psychological, and sexual abuse were less likely to be employed and more likely to have used the services of a domestic violence shelter than victims who reported less co-occurrence of types of abuse. Leone, Johnson, Cohan, and Lloyd (2004) found, in a sample of low-income minority women, that victims of IT were more likely to receive Aid to Families with Dependent Children (AFDC) than victims of SCV or those who did not experience violence. Delsol et al. (2003) reported that men classified in the IPV subtype characterized by elevations on antisocial and borderline/dysphoric personality disorders experienced three times more stressful negative life events than men classified in the other subtypes. Johnson (2008) found that IT, but not SCV, was linked to lower levels of educational attainment among perpetrators. Additionally, structural inequality influenced whether violence desisted or continued over time. Frias and Angel (2007) identified social class and racial/ethnic differences in the patterns of abuse experienced by women over time; women who experienced abuse at Time 1 but not at Time 2 in their longitudinal study were older, better educated, and experienced less financial strain than women who reported victimization at both waves. These findings raise questions about the ways in which structural inequalities are linked to distinct types of violence, poly-victimization, and the co-occurrence of types of abuse within families that should guide research in the coming decade.

Family Violence and Relationship Processes: Pregnancy, Marriage Formation, Cohabitation, and Divorce

Violence in families was more commonly studied as a dependent than an independent variable in research conducted through the 1990s, with the exception of studies that examined the negative consequences of abuse for well-being and the intergenerational transmission of abuse. In the 2000s, a number of studies examined how conflict, power, and violence within families were connected to the key issues studied by family researchers, including the formation and dissolution of marriage and cohabiting relationships, pregnancy and parenting, and relationship quality. An important innovation in the past decade was the increasing number of studies that used IPV as an independent variable to predict patterns of relationship formation and dissolution (DeMaris, 2000, 2001; Sanchez & Gager, 2000). In a series of studies, DeMaris (2000, 2001) examined IPV as a predictor of relationship dissolution using longitudinal data from the National Survey of Families and Households. His results provided evidence that IPV was an important predictor of separation for married and cohabiting couples. Additionally, DeMaris found that violence perpetrated by women and men had different effects on relationship dissolution. Men's IPV against female partners was associated with greater risk of separation in both marital and cohabiting relationships, whereas women's IPV against male partners was not linked to separation risk. Women's violence was associated with a reduced likelihood of entry into marriage among cohabiting couples (DeMaris, 2001). In a study focused on gender differences in the relationship between IPV and marital dissolution, Anderson (2007) found that men and women who were victims of minor or mutual IPV were equally likely to dissolve their marriages, whereas severe or asymmetrical IPV victimization predicted marital dissolution among women more than among men. Additionally, the presence of young children increased the odds of marriage dissolution among women victimized by severe or asymmetrical IPV but reduced the odds of dissolution among men. These results provided initial evidence that gender structured the effects of IPV on relationship dissolution and that these patterns varied for SCV and IT.

Research on how violence shaped the process of entry and exit from intimate relationships over time helped us to understand variation in the rates of IPV across different marital status categories. A consistent finding of studies over the past 20 years was that rates of IPV were higher in cohabiting than marital relationships. Kenney and McLanahan (2006) demonstrated that higher levels of IPV reported in current cohabiting as compared to marital relationships reflected multiple forms of selection bias rather than differences in the characteristics or dynamics of married versus cohabiting relationships (see also Brownridge, 2008). Cohabiting couples in less violent relationships were more likely to enter into marriage, and married couples in the most violent marriages were more likely to divorce, indicating that violence selected people out of the pool of married partners in cross-sectional studies. An innovative study by Cherlin et al. (2004) used survey and ethnographic data collected from low-income residents of Boston, Chicago, and San Antonio to study how experiences of violence selected women out of long-term, stable marital or cohabiting relationships. Cherlin and colleagues found that the timing of exposure to violence (childhood vs. adulthood) and the specific types of violence experienced (physical or sexual) influenced relationship formation. Women who experienced physical or sexual abuse or both in childhood or sexual abuse in adulthood were less likely to be married and more likely to be in short-term, serial-cohabiting relationships. Women who experienced physical abuse for the first time in adulthood were less likely than nonabused women to be in an intimate relationship. Their ethnographic results indicated that many women who were physically abused in adult relationships voluntarily removed themselves from the relationship market because of their abuse experiences. Cherlin et al. speculated that women who did not experience childhood abuse had the social and emotional resources to remove themselves from physically violent relationships formed in adulthood, whereas victims of childhood abuse or adult sexual abuse had less supportive social networks and greater mental health problems that prevented them from ending abusive relationships as adults. Their findings indicated that the specific type and timing of violence exposure was theoretically important to understanding the consequences of abuse for relationship formation.

Studies also found that dating violence was an important predictor of teen pregnancy. The majority of pregnancies among adolescents occurred in the context of dating violence (Jacoby, Gorenflo, Black, Wunderlich, & Eyler, 1999; Silverman, Raj, & Clements, 2004). A qualitative interview study of 53 adolescent women with a history of IPV victimization conducted by E. Miller et al. (2007) found that 26% of participants reported that their abusive partners intentionally tried to make them pregnant through behaviors like sabotaging birth control.

Research in the past decade has also examined violence as a predictor of poverty, welfare use, and unemployment. A number of studies linked abuse experienced in childhood or adulthood to lower earnings, employment instability, or welfare use among women (Brush, 2004; Hyman, 2000; Staggs & Riger, 2005). In a series of studies, Brush (2001, 2004) showed that abuse was associated with lower earnings and dropping out of welfare-to-work programs among poor women. One limitation of these studies was that they used samples of women only, precluding analysis of whether the economic consequences of abuse varied by gender.

Connections between violence and inequalities of gender, race, class, and sexual orientation are complex because violence can be conceptualized as both an independent and a dependent variable in relation to structural inequality. Neighborhood disadvantage, financial stress, and poverty were positively associated with perpetration of IPV and child abuse (Benson et al., 2003). The experience of victimization as a child, adolescent, or adult was also associated with greater risk of economic uncertainty and poverty later in life. Neighborhood level economic disadvantage explained higher rates of IPV perpetration among African Americans as compared to Whites (Benson et al., 2004), yet higher levels of violence in disadvantaged neighborhoods were also a cause of increasing structural racial inequality. High levels of violence in poor neighborhoods caused the most advantaged residents (who are likely to be White) to move away, resulting in more residential segregation by race and a higher concentration of poverty (Morenoff &

Sampson, 1997). The theorized bidirectionality of causation in the links between violence and social location presents a challenge for research in the next decade (Brush, 2004). Prospective longitudinal studies are needed to address this challenge. Using a prospective 3-year study of women on welfare, Staggs, Long, Mason, Krishnan, and Riger (2007) found that employment stability did not predict future IPV victimization, but IPV victimization predicted less stable future employment.

Reducing Family Violence: Policy Initiatives

Because of widespread public information campaigns and media attention, public awareness and knowledge about violence in families increased dramatically in the past few decades. Adult victims of domestic violence had greater social and legal resources, and educators and medical personnel were obligated to report cases of suspected child maltreatment. Recent victims of violence received greater cultural support to define their abusive treatment as criminal or deviant in comparison to victims of years past (Casey & Nurius, 2006). These changes mean that the context of abuse was vastly different in the 2000s than 20 or 30 years ago.

Although it is difficult to study changes in rates of domestic violence over time because of methodological issues and definitional disparities, a few recent studies suggested that social change and public interventions into family violence were successful in reducing the numbers of victims of child maltreatment and adult IPV, particularly domestic homicide. In a series of studies, Finkelhor and Jones (2006; Jones, Finkelhor, & Halter, 2006; Jones, Finkelhor, & Kopiec, 2001) investigated multiple explanations for the declines in reported child physical and sexual abuse in the United States over the past 15 years. They concluded, albeit cautiously, that evidence from national reporting agencies and self-report data supported the conclusion that there were real declines in child sexual abuse and possible declines in child physical abuse (see also Casey & Nurius, 2006; Dunne, Purdie, Cook, Boyle, & Najman, 2003). Research on declines over time in intimate partner homicide rates also suggested that some structural changes, such as the implementation of unilateral divorce legislation, were associated with reduced domestic homicides at the state level (Stevenson & Wolfers, 2006). In two studies on correlates of domestic homicide in large U.S. cities, Dugan, Nagin, and Rosenfeld (1999, 2003) found that the availability of shelter and hotline services for domestic violence and more aggressive arrest and prosecution lowered rates of intimate partner homicide. They argued that demographic changes that reduce "exposure" to domestic violence, including lower marriage rates, reduced the risk of intimate partner homicide. Conversely, Dugan et al. (2003) found that some policies, including greater willingness of prosecutors' offices to take on protection order cases and the reduction in AFDC payments, increased risk of domestic homicide for specific racial and marital status groups. These results suggested that, in some cases, policy changes resulted in a "retaliation effect" that exacerbated the risk of homicide. Jennings and Piquero (2008) found that declines in intimate partner homicide were lower in rural than urban areas, suggesting that declines in intimate partner homicide were specific to urban locales (cf. Frye & Wilt, 2001). These studies provided important initial evidence that cultural and structural changes may be reducing the rate of violence within families.

Conclusion

The past 50 years of family violence research was characterized by increasing differentiation and specialization of the research literature by distinct types of violence. In this review, I proposed that the most promising research of the 2000s moved away from this process of specialization and differentiation to focus instead on studying connections between different types of violence experienced by single victims, connections between child, adult partner, elder, parent, and sibling abuse, and connections between violence and larger structural inequalities. The ability to make these connections was aided by the use of new methods, including multilevel models that simultaneously examine individual and contextual characteristics, longitudinal panel studies that enable researchers to examine causal processes over time, and dyadic studies that obtain information about both partners in adult relationships. Additionally, ethnographic studies conducted during the past decade provided important insights into the connections that influence the experience of violence in the lives of people who struggle to make sense of their victimization and perpetration. Cherlin et al.'s (2004) ethnographic research was an important reminder of the benefits of triangulation in domestic violence research. Their 3-year ethnographic study of 256 low-income families involved surveys and field visits to a subsample of families. They found that, although a majority of the mothers had experienced abuse as children or adults, only 10% disclosed abuse during a semistructured interview early in the study. Abuse experiences were revealed to ethnographers only after they established trust with the study participants. These results suggested that most of our knowledge on IPV and child maltreatment is based on reports from only a small portion of those who experienced abuse. Cherlin et al. induced new theories about how the timing and types of violence experiences influenced relationship formation among women from their field data and replicated these patterns in their survey research. Similarly, J. Miller's (2008) ethnography of violence experienced by young African American girls identified how dating violence was interconnected with gender inequality and racialized urban poverty. These studies suggested the importance of studying violence in families using multiple methodologies, including triangulated qualitative and quantitative designs, to explore the complex connections between multiple types of violence, the life course, family formation, and structural inequalities.

Research in the next decade should further our understanding of these connections. For example, work on adult IPV typologies should be applied to other forms of family violence. It is important to know, for example, whether the typologies developed by Johnson (1995, 2008) and Holzworth-Munroe and Stuart (1994) can be integrated and whether these distinctions apply to child abuse, elder abuse, or sibling violence. Preliminary evidence suggests that work on poly-victimization in the child maltreatment field and on typologies in the adult IPV field may be tapping into similar underlying processes. Although Johnson's typology did not explicitly identify IT victims as poly-victims, his research showed substantial evidence that IT victims suffered both physical and emotional abuse and some weak evidence that victims of IT suffered higher levels of sexual abuse (Johnson, 2008).

Although studies in the past decade show that variation in abuse outcomes can be explained by the experience of poly-victimization (child abuse) or the use of typologies (adult IPV), we do not yet know *why* victims of some types or combinations of abuse suffer greater negative outcomes than other victims. For example, research to date suggested that IT had more negative outcomes than SCV, but it is currently unclear whether these outcomes are because of the greater severity of violence perpetrated in IT, the co-occurrence of violence and controlling behaviors or sexual abuse in IT, or the association between IT and structural disadvantage. Work on poly-victimization indicated that victims of physical and sexual abuse experience the greatest trauma, but the reasons for this are currently unclear. Are these effects simply cumulative, or are they interactive such that the impact of one type of abuse is greater in the context of another? How does the experience of one type of abuse change the meaning and impact of other types of abuse?

Additionally, it may be fruitful to integrate IPV typologies work with the life course framework that has been most commonly applied to dating and adolescent violence. Preliminary evidence indicating that IT is more common among married people and SCV characterizes cohabiting relationships, for example, could provide a basis for testing new hypotheses about how different types of violence influence relationship formation and dissolution. Finally, researchers should continue to apply multilevel models to assess hypotheses about how structural inequalities of race, class, gender, and sexual orientation influence the types of violence experienced in families and the causes and consequences of this abuse.

Our understanding of violence in families is enhanced by the recognition that the distinct types of violence that we study are not distinct in the lives of victims. Most victims of child abuse are also exposed to parental, sibling, or community violence, and sexual, physical, and emotional abuse are far too often interrelated experiences in the lives of victims. Research in the 2000s demonstrated the importance of these connections for our understanding of the causes and consequences of violence in families.

References

Allison, C. J., Bartholomew, K., Mayseless, O., & Dutton, D. G. (2008). Love as a battlefield: Attachment and relationship dynamics in couples identified for male partner violence. *Journal of Family Issues, 29,* 125–150.

Anderson, K. L. (2005). Theorizing gender in intimate partner violence research. *Sex Roles, 52,* 853–865.

Anderson, K. L. (2007). Who gets out? Gender as structure and the dissolution of violent heterosexual relationships. *Gender and Society, 21,* 173–201.

Anderson, K. L. (2008). Is partner violence worse in the context of control? *Journal of Marriage and Family, 70,* 1157–1168.

Anderson, K. L., & Umberson, D. (2001). Gendering violence: Masculinity and power in men's accounts of domestic violence. *Gender & Society, 15,* 358–380.

Appel, A. E., & Holden, G. W. (1998). The cooccurrence of spouse and physical child abuse: A review and appraisal. *Journal of Family Psychology, 12,* 578–599.

Archer, J. (2000). Sex differences in aggression between heterosexual partners: A meta-analytic review. *Psychological Bulletin, 126,* 651–680.

Archer, J. (2006). Cross-cultural differences in physical aggression between partners: A social role analysis. *Personality and Social Psychology Review, 10,* 133–153.

Atkinson, M. P., Greenstein, T. N., & Lang, M. M. (2005). For women, breadwinning can be dangerous: Gendered resource theory and wife abuse. *Journal of Marriage and Family, 67,* 1137–1148.

Baca-Zinn, M., & Thornton-Dill, B. (1996). Theorizing difference from multi-racial feminism. *Feminist Studies, 22,* 321–331.

Balsam, K. F., Rothblum, E. D., & Beauchaine, T. P. (2005). Victimization over the life span: A comparison of lesbian, gay, bisexual, and heterosexual siblings. *Journal of Consulting and Clinical Psychology, 73,* 477–487.

Benson, M. L., Fox, G. L., Demaris, A., & Van-Wyck, J. (2003). Neighborhood disadvantage, individual economic distress and violence against women in intimate relationships. *Journal of Quantitative Criminology, 19,* 207–235.

Benson, M. L., Wooldredge, J., Thistlewaite, A. B., & Fox, G. L. (2004). The correlation between race and domestic violence is confounded with community context. *Social Problems, 51,* 326–342.

Bonilla-Silva, E. (1997). Rethinking racism: Toward a structural interpretation. *American Sociological Review, 62,* 465–480.

Bookwala, J. (2002). The role of own and perceived partner attachment in relationship aggression. *Journal of Interpersonal Violence, 17,* 84–100.

Browning, C. R. (2002). The span of collective efficacy: Extending social disorganization theory to partner violence. *Journal of Marriage and Family, 64,* 833–850.

Brownridge, D. (2008). The elevated risk for violence against cohabiting women: A comparison of three nationally representative surveys of Canada. *Violence Against Women, 14,* 809–832.

Brush, L. D. (2001). Poverty, battering, race, and welfare reform: Black-White differences in women's welfare to work transitions. *Journal of Poverty, 5,* 67–89.

Brush, L. D. (2004). Battering and the poverty trap. *Journal of Poverty, 8*(3), 23–43.

Brush, L. D. (2005). Philosophical and political issues in research on women's violence and aggression. *Sex Roles, 52,* 867–873.

Capaldi, D. M., & Kim, H. K. (2007). Typological approaches to violence in couples: A critique and alternative conceptual approach. *Clinical Psychology Review, 27,* 253–265.

Casey, E. A., & Nurius, P. S. (2006). Trends in the prevalence and characteristics of sexual assault: A cohort analysis. *Violence and Victims, 21,* 629–644.

Cherlin, A. J., Burton, L. M., Hurt, T. R., & Purvin, D. M. (2004). The influence of physical and sexual abuse on marriage and cohabitation. *American Sociological Review, 69, 768–789.*

Cox, C. E., Kotch, J. B., & Everson, M. D. (2004). A longitudinal study of modifying influences in the relationship between domestic violence and child maltreatment. *Journal of Family Violence, 18, 5–17.*

Daro, D., Edleson, J. L. & Pinderhughes, H. (2004). Finding common ground in the study of child maltreatment, youth violence, and adult domestic violence. *Journal of Interpersonal Violence, 19,* 282–298.

Dasgupta, S. D. (2002). A framework for understanding women's use of nonlethal violence in intimate heterosexual relationships. *Violence Against Women, 8,* 1364–1389.

DeKeseredy, W. S., & Dragiewicz, M. (2007). Understanding the complexities of feminist perspectives on woman abuse: A commentary on Donald G. Dutton's *Rethinking domestic violence. Violence Against Women, 13,* 874–884.

Delsol, C., & Margolin, G. (2004). The role of family of origin violence in men's marital violence perpetration. *Clinical Psychology Review, 24,* 99–122.

Delsol, C., Margolin, G., & John, R. S. (2003). A typology of maritally violent men and correlates of violence in a community sample. *Journal of Marriage and Family, 65,* 635–651.

DeMaris, A. (2000). Till discord do us part: The role of physical and verbal conflict in union disruption. *Journal of Marriage and the Family, 62,* 683–692.

DeMaris, A. (2001). The influence of marital violence on transmissions out of cohabitation. *Journal of Marriage and Family, 63,* 235–246.

Dugan, L., Nagin, D. S., & Rosenfeld, R. (1999). Explaining the decline in intimate partner homicide: Effects of changing domesticity, women's status, and domestic violence resources. *Homicide Studies, 3,* 187–214.

Dugan, L., Nagin, D. S., & Rosenfeld, R. (2003). Exposure reduction or retaliation? The effects of domestic violence resources on intimate partner homicide. *Law & Society Review, 37,* 169–198.

Dunne, M. P., Purdie, D. M., Cook, M. D., Boyle, F. M., & Najman, J. M. (2003). Is child sexual abuse declining? Evidence from a population-based survey of men and women in Australia. *Child Abuse and Neglect, 27,* 141–152.

Dutton, D. G. (2006). *Rethinking domestic violence.* Vancouver: University of British Columbia Press.

Dutton, M. A., Kaltman, S., Goodman, L. A., Weinfurt, K., & Vankos, N. (2005). Patterns of intimate partner violence: Correlates and outcomes. *Violence and Victims, 20,* 483–497.

Edleson, J. L. (1999). The overlap between child maltreatment and woman battering. *Violence Against Women, 5,* 134–154.

Edleson, J. L., Mbilinyi, L. F., Beeman, S. K., & Hagemeister, A. K. (2003). How children are involved in domestic violence. *Journal of Interpersonal Violence, 18,* 18–32.

Ehrensaft, M. K., Cohen, P., Brown, J., Samiles, E., Chen, H., & Johnson, J. G. (2003). Intergenerational transmission of partner violence: A 20-year prospective study. *Journal of Consulting and Clinical Psychology, 71,* 741–753.

Felson, R. B. (2002). *Violence and gender reexamined.* Washington, DC: American Psychological Association.

Felson, R. B., & Outlaw, M. C. (2007). The control motive and marital violence. *Violence and Victims, 22, 387–407.*

Felson, R. B., & Pare, P. (2005). The reporting of domestic violence and sexual assault by nonstrangers to the police. *Journal of Marriage and Family, 67,* 597–610.

Fergusson, D. M., Horwood, L. J., & Ridder, E. M. (2005). Partner violence and mental health outcomes in a New Zealand birth cohort. *Journal of Marriage and Family, 67*, 1103–1119.

Finkelhor, D., & Jones, L. M. (2006). Why have child maltreatment and child victimization declined? *Journal of Social Issues, 62*, 685–716.

Finkelhor, D., Ormrod, R. K., & Turner, H. A. (2007). Poly-victimization: A neglected component in child victimization. *Child Abuse and Neglect, 31*, 7–26.

Freedner, N., Freed, L. H., Yang, Y. W., & Austin, S. B. (2002). Dating violence among gay, lesbian, and bisexual adolescents: Results from a community survey. *Journal of Adolescent Health, 31*, 469–474.

Frias, S. M., & Angel, R. J. (2007). Stability and change in the experience of partner violence among low-income women. *Social Science Quarterly, 88*, 1281–1306.

Friesthler, B., Merritt, D. H., & LaScala, E. A. (2006). Understanding the ecology of child maltreatment: A review of the literature and directions for further research. *Child Maltreatment, 11*, 263–280.

Friesthler, B., Needell, B., & Gruenewald, P. J. (2005). Is the physical availability of alcohol and illicit drugs related to neighborhood rates of child maltreatment? *Child Abuse and Neglect, 29*, 1049–1060.

Frieze, I. (2005). Female violence against intimate partners: An introduction. *Psychology of Women Quarterly, 29*, 229–237.

Frye, V., & Wilt, S. (2001). Femicide and social disorganization. *Violence Against Women, 7*, 335–351.

Graham-Kevan, N., & Archer, J. (2003). Intimate terrorism and common couple violence: A test of Johnson's predictions in four British samples. *Journal of Interpersonal Violence, 11*, 1247–1270.

Greenwood, G. L., Reif, M. V., Huang, B., Pollack, L. M., Canchola, J. A., & Catania, J. A. (2002). Battering victimization among a probability-based sample of men who have sex with men. *American Journal of Public Health, 92*, 1964–1969.

Hampton, R., Oliver, W., & Magarian, L. (2003). Domestic violence in the African American community. *Violence Against Women, 9*, 533–557.

Henderson, A. J. Z., Bartholomew, K., Trinke, S. J., & Kwong, M. (2005). When loving means hurting: An exploration of attachment and intimate abuse in a community sample. *Journal of Family Violence, 11*, 314–331.

Heyman, R. E., & Slep, A. M. S. (2002). Do child abuse and interparental violence lead to adulthood family violence? *Journal of Marriage and Family, 64*, 864–870.

Hoffman, K. L., & Edwards, J. N. (2004). An integrated theoretical model of sibling violence and abuse. *Journal of Family Violence, 19*, 185–200.

Holzworth-Munroe, A., & Meehan, J. C. (2004). Typologies of men who are maritally violent: Scientific and clinical implications. *Journal of Interpersonal Violence, 19*, 1369–1389.

Holzworth-Munroe, A., & Stuart, G. L. (1994). Typologies of male batterers: Three subtypes and the differences among them. *Psychological Bulletin, 116*, 476–497.

Hyman, B. (2000). The economic consequences of child sexual abuse for adult lesbian women. *Journal of Marriage and the Family, 62*, 199–211.

Jacoby, M., Gorenflo, D., Black, E., Wunderlich, C., & Eyler, A. E. (1999). Rapid repeat pregnancy and experiences of interpersonal violence among low-income adolescents. *American Journal of Preventive Medicine, 16*, 318–321.

Jennings, W. G., & Piquero, A. R. (2008). Trajectories of non-intimate partner and intimate partner homicide, 1980–1999: The importance of rurality. *Journal of Criminal Justice, 36*, 435–443.

Johnson, M. P. (1995). Patriarchal terrorism and common couple violence: Two forms of violence against women. *Journal of Marriage and the Family, 57*, 283–295.

Johnson, M. P. (2006). Conflict and control: Gender symmetry and asymmetry in domestic violence. *Violence Against Women, 12,* 1003–1018.

Johnson, M. P. (2008). *A typology of domestic violence: Intimate terrorism, violent resistance, and situational couple violence.* Boston, MA: Northeastern University Press.

Johnson, M. P., & Ferraro, K. J. (2000). Research on domestic violence in the 1990s: Making distinctions. *Journal of Marriage and the Family, 62,* 948–963.

Johnson, M. P., & Leone, J. M. (2005). The differential effects of intimate terrorism and common couple violence: Findings from the National Violence Against Women Survey. *Journal of Family Issues, 26,* 322–349.

Jones, L. M., Finkelhor, D., & Halter, S. (2006). Child maltreatment trends in the 1990s: Why does neglect differ from sexual and physical abuse? *Child Maltreatment, 11,* 107–120.

Jones, L. M., Finkelhor, D., & Kopiec, K. (2001). Why is sexual abuse declining? A survey of state child protection administrators. *Child Abuse & Neglect, 25,* 1139–1158.

Kaukinen, C. (2004). Status compatibility, physical violence, and emotional abuse in intimate relationships. *Journal of Marriage and Family, 66,* 452–471.

Kaukinen, C., & DeMaris, A. (2005). Age at first sexual assault and current substance use and depression. *Journal of Interpersonal Violence, 20,* 1244–1270.

Kenney, C., & McLanahan, S. L. (2006). Why are cohabiting relationships more violent than marriages? *Demography, 43,* 127–140.

Kim, H. K., & Capaldi, D. M. (2004). The association of antisocial behavior and depressive symptoms between partners and risk for aggression in romantic relationships. *Journal of Family Psychology, 18,* 82–96.

Kim, H. K., Laurent, H. K., Capaldi, D. M., & Feingold, A. (2008). Men's aggression toward women: A 10-year panel study. *Journal of Marriage and Family, 70,* 1169–1187.

Kimmel, M. (2002). "Gender symmetry" in domestic violence: A substantive and methodological research review. *Violence Against Women, 8,* 1332–1363.

Koenig, M. A., Ahmed, S., Hossain, B., & Khorshed Alam Mozumder, A. B. M. (2003). Women's status and domestic violence in rural Bangladesh: Individual-and community-level effects. *Demography, 40,* 269–288.

Kwong, M. J., Bartholomew, K., Henderson, A. J. Z., & Trinke, S. J. (2003). The intergenerational transmission of relationship violence. *Journal of Family Psychology, 17,* 288–301.

Langhinrichsen-Rohling, J., Huss, M. T., & Ramsey, S. (2000). The clinical utility of batterer typologies. *Journal of Family Violence, 15,* 37–53.

Lau, A. S., Takeuchi, D. T., & Alegria, M. (2006). Parent-to-child aggression among Asian American parents: Culture, context, and vulnerability. *Journal of Marriage and Family, 68,* 1261–1275.

Lauritsen, J. L., & Schaum, R. J. (2004). The social ecology of violence against women. *Criminology, 42,* 323–358.

Leone, J. M., Johnson, M. P., Cohan, C. L., & Lloyd, S. E. (2004). Consequences of male partner violence for low-income minority women. *Journal of Marriage and Family, 66,* 472–490.

Lewin, E. (2004). Does marriage have a future? *Journal of Marriage and Family, 66,* 1000–1006.

Macmillan, R. (2001). Violence and the life course: The consequences of victimization for personal and social development. *Annual Review of Sociology, 27,* 1–22.

Margolin, E., & Gordis, E. B. (2003). Co-occurrence between marital aggression and parents' child abuse potential: The impact of cumulative stress. *Violence and Victims, 18,* 243–258.

McCloskey, L. A., & Lichter, E. L. (2003). The contribution of marital violence to adolescent aggression across different relationships. *Journal of Interpersonal Violence, 18*, 390–412.

McHugh, M. C., Livingston, N. A., & Ford, A. (2005). A post-modern approach to women's use of violence: Developing multiple and complex conceptualizations. *Psychology of Women Quarterly, 29*, 323–336.

Melzer, S. A. (2002). Gender, work, and intimate violence: Men's occupational violence spillover and compensatory violence. *Journal of Marriage and Family, 64*, 820–832.

Miller, E., Decker, M. R., Reed, E., Raj, A., Hathaway, J. E., & Silverman, J. G. (2007). Male partner pregnancy-promoting behaviors and adolescent partner violence: Findings from a qualitative study with adolescent females. *Ambulatory Pediatrics, 7*, 360–366.

Miller, J. (2008). *Getting played: African American girls, urban inequality, and gendered violence*. New York: New York University Press.

Miller, J., & White, N. (2003). Gender and relationship violence: A contextual examination. *Criminology, 41*, 1212–1248.

Mills, L. (2003). *Insult to injury: Rethinking our responses to intimate abuse*. Princeton, NJ: Princeton University Press.

Morenoff, J. D., & Samson, R. J. (1997). Violent crime and the spatial dynamics of neighborhood transition: Chicago, 1970–1990. *Social Forces, 76*, 31–64.

Richmond, J. M., Elliot, A. N., Pierce, T. W., Aspelmeir, J. E., & Alexander, A. A. (2009). Polyvictimization, childhood victimization, and psychological distress in college women. *Child Maltreatment, 14*, 127–147.

Risman, B. (1998). *Gender vertigo: American families in transition*. New Haven, CT: Yale University Press.

Romito, P., & Grassi, M. (2007). Does violence affect one gender more than the other? The mental health impact of violence among male and female university students. *Social Science & Medicine, 65*, 1222–1234.

Saltzman, L. E., Mahendra, R. R., Ikeda, R. M., & Ingram, E. M. (2005). Utility of hospital emergency department data for studying intimate partner violence. *Journal of Marriage and Family, 67*, 960–970.

Sanchez, L., & Gager, C. T. (2000). Hard living, perceived entitlement to a great marriage, and marital dissolution. *Journal of Marriage and the Family, 62*, 708–722.

Schuck, A. (2005). Explaining Black-White disparity in maltreatment: Poverty, female-headed families, and urbanization. *Journal of Marriage and Family, 67*, 543–551.

Scott, E. K., London, A. S., & Myers, N. A. (2002). Dangerous dependencies: The intersection of welfare reform and domestic violence. *Gender & Society, 16*, 867–897.

Silverman, J. G., Raj, A., & Clements, K. (2004). Dating violence and associated sexual risk and pregnancy among adolescent females in the United States. *Pediatrics, 114*, 220–225.

Simonelli, C. J., Mullis, T., Elliot, A. N., & Pierce, T. W. (2002). Abuse by siblings and subsequent experiences of violence within the dating relationship. *Journal of Interpersonal Violence, 17*, 103–121.

Slep, A. M. S., & O'Leary, S. G. (2001). Examining partner and child abuse: Are we ready for a more integrated approach to family violence? *Clinical Child and Family Psychology Review, 4*, 87–107.

Smith, P. H., White, J. W., & Holland, L. J. (2003). A longitudinal perspective on dating violence among adolescent and college-age women. *Journal of American Public Health Association, 93*, 1104–1109.

Staggs, S. L., Long, S. M., Mason, G. E., Krishnan, S., & Riger, S. (2007). Intimate partner violence, social support, and employment in the post welfare-reform era. *Journal of Interpersonal Violence, 22*, 345–367.

Staggs, S. L., & Riger, S. (2005). Effects of intimate partner violence on low-income women's health and employment. *American Journal of Community Psychology, 36*, 133–145.

Stark, E. (2007). *Coercive control: How men entrap women in personal life*. Oxford, UK: Oxford University Press.

Stith, S. M., Rosen, K. H., Middleton, K. A., Busch, A. L., Lundeberg, K., & Carlton, R. P. (2000). The intergenerational transmission of spouse abuse: A meta-analysis. *Journal of Marriage and the Family, 62,* 640–654.

Stith, S. M., Smith, D. B., Penn, C. E., Ward, D. B., & Tritt, D. (2004). Intimate partner physical abuse perpetration and victimization risk factors: A meta-analytic review. *Aggression and Violent Behavior, 10,* 65–98.

Stevenson, B., & Wolfers, J. (2006). Bargaining in the shadow of the law: Divorce laws and family distress. *Quarterly Journal of Economics, 121,* 267–291.

Straus, M. A. (2007). Processes explaining the concealment and distortion of evidence on gender symmetry in partner violence. *European Journal of Crime Policy Research, 13,* 227–232.

Straus, M. A. (2008). Dominance and symmetry in partner violence by male and female university students in 32 nations. *Children and Youth Services Review, 30,* 252–275.

Swan, S. C., & Snow, D. L. (2002). A typology of women's use of violence in intimate relationships. *Violence Against Women, 8,* 286–319.

Swinford, S. P., DeMaris, A., Cernkovich, S. A., & Giordano, P. C. (2000). Harsh physical discipline in childhood and violence in later romantic involvements: The mediating role of problem behaviors. *Journal of Marriage and the Family, 62,* 508–519.

Teachman, J., & Crowder, K. (2002). Multilevel models in family research: Some conceptual and methodological issues. *Journal of Marriage and Family, 64,* 280–294.

Ulman, A., & Straus, M. A. (2003). Violence by children against mothers in relation to violence between parents and corporal punishment by parents. *Journal of Comparative Family Studies, 34,* 41–60.

Walsh, J. A., & Krienert, J. L. (2007). Child-parent violence: An empirical analysis of offender, victim, and event characteristics in a national sample of reported incidents. *Journal of Family Violence, 22,* 563–574.

Waltz, J., Babcock, J. C., Jacobson, N. S., & Gottman, J. M. (2000). Testing a typology of batterers. *Journal of Consulting and Clinical Psychology, 68,* 658–669.

White, J. W. (2009). A gendered approach to adolescent dating violence: Conceptual and methodological issues. *Psychology of Women Quarterly, 33,* 1–15.

Williams, L. W. (2003). Understanding child abuse and violence against women: A life course perspective. *Journal of Interpersonal Violence, 18,* 441–451.

Woodward, L. J., Fergusson, D. M., & Horwood, L. J. (2002). Romantic relationships of young people with childhood and adolescent onset antisocial behavior problems. *Journal of Abnormal Child Psychology, 30,* 231–243.

Yan, E., & Tang, C. S. (2003). Proclivity to elder abuse: A community study on Hong Kong Chinese. *Journal of Interpersonal Violence, 18,* 999–1017.

Chapter 3: Concluding Remarks

This chapter has presented us with compelling evidence of the complexities involved in understanding the relationship among crime, criminal behavior, and victimization from a multidimensional approach that accounts for variations in individual traits, as well as more broad structural elements of social environment. The causes and consequences of crimes such as bullying, intimate partner violence, and child abuse are better understood within a context of interrelated experiences that are distinct and variable from victim to victim; therefore, their prevention and intervention must account for these variations in a way that addresses the unique circumstances of each individual involved. Research within the field of victimology continues to grow in the direction of multilevel models of analysis that account for both individual and contextual characteristics of crime victimization, both in the immediate situation and over time, in order to better understand the behavior of both victims and offenders and how the relationship between the two can shape, alter, and affect the outcome of violence in their lives.

Criminal Justice System Response to Victims of Crime

Introduction

The field of victimology has a long-standing history of addressing questions concerning the treatment of crime victims in various social contexts. With a significant focus within criminal justice dedicated to the apprehension, trial, and conviction of the offender, attending to the needs of crime victims is sometimes considered an afterthought or secondary concern within criminal justice system policy, practice, response, and intervention. Effectually, the foundation of this discipline revolves around an understanding of the relationship between criminal events that lead to a victim's encounter with various components within the criminal justice system and the outcome of those encounters in terms of victim satisfaction and nonreporting. Ultimately, we must consider the role of police officers, prosecutors, judges, and other agents of criminal justice in providing a comprehensive response to victims of crime that gives them a sense of control over their lives, is emotionally sensitive to their position of vulnerability and distress, and creates a safe environment of trust and legitimacy.

Recent trends in the widespread dissemination of social media portraying a negative, strained relationship between law enforcement and citizens has created a particularly challenging demand to study the role of police in properly addressing the needs of crime victims during that initial encounter. The following reading explores the question of victim satisfaction with police, focusing on how the variable of emotional distress as a common reaction to victimization related to an individual's satisfaction with their interaction with police responders. The study presented challenges readers to engage in developing a more accurate awareness of the relevance of adopting a victim-centered approach that requires agents of criminal justice to focus on becoming more compassionate, empathetic, and sensitive to the emotional components of crime victimization.

Guiding Questions

As you read, consider the following questions:

1 What is the role of the victim in the criminal justice system, and how does this role influence victim satisfaction?

2 Can law enforcement responses to victims of crime shape the outcome of nonreporting?

3 Are there benefits to adopting a more victim-centered approach in dealing with crime?

4 How can we ensure that agents of criminal justice provide victims of crime the proper support services they need instead of merely "clearing" cases?

Key Terms

British Crime Survey (BCS)   The national crime data source in England and Wales, surveying households since 1981.

victim sensitivity training   Programs and practices operating in a variety of settings designed to enhance the response to victims of crime through adequate educational training.

Victim Injury, Emotional Distress, and Satisfaction with the Police

Evidence for a Victim-Centered, Emotionally-Based Police Response

Chad Posick and Christina Policastro

One central measure of legitimacy and professionalism of the criminal justice system is satisfaction with police encounters. Despite the relevance of satisfaction with the police in creating a fair and respected criminal justice system, little is known about what influences satisfaction with the police beyond demographic characteristics and procedural justice measures. This study explores victim satisfaction with the police using the 2009–2010 British Crime Survey. Specifically, the current research focuses on how emotional distress, a common reaction to victimization, is related to satisfaction with the police. Results reveal that emotional distress decreases satisfaction with the police and also interacts with confidence in the police such that individuals who are more distressed but have favorable attitudes of the police are satisfied with their encounters. The results suggest that a victim-centered police response, which is attentive to victim emotions, would provide an avenue to increasing police legitimacy and professionalism.

One of the most enduring issues in victimology and criminal justice is non-reporting of victimizations to the police (Block & Maxfield, 2011; Hart & Rennison, 2003). Many reasons for non-reporting are given when victims are asked in self-report surveys why they did not notify the police. Several of these reasons center on the thought that police will not take the incident seriously, not believe the victim, or not be able to help (Hagan & Albonetti, 1982). Despite widespread non-reporting even among crimes of serious violence (Catalano, 2008), research has shown that several demographic factors do increase reporting including age, gender, and marital status (Baumer, 2002; Rennison, 2007). Beyond individual characteristics, factors related to the crime and reactions to the crime influence reporting such as whether the victim sustained an injury (Baumer, 2002; Rennison, 2007) and whether the victim experienced high levels of emotional distress (Posick, 2013). The latter two factors are particularly relevant to the present study. If research indicates that victims who are injured and who experience emotional hardship are among the most likely to report their experiences—then how well are the police handling these situations and dealing with the emotional needs of victims? Further, how are injury and distress linked with satisfaction with the police and can the answers to these questions help inform policies and practices? This study uses data from the 2009–2010 British Crime Survey (BCS) to examine the relationship between victim injury, emotional distress, and satisfaction with the police. The purpose of the study is to uncover factors that are related to victim satisfaction with the criminal justice system and to advance the agenda on providing victim-centered responses to those affected by violence.

Satisfaction with the Police

Satisfaction with the police is important on several levels. First, and perhaps foremost, US society promotes equality and justice. Specific safeguards exist to protect against government intrusion into individuals' lives and against illegitimate use of force from officials who are granted power. Beyond the more philosophical reasons underlying the need to be concerned with satisfaction with the police, there are other reasons that have been illuminated by empirical studies. One of these is related to the finding that individuals who trust the police and are satisfied with the way that police handle situations in their community are more likely to cooperate with police activities such as assisting in investigations (Hinds, 2007; Tyler, 2004). Similarly, individuals who believe the police to be legitimate are more likely to abide by the law than those who are not satisfied with the way police interact with citizens (Tyler, 1990). It appears that those who are satisfied with the police are not only are more law-abiding but also are willing to assist in crime intervention and enforcement efforts.

Research indicates that the majority of individuals who encounter the police are satisfied with their interaction. In a recent study sponsored by the U.S. Bureau of Justice Statistics using a sample of individuals who had a recent encounter with the police, 9 in 10 respondents reported being satisfied with their interaction with the police (Eith & Durose, 2011). Similar findings are produced when considering general confidence in the police (Cao, Frank, & Cullen, 1996). In a recent study by Posick, Rocque, and McDevitt (2013) it was found that both procedural justice and confidence in the police positively predicted satisfaction with the police controlling for the effects of age, race, and gender.

Despite these findings on police legitimacy and confidence in the police, very little is known about each piece of the puzzle contributing to satisfaction with the police. One issue that has remained understudied is the role that emotional distress plays in satisfaction with the police. If individuals in distress reach out to the police more often than others, which research shows that they do (*see* Posick, 2013), it would serve the field well to know how these individuals, following their experience, perceive the police.

Linking Victim Injury and Emotional Distress to Satisfaction with the Police

Regardless of the type of violence perpetrated, the likelihood of significant physical injury to the victim remains low but the emotional impacts are often substantial (Daigle, 2012). Physical injury has also been shown to exacerbate emotional distress after victimization (Posick, 2013). Emotional distress takes on various forms and can culminate in many different poor health outcomes. Post-traumatic Stress Disorder is one reaction to victimization most commonly found in men who witness violence and in women who experience sexual victimization (Kessler, Sonnega, Bromet, Hughes, & Nelson, 1995). Victims often exhibit depressive symptoms after victimization including a reduction in self-worth and increased anxiety (Grills & Ollendick, 2002) as well as related symptoms such as restlessness, sweating, sleeping difficulties, and upset stomachs (Dryden-Edwards, 2007). While injury may be a statistically unlikely result of being victimized, emotional reactions *are* likely and have significant costs to victims.

Despite the seriousness of emotionality following victimization, very little is known about how victims experiencing emotional distress view the police. This knowledge is essential for a legitimate and effective criminal justice system and a lack of understanding this process presents a significant gap in the empirical literature. While studies on this topic are limited, hypotheses can be made about the relationship between emotional distress and satisfaction with the police from a theoretical standpoint.

First, it is expected that injury will increase emotional distress among the sample used in the current research. This hypothesis is based on prior research with the British Crime Survey (*see* Posick, 2013). Injury is more likely in violent crimes and those of an interpersonal nature, thus these types of victimizations are more likely to have an emotional toll on victims. Second, it is hypothesized that emotional distress will increase dissatisfaction with the police. This is based on work by Denkers and Winkel (1998) who found that victims of crime are often "unhappy" after their victimization experience. Finally, it is hypothesized that emotional distress will mediate the effect of injury on dissatisfaction. This follows the first hypothesis and is further based upon the finding that injury is a powerful predictor of distress (Davis, Taylor, & Lurigio, 1996). That is, injury is expected to be positively related to distress as highlighted by prior research (Davis et al., 1996) and that distress will be the mediating link to dissatisfaction in line with prior research by Denkers & Winkel (1998). The path conceptualization is depicted in Figure 5.1.

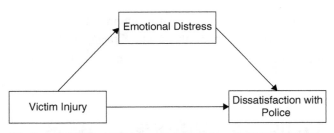

Note: Control variables and coefficients omitted from the figure. Model does not propose that emotional distress will fully mediate the effect of victim injury on victim dissatisfaction with the police.

Figure 5.1   Path Model.

Data and Methods

The current study uses data from the 2009–2010 British Crime Survey (BCS) to explore the relationships described above. This dataset is particularly well-suited to explore the theoretical questions proposed above and one of the few datasets to contain variables related to victim reactions to their experience. The BCS is currently an annual self-report survey conducted in England and Wales. Respondents are asked in face-to-face interviews to recall any personal victimization experiences in the previous 12 months. The total BCS sample consists of 49,024 individuals ages 16 years or older which constitutes a 76% response rate. The sample for the current study is based on those individuals who indicated that they reported their victimization to the police (n=5,833). The final sample for the current research is restricted to those participants who had complete data for the measures included in the analysis.

The focal dependent variable in this study is victim dissatisfaction with the police. This is assessed using one question from the survey that asked respondents, "Overall, were you/(the victim) satisfied or dissatisfied with the way the police handled this matter?" This variable is kept in ordinal form (ranging from 1=very satisfied to 4=very dissatisfied) and is distributed across categories in the following way (1=37.26%; 2=31.80%; 3=16.22%; 4=14.73%).

The focal independent variables (used as outcomes in the path analysis) are victim injury and emotional distress. Injury is assessed using a dichotomous variable (0=not injured; 1=injured). Emotional distress is a variety score of eight different emotions or emotional reactions experienced after the victimization incident including anger, shock, fear, depression, anxiety, loss of confidence, loss of sleep, and crying (where 0=did not experience the emotion/reaction; 1=did experience the emotion/reaction). Here, the victim was asked "Did you personally have any of these reactions after the incident?" The reliability coefficient for this variable is .70 and merged on a one-factor solution.

Several individual-level and incident-level covariates are used as statistical control variables. Demographic controls include sex (0=male; 1=female), age (range=16–96), and race (Black, Asian, and Other Race included in the models, White is excluded as the reference category). Other individual characteristics include whether the respondent was employed full-time (0=not full time; 1=full time), how long they have held their current residence (ranging from 1=less than 12 months to 7=20 years or longer), marital status (0=not married; 1=married), global confidence in the police (a summative scale of eight items which loaded on one factor ranging from 8–40 with a reliability coefficient of .92), and a measure of previous victimization (0=not a previous victim; 1=previous victim).

Table 5.1   Descriptive Statistics for Reported Victimizations (n = 5,833)

	MEAN	STANDARD DEVIATION	RANGE
Violent incident	0.193	0.395	0–1
Hate crime	0.031	0.190	0–1
Known offender	0.210	0.407	0–1
Close to home	0.756	0.429	0–1
Nighttime	0.590	0.492	0–1
Personal injury	0.082	0.274	0–1
Previous victimization	0.887	0.318	0–1
Confidence police	27.355	7.006	8–40
Residential tenure	4.505	1.985	1–7
Age	42.980	16.587	16–96
Female	0.550	0.498	0–1
Full-time employment	0.620	0.486	0–1
Asian	0.039	0.192	0–1
Black	0.020	0.141	0–1
White	0.918	0.274	0–1
Other	0.023	0.148	0–1
Married	0.403	0.491	0–1
Emotional distress	1.689	1.686	0–8
Dissatisfaction with police	2.094	1.058	1–4

Incident-level covariates include if the respondent believed the crime was a hate crime (0=no; 1=yes), if the offender was known to the victim (0=stranger; 1=acquaintance or family member/friend), if the offense occurred close to the victim's home (0=the incident occurred more than 15 minutes from the victim's home; 1=the incident occurred 15 minutes or less from the victim's home), if the incident occurred at night (0=the incident occurred when there was daylight; 1=the incident occurred when it was dark or dusk out), and a measure of whether the incident constituted a violent victimization (0=property victimization; 1=violent victimization). Descriptive statistics for our study variables are included in Table 5.1.

Analytic Strategy

The current study investigates the relationship between victim injury, emotional distress, and dissatisfaction with the police. It was hypothesized that victim injury would indirectly affect victim dissatisfaction with the police via the injury's influence on emotional distress. To test this hypothesis, the current study followed the method outlined by Baron and Kenny (1986) and consisted of a path analysis involving a series of multivariate regression models to test for direct and indirect effects. The first model estimated the direct effect of victim injury on emotional distress while controlling for incident and victim characteristics. Given the Poisson distribution of the outcome variable of the first model (i.e., emotional distress) a negative binomial regression model was estimated. This type of regression analysis is appropriate for outcomes based on counts and characterized by an excess of zeroes (*see* Gardner, Mulvey, & Shaw, 1995; Osgood, 2000). Next, ordinal logistic regression analyses were used in the second and third models to predict victim dissatisfaction with the police. The second model examined the direct effect of victim injury on victim dissatisfaction with the police while excluding the emotional distress measure from the analysis. In the final model, emotional distress was added to determine whether the effect of victim injury on dissatisfaction with the police was mediated by emotional distress. All analyses were completed using Mplus version 7.11.

Results

The results of the path analysis testing for mediation are presented in Table 5.2. The first column displays the results of the negative binomial regression model predicting emotional distress. All variables assessing characteristics of the victimization incident were significantly associated with emotional distress with the exception of the measure assessing whether the victimization occurred at night. As expected, victim injury was significantly and positively associated with emotional distress. Victim injury was associated with a 37% increase in the odds of emotional distress, holding all else constant. This is consistent with past research that suggests that injury leads to higher levels of emotional distress among victims of crime (Posick, 2013). With regard to other characteristics of the victimization incident violent victimizations, hate crimes, victimizations involving offenders known to the victim, and victimizations that occurred close to the victim's home were all associated with an increase in the odds of the victim reporting emotional distress. This finding is not surprising considering the personal nature of these types of victimization incidents.

Similar to the victimization incident variables, all of the victim characteristics included in the first model were significantly related to emotional distress, except for previous victimization. Finding that previous victimization was not significantly associated with distress seems to suggest that victims who have previously been victimized may be desensitized to some extent by their prior experiences with crime. Age, sex, and race were positively associated with emotional distress. For instance, being female was related to an approximately 51% increase in the odds of experiencing emotional distress, holding all else constant. Full-time employment, marital status, and residential tenure were all significantly and negatively related to experiencing emotional distress. Additionally, victims who were more confident with the police were less likely to report

Table 5.2 Direct and Indirect Effects Models

	EMOTIONAL DISTRESS (n = 4,367) (NEGATIVE BINOMIAL)		DISSATISFACTION (n = 4,275) (ORDINAL)		DISSATISFACTION (n = 4,275) (ORDINAL)	
	b(SE)	OR	b(SE)	OR	b(SE)	OR
Violent incident	0.255(0.045)***	1.290	0.009(0.108)	1.009	−0.025(0.108)	0.976
Hate crime	0.317(0.062)***	1.373	−0.037(0.159)	0.964	−0.083(0.160)	0.920
Known offender	0.174(0.037)***	1.190	0.241(0.086)**	1.272	0.214(0.086)*	1.238
Close to home	0.090(0.034)**	1.094	−0.025(0.073)	0.975	−0.035(0.073)	0.966
Nighttime	−0.002(0.029)	0.998	−0.011(0.062)	0.989	−0.010(0.063)	0.990
Personal injury	0.318(0.053)***	1.374	−0.452(0.137)**	0.637	−0.498(0.137)***	0.608
Previous victimization	−0.108(0.067)	0.898	0.386(0.172)*	1.471	0.407(0.172)*	1.503
Confidence police	−0.010(0.002)***	0.990	−0.164(0.005)***	0.849	−0.163(0.005)***	0.850
Residential tenure	−0.026(0.008)**	0.974	−0.030(0.017)	0.971	−0.026(0.017)	0.974
Age	0.002(0.001)*	1.002	−0.007(0.002)**	0.993	−0.007(0.002)**	0.993
Female	0.415(0.029)***	1.514	−0.046(0.059)	0.955	−0.099(0.061)	0.905
Full–time employment	−0.101(0.029)**	0.904	−0.060(0.064)	0.942	−0.047(0.064)	0.954
Asian	0.193(0.070)**	1.213	0.234(0.151)	1.264	0.205(0.151)	1.228
Black	0.217(0.091)*	1.242	0.270(0.204)	1.310	0.249(0.204)	1.283
Other	0.208(0.087)*	1.231	0.277(0.200)	1.320	0.249(0.200)	1.283
Married	−0.065(0.030)*	0.937	0.009(0.064)	1.009	0.021(0.064)	1.021
Emotional distress	–	–	–	–	0.077(0.019)***	1.080
Pseudo r²	–		0.294		0.297	

Note: *p<.05; **p<.01; ***p<.001; OR = odds ratio.

emotional distress compared to victims who reported lower confidence in the police. These findings seem to suggest that victims may be less distressed if they have emotional supports such as neighbors, spouses, and co-workers and believe that law enforcement will handle the offense appropriately and in a just manner.

The results of the second model examining the direct effect of victim injury on dissatisfaction with the police are reported in the second column of Table 5.2. Victim injury was significantly associated with dissatisfaction. Contrary to expectations, victims who were injured during the victimization incident were less likely to report that they were dissatisfied with the police than victims who were not injured. This may be related to the way that police officers handle cases involving injured victims. Research on arrest decisions in intimate partner violence cases has suggested that police are more likely to arrest in cases where the victim sustained injury (*see* Berk & Sherman, 1988; Buzawa & Austin, 1993; Buzawa & Hotaling, 2000). It may be that cases involving victim injury are taken more seriously by the police, thus victims feel more satisfied by the police response. The victim's age and confidence in the police were also significantly and negatively associated with dissatisfaction with the police. Older victims and victims with more confidence in the police were less likely to report dissatisfaction than younger victims and victims with lower confidence in the police. Whether the offender was known to the victim and whether the victim had previously been victimized were positively related to dissatisfaction. That is, victims who knew their offender and victims who had experienced a prior victimization were more likely to report that they were dissatisfied with the police response, compared to victims who did not know their offender and victims who had not previously been victimized.

The results of the full model estimating both direct and indirect effects are provided in the last panel of Table 5.2. The findings of the final model are very similar to the results of the second model predicting dissatisfaction. Overall, the results provide no support for the mediation hypothesis. The inclusion of emotional distress in the full model did not reduce the effect of victim injury on dissatisfaction with the police. As hypothesized, emotional distress was positively and significantly associated with dissatisfaction indicating that victims who reported higher levels of emotional distress were more likely to report being dissatisfied with the police response compared to victims who reported less emotional distress. Consistent with the previous model, injured victims were less likely to report being dissatisfied with the police compared to victims who were not injured.

To investigate whether the effect of emotional distress on dissatisfaction may be moderated by other victim characteristics, an additional model was estimated examining the effect of the interaction of victim confidence in the police and emotional distress on dissatisfaction, controlling for all of the victim and incident characteristics included in the previous models. Table 5.3 displays the results of the model including the multiplicative interaction term.[1] The multiplicative interaction term was significantly associated with dissatisfaction, holding all else constant. That is, the effect of emotional distress on satisfaction is conditioned by the victim's confidence in the police. This finding indicates that victims who reported higher levels of confidence in the police and higher levels of emotional distress were less likely to report being dissatisfied with the police response compared to victims who had lower levels of confidence in the police and lower levels of emotional distress, holding all else constant.

---

[1] For clarity, Table 5.3 omits the coefficients for the control variables. The results of the supplementary analysis were very similar to the findings reported in the last panel of Table 5.2 and there were no substantive differences between the models.

Table 5.3   Interaction Effect of Confidence in the Police and Emotional Distress on Satisfaction with the Police (n = 4,272)

	DISSATISFACTION	
	b(SE)	OR
Confidence in the police	−0.150(0.007)***	0.861
Emotional distress	0.261(0.070)***	1.298
Confidence in the police X emotional distress	−0.007(0.003)**	0.993
Pseudo r²	0.300	

Note: **p<.01; ***p<.001; OR=odds ratio

Discussion and Conclusion

The current study set out to investigate how victim emotional distress is related to feelings of satisfaction with the police. It was hypothesized that emotional distress would have a direct effect on satisfaction with the police and would also mediate the effects of injury on dissatisfaction. The results indicated that both injury and distress had significant direct effects on dissatisfaction but that distress did not mediate the effect of injury. To further explore a possible mechanism that explains victim satisfaction with the police, the current research explored an interaction between confidence in the police and police dissatisfaction. It was found that confidence in the police conditioned the effect of distress such that victims experiencing high emotional distress were satisfied with their encounter if they were confident in the police. In other words, even a highly emotional victim can have a very positive experience with the police if they believe them to be legitimate and professional.

The results of this study, coupled with past studies, indicate that emotional distress increases police reporting, as well as leads to greater dissatisfaction with the police. That is, highly emotional victims are more likely than other victims to reach out to the police for help but are less satisfied with the police response than other victims (see Posick, 2013). While this may suggest that emotional victims are somewhat inconsolable or that they will inevitably be unhappy with any interaction, the current analysis suggests that this is not likely to be true. The interaction analysis shows that even emotional victims can have a positive encounter with the police. The mechanism at work, at least partially, is confidence in the police.

Luckily, confidence in the police can be built and maintained by officers themselves and by police departments as a whole. Tyler (2004) suggests that perceptions of the criminal justice system as fair are affected by individuals' ability to participate in the process and have input in decisions, the degree of system transparency, how they are treated by criminal justice professionals, and whether they view criminal justice professionals as trustworthy. Training programs and policies aimed at positively influencing the public's perceptions of law enforcement officers and improving police-community relations are likely to increase confidence in the police, which in turn may ultimately improve victims' and citizens' satisfaction in their interactions with officers. Research indicates that positive direct and vicarious experiences with police have been shown to boost global attitudes toward the police (Rosenbaum, Schuck, Costello, Hawkins, & Ring, 2005). Further, the establishment of community-police partnerships has been found to lead to confidence in the police and perceptions of police legitimacy (Schafer, Huebner, & Bynum, 2003). According to the results of the current study, confidence in the police can lead to direct feelings of satisfaction with police encounters as well as promote positive experiences among the most distressed victims.

The results of the current research support a criminal justice response to victimization that is focused on the needs of victims. These needs are often psychological in nature consisting of reactions related to anger, depression, and anxiety, which should not go ignored by police when responding to victimization incidents. While a victim-centered response is not commonly recommended in the criminological literature (and perhaps even less so in police training) it has been thoughtfully recommended in the past. For example, Winkel (1991) recommended over 20 years ago that police interventions with victims should be victim-oriented and based on data related to victims' prior stressful experiences and life circumstances, which can influence distress. Further, Rosenbaum (1987) found that victim sensitivity training improved police perceptions of positive interactions with citizens. The current results suggest that training police on identifying specific forms of distress and intervening in a way that addresses those particular needs is an important step in increasing a fair and effective police response to victimization.

This research has contributed to an understanding of victim satisfaction with the police but should be considered along with the study limitations. First, there are emotions and reactions that could not be captured using the existing items in the BCS. Other measures might be differentially related to satisfaction. Second, it is unclear how the relationships explored here would translate to other countries and other samples. It may be that there are larger societal factors that play a part in confidence in the police and perceptions of legitimacy and professionalism. It would be surprising, however, if future research were to demonstrate that emotional distress has significantly different relationships to the variables used in the current study and it would be equally surprising if confidence in the police were to be found to have no effect on satisfaction or the moderation of emotional distress. However, future research should replicate this analysis using similar data sources from the US and other countries to empirically test these relationships. The shortcomings of this study suggest that future research can further uncover the important relationship between emotional distress and satisfaction with the police by using various measures of distress and additional control variables with diverse samples. Given the theoretical and policy implications of the current study, future research should seek to replicate and extend these findings.

References

Baron, R. M., & Kenny, D. A. (1986). The moderator-mediator variable distinction in social psychological research: Conceptual, strategic, and statistical considerations. *Journal of Personality and Social Psychology, 51*, 1173–1182.

Baumer, E. P. (2002). Neighborhood disadvantage and police notification by victims of violence. *Criminology, 405*, 579–616.

Berk, R. A., & Sherman, L. (1988). Police responses to family violence incidences: An analysis of an experimental design with incomplete randomization. *Journal of the American Statistical Association, 83*, 70–76.

Block, S., & Maxfield, M. G. (2011). National crime statistics: U.S. uniform crime reports and the National Crime Victimization Survey. In M. Natarajan (Ed.), *International Crime and Justice* (pp. 455–461). New York, NY: Cambridge University Press.

Buzawa, E., & Austin, T. (1993). Determining police response to domestic violence victims. *American Behavioral Scientist, 36*, 610–623.

Buzawa, E., & Hotaling, G. (2000). *The police response to domestic violence calls for assistance in three Massachusetts towns: Final report*. Washington, DC: National Institute of Justice.

Cao, L., Frank, J., & Cullen, F. T. (1996). Race, community context and confidence in the police. *American Journal of Police, 15*, 3–22.

Catalano, S. M. (2008). *Criminal victimization (2004)*. Darby, PA: Diane Publishing.

Daigle, L. E. (2011). *Victimology: A text/reader* (Vol. 9). Thousand Oaks, CA: Sage Publications.

Denkers, A. J., & Winkel, F. W. (1998). Crime victims' well-being and fear in a prospective and longitudinal study. *International Review of Victimology, 5*, 141–162.

Dyden-Edwards R. (2007). Anxiety. Retrieved from http://www.Emedicinehealth.com/anxiety/article_em.htm.

Eith, C., & Durose, M. (2011). *Contacts between police and the public, 2008*. Washington, DC: Office of Justice Programs, Bureau of Justice Statistics, U.S. Department of Justice.

Gardner, W., Mulvey, E. P., & Shaw, E. C. (1995). Regression analyses of counts and rates: Poisson, overdispersed poisson, and negative binomial models. *Psychological Bulletin, 118*, 392–404.

Grills, A. E., & Ollendick, T. H. (2002). Peer victimization, global self-worth, and anxiety in middle school children. *Journal of Clinical Child and Adolescent Psychology, 31*, 59–68.

Hagan, J., & Albonetti, C. (1982). Race, class, and the perception of criminal injustice in America. *American Journal of Sociology, 88*, 329–355.

Hart, T. C., & Rennison, C. (2003). *Reporting crime to the police, 1992–2000* (Special Report NCJ-195710). Washington, DC: Bureau of Justice Statistics.

Hinds, L. (2007). Public satisfaction with police: The influence of general attitudes and police-citizen encounters. *International Journal of Police Science & Management, 11*, 54–66.

Kessler, R. C., Sonnega, A., Bromet, E., Hughes, M., & Nelson, C. B. (1995). Posttraumatic stress disorder in the National Comorbidity Survey. *Archives of General Psychiatry, 52*, 1048–1060.

Osgood, D. W. (2000). Poisson-based regression analysis of aggregate crime rates. *Journal of Quantitative Criminology, 16*, 21–43.

Posick, C., (2013). Victimization and police reporting: The role of negative emotionality. *Psychology of Violence*. DOI: 10.1037/a0031770.

Posick, C., Rocque, M., & McDevitt, J., (2013). One scale fits all? Assessing racial differences in the measurement of attitudes toward the police. *Race & Justice*. DOI: 10.1177/2153368713494214.

Rennison, C. (2007). *Victim and household characteristics: Reporting violence to the police. Illinois crime victimization survey 2002 data analysis*. Chicago, IL: Illinois Criminal Justice Information Authority.

Rosenbaum, D. P. (1987). Coping with victimization: The effects of police intervention on victims' psychological readjustment. *Crime & Delinquency, 33*, 502–519.

Rosenbaum, D. P., Schuck, A. M., Costello, S. K., Hawkins, D. F., & Ring, M. K. (2005). Attitudes toward the police: The effects of direct and vicarious experience. *Police Quarterly, 8*, 343–365.

Schafer, J. A., Huebner, B. M., & Bynum, T. S. (2003). Citizen perceptions of police services: Race, neighborhood context, and community policing. *Police Quarterly, 6*, 440–468.

Tyler, T. R. (1990). *Why people obey the law*. New Haven, CT: Yale University Press.

Tyler, T. R. (2004). Enhancing police legitimacy. *Annals of the American Academy of Political and Social Science, 593*, 84–99.

Winkel, F. W. (1991). Police, victims, and crime prevention: Some research-based recommendations on victim-orientated interventions. *British Journal of Criminology, 31*, 250–265.

Chapter 4: Concluding Remarks

The role of victim satisfaction with the outcome of their various encounters with agents of criminal justice is an integral component of study within the field of victimology. From the research presented in this chapter, we can clearly see that victimization carries with it a heightened state of emotional distress that needs specialized care and attention in order to properly meet the needs of victims and ensure their adequate treatment throughout the process of interacting with police officers, court officials, and service providers. The level of trust that victims feel plays an important role in the outcome of their healing and well-being; therefore, measures must be taken to ensure the appropriate level of training and preparation to increase victim confidence in criminal justice system professionals and providers. This chapter inspires us to adapt a victim-centered approach to criminal offending that includes the victim at every stage of the process and ensures a fair and adequate response to their physical, psychological, and personal needs.

Victim Rights

Introduction

For many years now, the subject of protecting the rights of victims of crime has been at the forefront of academic, legal, and scholarly discourse. Today, the federal government, as well as each state, has enacted laws that define a set of rights and protections guaranteed to victims as they navigate throughout the criminal justice process and during court proceedings. These rights extend to victims and their families, and encompass all those individuals who are directly or indirectly affected by a harm caused by another person. The goal is to ensure that individuals affected by crime stay informed; are treated with dignity, sensitivity, and respect; and are protected from further harm and compensated from any harm committed by the offender. Historically, the crime victims' rights movement began in the 1970s as a response to a case where the Supreme Court effactually defined victims of crime as mere witnesses or pieces of evidence (*Linda R. S. v. Richard D.*, 410 U.S. 614 1973).

Over the next decades, social activism, the civil rights and feminist movements, as well as a general consciousness about the rights of victims of crime, laid the foundation for changes in legal principles, policies, and practices, as well as redefined cultural norms and attitudes toward victims of crime, forming a nexus for the evolution of laws protecting the rights of victims for years to come. An offspring of these changes is reflected in the recent application of Title IX in various contexts and the emphasis on proactive changes that need to be made to ensure that victims of sexual violence are protected. The reading selection in this chapter explores various issues pertaining to the definition of Title IX, the responsibility of college campuses in addressing sexual violence under Title IX, and the evolution of the definition of sexual discrimination as outlined in Title IX.

Guiding Questions

As you read, consider the following questions:

1   What do you think encompasses the definition of victims' rights?

2   Are there ways we can ensure that victims receive proper care and treatment during criminal justice proceedings?

3   What duties and obligations to victims of sexual violence has Title IX legislation added to practices on college campuses?

4   Do you feel that society should do more to protect victims of crime? If so, what can we do?

Key Terms

Dear colleague letter   A form of government correspondence where a letter is sent by a colleague form one legislative body to another when there is an issue under inquiry and debate.

Office for Victims of Crime   A U.S. Department of Justice agency established in 1988 as part of the Victims of Crime Act to assist crime victims by providing national research support, leadership in victim advocacy, and funding to victims of crime.

Title IX   A federal law that prohibits discrimination on the basis of sex in education and requires schools to proactively adopt policies, practices, and procedures that address and eliminate sexual violence on campus.

From Sexual Harassment to Sexual Violence

The Evolution of Title IX's Response to Sexual Victimization

Michelle Hughes Miller

Introduction

With the advent of the Dear Colleague Letter (2011 DCL) from the U.S. Department of Education's (DOE) Office for Civil Rights (OCR) in 2011, institutions of higher education began the process of reconceptualizing their Title IX processes to more directly address sexual violence on college campuses, including peer-on-peer sexual assault (DOE 2011a). In this chapter, I discuss the evolution of the OCR's Title IX demands on universities in relation to sexual violence, but I do so by querying the widely cited claim that the 2011 DCL was a seismic shift in the OCR's expectations for universities. Though there is no doubt that the 2011 DCL ushered in an era of significant and intensive transformation of Title IX prevention and response to sexual violence on college campuses, such changes in implementation do not require a shift in the OCR's understanding or articulation of sexual violence as an element of Title IX. In other words, though the 2011 DCL provided guidance to universities on changing institutional practices, did it in fact reflect a change in the OCR's articulation of Title IX and sexual violence compared to earlier communications?

To answer this question, I analyze the most relevant communications the OCR had with universities prior to the 2011 DCL to detail the evolution of discourse about sexual violence and Title IX in those documents. How did the OCR's guidance for universities on Title IX incorporate sexual violence, and when? By focusing on the discourse in various OCR communications from 1997 to 2011, I am able to both trace the evolution of OCR discourse on sexual violence and understand the context of the 2011 DCL. I use summative content analysis to consider the manifest and latent content of language included within OCR communications, focusing on documents related to or predating the 2011 DCL (see Hsieh and Shannon 2005 for a discussion of summative content analysis). I focus on the use and development of the construct "sexual violence" within these documents. To be clear, I do not discuss the legal or administrative rulings on Title IX (see Smith, Chapter 17 in this volume, for such a review). Instead, I am interested in how the OCR itself, tasked as it is with enforcing and providing information and guidance to schools and universities, talks about issues of sexual violence to its constituents through its published communications. I begin with a brief background on Title IX before I discuss in detail the definitional elements of importance within the 2011 DCL. I then trace the discourse in the 2011 DCL back to its sources in prior OCR communications and documents, noting any shifts and clarifications. Finally, I consider, at the end of this chapter, how the 2011 DCL with its particular focus on sexual violence came to be, focusing on the legal, political, cultural, and advocacy context within which it was written and, ultimately, distributed to universities, thus setting in motion "shock-waves" across the academic community (Jonson-Reid et al. 2016, 235).

I first became interested in sexual harassment policy at my former institution, Southern Illinois University Carbondale, where I chaired a committee tasked with providing recommendations to revise the institution's sexual harassment policy and procedures. At the University of South Florida (USF), I recently served on and chaired the Presidential Advisory Committee on Title IX. Throughout this time actively working on Title IX issues, including two years' dedicated time working on defining and responding to sexual harassment policy in the company of Title IX scholars and practitioners, I can honestly say that the issue of student-on-student sexual assault as an element of Title IX barely came up. That is, until 2011, when the DCL crossed our desks. Since then I have watched USF respond to these new articulations of expected Title IX response, and I have witnessed student activists—many of whom are survivors of sexual violence—hold their universities accountable. In Chapter 10, the story told by Dr. Carmen Suarez, Vice President of Global Diversity and Inclusion at Portland State University, nicely discusses changes to institutional response at her university, and the activist narrative by Ava Blustein in Chapter 16 shares the empowerment that can come from collective action on this topic.

Background

The 2011 DCL was written by the OCR under the guidance of Russlyn Ali, who signed the letter, although she was clear in remarks she made to the press that the guidance was developed by a "team of staffers" charged with reviewing prior OCR communications on sexual violence (Lombardi 2010). Ali was appointed to the position of assistant secretary for civil rights in 2009 by President Barack Obama. The format of the DCL as a letter represents a frequently used format by the OCR, simultaneously invoking a shared obligation to address sexual violence ("Dear Colleague") and a formal description of OCR expectations on how and why to do so. Such a letter is not to be taken lightly: "While this ... DCL does not in and of itself carry the force of law, the reality is that guidance interpreting a law issued by the very agency that is empowered to enforce that law warrants significant attention and action" (Association of Governing Boards 2015, 9).

As also discussed by Smith in Chapter 17, the letter begins by reminding its intended audience—representatives from school districts, colleges, and universities—of the purpose of Title IX within the broader social and governmental goal of "educational environments free from discrimination" (DOE 2011a, 1). The antidiscrimination clause in Title IX, Education Amendments of 1972, says this:

> No person in the United States shall, on the basis of sex, be excluded from participation in, be denied the benefits of, or be subjected to discrimination under any education program or activity receiving Federal financial assistance. (DOE 1998, para. 2)

The 1972 Education Amendments go on to define "education program or activity" (Department of Labor 1972, section 1687) and to identify institutions that would not be covered by this policy (namely, certain religious institutions, military institutions, and historically single-sex institutions). Within this broader mission to create discrimination-free educational environments carried out by the OCR within the DOE, Title IX prohibits discrimination based on sex and, by doing so, prohibits discrimination arising from sexual harassment.

Discourse in the 2011 DCL

> The sexual harassment of students, including sexual violence, interferes with students' right to receive an education free from discrimination and, in the case of sexual violence, is a crime. (DOE 2011a, 1)

In this one statement, in the first paragraph of the 2011 DCL, readers are reminded of two things: (1) sexual harassment is a form of sex discrimination, which is prohibited by Title IX; and (2) sexual violence is a form of sexual harassment—thus, it too is prohibited by Title IX. The first of these points is nothing new, as universities have been aware of federal expectations to address sexual harassment under Title IX for decades—thanks to the work of MacKinnon (1979) and others (see Simon 2003)—and have been held accountable for doing so in U.S. Supreme Court rulings such as *Franklin v. Gwinnett Public Schools* (1992) and *Davis v. Monroe County Board of Education* (1999, for student-on-student harassment). But the second point has a more ambiguous history within Title IX guidances from the OCR, as I discuss in this chapter.

In the second paragraph of the 2011 DCL, the OCR repeats itself, saying: "Sexual harassment of students, which includes acts of sexual violence, is a form of sex discrimination prohibited by

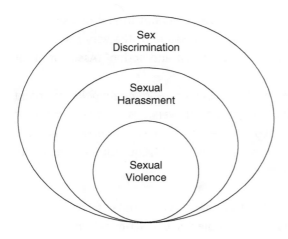

Figure 6.1 Visualization of the Discursive Relationship between Sexual Violence and Sex Discrimination in the 2011 DCL

Title IX" (DOE 2011a, 1). With this argument, the OCR effectively presents an understanding for universities of the interconnections between sex discrimination, sexual harassment, and sexual violence. Figure 6.1 illustrates those interconnections. In the 2011 DCL, the relation between sexual violence and sex discrimination (or coverage of sexual violence under Title IX) is explicit only because of the definitional acceptance of sexual violence as a form of sexual harassment. In other words, the hostile environment arguments that link sexual harassment to sex discrimination create the umbrella under which sexual violence also resides, as a form of sexual harassment.

Having alerted readers twice to the second point that sexual violence is prohibited by Title IX, the purported purpose of the 2011 DCL is disclosed:

> In order to assist recipients, which include school districts, colleges, and universities ... in meeting these obligations [to address discrimination], this letter explains that the requirements of Title IX pertaining to sexual harassment also cover sexual violence, and lays out the specific Title IX requirements applicable to sexual violence. (DOE 2011a, 1)

The document then defines sexual violence:

> Sexual violence, as that term is used in this letter, refers to physical sexual acts perpetrated against a person's will or where a person is incapable of giving consent due to the victim's use of drugs or alcohol. An individual also may be unable to give consent due to an intellectual or other disability. (DOE 2011a, 1)

The document provides examples of sexual violence, and couples these examples with yet a third statement about the relationship between sexual violence and sexual harassment within Title IX: "A number of different acts fall into the category of sexual violence, including rape, sexual assault, sexual battery, and sexual coercion. All such acts of sexual violence are forms of sexual harassment covered under Title IX" (DOE 2011a, 1–2). Stating three times in short succession the relationship between sexual violence, sexual harassment, and sex discrimination marks this discourse as important. And, indeed, in a footnote, the 2011 DCL calls itself a "significant guidance document" (DOE 2011a, 1). In conjunction with the use of the term "explains" in the prior quote, the letter does appear to express a new (or updated) understanding of sexual violence within Title IX.

But the DCL also is clear that the letter is only providing *more* guidance on these issues to college campuses, grounding itself in its prior communications and also implying that this is not a new issue for the OCR, nor for educational institutions. In explaining this point, the letter points to the OCR's *Revised Sexual Harassment Guidance* (DOE 2001). The 2011 DCL (DOE 2011a, 2) purportedly only "supplements" this 2001 document because sexual harassment and sexual violence "requirements are discussed in detail" in the 2001 guidance. In other words—the 2011 DCL should be read as only providing additional guidance and practical examples to existing OCR regulations. This language suggests that sexual violence has been an element of concern for the OCR and Title IX all along, and the 2011 DCL is only being done to provide additional guidance and recommendations in this area. Indeed, the 2011 DCL specifies that sexual harassment and sexual violence should be addressed by the same set of policies and procedures in an institution: "OCR therefore recommends that a recipient's nondiscrimination policy state that prohibited sex discrimination covers sexual harassment, including sexual violence, and that the policy include examples of the types of conduct that it covers" (DOE 2011a, 7). In saying this, the OCR reinforces its construction of sexual violence within sexual harassment, and "recommends" that universities model this construction explicitly within their Title IX policies, if they have not already done so.

There is a disjunction here in the discourse for the OCR. The repetitiveness of the construction of sexual violence under the umbrella of sexual harassment and sex discrimination appears to mark it as not only significant but also transformative. And that is how many institutional actors have responded to the 2011 DCL—as a document that transforms how educational institutions should respond to sexual violence. In the public discussion of the 2011 DCL when it was first distributed, the portrayal by federal actors was absolutely about the presentation of something new. In a press release on April 4, 2011, Vice President Joseph Biden and Secretary of Education Arne Duncan described the 2011 DCL as "the first specifically advising schools, colleges and universities that their responsibilities under Title IX include protecting students from sexual violence" (DOE 2011b, para. 2). However, in making this argument in the 2011 DCL, the OCR is forced to face its own history of communication about Title IX. In doing so, the OCR had to assess the extent to which sexual violence has been an element of concern all along, an analysis I present in the next section.

The 2001 and 1997 Guidances

Directly referenced in the 2011 DCL is the 2001 guidance, which is, in fact, a revision of the 1997 guidance. As the 2001 guidance says in its preamble, "We revised the [1997] guidance in *limited respects* in light of subsequent Supreme Court cases relating to sexual harassment in schools"

(DOE 2001, i; emphasis added). Thus, if the 2001 document only involved limited revisions to the 1997 guidance, and the 2011 DCL only supplemented the 2001 document, there should be a clear connection in the language of both sexual harassment and sexual violence in the 1997 and 2001 guidances and the 2011 DCL. Failure to find peer-on-peer sexual violence within these documents cached within sexual harassment policy and procedures, however, would speak to the novelty of the 2011 DCL's discourse.

Both prior guidances indicate that the 2011 DCL is both new and not new, which perhaps explains its disjunctive language. The 1997 guidance, in particular, uses very different language from the 2011 DCL when it comes to both sexual harassment and sexual violence, although the roots of the 2011 DCL are present. For the 1997 guidance, the focus is strictly on sexual harassment, which it divides into two forms: quid pro quo and "hostile environment sexual harassment," the latter of which is the legal mechanism by which both sexual harassment and sexual violence become elements of Title IX. Hostile environment sexual harassment is defined in the 1997 guidance as:

> Sexually harassing conduct (which can include unwelcome sexual advances, requests for sexual favors, and other verbal, nonverbal, or physical conduct of a sexual nature) by an employee, by another student, or by a third party that is sufficiently severe, persistent, or pervasive to limit a student's ability to participate in or benefit from an education program or activity, or to create a hostile or abusive educational environment. (DOE 1997, para. 2)

Contained in this definition is the phrase "physical conduct of a sexual nature," a euphemism for sexual violence and as explicit as the document gets definitionally. Also present is the recognition that the harasser (the preferred term in the 2011 DCL) may be another student—an issue of extreme importance in the 2011 DCL. The 1997 guidance further acknowledges that sexual harassment can be from the same sex, and can include "harassing conduct of a sexual nature" against lesbian, gay, bisexual, and transgender (LGBT) individuals, as long as it is severe, persistent, and pervasive (DOE 1997, para. 9). The 1997 guidance also defines gender-based harassment, which it characterizes as "acts of verbal, nonverbal, or physical aggression, intimidation, or hostility based on sex, but not involving conduct of a sexual nature" (para. 10) that is directed at individuals because of their sex. Why gender-based harassment could not include "physical conduct of a sexual nature" is unclear, as research suggests that sexual violence is a type of heteronormative attack, except for the understanding that the OCR's response to sexual harassment has been, from the beginning, heterosexist (Carrigan Wooten 2016).

Two key issues arise for the 1997 guidance. First, it discusses the question of "welcomeness" of the conduct. The authors of the guidance recognize that a person may go along with harassment to avoid a negative outcome. This contextualization of victims' behaviors is important because, as Estrich (1991) explained before the guidance was published, unwelcomeness is a "doctrinal stepchild of the rape standards of consent and resistance" (27) and, as such, puts the burden on victims to explain their conduct. Second, the 1997 guidance considers severe, persistent, and pervasive to be requirements for conduct to be considered sexually harassing, though it concludes—again, in alignment with the 2011 DCL—that a single severe incident such as a rape can signify a sexually hostile environment.

For the 1997 guidance, the concern is predominantly language, especially language as a form of conduct that is harassing. Most of the examples within the document reflect this focus on language. But conduct—or in this case, "conduct of a sexual nature"—is not ignored, with "sexual advances" discussed along with touch and sex. The body of the document does not discuss sexual assault. The word "rape" itself only appears in the footnotes, and then only in reference to the first Supreme Court ruling on Title VII and sexual harassment in which the justices endorsed the legal construct of hostile environment sexual harassment, *Meritor Savings Bank v. Vinson* (1986). In this case, the plaintiff claimed her supervisor subjected her to a hostile environment by, in part, making sexual demands on her and raping her on more than one occasion. Thus, the 1997 guidance includes rape in its description of the coverage of *Meritor*:

> Footnote 6; See e.g. ... *Meritor Savings Bank FSB v. Vinson*, 477 U.S. 57, 60–61 (1986) (demands for sexual favors, sexual advances, fondling, indecent exposure, sexual intercourse, rape sufficient to raise hostile environment claim under Title VII). (DOE 1997, 12047)

Note that for the courts, the legality of the conduct and whether it constituted sexual harassment was directly related to its characteristics in terms of hostile environment, namely, whether it met the severity or pervasiveness test (Bartels 1987).

"Sexual assault" as a construct fares a little better in the 1997 guidance. Though it is strikingly absent in the discussion of the definition of sexual harassment or in examples of sexual harassment, it does appear in the procedural section, affecting how schools should respond to claims, handle mediation, or discuss case outcomes. For instance, in a section on responding to claims, the 1997 guidance says:

> It may be appropriate for a school to take interim measures during the investigation of a complaint. For instance, if a student alleges that he or she has been sexually assaulted by another student, the school may decide to immediately place the students in separate classes or in different housing arrangements on a campus, pending the results of the school's investigation. (DOE 1997)

Later, in a discussion of strategies to handle grievances, the document says: "In some cases, such as alleged sexual assaults, mediation will not be appropriate even on a voluntary basis." A third notation, hidden deep within footnote 84, which is about schools' Family Educational Rights and Privacy Act (FERPA) responsibilities for releasing information to complainants about disciplinary action imposed on a student found guilty, does allow for the release of this information if "(2) the harassment involves a crime of violence or a sex offense in a postsecondary institution."

Collectively, the 1997 guidance fails to place peer-on-peer sexual violence under the umbrella of sexual harassment either definitionally or explicitly in the way that the 2011 DCL does, but in discussing responses to sexual harassment, the document clearly gives schools notice that such incidents will require institutional responses. The disconnect between absent policy language and present procedural expectations downplays the importance of sexual violence prevention and response for institutional actors charged with enacting Title IX. Though the procedural discussion and footnotes mention sexual violence, nowhere in the document is the abject connection between the concepts specified.

So how was the 1997 guidance changed in 2001 in relation to the issue of sexual violence? Actually, sexual violence is covered in almost exactly the same muted way in the 2001 guidance, making it a truly "limited" revision of the 1997 guidance on this definitional issue. First, "rape" appears in the 2001 guidance only twice—both of them in footnotes, and both for issues at least marginally covered in 1997 (citing *Meritor* again, and in terms of procedural responses to housing changes for victims of rape as an interim measure). The term "violence" occurs twice also, both in response to concerns about FERPA and Title IX conflicts. Finally, the explicit term "sexual assault" appears only in procedural discussions of classroom or living arrangement changes and in terms of mediation. In other words, the 2001 guidance does not open up its definition of sexual harassment in ways that would guide a university to understand it needed to directly address sexual assault under Title IX. However, both of these guidances use explicit examples of sexual violence to detail the OCR's recommended responses to such violence. So, without making the discursive connection that is so clear in the 2011 DCL, both of these documents included a procedural connection that gave universities fair warning.

What the 2001 guidance does is create a useful definition of sexual harassment early in the document (DOE 2001, 2), a definition that moves us away from types of sexual harassment (quid pro quo and hostile environment), although it retains the use of euphemisms in its incorporation of sexual violence:

> Sexual harassment is unwelcome conduct of a sexual nature. Sexual harassment can include unwelcome sexual advances, requests for sexual favors, and other verbal, nonverbal, or *physical conduct of a sexual nature.* (DOE 2001, 2; emphasis added)

This euphemism of "physical conduct of a sexual nature" is as close as both of the guidances get to acknowledging that sexual violence is a form of sexual harassment. Yet there is some progress in 2001: this definition, unlike the 1997 guidance, is linked via footnote to the *Meritor* cite, which includes rape as conduct that can create a hostile environment. In doing so, the definition of sexual harassment itself creates an opening, albeit a vague one using a Title VII case, for universities to understand expectations that they address sexual assault under their sexual harassment policies.

Other Documents on the Journey to the 2011 DCL

It is important to keep in mind that the issue of sexual assault on campus was well-known before the publication of the 2011 DCL, and was even recognized by the OCR before 2001. For instance, in the 2000 DCL in "Reminder of Responsibilities under Section 504 of the Rehabilitation Act of 1973 and Title II of the Americans with Disabilities Act," the OCR noted that disability harassment included "sexual and physical assault" (DOE 2000, 1). Nowhere in this 2000 DCL, however, did the OCR link Title II to Title IX. In addition, a 2002 National Institute of Justice report (followed in 2005 by a widely publicized summary of this report) by Karjane, Fisher, and Cullen (2002) discussed the prevalence of campus sexual violence and universities' responses. This report, however, failed to turn to Title IX in its recommendation section as it laid out policy and procedure "best practices," hinting at the continuing disconnect between Title IX and campus sexual assault response in 2005. Title IX, as a mechanism to address campus sexual assault, was also not on the radar in the Handbook for Campus Safety and Security Reporting (Westat and Mann 2011), which was published just two months before the 2011 DCL and discussed Clery Act expectations for reporting sexual assault, responding to victims, and adjudicating offenses. It is telling that this document did not identify Title IX as a related and relevant federal law that could or should be used to address campus sexual assault in 2011.

Most of the OCR Title IX-related DCLs published between 2001 and 2011 that I reviewed also did not address the issue of sexual violence. These DCL documents include a 2004 letter regarding Title IX grievance procedures; a 2006 letter that reasserts the importance of sexual harassment response; a 2007 letter celebrating Title IX history and potential, including its "substantial focus to the issue of sexual harassment in schools" (DOE 2007, para. 8); and a 2010 letter on bullying as it relates to Title IX. There is one notable exception, however; in 2008, the OCR released *Sexual Harassment: It's not Academic* (DOE 2008), the fourth version of this document (Henrick 2013). There are two places within this document where the issue of sexual violence is addressed. In a section titled "What if the Sexual Conduct Is Criminal in Nature?" the authors state: "Sexual harassment includes conduct that is criminal in nature, such as rape, sexual assault, dating violence, and sexually motivated stalking" (DOE 2008, 4), and note that if schools report the incidents to the police, they are still obligated to follow Title IX policies.

Later, the document illustrates the concept of severity as it relates to hostile environment by using the example of a high school student sexually assaulting a fellow student in a classroom (DOE 2008, 7). However, it should be noted that severity of sexual violence is not a given; the wording in court decisions (including Title VII decisions that often serve as guidance for Title IX decisions; see 2011 DCL, footnote 10; DOE 2011a, 3) remains frustratingly ambiguous regarding the issue of severity in cases of sexual violence, including the use of qualifiers such as "deemed sufficient," "can create," or "may be enough" (see, e.g., *Jennings v. University of North Carolina*; *Berry v. Chicago Transit Authority*; and *Turner v. Saloon Ltd.*, respectively). Nevertheless, the 2008 example makes clear that sexual assault affects the victim's ability to participate in the educational environment, as she is "afraid of attending any classes or coming into contact with the harasser" (DOE 2008, 7).

While these two components of the 2008 document appear to serve as a bridge between the OCR's discussion of sexual violence in the 1997 and 2001 guidances and the 2011 DCL, there are two problems with this perception. First, the 2008 document continues the tradition of the guidances and avoids explicit inclusion of sexual violence within its definition of sexual harassment. Specifically, in the 2008 document, sexual harassment is defined as conduct that is: "(1) sexual in nature; (2) unwelcome; and (3) denies or limits a student's ability to participate in or benefit from a school's education program" (DOE 2008, 3). Though sexual violence has these characteristics, it is notably absent from the examples of sexual conduct provided to illustrate these elements (3). The closest item on the list is the phrase "touching of a sexual nature," which is woefully inappropriate in representing sexual violence. Instead, the document positions sexual violence as a criminal act in a separate section, linking it to behaviors such as dating violence. Though this section explicitly ties sexual harassment to sexual violence, its separation from the definitional elements of the document belies that connection. Second, the rest of the document, with the exception noted earlier, uses the term harassment. As the authors of the guidance take institutional actors through their obligations under Title IX, there is little further recognition that violent victimization may have occurred, with its resultant trauma and physical harm. In contrast, the terminology used in the 2011 DCL is most frequently "sexual harassment and violence," which serves to reinforce the relationship between the two constructs while it constructs sexual violence as a distinctive concern under Title IX.

So, How Did the 2011 DCL Come to Be?

In several of the chapters in *The Crisis of Campus Sexual Violence: Critical Perspectives on Prevention and Response*, edited by Carrigan Wooten and Mitchell (2016), the authors begin from the assumption that the 2011 DCL began campuses' work on sexual violence. I do not disagree. While I have argued in this chapter that earlier OCR Title IX communications implicitly incorporated sexual violence, explicit OCR guidance was lacking until the 2011 DCL, which then set in motion the policy and procedural changes that we discuss in this volume. As stated in the OCR Fact Sheet entitled "Sexual Violence: Background, Summary and Fast Facts" that was released contemporaneously with the 2011 DCL, the "ED is issuing the DCL to *explain* that the requirements of Title IX cover sexual violence and to *remind* schools of their responsibilities to take immediate and effective steps to respond to sexual violence in accordance with the requirements of Title IX" (DOE 2011c, 1; emphasis added). In "explaining" and "reminding" campus authorities, the 2011 DCL both claims its own history recognizing sexual violence within sexual harassment and validates the perception that this is also, in fact, something new. But, that still leaves us with the question, why did the OCR take this vital step in 2011? While my analysis of the OCR documents cannot answer this question, there are other scholars and pundits who have pointed to a confluence of factors.

The earliest of these factors may simply be the growing case law related to campus sexual violence that started in the late 1990s but was "settled law" by the mid-2000s (Lewis, Schuster, and Sokolow 2010). The National Center for Higher Education Risk Management (NCHERM; Lewis, Schuster, and Sokolow 2010) predicted that Title IX would be used to address sexual violence in their report to higher education institutions in 2000—eleven years before the 2011 DCL. In 2010, they repeated this argument and demonstrated that within the courts, at least, Title IX was being used in tort cases to assess institutional liability, as in *Simpson; Gilmore v. University of Colorado Boulder*. Other insiders fully expected that Title IX would or should be used to address sexual violence. Wies (2015), speaking from the perspective of an advocate, reflected on a variety of conversations she had with peers about the use of the "deliberate indifference" expectation of Title IX to hold universities accountable in sexual violence cases well before the 2011 DCL. So, within the campus security domain and the direct service provider domain, there was the understanding even before the 2011 DCL that case law was dictating that universities should respond to sexual violence using Title IX.

In addition, a political shift occurred in 2009, when President Barack Obama took office. Within a year of taking office, President Obama's appointee, Education Secretary Arne Duncan began referencing the DOE's response to school sexual violence in remarks he made before various public entities, such as his speech to the National Urban League in 2010. He claimed that "our Office for Civil Rights has itself under gone a transformation. We have renewed its focus on enforcing civil rights laws and advancing equity" (DOE 2010). Efforts by Ali to guide her staff in the development of the 2011 DCL reflected this new political reality.

At the same time, others were also putting forward legislative and institutional changes, including the OCR itself. In November 2010, Representative Tom Perriello proposed the Campus Sexual Assault Violence Elimination Act (SaVE) to amend the Clery Act. Though the SaVE Act was not passed until 2013, publicity about the 2010 proposal added to the growing political climate urging change (see Chapter 8 by Hughes Miller and Cook for a discussion of the Campus SaVE Act). And the OCR itself pointed to the DOE's 2010 settlements with Notre Dame and Eastern Michigan as models "for how colleges, universities, and the department [will] deal with allegations of campus sexual assault" (Lombardi 2010, para. 6). In these settlements, the DOE fined the two institutions for violations under the Clery Act, and also required them to make changes in their Title IX processes to better address sexual violence. In a December 2010 interview with the Center for Public Integrity, Ali noted that these were "big-picture reform(s)" (Lombardi 2010, para. 14) that would guide the next OCR guidance—what was to become the 2011 DCL.

Finally, within this political realm was also a growing loudness about the prevalence of sexual violence on college campuses. The 2011 DCL itself justifies its focus on sexual violence using statistics on the rates of rape and sexual assault from studies done between 2007 and 2010, saying: "The statistics on sexual violence are both deeply troubling and a call to action for the nation" (DOE 2011a, 2). The phrase "a call to action" implies an immediacy to the concern that ignores the long history of sexual violence on college campuses. But it also acknowledges con temporary research as a justification for the actions required by the 2011 DCL. The Center for Public Integrity's report in 2010, which blatantly called out universities for failing to respond to sexual assault under their Title IX guidelines, has been given significant credit for both sparking and elevating the voices demanding change. Laura Dunn (2014), whose story was one of those profiled in the center's report, argued that such high-profile publicity challenged the status quo. The six-part report, which culminated in a National Public Radio (NPR) piece, was presented in a Senate Judiciary Subcommittee Hearing in September 2010.

Together, these legal, political, and cultural factors created a milieu within which the OCR acted. Though I have argued here that the inclusion of sexual violence under Title IX was not new to the OCR's understanding of sexual harassment, the impetus to articulate this relationship and provide recommendations on implementation for the "unique" topic of sexual violence in the 2011 DCL does illustrate the political and cultural nature of this document.

Conclusion

The framework to address campus sexual violence using Title IX has been present since at least 1997 in OCR communications with universities. The discursive construction of sexual violence as a form of sex discrimination has been present even longer, especially if one considers case law related to Title VII (e.g., *Meritor*) that has direct correlations to Title IX. Educational pundits like NCHERM also have described and predicted this framework relying on case law and OCR communications well before the 2011 DCL. Nevertheless, it is clear that little emphasis or guidance was given to campuses by the OCR on *how* to respond to sexual violence, or even clear instructions *to* respond to sexual violence, until the 2011 DCL.

The articulation of campus responsibilities to address sexual violence under Title IX was made explicit in the 2011 DCL and has been reiterated since in even more detail, such as in the April

2014 Q&A document (DOE 2014). The 2014 Q&A discursively expands the definition of sexual violence to include sexual abuse and coercion and posits a direct relationship between sexual violence and sex discrimination: "All such acts of sexual violence are forms of sex discrimination prohibited by Title IX" (DOE 2014, 1), eliminating the need to retain the phrase "sexual harassment and violence" used in the 2011 DCL. This recent discursive shift may presage a potential bifurcation in the OCR's presentation of sexual harassment and sexual violence, with sexual violence reserved primarily for student-on-student conduct. Note, for instance, the terminology invoked in the 2014 discussion of school employee (as opposed to peer) sexual harassment:

> Although this document and the DCL focus on student-on-student sexual violence, Title IX also protects students from other forms of sexual harassment (including sexual violence and sexual abuse), such as sexual harassment carried out by school employees.... Sexual harassment by school employees can include unwelcome sexual advances; requests for sexual favors; and other verbal, nonverbal, or physical conduct of a sexual nature, including but not limited to sexual activity. (DOE 2014, 3)

In talking about Title IX violations by school employees, there may be resistance to referencing sexual violence, as this return to euphemisms illustrates.

Henrick (2013, 60) claims that the 2011 DCL "impose[s] new legal obligations" on institutions. While his concern relates to policy changes that affect student defendants, his point is overstated, according to my analysis. The 2011 DCL "explained" its own prior constructions of sexual violence that, while muted and nondefinitional, explicitly existed prior to 2011. This document has certainly been interpreted as a shift in OCR policy by many institutions, but that also is a problematic claim. Indeed, once sexual harassment was defined as an element of sex discrimination, the stage was set for further articulation of students' experiences. And because Title IX is civil rights legislation, it provides an opportunity to express "the desire of victims and their movements to end these forms of violence, not simply through individualized punishment but by securing collective justice" (Brodsky and Deutsch 2015, 144). Title IX adds a powerful tool to address this widespread and significant problem.

References

Association of Governing Boards of Universities and Colleges. (2015). History and context of sexual misconduct. Available at http://agb.org/sites/default/files/agb-statements/statement_2015_sexual_misconduct.pdf.

Bartels, V. T. (1987). *Meritor Savings Bank v. Vinson:* The Supreme Court's recognition of the hostile environment in sexual harassment claims. *Akron Law Review, 23* (3), 575–589.

Berry v. Chicago Transit Authority. (2010). 618 F.3d 688.

Brodsky, A., & Deutsch, E. (2015). The promise of Title IX: Sexual violence and the law. *Dissent, 62*(4), 135–144.

Carrigan Wooten, S. (2016). Heterosexist discourses: How feminist theory shaped campus sexual violence policy. In S. Carrigan Wooten & R. W. Mitchell (Eds.), *The crisis of campus sexual violence: Critical perspectives on prevention and response* (pp. 33–51). New York: Routledge.

Carrigan Wooten, S., & Mitchell, R. W., eds. (2016). *The crisis of campus sexual violence: Critical perspectives on prevention and response.* New York: Routledge.

Center for Public Integrity. (2010). *Sexual assault on campus.* Available at http://www.publicintegrity.org/accountability/education/sexual-assault-campus.

Davis v. Monroe County Board of Education. (1999). 526 U.S. 629.

Department of Education, Office for Civil Rights (DOE, OCR). (1997). *Sexual harassment guidance 1997.* Available at http://www2.ed.gov/about/offices/list/ocr/docs/sexhar01.html.

_____. (1998). *Title IX and sex discrimination.* Available at http://www2.ed.gov/about/offices/list/ocr/docs/tix_dis.html.

_____. (2000). *Prohibited disability harassment.* Available at http://www2.ed.gov/about/offices/list/ocr/docs/disabharassltr.html.

_____. (2001). *Revised sexual harassment guidance: Harassment of students by school employees, other students, or third parties.* Available at https://www.atixa.org/wordpress/wp-content/uploads/2012/01/OCR-2001-Revised-Sexual-Harassment-Guidance-Title-IX.pdf.

_____. (2007). *Dear Colleague Letter.* Available at http://www2.ed.gov/about/offices/list/ocr/letters/colleague-20070622.html.

_____. (2008). *Sexual harassment: It's not academic.* Available at http://www2.ed.gov/about/offices/list/ocr/docs/ocrshpam.html.

_____. (2010). *Secretary Arne Duncan's remarks at the National Urban League Centennial Conference.* Available at http://www.ed.gov/news/speeches/secretary-arne-duncans-remarks-national-urban-league-centennial-conference.

_____. (2011a). *Dear Colleague.* Available at http://www2.ed.gov/about/offices/list/ocr/letters/colleague-201104.pdf.

_____. (2011b). *Vice President Biden announces new administration effort to help nation's schools address sexual violence.* Available at http://www.ed.gov/news/press-releases/vice-president-biden-announces-new-administration-effort-help-nations-schools-address-sexual-violence.

_____. (2011c). *Sexual violence: Background, summary and fast facts.* Available at https://www.whitehouse.gov/sites/default/files/fact_sheet_sexual_violence.pdf.

_____. (2014). *Questions and answers on Title IX and sexual violence.* Available at http://www2.ed.gov/about/offices/list/ocr/docs/qa-201404-title-ix.pdf.

Department of Labor. (1972). *Title IX, Education Amendments of 1972* (Title 20 U.S.C. Sections 1681–1688). Available at http://www.dol.gov/oasam/regs/statutes/titleix.htm.

Dunn, L. L. (2014). Addressing sexual violence in higher education: Ensuring compliance with the Clery Act, Title IX and VAWA. *Georgetown Journal of Gender and the Law, 15,* 563–584.

Estrich, S. (1991). Sex at work. *Stanford Law Review, 43,* 813.

Franklin v. Gwinnett Public Schools. (1992). 503 U.S. 60.

Henrick, S. (2013). A hostile environment for student defendants: Title IX and sexual assault on college campuses. *Northern Kentucky Law Review, 40*(1), 49–92.

Hsieh, H-F., & Shannon, S. E. (2005). Three approaches to qualitative content analysis. *Qualitative Health Research, 15* (9), 1277–1288.

Jennings v. University of North Carolina. (2007). 444 F.3d 255.

Jonson-Reid, M., Lauritsen, J. L., Edmond, T., & Schneider, F. D. (2016). Public policy and prevention of violence against women. In A. A. Eyler, J. F. Chriqui, S. Moreland Russell, & R. C. Brownson (Eds.), *Prevention, policy and public health,* (pp. 229–248). New York: Oxford.

Karjane, H. K., Fisher, B. S., & Cullen, F. T. (2002). *Campus sexual assault: How America's institutions of higher education respond* (Final Report, NIJ Grant No. 1999-WA-VX-0008). Newton, MA: Education Development Center.

Lewis, W. S., Schuster, S. K., & Sokolow, B. A. (2010). *Gamechangers: Reshaping campus sexual misconduct through litigation.* The NCHERM 10th Anniversary Whitepaper, 2000–2010. Available at http://students.msstate.edu/clic/pdf/2010_NCHERM_Whitepaper_Gamechangers.pdf.

Lisa Simpson; Anne Gilmore v. University of Colorado Boulder. (2007). No. 06-1184, No. 07-1182; 2007 U.S. App. LEXIS 21478. U.S. Ct. of Appeals, 10th Circuit.

Lombardi, K. (2010). *Education Department touts settlement as "model" for campus sex assault policies: Feds reach agreement with Notre Dame College in Ohio and Eastern Michigan University.* Available at http://www.publicintegrity.org/2010/12/08/2266/education-department-touts-settlement-model-campus-sex-assault-policies.

MacKinnon, C. A. (1979). *Sexual harassment of working women: A case of sex discrimination.* New Haven, CT: Yale University Press.

Meritor Savings Bank v. Vinson. (1986). 477 U.S. 57.

Simon, A. E. (2003). *Alexander v. Yale University*: An informal history. In C. A. MacKinnon & R. B. Siegel (Eds.), *Directions in sexual harassment law* (pp. 51–59). New Haven, CT: Yale University Press.

Turner v. Saloon Ltd. (2010). 595 F.3d 679.

Westat, D. W., & Mann, J. L. (2011). *The handbook for campus safety and security reporting.* Washington, DC: U.S. Department of Education, Office of Postsecondary Education.

Wies, J. R. (2015). Title IX and the state of campus sexual violence in the United States: Power, policy, and local bodies. *Human Organization 74* (3): 276–286. Available at http://dx.doi.org/10.17730/0018-7259-74.3.276.

Chapter 5: Concluding Remarks

Emerging trends in defining policies and procedures to protect victims of crime as mandated by federal guidelines are reflected in recent developments in the widespread enforcement of Title IX rules and regulations. As a society, we are making strides in the progressive movement toward ensuring that crimes such as sexual violence are at the cusp of discussions for the development of legislation that ensure that individual rights are protected and that victims' rights are equally enforced. As we move forward with these trends, there is a need for criminal justice practice and academic debate to collectively reflect these changing dynamics to better articulate a framework within which evidence-based research can advance the goals of justice for victims of crime.

CHAPTER 6

Restorative Justice and Crime Victimization

Introduction

The cultural and social norms within any given society dictate the definitions by which we come to perceive certain groups of individuals, their characteristic traits, as well as how we interact with them and come to identify their common attributes. This influences many aspects of how we structure rules and regulations that govern these interactions and come to delineate the boundaries upon which we build and establish mechanisms of support and responses to social problems. In our studies, the term "victim" conjures up a variety of images that hinge upon very similar ideals of harm, weakness, and vulnerability. However, this image often clouds our ability to discern the diversity of response that occurs when individuals experience crime victimization and the various emotions that are associated with it that make each individual victim unique in his or her own encounter with crime.

One approach that has made its way to the forefront of criminal justice policy and practice over the past few decades is restorative justice. While the various theoretical principles and mechanisms of restorative justice interventions are not new, the need to identify and assess victim experiences with restorative justice programs has become of great interest to criminal justice practitioners and researchers in recent times. This interest stems from the recognition that victims' experiences with crime are quite varied and diverse, and therefore necessitate a better understanding of the unique qualities of crime victimization and its impact on the response to interventions designed to heal, empower, and restore victims of crime. In this reading, we will explore the generalized needs of victims of crime and take a closer look at what makes these needs distinct for different types of victims and different types of victimization. We will also examine the application of restorative justice theory and practice as perceived by individuals who have been impacted by the emotional distress of crime victimization.

Guiding Questions

As you read, consider the following questions:

1   What is the role of restorative justice in helping victims of crime?

2   How satisfied are victims of crime with the methods of reparation provided by the courts?

3   Do we currently do enough to meet the emotional and physical needs of victims?

4   Are there steps that need to be taken to improve victim satisfaction with criminal justice procedures?

5   In what ways is restorative justice as in intervention more suitable for meeting the needs of victims than formal criminal justice proceedings?

Key Terms

behavioral self-blame (BSB)   When a victim attributes their victimization to controllable aspects, such as their own conduct, lifestyle, and actions.

characterological self-blame (CSB)   When a victim attributes their victimization to uncontrollable aspects of their own personal traits such as race, gender, or sexual orientation.

reintegrative shaming   A philosophical approach to punishment that expresses the disapproval of a behavior while also providing the opportunity for correction and acceptance.

restorative justice   A theoretical and practical approach to justice that focuses on repairing harm and restoring victims with the goal of reintegrating offenders back into the community.

secondary victimization   The experience of victims during formal court proceedings that places them in a position of fear and vulnerability similar to becoming victim once again.

Evaluating Victims' Experiences in Restorative Justice

Antony Pemberton, Frans-Willem Winkel, and Marc S. Groenhuijsen

Introduction: Victims and Restorative Justice

There seems to be little doubt that restorative justice is intended to be in the interests of victims of crime. In academic textbooks the two are often paired[1] and legislation concerning restorative justice pays homage to the plight and position of victims of crime.[2] Repairing the harm caused by crime is central to restorative justice, and assisting victims in their recovery is considered to be a core element[3].

In contrast, theoretical work and evaluation research concerning victims of crime is scarce. As Dignan (2005) points out, the three main intellectual traditions underlying restorative justice are quite ambivalent to the plight and position of victims of crime. Neither the civilization thesis championed by Hulsman, Bianchi and Mathiesen, the communitarian theories, most famously advocated by Christie (1977) in 'Conflicts as property', nor the moral-discourse theories, like Braithwaite's (1989) reintegrative shaming theory, are aimed at achieving direct benefits for victims of crime[4]. Any added value for victims is a by-product.

Repair or Revenge?

The most developed view on victims in restorative justice has been put forward by Heather Strang in her research into the RISE-projects in Australia and subsequently developed by Strang, Lawrence Sherman and their associates in a number of publications (see Strang, 2002, Strang and Sherman, 2003, Sherman, Strang et al, 2005,

Strang, Sherman et al, 2006). Central in their view is a set of victim needs, derived from research which highlighted the satisfaction and in particular the dissatisfaction of victims with the criminal system. First of all there are a number of process-related needs (Strang, 2002):

- Victims want a less formal process where their views count;
- Victims want more information about both the processing and outcome of their cases;
- Victims want to be treated respectfully and fairly;
- Victims want to participate in their cases.

Second there are a number of outcome related needs:

- Victims want material restoration;
- Victims want emotional restoration, including an apology.

Strang (2002) suggested that restorative justice addresses these needs and would outperform the criminal justice procedures on most if not all these counts. Using this as a starting point Strang, Sherman and their colleagues undertook some of the most methodologically rigorous testing of restorative justice, in various sites across Australia (the Reintegrative Shaming Experiments or RISE) and the United Kingdom. Utilizing randomized controlled trials (RCT's) they compared victims' experiences within restorative justice and criminal justice[5]. On most, if not all, factors the restorative justice conditions outperformed the criminal justice conditions. Victims felt more involved and satisfied and less fearful and angry after a restorative justice conference compared to their experience within the criminal justice system.

These results are promising, as they show real benefits for participating victims in comparison to those afforded by the criminal justice system. However as Strang et al (2005) themselves point out research into restorative justice will remain work in progress and is very much open to its own improvement through better knowledge of its consequences. Contributing to this endeavour is the focus of this article. A number of issues are discussed, relating to Strang and Sherman's work, which have bearing on theory and/or evaluation research into victims of crime. First there are two general points. These relate to differences between individual victims and the difficulties associated with the comparison of restorative justice and criminal justice 'paradigms'. Second the needs Strang attributed to victims are discussed. This will not amount to a challenge of the general accuracy of these needs or the results of restorative justice in meeting these needs. Instead it will be shown that the relationship between victims and these needs and the extent to which restorative justice can be expected to meet these needs is less straightforward than Strang's initial list implies.

Victim Variety

Victims vary and so do their needs. This is not just stating the obvious. In fact Young (2002) criticized restorative justice literature for using too homogenous conceptions of victims, fol-lowed by generalized, sweeping statements about the beneficial effects of restorative justice for all victims. Victims' psychological reactions to crime are the result of three sets of factors. Not only are the differences in the crimes experienced important, but also victims' experiences in the aftermath of crime and factors associated with victims' personality factors (see Winkel, 2002, Ozer, Best, Lipsey & Weiss, 2003). In the first place this means that the six features of what victims want (see above) should be qualified as the extent and sometimes even the direction of what individual victims want is dependent on the interplay of the triple set of factors. For example Strang (2002) asserts that victims are not as vengeful as often is thought. This is born out for most victims or for the average victim, but, as research into trait vengefulness shows there are people who are simply more prone to wanting revenge than others (McCullough, Bellah, Kilpatrick and Johnson, 2001). Similarly the chance people will forgive wrongdoers is also related to their innate trait capacity for forgiveness (McCullough et al, 2001). In the section on emotional restoration these features will be discussed more extensively, but the relevance here is the importance of assessing these and other traits among victims. In particular, doing so could shed light on the differences in victims' reactions to restorative justice procedures.

Allowing for personality and individual differences may also impact the research question in comparisons between criminal justice and restorative justice. In Strang and Sherman's research the question is which system or paradigm outperforms the other. Introducing individual differences affects this, as it could be that it is more relevant to ascertain what the best fitting option is, depending on the characteristics of the victim, the offender, and the crime committed. Instead of asking ourselves if restorative justice should be preferred to criminal justice, we could ask ourselves under what circumstances restorative justice is better suited and under what circumstances criminal justice or some combination of the two is best. A variant of this is the question of what features of restorative justice are most effective for which situation.

The Comparison of Restorative Justice with Criminal Justice

As mentioned above, in restorative justice literature there is a tendency to compare restorative justice procedures with the 'traditional' criminal justice system, with the goal of seeing which system achieves the most favorable results. Underlying this tendency is a strong sense that restorative justice is a different paradigm or lens for viewing crime and conflict (Zehr, 1990). Strang and Sherman state in their discussion of the shortcomings of the criminal justice system that:

> It seems unlikely that the needs and preferences of victims will be well met by piecemeal reforms. It seems more likely that a new paradigm of justice is required to transform the values and jurisprudence of criminal justice to include victims as stakeholders equal to offenders and the community.
>
> (Strang and Sherman, 2003, p. 25).

There are a number of issues, related to this 'clash of the paradigms', which are relevant to the evaluation of victim experiences in restorative justice procedures. The two most important relate to variety within criminal justice systems in space and time, and the multiple simultaneous differences between restorative justice and traditional criminal justice, in particular when restorative justice is implemented as a replacement.

A Myriad of Criminal Justice Systems

Asserting that restorative justice processes vary is stating the obvious. A lot of time at academic conferences on restorative justice is devoted to the discussion of the definition and the variety of ways and different situations restorative justice procedures and techniques are used, many of which lie outside the domain of criminal law. Traditional penal systems vary, from one jurisdiction to another, but also within jurisdictions. The most common example of variety between jurisdictions is the difference between inquisitorial and adversarial systems, while the difference between adult and juvenile systems is the most obvious example of variety within jurisdictions (see e.g. Cavadino and Dignan, 2005). These differences also affect the position of victims within these penal systems. Strang's portrayal of victims as 'being effectively silenced by a system that relegates them to witnesses subject to strict evidentiary rules' (2002: 9–10), only bears resemblance to the situation of victims within the Anglo-Saxon common law world. In continental Europe, in contrast, victims can and do play additional roles. Examples of these additional procedural possibilities are the adhesion procedure or the role of private prosecutor[6].

The position of victims within the criminal justice system not only varies in space but also in time. The criticism levelled at the position of victims in the 1980s, for example in Shapland, Wilmore and Duff's (1985) much-cited study, has led to changes in the position of victims and the way they are treated. Strang (2002) refers to victim impact statements, but the changes are not restricted to these measures and have had general bearing on the way that police and prosecution approach victims. In particular the amount of information given to and received from victims has increased, the way they are questioned has improved and the same is true about their possibilities for compensation. Again this varies from one country to another[7]. The point here is not necessarily that differences between and changes within criminal justice systems may complicate a blanket comparison of restorative justice to criminal justice, although the strong Anglo-Saxon slant in evaluation research of victim experiences does pose some problems for a direct translation of the results to other systems. Rather it is important to consider that current criminal justice practices are not neutral 'waiting list' conditions. In the testing of medical instruments, to which Strang and Sherman themselves compare the RCT's they conducted, it is not common that two medicines are compared to each other directly, at least not without the inclusion of a group of participants who do not receive treatment at all. This is due to the problems that a direct comparison causes for the interpretation of the results. Does medicine

A perform significantly better than medicine B and should A therefore be prescribed rather than B or is medicine B significantly worse option than A, and should B therefore definitely not be prescribed?

The relevance of this is that criminal justice, as Strang and Sherman themselves discuss at length, may have negative effects on victims (Strang, 2002 and Strang and Sherman, 2003). It is no coincidence that the term 'secondary victimization' was coined to describe victims' experiences within the criminal justice system (Orth, 2002). This last feature only strengthens the argument for restorative justice as a preferred alternative to criminal justice, but the unique effect of the criminal justice system could change the conclusion from restorative justice being a better alternative, to restorative justice being not as harmful as the criminal justice system. This feature makes the comparison with other measures outside of the criminal justice system with overlapping goals, e.g. victim support or counselling, difficult. The way out of this is to introduce a 'real' waiting list condition, i.e. a condition in which victims do not take part in either restorative or criminal justice proceedings. This is hardly a hypothetical situation. The typical experience of victims in reality is not the criminal justice process and definitely not the sentencing stages of this procedure, but no justice involvement at all (Fattah, 1997).

RJ versus CJ: Many Differences at the Same Time

Restorative justice procedures differ on various dimensions from the criminal justice system. Some of these dimensions are directly related to the proposed paradigmatic differences between restorative and criminal justice. Within restorative justice crime is viewed as a conflict between individuals rather than a violation against the state and the central goal of restorative justice is to repair harm and reconcile individuals rather than to assign guilt and blame and punish wrongdoers[8]. However, like von Hirsch, Ashworth and Shearing (2003) observe, there are also a number of dimensions that are not inherent to the paradigms. The most obvious is the far larger amount of time and attention given to the participants in a restorative justice conference than is normally the case within the criminal justice system. In addition a number of practical differences do not require restorative justice to replace criminal justice. The face-to-face meeting between victims and offenders, the discussion of the event and the subsequent apology are all possible when restorative justice conferences are held in addition to criminal justice proceedings or even when the meeting has no implications at all for the criminal justice process. An important question is then which of these dimensions account for the advantageous results of restorative justice in the RCTs that Strang, Sherman and associates conducted. Are these advantages caused by paradigm-related features or by non-paradigm related features?[9] How important are the essential restorative justice features of conferencing and mediation?

A relevant result in this context is found by Strang, Sherman and associates (2006) themselves. They conducted RCT's in four different situations, focusing again on a comparison between the restorative justice condition with the criminal justice system. They found compelling evidence for the benefits of restorative justice over criminal justice. In all four situations restorative justice conditions outperformed the normal criminal justice procedures. In three of the RCT's the restorative justice conferences were held in addition to the criminal justice procedure, not as a replacement. One (the original RISE-project in Australia) did implement restorative justice as a replacement of the normal criminal justice procedure. An interesting finding was that the results for all four situations were similar. That is: the RCT's where the restorative justice procedure was an additional measure obtained the same results as the RCT where it was a replacement. This can be interpreted as proof or indication of the general superiority of restorative justice procedures in different situations, which is the way Strang et al (2006) see it, but an alternative interpretation is also possible. It appears that it does not have an added advantage to implement RJ as an alternative rather than as an additional measure, which is what would be predicted by a completely paradigmatic explanation of the benefits of participating in an RJ conference.

In general, the argument for 'RJ as the preferred paradigm' would be greatly enhanced if it could be shown that the necessarily paradigmatic features of restorative justice significantly contribute to the benefits of participation in restorative justice. In other words, there is a need to isolate the 'working elements' of restorative justice. Experiments could be devised in which aspects of restorative justice conferences are manipulated. Schweizer (2006) is an example of this type of research.

Another avenue is a trial including a condition that has the non-paradigmatic features of a restorative justice conference, but not the paradigmatic features. This would entail testing what the effects are of facilitated meetings between victims and offenders, in which they discuss the causes and consequences of the crime, without these meetings having any consequences for the criminal justice procedure. As will be discussed in the section on emotional restoration, the observed results concerning victims, like the effects on anxiety or anger, could be explained by the social-psychological dynamics of this meeting alone.

The Question of Participation

Of the typically process-related features (respectful treatment, information and participation) the first two are rather straightforward. There is not much discussion about the fact that, given the choice, victims will prefer to be treated in a manner that respects their situation and will prefer to receive sufficient and timely information concerning their case, if they so desire. Participation is a more complicated concept. The fact that victims feel they are lacking sufficient participation in their case as it progresses through the criminal justice system leads to the obvious conclusion that they would prefer a higher level of participation than is currently available, but not that ever more participation is always in victims' interests. The benefits of increased participation from a procedural justice perspective (see Tyler, 1990 or Röhl, 1997) should be offset against the psychological stress that may accompany this increased participation (Orth, 2002). This is most obvious in the situation of victims 'participating' as interrogated witnesses (Herman, 2003), but also in more victim-friendly forms of participation this factor should be taken into account. As we will argue in the section on emotional restoration a face-to-face meeting with the offender can offer real benefits for victims, but may also pose risks, depending on the behavior of the offender and the reasons for committing the crime. For certain types of severe harassment, like stalking (see Mullen, Pathé and Purcell, 2000) direct contact with the offender must be undertaken with extreme caution, because of the stress that seeing the offender can cause victims.

The Preferred Level of Participation

Aside from the structure of the participation and the stress that may accompany it, it is an open question what the preferred level of participation of victims is. Edwards (2004) for example cites, Arnstein (1971), who describes a ladder of eight levels of participation[10]. Are victims increasingly satisfied as they gain a higher level of participation? Or is there an optimum point along the way that is preferable to positions further up the ladder of participation?[11] Bear in mind that the highest rungs—decision power and citizen control—not only allow for more participation and control of the situation, but also have an added burden of responsibility. Furthermore victims may not necessarily view processes as having a higher degree of fairness if they are allowed to have a higher degree of control, as they may deem it fairer for someone who has a less biased view of the situation to make the decision in their case. This also relates to the question of the 'working element' in restorative justice. If victims really view crime in private terms, viewing crime as conflict that is rightly theirs and has been stolen by the criminal justice system, as Christie (1977) implied, we would expect their level of desired participation to be high. Decision power would be their preferred level of participation. This does not seem to be the case.

Research by Wemmers and Cyr (2004) showed that given the choice victims prefer the situation where they are allowed input in the process, in the sense of having their say, but generally prefer decision-making power in their cases to reside elsewhere.

Again individual circumstances will impact the preferred level of participation. Within Wemmers and Cyr (2004)'s research subjects, there were those who would prefer decision power. Determining the influence of participation on the evaluation of restorative justice procedures then should include matching the victim's preferences with the degree of participation allotted to them.

Outcomes: Material Restoration

Compensation of losses is also a complicated matter. Strang (2002) includes this as an outcome measure, but wonders whether this is in fact appropriate as victims may prefer compensation of a symbolic nature to full material compensation. Similarly she quotes Braithwaite who asserts that 'some victims will prefer mercy to insisting on getting their money back; indeed it may be that 'act of grace' which gives them a spiritual restoration that is critical for them'[12]. Furthermore the comparison between criminal justice and restorative justice on this issue neglects the possibility that participation in restorative justice procedures may change victims' preferences for receiving compensation.

As repeatedly stated, most victims wishes and needs will at least in part be influenced by the personal characteristics of victims. This is also the case for the issue of material restoration. It stands to reason that the extent of the damage in relation to the victim's income and the possibilities of obtaining compensation from other sources will influence the victims need for full compensation from the offender. In addition their needs will be modified by their assessment of the possibilities the offender has to reimburse them. In this sense restorative justice procedures may well influence victims' preferences merely by the more realistic picture they provide of the offenders solvability.

A possible important factor is the type of crime the victim has suffered. In particular victims of property crime may differ from victims of violent crime. This is illustrated by the differences in reasons for reporting the crime in the first place. Wittebrood found that 70% property crime victims reported the crime to retrieve the lost or stolen materials, be compensated for damages or for insurance purposes (see Wittebrood, 2006). For victims of violent crime this percentage is understandably much lower. For this group of victims other reasons, for example 'I felt the offender should be punished' and 'I felt the severity of the offence merited reporting to the police' were more important. The relevance of material restoration may vary according to the stated reasons for reporting crime. Braithwaite is quite right that forgiving the offender is in the victims own interest as the section on emotional restoration will show. However, where it may well be true that certain victims experience the act of foregoing full compensation as a cathartic act of forgiveness, it seems equally likely that, for other victims, receiving (full) compensation may in fact be a prerequisite for forgiveness. Victims may feel that it is unjust to forgive the offender before he has repaid the damage[13]. Lacking full compensation may make it more difficult to believe the apology the offender may offer, as the victim may feel it is just talk[14]. As the most important defining feature of the positive effect of an apology is the extent to which the victim finds it sincere and believable, lacking compensation may amount to barrier for forgiveness. In any case, comparable to the discussion of participation, victims' preferences concerning material restoration is a necessary element of an explanation of the effect of material restoration on evaluation of restorative justice procedures.

Outcomes: Emotional Restoration

Maybe the most important feature of a restorative justice conference for victims is the possibilities of emotional restoration that it offers. In their most recent studies Strang and Sherman and associates have emphasized this matter and offered more theoretical elaboration of the proposed benefits. In their theoretical approach they draw on two bodies of research. The first is psychological, concerning cognitive theories of post" traumatic stress disorder (PTSD). Sherman, Strang et al (2005) use this body of research to explain the effect of restorative justice on the victims fear of the offender. The second is sociological. Randall Collins' theory of interaction ritual chains is applied to victims' experiences within restorative justice conferences (see Collins, 2004). The interaction ritual theory is used, amongst others, to explain the effect of restorative justice procedures on victims' anger (see Sherman, Strang et al, 2005 for further elaboration).

In a recent article Pemberton, Winkel and Groenhuijsen (2006) have sought to explain victims experiences within restorative justice using solely psychological concepts. Pemberton et al (2006) derive their theory from two dominant victim reactions to crime: anxiety and anger. The remainder of this section discusses this approach, contrasting it at various points with Strang and Sherman's theoretical framework.

Control, Attributions, PTSD

Post-traumatic stress is a common reaction to traumatic events like assaults or severe accidents. In the aftermath of crime, many victims experience at least some of the following symptoms: re-experiencing the event, repeated and unwanted intrusive thoughts, hyper-arousal, emotional numbing and avoidance of stimuli which could serve as reminders of the traumatic experience. Most people recover within the first weeks or months after the crime, but a sizable minority of victims goes on to develop post-traumatic stress disorder (PTSD). Then these symptoms occur over a longer period of time, sometimes even years, meaning that the victims that suffer from PTSD have their social and occupational function severely impaired (Ehlers and Clark, 2000). Counselling, treatment and therapy for victims of crime therefore focuses on the prevention or cure of PTSD.

Two features of the theorizing surrounding PTSD are particularly relevant to explanations of victims' experiences within restorative justice. These subjects are perceived control over the event and attributions concerning the cause of the crime.

The Relevance of Perceived Control

Theories regarding the role of perceived control in adjustment to stressful life events typically hypothesized that events perceived to be uncontrollable are more distressing than those that are controllable (Foa, Zinbarg, & Rothbaum, 1992). In these models the perceived lack of control-lability is a risk factor for the development of PTSD. Conversely, the more controllable an event is for the victim, the more likely it is he or she will not develop PTSD. However Frazier, Berman, and

Steward (2002) showed that control is a complex construct. The relationship between control and stressful life events and PTSD is moderated by the temporal dimension of control[15].

The temporal model divides control into past control (Could I have prevented this from happening?), future control (Can I keep this from happening again?) and present control (What can I do about the situation now?). The different types of control influence the extent to which control is adaptive. They are not correlated with each other, meaning it is possible for victims to feel confident about their ability to cope with the present situation, without thinking they could have prevented the crime from happening. Frazier (2003) shows that it is most adaptive to focus on aspects of an event that are controllable at this moment. Victims who state 'I am confident that I will get over this if I just work at it' or 'I have taken steps to protect myself since the assault' show better recovery results than those who disagree with these statements. A first relevant element about participation in restorative justice procedures is that mere participation may be viewed as a possibility for asserting a sense of present control. Through the voluntary nature of participation in restorative justice procedures, victims may view participation as a step they can take to prevent the reoccurrence of crime.

Future control is a more complicated matter, as control over future reoccurrence is moderated by beliefs concerning the likelihood of reoccurrence. Victims, who think the crime is not likely to happen again and feel confident about their ability to control it if it did reoccur, fare better than those who do not. Again this feature is relevant for restorative justice procedures. Participation in restorative justice procedures seems to influence victims' assessment of the chance of the reoccurrence of the crime (see Strang, 2002).

The most complicated matter is the issue of past-control. The question—Could the event have been prevented?—can also be conceptualized in terms of attributions about the cause of a trauma. A first distinction within these attributions is whether they are focused on the offender, which in the terms of the temporal model is called 'vicarious' past control or the victim him or herself. Within the self-focused attributions an important division is Janoff-Bulman's distinction between characterological self-blame (CSB) and behavioural self-blame (BSB) (Janoff-Bulman 1979 and 1992). Within CSB the victim attributes the victimization to uncontrollable aspects of the self, like character, race, gender or sexual orientation. These are matters over which the victim has no control. CSB is associated with PTSD and other trauma-related mental health problems, with the victim having cognitions like 'I attract disaster' or 'Everyone can see I am a victim' (Ehlers and Clark, 2000). BSB, on the other hand, refers to the extent to which the victim attributes the crime to controllable aspects of the self, like conduct or behaviour. Janoff-Bulman assumed that BSB would be adaptive for victims. Assigning the causes of the event to features of the self that may be changed, would allow victims to feel confident they could control and prevent the reoccurrence of similar events and would give them a sense of present control.

This line of reasoning has strong intuitive appeal, but is not born out by recent research (Frazier et al, 2002). BSB may be more adaptive than CSB, but also gives rise to counterfactual thinking (Roese, 1997). The victim may focus on 'what if'-questions. 'What if I hadn't gone out that night?', 'What if I had resisted more?', and the like. This kind of emphasis on the past and attempts to control it, does not give clues to adaptive behaviour in the present. Rather it means that the victim's attention is focused elsewhere. In other words behavioural self-blame does not necessarily lead to present-control. In sum: the results show both types of self-focused past control to be associated with poorer coping in the present, with CSB having added disadvantages over BSB.

In essence there are three ways the victim may view the offender of a crime. First of all victims may over-generalise the event and as consequence perceive a range of normal events as more dangerous than they are (Ehlers and Clark, 2000). In this mind-frame the offender is part of a large group of offenders who together make the world a dangerous place, make the probability of future victimization high and make the victim feel like nowhere is safe. For coping with the consequences of crime this first kind of attribution is the least adaptive. It incites fear in the victim and prolongs the negative consequences of victimization as the victim avoids similar situations to the one in which the crime took place and withdraws from previously liked activities. This type of overgeneralization is associated with the onset of PTSD. In the second and third set of attributions the victim doesn't see the world as a place filled with evil offenders, but attributes the victimization to either the individual offender's character or to his/her behaviour, i.e. 'the offender is a bad person' in the second set and 'the offender did a bad thing' in the third. Frazier (2003) showed that the second set of attributions is associated with higher levels of distress in victims. In the section on anger it will be shown that the third set of attributions can be assumed to be the most adaptive of the attributions of 'vicarious past control'.

The Relevance to Restorative Justice

The link between the previously described body of research and restorative justice procedures lies in the possibilities these procedures offer for clarification of the causes of the crime. The offender is in a unique position to confirm or disaffirm the victim's attributions concerning what happened. Sherman and Strang et al (2005) state:

> victims almost always seem reassured when the offender says they did not target the victim for any particular reason, when the crime occurred as an almost random intersection of offender and victim in time and space (p. 369).

In other words the offender's story may have effects on the victim's self-focused attributions. The account may assure the victim that he or she is not uniquely vulnerable, as the offender may not have targeted the victim for any special reason, and as a consequence lead to lower levels of CSB. Furthermore, a better understanding of the causes of the crime, can release the victim from the burden of ruminating about 'what if'-questions, which will lead to lower levels of BSB. This may help the victim to focus more on present coping as well as having the added benefit of providing insight into the prevention of repeats in the future. However this line of reasoning depends to a large extent on the offender's actual motivation. If, for example, the crime was hate-motivated, the offender's account seems more likely to reinforce than reduce CSB and if the crime was explicitly motivated by the victim's behaviour (for example, the victim was drunk or left the door unlocked) it could lead to more rather than less BSB.

Similarly with the offender focused attributions, meeting the offender and hearing an account in a restorative justice conference may allow victims to move from over generalising the crime (the world is a dangerous place) to the second and third set of assumptions. Like Sherman and Strang et al (2005) point out 'a RJ-conference has all the elements necessary for de-conditioning the fearful associations in victims' 'recalling of the event'. Hearing the offender's reasons for the crime may convince the victim that the offender is not basically a bad person and is sincerely sorry for the harm caused by the crime. But again this depends on the actual reasons the offender may have had for committing the crime. Pemberton et al (2006) describe the case of a burglary that caused the victim additional harm due to the fact that the original occupant had passed away shortly before the crime. The victim, the deceased person's partner, felt that their apartment had been targeted due to the fact that the burglar knew about this. This increased her anxiety as she saw this as a sign that the offender was sufficiently evil to perpetrate a crime against people who are stricken with grief. A restorative justice conference could then decrease her anxiety. Offenders normally burgle apartments based on no more information than that they are accessible and empty and the offender could assure here that he had not intended the additional harm caused by her partner's recent demise. However there are also offenders that do use additional information. If the offender for example knew the apartment was empty because he heard or read about the death the victim's suspicions will be confirmed rather than disaffirmed.

In conclusion there are four avenues through which restorative justice procedures could impact victims' anxiety. First participation in restorative justice may be seen as an instance of present control. It may be an avenue for a victim to assert a sense of control over his or her recovery process. Secondly the effects of restorative justice procedures on anxiety could be caused by the effects participation has on future control. In particular victims assessment of the chance of reoccurrence seems to be influenced by meeting the offender in a restorative justice procedure. Thirdly the offender's stated motivation may impact victims self-focused attributions. This impact does not necessarily have to be positive. Where the offender targeted the victim for reasons associated with the victim's character or behavior the effect may well be increased rather than decreased anxiety.

Finally the same observation holds for the effect on offender-focused attributions. Meeting the offender may well allow the victim to stop over-generalizing the event or to attribute the crime to the offender's behavior rather than his character. However, the offender's stated motivation may also confirm the victim's initial fears.

Anger: Rumination, Forgiveness and Apologies

The perception that one has been treated disrespectfully or insulted is the most common source of anger (Miller, 2001). Fitzgibbons (1986) defines anger as a strong feeling of displeasure aroused by a sense of injury or wrong. It follows that anger is a common response to criminal victimization as this at least involves disrespectful treatment. Surprisingly though, research concerning anger after victimization is scarce, definitely when compared to the abundance of fear of crime and post-traumatic stress literature (Goodey, 2005). In one of the exceptions Jason Ditton and colleagues found that victims typically more often reacted with anger than with fear toward victimization (Ditton et al 1999a and 1999b).

A construct that has emerged recently combines anger with rumination, which involves a repetitious dwelling on the negative things in one's life. According to Sukhodolsky et al. (2001) anger rumination can be defined "as unintentional and recurrent cognitive processes that emerge during and continue after an episode of anger experience". Sukhodolsky et al propose a four factor model of anger rumination that consists of angry afterthoughts, angry memories, revenge fantasies and understanding of causes. The afterthoughts involve the victim maintaining thoughts about or re-enacting the episode of anger. Angry memories involve the individual constantly dwelling over the experienced injustice. In the revenge fantasies the victim will dream or fantasize about how to retaliate against the perceived transgressor. Finally the sub-scale of understanding of causes is concerned with people who dwell on the reasons they were treated badly and the reasons why this happened.

There are two reasons why anger rumination is relevant for the understanding of victims' experiences in restorative justice. First: because of the negative correlations between anger rumination and forgiveness (Barber et al, 2005). Anger rumination can act as barrier for forgiveness. Enhancing forgiveness may on the other hand release victims from the burden of the unwanted and intrusive angry feelings and thoughts associated with anger rumination. As is shown in the following section, forgiveness, in an intra-psychic sense, is particularly relevant to victim experiences in restorative justice. Secondly anger rumination has interesting parallels to various features of the temporal model of control discussed in the previous section. In particular, the unwanted and intrusive thoughts concerning the event, counterfactual thinking and the desire to control the past, are similar. The inclusion of anger rumination in the temporal model of perceived control allows the combination of victims' experiences of anger and fear into one general psychological model of reactions to victimization.

Forgiveness

Forgiveness, in a psychological sense, can he defined as a willingness to abandon one's right to resentment, negative judgement and indifferent behaviour toward the offender, while fostering the undeserved qualities of compassion and generosity to him or her (Exline and Baumeister, 2000). Put more simply the three words 'I forgive you' express three separate things:

1   I have suffered harm or injury.
2   You are the source of that harm or injury.
3   But I am choosing to release you from your debt to me.

Forgiveness may be confused with a number of closely related constructs. It is different from excusing, which supposes that the offender had good reason to commit the offence, from condoning, which implies justifying the offence, or reconciliation, which implies restoring a relationship (Exline and Baumeister, 2000). This last differentiation is particularly important to restorative justice, as reconciliation is used in a number of studies as outcome measure for victims and offenders (Kurki, 2003 and Daly, 2005). From an intra-psychic point of view using forgiveness rather than reconciliation has a number of advantages. First, there may not have been a relationship as such to restore between victim and offender, which does not prevent the victim from forgiving the offender. Second, where there was a relationship the victim may choose to simultaneously forgive the offender and end the relationship. In both cases the construct of reconciliation does not adequately tap the positive aspects the act of forgiving may have for the victim.

Forgiveness is associated with a number of positive features for the person who forgives. Measures of forgiveness are negatively correlated with vengefulness and angry rumination, as forgiving releases victims from negative and intrusive angry thoughts about the offence and the offender. (McCullough et al, 2001; Barber et al, 2005)[16]. Forgiveness is associated with reduced depression and anxiety (Freedman & Enright, 1996; Hebl & Enright, 1993), heightened self-esteem (Karremans, Van Lange, Ouwerkerk, & Kluwer, 2003), and improved life satisfaction (Karremans et al., 2003). Through the release of negative emotions it may even promote physical health (Baumeister, Exline, & Sommer, 1998; Thoresen, Harris, & Luskin, 2000). In sum: forgiving the offender in general makes good sense for victims.

Even so it makes no sense to apply external pressure on victims to forgive because of the associated benefits. In the first place external pressure will not lead to forgiving (Opdebeeck et al, 2002), but to condoning or excusing, which neither are associated with the positive effects of forgiveness. Second, as shall be elaborated below, there is the moral issue. It may be morally right to withhold forgiveness (Exline and Baumeister, 2000).

The Relevance to Restorative Justice

Forgiveness already features within the restorative justice literature (Gehm, 1992). However, it is common to view it as a part of reconciling relationships or to view related aspects like apologies, in a sociological sense, rather than a psychological sense. In Strang and Sherman's work for example it is included within Collins Interaction Ritual Theory. The remainder of this section discusses two important aspects of forgiveness, namely the relationship between forgiveness and apologies and the relationship between forgiveness and justice values, to demonstrate the relevance of including the intra-psychic side to forgiveness in explanations of victims' experiences in restorative justice.

In the first place common sense tells us that a good way to achieve forgiveness is through the offender offering an apology to the victim, which is confirmed by research (Exline and Baumeister, 2000, Darby & Schlenker, 1982, McCullough et al, 1997). In restorative justice procedures apologizing by the offender is quite common. In the RISE-experiments 72% of participating offenders apologized for what they had done (Strang, 2002), in the South Australian Juvenile Justice (SAJJ) programme the figures were slightly lower, with spontaneous apologies being offered in 40% of cases and a further 28% having the apology 'drawn out' (Daly, 2003).

An important qualification of the positive effect of apologies on victims is the way it is interpreted by the victim. First it is important to ascertain if what has been offered by the offender is essentially an apology, rather than an excuse[17]. Second a relevant question is whether the victim sees the apology as sincere or not. Sincere apologies are associated with forgiveness but insincere apologies are not and serve as an added barrier to forgiveness (Exline and Baumeister, 2000) with victims reacting with more rather than less indignation to this kind of apology (Baron, 1988 and Cohen, 1986). Receiving an insincere apology therefore, is not a neutral but a negative experience for victims, and could be said to amount to secondary victimization (Opdebeeck et al, 2002). In only a minority of the cases in the Australian restorative justice experiments, victims considered offenders apologies to be sincere (41% in RISE, with an additional 36% being 'somewhat sincere', 27% in SAJJ). Important here is the considerable chance of perceptual difference between victims and offenders. Even when offenders sincerely apologize, many victims will not believe them. In the SAJJ experiments Daly contrasted the views of victims with those of offenders and found that they disagreed in 30% of the cases on the sincerity of the apology[18].

Second is the relationship between forgiveness and justice values. This relationship is not straightforward. Recent research shows that the effect of justice values depends on the type of justice values triggered (Karremans & Van Lange, 2005). If these are predominantly punishment or retribution oriented—offenders of these types of crimes should be sent to prison—justice values will serve as a barrier (Exline and Baumeister, 2000). The victim will feel something like, I can't forgive him, because he deserves to be punished. Conversely it will be easier for victims focusing on retributive values to forgive the offender if they see that the offender has been punished and/ or has compensated for the harm done. However justice values can also be related to social justice, human rights or procedural justice instead of retribution. In these cases aspects of justice will stimulate rather than hinder forgiveness. Restorative justice processes in general deliver high levels of procedural justice (see Strang, 2002). Furthermore, the restorative justice philosophy tends to emphasize non-retributive values. On both counts participating in a restorative justice process could foster forgiveness by stimulating justice values that are associated with higher levels of forgiveness. The importance of justice values for forgiveness is also emphasised by the relationship between offence severity and justice values. Criminological research shows that the severity of offences is associated with the likelihood of people emphasizing retributive justice values and desiring the offender to go to prison, (e.g. Mattinson & Mirrlees-Black, 2000). With less severe offences, values like repair and rehabilitation become more important.

The following hypothesis may be offered. Restorative justice can help victims to forgive offenders, and therefore contribute to recovery as forgiveness is associated with a number of benefits for victims. However this contribution is more likely for situations in which the offender has already been punished and/or paid full compensation or for less severe offences, as justice values will not provide a moral barrier for forgiveness in these cases. This hypothesis provides a possible explanation for recent research that shows victims of more severe crimes profit less from their participation than those who suffer lesser crimes. Daly (2005) reported that only 29% of the most distressed victims, who had suffered the more severe crimes, said they fully recovered a year after taking part in the restorative justice process. 66% of all participating victims said they fully recovered. Furthermore 77% of all victims attributed the recovery to participating in the restorative justice process, while only 49% of the 'high distress' victims did the same.

The discussion of anger and forgiveness can be summarized in three main conclusions. First of all it is relevant to measure forgiveness in a psychological sense as an outcome measure of restorative justice procedures, using relevant methodology[19]. Second the offering of an apology is important, but has to be qualified by the extent which it is an apology rather than an excuse and by the victims' interpretation of the sincerity of the apology. Finally the relationship between forgiveness and justice values, compensation or retribution and offence severity needs further exploration.

Endnotes

1 See Zedner, 2002, Dignan, 2005 and Goodey, 2005.

2 See e.g. the Council of Europe recommendation on mediation and the draft UN basic principles on restorative justice.

3 See Daly, 2006, for an overview of the core elements of restorative justice.

4 See Dignan, 2005, Christie, 1977 and Braithwaite, 1989 for a discussion of these intellectual traditions.

5 In the RCT's the offenders where divided at random across court and conference conditions.

6 See Brienen and Hoegen, 2000 for more examples.

7 See Brienen and Hoegen, 2000 for an extensive discussion of the situation at the turn of the century in 22 European Jurisdictions.

8 These and other differences are highlighted by many authors, see e.g. Zehr, 1990.

9 A similar point is made by Hayes and Daly (2003) concerning offenders.

10 Respectively: manipulation, therapy, information, consultation, placation, partnership, delegated power and citizen control.

11 Strang, 2002 in fact addresses this issue as well.

12 Strang, 2002, p. 54, Braithwaite, 1999, p. 20.

13 See Karremans & van Lange, 2005.

14 Duff, 2003, makes a similar argument.

15 See Brickman et al, 1982 and Zimbardo and Boyd, 1999, for a discussion of the temporal model and Frazier, 2003 and Frazier et al, 2004 for further empirical testing of the model.

16 It is relevant to stress here that forgiveness, see e.g. the Transgression Related Interpersonal Motivations (TRIM) Scale (McCullough et al, 1997), is measured as a continuous construct, rather than a forgiveness- no forgiveness dichotomy.

17 A relevant contribution in this respect is Smith, 2005. He offers an interesting discussion of what he describes as a 'categorical apology'.

18 This could be a particular instance of the more general perceptual mismatch between victims and offenders. Where offenders have a tendency to engage in self-serving distortions, which allow them to diminish their responsibility (Baumeister, 1998), victims do exactly the reverse and tend to exaggerate the severity of the offence (Stillwell & Baumeister, 1997).

19 For example the TRIM- scale, see McCullough et al, 1997.

References

Aertsen, I., Mackay, R., Pelikan, C., Willemsens, J., & Wright, M. (2004). *Rebuilding community connections-mediation and restorative justice in Europe*. Strasbourg, France: Council of Europe publishing.

Amstein, S. (1971). A Ladder of Citizen Participation in the USA., *Journal of the Royal Town Planning Institute*, 57: 176.

Barber, L., Maltby, J., & Macaskill, A. (2005). Angry memories and thoughts of revenge: The relationship between forgiveness and anger rumination. *Personality and Individual Differences, 39*, 253–262.

Baron R. A. (1988). Attributions and organizational conflict: the mediating role of apparent sincerity. *Organizational Behavior and Human Decision Processes, 69*, 272–279.

Baumeister, R. F. (1998). The self. In D. T. Gilbert & S. T. Fiske (Eds.), *The handbook of social psychology* (Vol. 2, 4th ed.). Boston: McGraw-Hill.

Baumeister, R. F., Exline, J. J., & Sommer, K. L. (1998). The victim role, grudge theory, and two dimensions of forgiveness. In E. L. Worthington (Ed.), *Dimensions of forgiveness: Psychology research and theoretical perspectives*. Philadelphia: Templeton.

Bottoms, A. E. (2003). Some sociological reflections on restorative justice. In A. Von Hirsch, J. Roberts, A. E. Bottoms, K. Roach, & M. Schiff (Eds.), *Restorative justice and criminal justice: competing or reconcilable paradigms?* Oxford: Hart Publishing.

Braithwaite, J. (1989). Crime, Shame, and Reintegration, Cambridge: Cambridge University Press.

Braithwaite, J. (1999). Restorative justice: Assessing optimistic and pessimistic accounts. In M. Tonry (Ed.), *Crime and justice: A review of research, 25.* Chicago: University of Chicago Press.

Braithwaite, J. (2002) *Restorative justice and responsive regulation.* New York: Oxford University Press.

Brickman, P., Rabinowitz, V. C., Karuza, J., Jr., Coates, D., Cohn, E., & Kidder, L. (1982). Models of helping and coping. *American Psychologist, 37,* 368–384.

Cavadino, M., & Dignan, J. (2005). *Penal systems. A comparative approach.* London/Thousand Oaks/New Delhi: Sage Publications.

Christie, N. (1977). Conflicts as property. *British Journal of Criminology, 17,* 1–17.

Christie, N. (1986). The ideal victim. In *From crime policy to victim policy.* Basingstoke: Macmillan.

Council of Europe Committee of Ministers (1999). Mediation in penal matters, *Recommendation No R(99) 19,* adopted 15 September 1999.

Cohen R. L. (1986). Power and justice in intergroup relations. In H. W. Bierhoff, R. L. Cohen, & J. Greenberg (Eds.), *Justice in social relations.* New York: Plenum.

Collins, R. (2004). *Inter action ritual chains.* Princeton, New Jersey, USA: Princeton University Press.

Daly, K. (2001). Conferencing in Australia and New Zealand: Variations, research findings, and prospects. In A. Morris & G. Maxwell (Eds.), *Restorative justice for juveniles: Conferencing, mediation, and circles.* Oxford, UK: Hart Publishing.

Daly, K. (2002). Restorative justice: the real story. *Punishment & Society, 4,* 55–79.

Daly, K. (2003). Mind the gap: restorative justice in theory and practice. In A. von Hirsch, J. Roberts, A. E. Bottoms, K. Roach, & M. Schiff (Eds.), *Restorative justice and criminal justice: competing or reconcilable paradigms?* Oxford, Hart Publishing.

Daly, K. (2005). A tale of two studies: restorative justice from a victim's perspective. In E. Elliott & R. Gordon (Eds.), *Restorative justice: emerging issues in practice and evaluation.* Cullumpton, UK: Willan Publishing.

Daly, K. (2006). The limits of restorative justice. In D. Sullivan & L. L. Tifft (Eds.), *The handbook of restorative justice: a global perspective.* New York: Routledge.

Darby, B. W., & Schlenker, B. R. (1982). Childrens reactions to apologies. *Journal of Personality and Social Psychology, 43,* 742–753.

Dignan, J. (2005). *Understanding victims and restorative justice.* Maidenhead: Open University Press.

Ditton, J., Bannister, J., Gilchrist, E. & Farrall, S. (1999a). Afraid or angry? Recalibrating the 'fear' of crime. *International Review of Victimology, 6:* 83–99.

Ditton, J., Farrall, S., Bannister, J., Gilchrist, E., & Pease, K. (1999b). Reactions to victimisation: Why has anger been ignored? *Crime Prevention and Community Safety: An International Journal, 1*(3), 37–54.

Duff, R. A. (2003). Restoration and retribution. In A. von Hirsch, J. Roberts, A. E. Bottoms, K. Roach, & M. Schiff (Eds.), *Restorative and criminal justice: competing or reconcilable paradigms.* Oxford, UK: Hart Publishing.

Ehlers, A., & Clark, D. M. (2000). A cognitive model of posttraumatic stress disorder. *Behavior Research and Therapy, 38,* 319–345.

European Union (2001). *Council Framework Decision of 15 March 2001 on the standing of victims in criminal proceedings,* (2001/220/JHA).

Exline, J. J., & Baumeister, R. F. (2000). Expressing forgiveness and repentance: benefits and barriers. In M. E. McCullough & C. E. Thoresen (Eds.), *Forgiveness theory: research and practice*. London: Guildford Press.

Fattah, E. A. (1997). Toward a victim policy aimed at healing, not suffering. In R. C. Davis, A. J. Lurigio, & W. G. Skogan (Eds.), *Victims of crime*, Thousand Oaks, CA: Sage.

Fitzgibbons, R. P. (1986). The cognitive and emotive uses of forgiveness in the treatment of anger. *Psychotherapy, 23*, 629–633.

Foa, E. B., Zinbarg, R., & Rothbaum, B. O. (1992). Uncontrollability and unpredictability in post-traumatic stress disorder: An animal model. *Psychological Bulletin, 112*, 218–238.

Frazier, P., Berman, M., & Steward, J. (2002). Perceived control and posttraumatic stress: A temporal model. *Applied & Preventive Psychology, 10*, 207–223.

Frazier, P. A. (2003). Perceived control and distress following sexual assault: A longitudinal test of a New model. *Journal of Personality and Social Psychology, 84*, 1257–1269.

Frazier, P., Steward, J., & Mortensen, H. (2004). Perceived control and adjustment to trauma: a comparison across events. *Journal of Social and Clinical Psychology. 23*, 303–324.

Freedman, S., & Enright, R. D. (1996). Forgiveness as an intervention goal with incest survivors. *Journal of Consulting and Clinical Psychology, 64*, 938–922.

Gehm, J. R. (1992). The function of forgiveness in the criminal justice system. In H. Messner & H. Otto (Eds.), *Restorative justice on trial*. Dordrecht, the Netherlands: Kluwer.

Goodey, J. (2005). *Victims and victimology: Research, policy, practice*. Harlow, UK: Pearson.

Hayes, H., & Daly, K. (2003). Youth justice conferencing and reoffending. *Justice Quarterly, 20*(4), 725–764.

Hebl, J. H., & Enright, R. D. (1993). Forgiveness as a therapeutic goal with elderly females. *Psychotherapy, 30*, 658–667.

Hill, R. (2002). Restorative justice and the absent victim: New data from the Thames Valley. *International Review of Victimology, 9*, 273–288.

Hoyle, C. (2002). Securing restorative justice for the non-participating' victim. In C. Hoyle & R. Young (Eds.), *New visions of crime victims*, Oxford, UK: Hart Publishing.

Janoff-Bulman, R. (1979). Characterological versus behavioral self-blame: Inquiries into depression and rape. *Journal of Personality and Social Psychology, 37*, 1798–1809.

Janoff-Bulman, R. (1992). *Shattered assumptions: Towards a new psychology of trauma*. New York: Free Press.

Karremans, J. C., Van Lange, P. A. M., Ouwerkerk, J. W., & Kluwer, E. S. (2003). When forgiving enhances psychological well being: The role of interpersonal commitment. *Journal of Personality and Social Psychology, 84*, 1011–1026.

Karremans, J. C., & Van Lange, P. A. M., (2005). Does activating justice help or hurt in promoting forgiveness? *Journal of Experimental Social Psychology, 41*, 290–297.

Kurki, L. (2003). Evaluating restorative justice practices. In A. von Hirsch, J. V. Roberts, A. Bottoms, K. Roach, & M. Schiff (Eds.), *Restorative and criminal justice: competing or reconcilable paradigms*. Oxford, UK: Hart Publishing.

Latimer, J., Dowden, C., & Muise, D. (2005). The effectiveness of restorative justice practices: a meta-analysis. *The Prison Journal, 85*, 127–144.

Marandos, R., & Perry, A. (2002). *"Assessing the effectiveness of interventions designed to support victims of crime: a systematic review of psychological outcomes"*, proposal approved in 2002 by the Campbell Collaboration, published at www.campbellcollaboration.org/doc-pdf/assessvictimsprot.pdf

Mattinson, J., & Mirrlees-Black, C. (2000). *Attitudes to crime and criminal justice*, Home Office, London, UK.

McCullough, M. E., Pargament, K. I., & Thoresen, C. E. (2000). The psychology of forgiveness: History, conceptual issues, and overview. In M. E. McCullough & C. E. Thoresen (Eds.), *Forgiveness theory: research and practice*. London: Guildford Press.

McCold, P. (2003). A survey of assessment research on mediation and conferencing. In L. Walgrave (Ed.), *Repositioning restorative justice*. Cullumpton, UK: Willan.

McCullough, M. E., Bellah, C. G., Kilpatrick, S. D., & Johnson, J. L. (2001). Vengefulness: Relationships with forgiveness, rumination, well-being, and the big five. *Personality and Social Psychology Bulletin, 27*, 601–610.

McCullough, M. E., Worthington, E. L., & Rachal, K. C. (1997). Interpersonal forgiving in close relationships. *Journal of Personality and Social Psychology, 73*, 321–336.

McCullough, M. E., Sandage, S. J., Brown, S. W., Rachal, C. K., Worthington, E. L., & Hight, T. L. (1998). Interpersonal forgiving in close relationships: II Theoretical elaboration and measurement. *Journal of Personality and Social Psychology, 75*, 1586–1603.

Miller, D. T. (2001). Disrespect and the experience of injustice. *Annual review of psychology, 52*, 527–553.

Opdebeeck, A., Vervaeke, G., & Winkel, F. W. (2002). Bemiddeling in het Strafrecht. In P. J. van Koppen, D. J. Hessing, H. L. G. L. Merkelbach, & H. F. M. Crombag (Eds.), *Het recht van hinnen: Psychologie van het recht*. Deventer, the Netherlands: Kluwer.

Orth, U. (2002). Secondary victimization of crime victims by criminal proceedings. *Social Justice Research, 15*(4), 313–325.

Ozer, E. J., Best, S. R., Lipsey, T. L., & Weiss, D. S. (2003). Predictors of posttraumatic stress disorder and symptoms in adults: A meta-analysis. *Psychological Bulletin, 129*, 52–73.

Pemberton, A., Winkel, F. W., & Groenhuijsen, M. S. (2006). Op weg naar slachtoffergerichte theorievorming in het herstelrecht. *Tijdschrift voor Herstelrecht, 6*(1), 48–64.

Roese, N. J. (1997). Counterfactual thinking. *Psychological bulletin, 121*(1), 133–148.

Röhl, K. F. (1997). Procedural justice: Introduction and overview. In K. F. Röhl & S. Machura (Eds.), *Procedural justice*. Aldershot, UK: Ashgate.

Schweizer, S. (2006). *Effects of guided writing and apology on forgiveness: Are they mediated by anger ruminations, thoughts of revenge, type D personality and PTSD symptomology?* Unpublished thesis, Tilburg University.

Shapland, J., Wilmore, J., & Duff, P. (1985). *Victims in the criminal justice system*. Aldershot, UK: Gower.

Sherman, L. W., Strang, H., Angel, C., Woods, D., Barnes, G. C., Bennett, S., & Inkpen, N. (2005). Effects of face-to-face restorative justice on victims of crime in four randomized, controlled trials. *Journal of Experimental Criminology, 1*, 367–395.

Smith, N. (2005). The categorical apology. *Journal of Social Philosophy, 36*, 473–496.

Stillwell, A. M., & Baumeister, R. F. (1997). The construction of victim and perpetrator memories: Accuracy and distortion in role-basedaccounts. *Personality and Social Psychology Bulletin, 23*, 1157–1172.

Strang, H. (2002). *Repair or revenge: Victims and restorative justice*. Oxford: Oxford University Press.

Strang, H. & Sherman, L. W. (2003). Repairing the harm: Victims and restorative justice. *Utah Law Review, 1*, 15–42.

Strang, H., & Sherman, L. (2004) *Protocol for a Campbell Collaboration Systematic Review: Campbell Collaboration Systematic Review: Effects of Face-to-Face Restorative Justice for Personal Victim Crimes*, draft #4, November, see http://www.campbellcollaboration.org/doc-pdf/restorativejusticeprot.pdf.

Strang, H., Sherman, L. W., Angel, C., Woods, D., Bennett, S., Newbury-Birch, D., & Inkpen, N. (2006). Victim evaluations of face-to-face restorative justice conferences: A quasi-experimental analysis. *Journal of Social Issues, 62*(2), 281–306.

Sukhodolsky, D. G., Golub, A., & Cromwell, E. N. (2001). Development and validation of the anger rumination scale. *Personality and Individual Differences, 31*, 689–700.

Thoresen, C. E., Luskin, F., & Harris, A. H. S. (1998). Science and forgiveness interventions: Reflections and recommendations. In E. L. Worthington, Jr. (Ed.), *Dimensions of forgiveness: Psychology research and theoretical perspectives*. Philadelphia: Templeton.

Tyler, T. R. (1990). *Why people obey the law*. New Haven: Yale University Press.

United Nations (2002). *Basic Principles on the Use of Restorative Justice Programmes in Criminal Matters*. United Nations Economic and Social Council.

Wemmers J. & Cyr. K. (2004). Victims' perspective on restorative justice: How much involvement are victims looking for? *International Review of Victimology, 11*, 1–16.

Winkel, F. W. (2002). *Slachtofferhulp bij hardnekkige klachten: Over visie, witte beren, stroop en tegenpolen*. Inaugural lecture, Free University Amsterdam.

Wittebrood, K. (2006). *Slachtoffers van criminaliteit*. SCP: The Hague.

Young. R. (2002). Testing the limits of restorative justice: the case of corporate victims. In C. Hoyle & R. Young (Eds.), *New visions of Crime victims*. Oxford: Hart Publishing.

Zedner, L. (2002). Victims. In M. Maguire, R. Morgan, & R. Reinder (Eds.), *The Oxford Handbook of Criminology* (3rd edition). Oxford: Oxford University Press.

Zehr, H. (1990). *Changing lenses: a new focus for crime and justice*. Scottsdale, PA: Herald Press.

Zimbardo, P. G., & Boyd, J. N. (1999). Putting time in perspective: A valid, reliable individual-differences metric. *Journal of Personality and Social Psychology, 77*, 1271–1288.

Chapter 6: Concluding Remarks

Providing culturally competent, relevant, and holistic services to victims of crime that account for and recognize the many obstacles and barriers they face along the path to healing and repair has been at the forefront of academic discourse and research for quite some time now. An integral part of this discussion is the recognition that victims' experiences with crime differ, and the response to their needs can determine their course of emotional restoration. This chapter presented us with restorative justice principles and practices that bring to the surface many of the unaddressed, often neglected dynamics of victim feelings of hurt and self-blame that can be resolved through meaningful encounters between victims and offenders. Through the experiences of being heard and listening to expressions of remorse by the offender, victims can begin the proper path to therapeutic recovery, gaining a sense of dignity and empowerment.

The Overlap in Victimization and Offending

Introduction

One of the most consistent and well-documented findings in the research literature is the relationship between crime victimization and criminal offending. This phenomenon has been referred to as the victim–offender overlap. Studies of crime trends have time and again revealed that the experience of victimization is somehow related to participation in criminal behavior. Likewise, involvement in criminal activity increases the risk of becoming the victim of crime. Various theoretical paradigms have been proposed to offer some explanation for these underlying trends. Some have focused on lifestyles and routine activities that increase both risk for victimization and offending. Others have researched the common characteristics and shared experiences of victims and offenders that make them both more likely to encounter victimization and become involved in crime.

One area of focus in victim studies literature has been domestic violence within relationships between intimate partners. Studies have found this type of violence to be generational and one of the most recurrent forms of criminal behavior. The question of criminal desistence becomes particularly problematic in such cases where we are left with the question of how trauma affects individuals in a way that leads them to either become an aggressor or continue in their role as victim. The study presented in this chapter explores the continuation of intimate partner violence experienced in adolescence into adulthood and the relationship between experiencing victimization as a teenager and the perpetration of violence in later years. The authors examine various concepts within the study of intimate partner violence, including personal traits such as gender, age, and race that lead to variations in the incidence of aggression, as well as social variables such as parent–child violence, family structure, and parental education, and how these variables can affect the continuity of behavior in the experience of both victimization and offending.

Guiding Questions

As you read, consider the following questions:

1   How can the trauma of experiencing crime victimization lead to criminal offending?

2   What aspects of social environment and routine activity are related to the overlap in becoming a crime victim and perpetrating crime?

3   Are there certain types of crimes that can better inform the overlap in victimization and offending?

4   In what ways can criminal justice policies and practices address crime victimization so as to mediate those variables that can lead to criminal offending?

Key Terms

commitment theory   An approach to understanding domestic violence that states that the more invested a couple is in a relationship, such as living together, sharing resources, or being married, the less likely they are to terminate an abusive relationship.

cross-sectional study   A descriptive study that captures information about a group of individuals in a given time period.

victim–offender overlap   The research finding that there is a positive relationship between experiencing crime victimization and the perpetration of criminal behavior, and vice versa.

The Continuation of Intimate Partner Violence from Adolescence to Young Adulthood

Ming Cui, Mellissa Gordon, Koji Ueno, and Frank D. Fincham

Little attention has been paid to whether violence in adolescent romantic relationships is associated with relationship violence later in young adulthood. This study examined the continuation of intimate partner violence (IPV) from adolescence to young adulthood. Using data from the National Longitudinal Study of Adolescent Health, results from negative binomial models and propensity score models showed that being victimized by relationship partners in adolescence was significantly associated with both perpetration and victimization in romantic relationships in young adulthood. Women reported higher levels of perpetration and lower levels of victimization than men did. Those who were living together (married or cohabiting) reported higher levels of victimization and perpetration than those who were dating. Further, such associations existed beyond the effects of parent–child violence and general aggression tendencies, suggesting the continuation of relationship-specific violence. Finally, these patterns persisted after controlling for participants' age, race and ethnicity, parental education, and family structure.

Establishing and maintaining romantic relationships are central developmental tasks for young adults (Conger, Cui, Bryant, & Elder, 2000). One particularly important behavior in relationships is intimate partner violence (IPV), which has been associated with a variety of negative developmental outcomes, such as anxiety and depression (e.g., Holt & Espelage, 2005; Makepeace, 1983; Silverman, Raj, Mucci, & Hathaway, 2001). Further, IPV is a major impediment not only to healthy individual development, but also to public health. It is estimated that IPV costs $5.8 billion each year for injury treatment, counseling, and intervention programs (Arias

& Corso, 2005). Understanding IPV among young adults is particularly important because such understanding could provide information for prevention and intervention programs geared towards reducing IPV.

Research has focused on the influence of family of origin as the major precursor of IPV in young adulthood (e.g., Cui, Durtschi, Lorenz, Donnellan, & Conger, 2010). Even though these studies have established an association between violence in the family of origin and IPV in later adulthood, little attention has been paid to the effect of a more proximal factor—IPV in earlier romantic relationships during adolescence. As a result, little evidence is available about the effect of an individual's previous experiences of relationship violence on current relationship violence (Halpem, Spriggs, Martin, & Kupper, 2009; Meier & Allen, 2009; Williams, Craig, Connolly, Pepler, & Laporte, 2008). As Spriggs, Halpem, and Martin (2009) noted, researchers know very little about the longitudinal course of relationship violence from adolescence to adulthood. In contrast to research efforts focusing on violence in the family of origin and IPV later in young adulthood, few studies have examined IPV as it emerges in adolescence and is potentially maintained into young adulthood (Williams et al.).

One reason for the lack of studies in this area is that romantic relationships in adolescence have been regarded as trivial and transitory; therefore, the topic of adolescent romance itself has been ignored until the last several decades (Furman, Brown, & Feiring, 1999). Further, most studies are cross-sectional and do not follow individuals from adolescence to young adulthood. In the few longitudinal studies that do exist, the time period was often not long enough to capture the full range of young adulthood (Williams et al., 2008). Finally, because analyses have usually been based on college students or other rather homogeneous samples, knowledge reflecting the broader population is limited (see Cleveland, Herrera, & Stuewig, 2003; Halpern et al., 2009). To fill the gap in the current literature, this study uses a large, nationally representative, longitudinal sample to examine the long-term effects of IPV in adolescence on IPV in young adulthood.

The Continuation of Intimate Partner Violence from Adolescence to Young Adulthood

IPV is defined in the current study as verbal (e.g., verbal threats) and physical (e.g., hitting, slapping) violence toward one's romantic partner. Social learning theory (Bandura, 1977) proposes that behaviors are learned, reinforced, and cumulated through prior experiences such as dyadic interactions in relationship contexts. Adolescents who have experienced violence in previous relationships may regard such behaviors as acceptable and allow such behaviors in future relationships (Gomez, 2011; Graves, Sechrist, White, & Paradise, 2005). Therefore, being a victim in a violent relationship is likely to lead to being a victim and also a perpetrator in current relationships as well as in future relationships. Consistent with social learning theory, the life course perspective (Elder & Giele, 2009) also proposes that adolescent romantic relationships hold developmental currency for relationships in later adulthood and that adolescents could reinforce and reciprocate violent behaviors in relationships, further leading to more violence victimization and perpetration in future relationships. In addition, the life course perspective emphasizes "cumulative disadvantage," and thus earlier victimization could have influence on subsequent relationships cumulatively and negatively over the life course. Despite these theoretical predictions, there is scant empirical evidence linking adolescent IPV to young adult IPV (Meier & Allen, 2009). The present study addresses this issue. Based on social learning theory and the life course perspective, continuity in relationship violence from adolescence to young adulthood is expected.

With the current literature mainly focusing on the intergenerational transmission of violence (e.g., Cui et al., 2010), the more proximal and potentially more powerful effect of IPV experienced in earlier romantic relationships in adolescent years has not received the attention it deserves (Halpem et al., 2009). In a shortterm longitudinal study, O'Leary and Slep (2003) followed adolescents who remained in a relationship for 3 months and found that physical aggression was highly stable. Even though the findings from this study demonstrated short-term continuity in relationship violence, studies on continuity across relationships and over longer periods (i.e., extending beyond the adolescent years into young adulthood) are much needed. Only a few studies to date have examined the continuation of IPV from adolescence to young adulthood. These studies have shown that IPV experienced in a previous relationship was a major predictor of violence in one's current relationship (e.g., Bookwala, Frieze, Smith, & Ryan, 1992; Cano, Avery–Leaf, Cascardi, & O'Leary, 1998; Gomez, 2011; O'Leary et al., 1989). Specifically, some studies have found continued violence victimization from adolescence to young adulthood (Graves et al., 2005; Halpem et al., 2009; Spriggs et al., 2009). For example, a study by Smith, White, and Holland (2003) examined physical dating violence from high school through college. They found that women who were physically assaulted in romantic relationships as adolescents were more likely to experience victimization in romantic relationships in college.

Even though these studies have examined IPV from adolescence to young adulthood, they display several limitations. First, many studies focused on violence prevalence (Brown et al., 2009; Cleveland et al., 2003; Halpem et al., 2009). Focusing on violence prevalence is important, but it tends to overlook the level of violence, which is equally important, especially when one wants to examine variations in the degree of violence among individuals. In order to complement previous studies on prevalence, this study examines relationship violence on a continuum. Second, some studies have not differentiated victim and perpetrator roles and have only measured a general violence level (e.g., Fusco, 2010). Such studies are useful when looking at violence at the couple level, but differentiating individual level violence by victimization and perpetration is important to examine violence initiation, interaction, and other potential differences, such as gender difference (Kimmel, 2002). Some studies have differentiated victimization and perpetration but only investigated one but not both (e.g., Spriggs et al., 2009). To gain more information on both victimization and perpetration, this study includes both victimization and perpetration in young adult relationships. Third, when examining the association between relationship violence in adolescence and in young adulthood, some studies used cross-sectional data based on retrospective reports of adolescent experiences (Cano et al., 1998). Cross-sectional studies using retrospective accounts are subject to numerous cognitive heuristics (e.g., availability and accessibility heuristics) and are unlikely to estimate the association accurately. Further, the vast majority of relationship violence research has used college samples (see Cleveland et al.). Findings from such samples cannot be generalized to the larger population. Taken together, cross-sectional and nonrepresentative samples are not well suited for studying a problem with such important public health implications. Several studies have extended earlier findings by using large, nationally representative, and longitudinal samples (Brown et al., 2009; Gomez, 2011; Halpem et al., 2009; Spriggs et al., 2009). These studies, however, only used samples of young adults in their mid-20s (e.g., ages 18 to 27). With the trend of delaying marriage until mid- and late 20s (Cherlin, 2010), such samples may only cover relatively early marriages, which may affect the implication of the findings. To capture the full range of young adulthood and explore various types of relationships, this study used longitudinal data based on a large, nationally representative sample to examine relationship violence among young adults in their mid-20s to mid-30s.

Gender Differences, Relationship Type, and Other Factors Related to IPV

Social role theory has been used to explain gender difference in behaviors (Eagly, 1987). It proposes that gender differences in IPV are the result of gender-role expectancy. Specific to IPV, Archer (2006) proposes that there are an equal number of or more male victims relative to female victims in relationships because of increases in women's power, especially in Western societies. This is consistent with the gender symmetry approach found in family conflict theory (Straus, 2009; also see White, 2009), which proposes equal or higher rates of IPV by women. Indeed, several recent studies on gender differences in IPV have found overall higher rates of female perpetration and lower rates of female victimization (e.g., Archer, 2006; Cui et al., 2010; Cunradi, 2007). Such findings apply to severe violence such as kicking, choking, and causing injuries as well as to minor violence (see Straus for a review). But the findings in the literature are inconsistent, with some studies suggesting greater male perpetration, especially regarding severe violence (Archer, 2000; Stark, 2007; Tjaden & Thoennes, 2000; White, Smith, Koss, & Figueredo, 2000). Thus, past findings are somewhat mixed, which may indicate differences in the samples. This study added to the literature by analyzing data from a nationally representative sample.

Commitment theory (Johnson & Ferraro, 2000) and the investment model of relationships (Rusbult, 1980) both propose that when couples are living together, they share resources and have invested a significant amount of time and energy in the relationship. Therefore, married and cohabiting couples are less likely than dating couples to terminate a violent relationship due to greater levels of commitment and investment as well as more barriers to exiting the relationship (Kurdek, 1998). Consistent with such theoretical frameworks, studies have shown that married and cohabiting couples demonstrated a higher level of violence than dating couples (Arriaga, 2002). Nevertheless, findings are not always consistent. Frias and Angel (2005) suggested that cohabitors and daters did not differ in violence, but both cohabitors and daters reported lower levels of victimization than married couples did. Relationship type differences in IPV are examined in the current study.

Other factors have also been shown to be associated with relationship violence. First, individuals with a history of general aggression tend to be more likely to act aggressively toward a romantic partner (Cleveland et al., 2003). Several studies have suggested a possible association between general aggression and relationship violence (Capaldi, Kim, & Shortt, 2004). Second, parent–child violence has been shown to be associated with adolescent and young adult IPV (Cui et al., 2010; Gomez, 2011). Still, other factors that could affect the association of IPV in adolescence and young adulthood include age (Spriggs et al., 2009), race and ethnicity (Frias & Angel, 2005), parental education (Heyman & Slep, 2002; Simons, Lin, & Gordon, 1998), and family structure (Halpem, Oslak, Young, Martin, & Kupper, 2001). These potential confounding factors are considered in the current study.

In sum, in the present study, the continuity in IPV from adolescence to young adulthood is examined. In addition, potential gender and relationship type differences are examined. Many important covariates (i.e., parent–child violence, adolescent general aggression, age, race and ethnicity, parental education, and family structure) are included in the analyses to ensure that the proposed continuation of relationship violence is not an artifact of these factors. Based on theories and recent studies, the following hypotheses are proposed:

> Hypothesis 1: IPV victimization in adolescent romantic relationships is positively associated with both victimization and perpetration in young adult IPV.

> Hypothesis 2: Women demonstrate higher levels of perpetration and lower levels of victimization than men in young adult IPV.

> Hypothesis 3: Young adults who are married or cohabiting demonstrate higher levels of victimization and perpetration than those who are dating.

Method

Sample and Procedures

To evaluate the hypotheses, data were drawn from the National Longitudinal Study of Adolescent Health (Add Health). Add Health is a school-based longitudinal study of a nationally representative sample of adolescents in grades 7–12 in the United States during the 1994–1995 school year. Detailed descriptions of the sample and procedures can be found in Harris et al. (2008)

and at the web site http://www.cpc.unc.edu/projects/addhealth/design. Briefly, a sample of 132 high schools and middle schools from the United States was selected with unequal probability of selection. Incorporating systematic sampling methods and implicit stratification into the Add Health study design ensured that this sample is representative of U.S. schools with respect to region of country, urbanicity, school size, school type, and ethnicity.

At Wave I, in-home interviews ($N = 20,745$) were administered to students in grades 7–12 in 1994–1995. The topics included social and demographic characteristics of respondents, household structure, family composition and dynamics, risk behaviors, sexual partnerships, and formation of romantic partnerships. Wave II surveyed students from the original sample (except for those who had graduated) in 1996. Data were collected from respondents during an in-home interview ($n = 14,738$). In 2001–2002, 15,197 respondents from the original sample, 18 to 27 years old, were reinterviewed in Wave III. In 2007–2008, Wave IV data were collected from respondents ($n = 15,701$), who were between ages 24 and 32.

The current study used data from all waves: Wave I included most demographic variables, Wave II included adolescent IPV, and Waves III and IV included young adult outcome variables. Participants were included in the present analysis if they had participated in all waves and had valid sampling weights. These criteria resulted in a sample of 9,421 participants. In order to address the research questions on violence from adolescence to young adulthood, the sample in this study was further restricted to those who were 18 or younger at Wave II (i.e., adolescents; see also Spriggs et al., 2009; $n = 7,232$). Of the 7,232 participants, 4,468 had reported at least one romantic relationship at Wave II and therefore were included in the analyses. Of the 4,468 participants from adolescents (Wave II) to young adulthood (Wave III and Wave IV), 3,563 in Wave III and 4,048 in Wave IV had complete data on all variables of interests. Attrition analyses suggested that male participants, African Americans, and those in lower grade levels in earlier waves were more likely to have dropped out from the survey. The use of longitudinal weights minimized attrition biases. The final operational samples included 3,563 participants at Wave III and 4,048 participants at Wave IV.

Measures

Relationship Violence Victimization in Adolescence (Wave II)

At Wave II, adolescents were asked to report up to three romantic relationships. For each relationship, they were asked five questions on violence victimization (Conflict Tactic Scale; Straus, Hamby, Boney-McCoy, & Sugarman, 1996; e.g., Did your partner threaten you with violence? Did your partner push or shove you?). The answers were coded as 0 = *no* and 1 = *yes*. The five items were added together to create a count of violence victimization. If the adolescents only reported one relationship, the report of violence victimization of that one relationship was used. If the adolescents reported two or three relationships, the scores for violence victimization were averaged across relationships.

Relationship Violence Victimization and Perpetration in Young Adulthood (Wave III)

At Wave III, both victimization and perpetration of relationship violence were assessed. Participants were asked to report their IPV in as many relationships as they reported having had since Wave I. The participants were asked four items on *violence victimization* (e.g., How often did your partner slap, hit, or kick you? How often did you have an injury, such as sprain, bruise, or cut because of a fight with your partner?). The responses ranged from 0 = *never* to 6 = *more than 20 times in the last year of the relationship*. The scores of the four items were added together to create a composite score, with a higher score indicating a higher level of violence victimization. Similar to the measure in adolescence, if the participants reported more than one relationship, the scores for victimization were averaged across relationships. The alpha coefficient was $\alpha = .80$. Likewise, participants were also asked the same four items on *violence perpetration* (e.g., How often did you slap, hit, or kick your partner?) with the same coding scheme. The scores were created the same way as victimization. The alpha coefficient was $\alpha = .68$.

Relationship Violence Victimization and Perpetration in Young Adulthood (Wave IV)

At Wave IV, both victimization and perpetration of relationship violence were also assessed. Unlike the Wave III questions that asked about as many relationships as the participants had, the Wave IV questions asked about one current relationship. If participants reported multiple relationships, priority was given first to marriage, then to cohabitation, and then to relationships with pregnancy and dating relationships. If two or more relationships fell into the same type of relationship, the longer or longest relationship was selected. The items were the same as in Wave III with a slightly different coding: from 0 = *never* to 7 = *more than 20 times in the last year of the relationship*. As in Wave III, the scores were summed to create the measures of victimization and perpetration. The alpha coefficients were $\alpha = .76$ for victimization and $\alpha = .69$ for perpetration.

Parent–Child Violence (Wave III)

Unfortunately, information on parent–child violence was not collected at Wave I. Instead, participants were asked in Wave III to retrospectively report how often their parents or other adult caregivers slapped, hit, or kicked them by the time they were in the sixth grade. The item was recoded as 0 = *never happened*, 1 = *one time*, 2 = *two times*, 3 = *three to five times*, 4 = *six to ten times*, and 5 = *more than ten times*, with a higher score indicated a higher level of parent–child violence.

General Aggression (Wave II)

Adolescents were asked to report on three items (i.e., during the past 12 months, how often did you get into a severe physical fight? How often did you use or threaten to use a weapon to get something from someone? How often did you take part in a fight where a group of your friends was against another group?). The responses ranged from 0 = *never* to 3 = 5 *or more times*. The scores from the three items were summed together. The alpha coefficient was α = .64.

Other Variables

Gender was coded as 0 = *male participant* and 1 = *female participant*. *Relationship type* was assessed by three dummy variables at Wave IV: married, cohabiting, and dating (reference category). Age was assessed in years at Wave II. Other demographic variables were assessed at Wave I. *Race and ethnicity* were assessed by five dummy variables for Hispanic, White (reference category), African American, Asian, and others. In order to control for family effects, the analysis also included family structure and parents' education. *Family structure* was assessed by five dummy variables for two-parent families (reference category), step-families, single-mother families, single-father families, and other families. *Parents' education* was assessed by asking the target adolescent about his or her mother's and father's years of schooling. Based on the higher number of years of schooling of mother and father, the responses were coded into four dummy variables: college education or more, some college education, high school graduation (reference category), or less than a high school education (Cui, Ueno, Fincham, Donnellan, & Wickrama, 2012).

Analytic Strategy

Following the advice of Add Health researchers (Chantala, 2006), Stata's "svy" estimation was used to adjust the analysis for the multistage stratified sampling design. Specifically, the estimation method used longitudinal sampling weights to correct for the unequal chance of being selected into the sample and remaining in the sample across waves, and it employed the Taylor series linearization method to adjust standard errors for data clustering (e.g., students nested in schools). The estimation method also helped specify the analytical subpopulation (age 18 or younger at Wave II) so the results could be generalized to this subpopulation. For the primary analysis, negative binomial models were used to address the extremely skewed distribution in the dependent variable—a large number of 0's (no violent behavior) and a small number of very high values (high levels of violence; see Cui et al., 2012).

Further, one major concern of the current study is that the differences between adolescents who experienced IPV and those who did not may be due to pre-existing differences in their background characteristics (therefore, individuals selected themselves or were selected into IPV in adolescence and young adulthood). To address this concern, propensity score matching models were also estimated. Propensity score matching approximates an experimental design by using observed variables to generate a treatment group (adolescents who reported IPV) and a control group (adolescents who did not report IPV). It makes the treatment and control groups as similar as possible by matching their propensity for the treatment or the key independent variable (Morgan & Harding, 2006). Three types of matching techniques were used: nearest-neighbor matching, radius matching, and kernel matching (Becker & Ichino, 2002; Turney, 2012). The nearest-neighbor matching technique estimates young adult victimization and perpetration by comparing each treatment observation to a control observation with the closest propensity score. Radius matching compares each treatment observation with control observations within a specific radius. Kernel matching compares each treatment observation with all control observations but weights these observations according to their distance from the treatment observation.

Results

Descriptive Statistics

Table 8.1 provides descriptive information about the sample. The means for violence were relatively low but with big variations. This suggested that the use of negative binomial regression would be appropriate. In addition to the mean levels reported in Table 8.1, prevalence statistics (not shown in Table 8.1) suggested that in adolescence (Wave II), 70% reported no IPV victimization, whereas the remaining 30% reported[4] "yes" to at least one violence victimization item. In young adulthood (e.g., Wave IV), 70% reported no victimization or perpetration (0 times), 5% reported perpetration only, 13% reported victimization only, and 12% reported both victimization and perpetration. Such findings on IPV prevalence are similar to those from previous studies (e.g., Whitaker, Haileyesus, Swahn, & Saltzman, 2007). Information regarding other variables is also provided in Table 8.1. The average age of adolescents at Wave II was 16.07 with a range from 13 to 18. Slightly over half (55.66%) were female adolescents. Regarding relationship type at Wave IV, 50.70% were married, 36.94% were cohabiting, and 12.36% were dating.

Negative Binomial Models

Table 8.2 provides the results for the effects of adolescent violence victimization on young adult violence victimization separately for Wave III and Wave IV. Regarding the results in Wave IV, there are several important findings. First, violence victimization at Wave II was significantly associated with violence victimization at Wave IV ($b = .239$, $exp(b)$ or odds ratio $(OR) = 1.270$, $p < .001$). The odds ratio of 1.270 shows that a one unit increase in violence victimization in adolescence was associated with a 27% increase in the predicted risk of violence victimization in young adult relationships. Women reported significantly lower levels of victimization at Wave IV. Regarding relationship type in Wave IV, married and cohabiting young adults reported a higher level of victimization than dating couples. Further, parent–child violence and adolescent general aggression also significantly predicted victimization. A similar pattern was found in Wave III (except for relationship type, which was not applicable due to multiple relationships reported in Wave III).

Findings on young adult perpetration are presented in Table 8.3. For young adults aged 24 to 32 in Wave IV, adolescent victimization was significantly related to young adult perpetration in Wave IV ($b = .159$, $OR = 1.172$, $p < .01$). Women reported significantly higher levels of perpetration than men did. People in marital and cohabiting relationships reported higher levels of perpetration than those in dating relationships. Parent–child violence and general aggression during adolescence also significantly predicted perpetration. A similar pattern was found in Wave III.

Table 8.1 Descriptive Information on Study Variables (Weighted) *(n = 3,520)*

VARIABLES	M OR %	SD	RANGE
Adolescent violence victimization (Wave II)	0.412	0.818	0–5
Young adult violence victimization (Wave III)	0.946	2.019	0–21
Young adult violence perpetration (Wave III)	0.667	1.423	0–14
Young adult violence victimization (Wave IV)	1.193	2.767	0–28
Young adult violence perpetration (Wave IV)	0.705	1.920	0–27
Gender			
Female participants	55.66%		
Male participants (reference)	44.34%		
Relationship type			
Married	50.70%		
Cohabiting	36.94%		
Dating (reference)	12.36%		
Parent–child violence	0.768	1.413	0–5
Adolescent general aggression	0.631	1.146	0–9
Age	16.07	1.176	13–18
Race and ethnicity			
White (reference)	73.32%		
Hispanic	10.70%		
African American	12.54%		
Asian	2.27%		
Other races and ethnicities	1.17%		
Parents' education			
College or more	36.84%		
Some college	21.87%		
High school graduation (reference)	30.90%		
Less than a high school education	10.39%		
Family structure			
Two biological parents (reference)	57.29%		
Stepfamilies	17.75%		
Single-mother families	19.19%		
Single-father families	2.67%		
Other families	3.10%		

Note: The descriptive statistics were based on those who had valid weights and completed data on all four waves, so the *n* in this table is smaller than those used in subsequent analyses where only Wave III or Wave IV (but not both) was used in the model. Relationship type was measured at Wave IV.

Table 8.2 Negative Binomial Regression of the Association Between Adolescent Violence Victimization and Young Adult Victimization at Wave III (n = 3,563) and Wave IV (n = 4,048)

VARIABLES	WAVE III n = 3,563			WAVE IV n = 4,048		
	b	SE	OR	b	SE	OR
Adolescent victimization	0.282***	0.040	1.326	0.239***	0.049	1.270
Gender	−0.396***	0.110	0.673	−0.484***	0.112	0.616
Relationship type						
Married				0.607**	0.192	1.835
Cohabiting				0.695***	0.197	2.004
Parent–child violence	0.153***	0.024	1.165	0.078*	0.034	1.081
Adolescent general aggression	0.142***	0.033	1.153	0.191***	0.042	1.210
Age	−0.112**	0.041	0.894	−0.003	0.045	0.997
Race and ethnicity						
Hispanic	0.155	0.144	1.168	0.135	0.133	1.145
African American	0.050	0.141	1.051	0.432***	0.114	1.540
Asian	−0.310	0.238	0.733	−0.199	0.299	0.820
Other	−0.111	0.465	0.895	0.501	0.257	1.650
Parents' education						
College or more	0.097	0.124	1.102	−0.322**	0.124	0.725
Some college	0.004	0.137	1.004	−0.127	0.142	0.881
Less than high school	0.292	0.174	1.339	0.178	0.166	1.195
Family structure						
Stepfamilies	0.146	0.114	1.157	0.141	0.128	1.151
Single-mother families	0.228	0.114	1.256	0.182	0.134	1.200
Single-father families	0.136	0.312	1.146	0.224	0.357	1.251
Other	−0.008	0.286	0.992	0.371	0.233	1.449
Constant	0.918	0.689		−0.540	0.769	
	$F(16,115) = 11.61, p < .001$			$F(18, 113) = 9.03, p < .001$		

Note: *$p < .05$. **$p < .01$. ***$p < .001$.

In addition to the results presented in Tables 8.2 and 8.3, several additional analyses were conducted. First, considering individual variability in the degree of IPV (Gomez, 2011), the items of victimization and perpetration were split into two subscales: less severe violence (threatened with violence; slapped, hit, kicked partner) and more severe violence (forced sexual behavior, fights resulting in injuries). The two subscales were then treated as separate outcomes. The analyses showed similar results for less severe violence and more severe violence (e.g., for

Table 8.3 Negative Binomial Regression of the Association Between Adolescent Violence Victimization and Young Adult Preparation at Wave III (n = 3,563) and Wave IV (n = 4,048)

VARIABLES	WAVE III n = 3,563			WAVE IV n = 4,048		
	b	SE	OR	b	SE	OR
Adolescent victimization	0.213***	0.042	1.237	0.159**	0.060	1.172
Gender	0.823***	0.108	2.277	0.432***	0.129	1.540
Relationship type						
Married				0.587**	0.279	1.799
Cohabiting				0.754**	0.291	2.125
Parent–child violence	0.180***	0.028	1.197	0.118**	0.038	1.125
Adolescent general aggression	0.106**	0.033	1.112	0.104*	0.052	1.110
Age	−0.115*	0.045	0.891	−0.0380	0.049	0.963
Race and ethnicity						
Hispanic	0.130	0.146	1.139	0.410**	0.150	1.507
African American	0.530***	0.126	1.699	0.565***	0.141	1.759
Asian	−0.217	0.204	0.805	−0.224	0.310	0.799
Other	−0.123	0.528	0.884	0.898*	0.360	2.455
Parents' education						
College or more	−0.099	0.120	0.906	−0.133	0.147	0.875
Some college	−0.112	0.130	0.894	−0.103	0.135	0.902
Less than high school	0.273	0.143	1.314	0.101	0.190	1.106
Family structure						
Stepfamilies	−0.165	0.094	0.848	0.262	0.150	1.30
Single-mother families	−0.128	0.126	0.880	0.193	0.145	1.213
Single-father families	0.044	0.263	1.045	−0.450	0.359	0.638
Other	−0.273	0.238	0.761	−0.0660	0.241	0.936
Constant	0.543	0.745		−1.052	0.878	
	$F(16, 115) = 12.70, p < .001$			$F(18, 113) = 4.27, p < .001$		

Note: *$p < .05$. **$p < .01$. ***$p < .001$.

Wave IV: $b = .255$ for adolescent victimization on young adult less severe victimization; $b = .256$ for adolescent victimization on young adult more severe victimization; $b = .205$ for adolescent victimization on young adult less severe perpetration; $b = .231$ for adolescent victimization on young adult more severe perpetration; $p < .001$ for all).

Additionally, when creating violence measures in Waves II and III, the analyses presented above used averaged violence across multiple relationships in order to obtain a more stable estimate. Another set of analyses was conducted using an alternative approach, in which the most violent relationship among the multiple relationships was selected. The results showed similar patterns of findings as reported in Tables 8.2 and 8.3 ($b = .219, p < .001$ for adolescent maximum victimization on young adult maximum victimization; $b = .163, p < .001$ for adolescent maximum victimization on young adult maximum perpetration).

Propensity Score Matching

In addition to the results reported in Tables 8.2 and 8.3, propensity score matching was conducted to examine whether the above significant findings were robust to selection effect. First, a dichotomous variable of adolescent victimization (0 = *no IPV, control group;* 1 = *IPV, treatment group*) was created. Before running propensity score matching models, negative binomial models were run to make sure that this dichotomous version of adolescent victimization variable was also significantly associated with young adult victimization and perpetration in the same way that the continuous version of the variable was. With significant findings, propensity score matching was then used. Specifically, the propensity scores were generated using a logistic regression model and included the following variables: parent–child violence, general aggression tendency, age (and age squared for Wave III), gender, race and ethnicity, parents' education, and family structure. Once the balancing property was satisfied, the propensity scores were generated. Three types of matching procedures were then used: nearest-neighbor matching, radius matching, and kernel matching (Morgan & Harding, 2006; Turney, 2012).

Table 8.4 shows the results. For example, the average treatment effect for the treated (ATT; see Becker & Ichino, 2002) estimates for adolescent IPV ranged from .379 to .651 (*p* <.001 for all)

Table 8.4   Propensity Score Matching Models Estimating the Consequences of Adolescent Victimization for Young Adult IPV at Wave III and Wave IV

| | TREATMENT | CONTROL | YOUNG ADULT IPV | | | |
	n	n	VICTIMIZATION	SE	PERPETRATION	SE
Adolescent IPV-Wave III						
Nearest-neighbor matching	1,158	908	.379***	.104	281***	.078
Radius matching	1,158	2,831	.651***	.080	.409***	.060
Kernel matching	1,158	2,831	.584***	.066	.355***	.052
Adolescent IPV-Wave IV						
Nearest-neighbor matching	1,183	943	.619***	.138	.460***	.101
Radius matching	1,183	2,828	.746***	.115	427***	.085
Kernel matching	1,183	2,828	.635***	.110	381***	.075

Note: Adolescent IPV (victimization) is dichotomized into a control group (no IPV) and a treatment group (IPV). ***p<.001.

for young adult victimization at Wave III. All three strategies—nearest-neighbor matching, radius matching (radius = 0.1), and kernel matching (bandwidth = 0.06)—yielded the same patterns of findings. The significant findings suggested that, compared with those who did not experience adolescent victimization, adolescents who experienced victimization showed more victimization and perpetration in young adulthood. Taken together, these propensity score models suggested that when adolescents who experienced victimization were matched with adolescents who did not experience victimization, there remained a highly significant association between adolescent victimization and young adult IPV.

Discussion

Hypotheses were proposed that experiences of relationship violence victimization in adolescence would be associated with IPV in young adulthood. Using a sample from Add Health, results from negative binomial regression supported the hypothesis that there was continuity in IPV from adolescence to young adulthood. The results are consistent with social learning theory and the life course perspective and have several important implications for the current understanding of IPV.

First, the findings suggest that being a victim of violence in romantic relationships during adolescence was a significant predictor of violence victimization in romantic relationships in young adulthood. Such a finding is consistent with previous findings on continuity of relationship violence victimization from adolescence to young adulthood (Spriggs et al., 2009). For example, being a victim of relationship violence may lead adolescents to believe that violence is a normal part of romantic relationships and therefore lead them to be less resistant to partner violence in later relationships (Roscoe & Benaske, 1985). The findings from this study advance the current literature in that the sample extended the study period from adolescence to the whole range of young adulthood. The findings provide strong support for the long-term effects of early violence victimization on violence victimization in later young adulthood years.

Second, the findings suggested that being a victim in relationships during adolescence was also predictive of violence perpetration in relationships in young adulthood. Thus, being a victim of relationship violence can also lead to being a perpetrator of violence in future romantic relationships. This is consistent with several studies that found victimization to be a strong predictor of violent behavior (i.e., perpetration; e.g., Bookwala et al., 1992; Cano et al., 1998; Gómez, 2011). One reason could be that, having experienced violence by their partners (i.e., violence victimization), adolescents may learn such violent behavior from their partners and become violent themselves in their current as well as future relationships. Indeed, being a victim in a relationship can create violent interactions that lead to greater likelihood of both victimization and perpetration.

Notably, the association between adolescent violence and young adult violence in relationships found in this study was observed after taking into account parent—child violence and the participants' own general aggression tendencies. Studies have found that experiencing parent—child violence was a strong predictor of later IPV (Cui et al., 2010). Similarly, participants' general aggression was also controlled for in this study because it has been shown to be associated with IPV (Capaldi et al., 2004). Taken together, the significant findings suggested that the continuity of IPV is relationship specific and extends beyond the influence of parent—child violence and general aggression. That is, individuals likely learn relational schemas that provide the basis for if—then inferences regarding the use of IPV in their relationships (Baldwin, 1992).

The findings on gender differences were consistent with several recent studies (e.g., Archer, 2006; Cui et al., 2010; Cunradi, 2007), in that women demonstrated higher levels of perpetration and lower levels of victimization than men did. Such findings were also consistent with social role theory (Eagly, 1987) and family conflict theory (Straus, 2009; White, 2009). One possible reason is that women feel more empowered in relationships, and therefore are more likely to initiate verbal and physical aggression or use violence as a means of conflict resolution (Archer, 2006). Nevertheless, given the inconsistent findings in the existing literature, more studies on this topic are needed.

Regarding relationship type, the findings suggested that couples living together demonstrated higher levels of IPV than dating couples. This is consistent with commitment theory (Johnson & Ferraro, 2000), the investment model (Rusbult, 1980), and several previous studies (e.g., Kurdek, 1998). Indeed, when couples live together, they have more interactions and therefore more opportunities for IPV. Further, couples living together have more shared resources, thus making them less likely to leave the relationship. As previous researchers have argued, these couples perhaps have greater demands for solving their problems rather than simply terminating the relationship. No moderating effects by relationship status were found in this study. This suggested that relationship type was associated with young adult couples' mean level IPV but did not change the association between adolescent IPV and young adult IPV.

This study has several methodological strengths. First, the study included both victimization and perpetration in young adult relationships. Such an approach allowed specific violent behavior rather than a general combined violent interaction to be investigated (Fusco, 2010). Specifically, a link between adolescent victimization and young adult perpetration in addition to young adult victimization was demonstrated. Also worth mentioning, one sexual violence item was included in young adult IPV. Inclusion of this item was important, as many studies have overlooked sexual violence. Second, this study took into consideration several important covariates, including parent—child violence and general aggression. The findings were particularly informative when they were shown to exist over and beyond associations with parent—child violence and own general aggression tendencies. Third, the study focused on variations in absolute violence levels, which complements existing studies, most of which focus on prevalence (e.g., Halpem et al., 2009). Fourth, propensity score matching was used to draw stronger conclusions about the association between adolescent IPV and young adult IPV beyond selection effect. Finally but importantly, this study used longitudinal data from a large, nationally representative sample that covered a period of more than 10 years. The findings therefore provide an additional contribution to the current literature where most studies had data limitations such as cross-sectional design, retrospective reports, nonrepresentative samples, and truncated age range.

Nevertheless, the findings should be viewed in the light of several limitations. First, the measures used in this study were all from participants' self-reports. Self-report of socially undesirable behavior could result in underreporting of such behavior (Cui, Lorenz, Conger, Melby, & Bryant, 2005). The interpretation of gender differences could be complicated, especially when underreporting varies by gender (Gomez, 2011). Second, this study included measures of adolescent violence victimization but not perpetration, due to lack of information in the data set. Specifically, the omission of adolescent perpetration may have led to the overestimation of the association between adolescent victimization and young adulthood perpetration because the study could not control for adolescent perpetration. For example, adolescent violence perpetration could be associated with young adult perpetration. Further, violence perpetration could lead to victimization (e.g., partner hitting back). More complete analyses require both adolescent victimization and perpetration as predictors of victimization and perpetration in romantic relationships in young adulthood (Gomez; Graves et al., 2005). Third, even though parent–child violence was included in the current study, it was retrospectively reported. Such retrospective reports could increase recall bias. Further, future studies may consider including partner characteristics (e.g., partner's age, general aggression) to examine whether they moderate the continuity of violence. Use of partners' reports of violence should also be considered in order to examine the robustness of the present findings. Fourth, even though the study used a longitudinal design, the analyses focused on the association of IPV behaviors from adolescence to young adulthood and did not examine within-person changes. Future studies are needed to investigate the changes in levels of IPV over time to gain a better understanding of the developmental trend of such behavior. Finally, even though the findings of this study established the continuity of IPV, the mechanisms explaining such continuity were not examined. Future research should explore the potential mechanisms to explain such continuity in IPV.

Despite these limitations, the study provided important evidence on the continuation of violence from adolescent relationships to young adult relationships. The findings suggested that experiences of relationship violence may form part of a lifelong continuum that continues from violent adolescent romantic relationship experiences to violence in relationships formed in adulthood (Halpem et al., 2001). Given the continuation and degree of violence among young adults, adolescents are a critical group for intervention.

Note

This research was supported by a grant (1R03HD064836) from the Eunice Kenney Shriver National Institute of Child Health and Human Development. This study uses data from Add Health, a program project directed by Kathleen Mullan Harris and designed by J. Richard Udry, Peter, S. Bearman, and Kathleen Mullan Harris at the University of North Carolina at Chapel Hill, and funded by a grant P01-HD31921 from the National Institute of Child Health and Human Development, with cooperative funding from 23 other federal agencies and foundations. Special acknowledgement is due Ronald R. Rindfuss and Barbara Entwisle for assistance in the original design. Information on how to obtain the Add Health data files is available on the Add Health web site (http://www.cpc.unc.edu/addhealth). No direct support was received from grant P01-HD31921 for this analysis.

References

Archer, J. (2000). Sex differences in aggression between heterosexual partners: A meta-analytic review. *Psychological Bulletin, 126,* 651. doi:10.1037//0033-2909.126.5.651

Archer, J. (2006). Cross-cultural differences in physical aggression between partners: A social-role analysis. *Personality & Social Psychology Review, 10,* 133–153. doi: 10.1207/sl5327957psprl002_3

Arias, I., & Corso, P. (2005). Average cost of per person victimized by an intimate partner of the opposite gender: A comparison of men and women. *Violence & Victims, 20,* 379–391. doi:10.1891/vivi.2005.20.4.379

Arriaga, X. B. (2002). Joking violence among highly committed individuals. *Journal of Interpersonal Violence, 17,* 591–610. doi:10.1177/0886260502017006001

Baldwin, M. W. (1992). Relational schemas and the processing of social information. *Psychological Bulletin, 112,* 461–484. doi:10.1037//0033-2909.112.3.461

Bandura, A. (1977). *Social learning theory.* Englewood Cliffs, NJ: Prentice-Hall.

Becker S., & Ichino, A. (2002). Estimation of average treatment effects based on propensity scores. *Stata Journal, 2,* 358–377. Retrieved from http://www.stata-joumal.com/article.html?article=st0026

Bookwala, J., Frieze, I. H., Smith, C., & Ryan, K. (1992). Predictors of dating violence: A multivariate analysis. *Violence and Victims, 7,* 297–311.

Brown, A., Cosgrave, E., Killackey, E., Purcell, R., Buckby, J., & Yung, A. R. (2009). The longitudinal association of adolescent dating violence with psychiatric disorders and functioning. *Journal of Interpersonal Violence, 24,* 1964–1979. doi:10.1177/0886260508327700

Cano, A., Avery-Leaf, S., Cascardi, M., & O'Leary, K. D. (1998). Dating violence in two high school samples: Discriminating variables. *Journal of Primary Prevention, 18,* 431–446. doi: 10.1023/AT022653609263

Capaldi, D. M., Kim, H. K., & Shortt, J. W. (2004). Women's involvement in aggression in young adult romantic relationships. In M. Putallaz and K. L. Bierman (Eds.), *Aggression, antisocial behavior and violence among girls* (pp. 223–241). New York: Guilford Press.

Chantala, K. (2006). *Guidelines for analyzing Add Health data.* Chapel Hill: Carolina Population Center, University of North Carolina at Chapel Hill.

Cherlin, A. J. (2010). Demographic trends in the United States: A review of research in the 2000s. *Journal of Marriage and Family, 72,* 403–419. doi:10.111 l/j.l741–3737.2010.00710.x

Cleveland, H. H., Herrera, V. M., & Stuewig, J. (2003). Abusive males and abused females in adolescent relationships: Risk factor similarity and dissimilarity and the role of relationship seriousness. *Journal of Family Violence, 18,* 325–339.

Conger, R. D., Cui, M., Bryant, C. M., & Elder, G. H., Jr. (2000). Competence in early adult romantic relationships: A developmental perspective on family influences. *Journal of Personality and Social Psychology, 79,* 224–237. doi:10.1037//0022-3514.79.2.224

Cui, M., Durtschi, J. A., Lorenz, F. O., Donnellan, M. B., & Conger, R. D. (2010). Intergenerational transmission of relationship aggression: A prospective longitudinal study. *Journal of Family Psychology, 24,* 688–697. doi:10.1037/a0021675

Cui, M., Lorenz, F. O., Conger, R. D., Melby, J. N., & Bryant, C. M. (2005). Observer, self, and partner reports of hostile behaviors in romantic relationships. *Journal of Marriage and Family, 67,* 1169–1181. doi: 10.1111/j.1741-3737.2005.00208.x

Cui, M., Ueno, K., Fincham, F. D., Donnellan, M. B., & Wickrama, K. A. S. (2012). The association between romantic relationships and delinquency in adolescence and young adulthood. *Personal Relationships, 19,* 354–366. doi: 10.1111/j.1475-6811.2011.01366.x

Cunradi, C. B. (2007). Drinking level, neighborhood social disorder, and mutual intimate partner violence. *Alcoholism: Clinical and Experimental Research, 31,* 1012–1019. doi: 10.1111/j.1530-0277.2007.00382.x

Eagly, A. H. (1987). *Sex differences in social behavior: A social-role interpretation.* Hillsdale, NJ: Erlbaum.

Elder G. & Giele, J. (Eds.). (2009). *The craft of life course research.* New York: Guilford Press.

Frias, S. & Angel, R. J. (2005). The risk of partner violence among low-income Hispanic subgroups. *Journal of Marriage and Family, 67,* 552–564. doi:10.111 l/j.l741–3737.2005.00153.x

Furman, W., Brown, B. B., & Feiring, C. (1999). *The development of romantic relationships in adolescence.* Cambridge, UK: Cambridge University Press.

Fusco, R. A. (2010). Intimate partner violence in interracial couples: A comparison to White and ethnic minority monoracial couples. *Journal of Interpersonal Violence, 25,* 1785–1800. doi:10.1177/0886260509354510

Gómez, A. M. (2011). Testing the cycle of violence hypothesis: Child abuse and adolescent dating violence as predictors of intimate partner violence in young adulthood. *Youth & Society, 43,* 171–192. doi: 10.1177/0044118X09358313

Graves, K. N., Sechrist, S. M., White, J. W., & Paradise, M. J. (2005). Intimate partner violence perpetrated by college women within the context of a history of victimization. *Psychology of Women Quarterly, 29,* 278–289. doi: 10.1111/j.1471-6402.2005.00222.x

Halpem, C., Oslak, S. G., Young, M. L., Martin, S. L., & Kupper, L. L. (2001). Partner violence among adolescents in opposite-sex romantic relationships: Findings from the National Longitudinal Study of Adolescent Health. *American Journal of Public Health, 91,* 1679–1685. doi:10.2105/AJPH.91.10.1679

Halpem, C. T., Spriggs, A. L., Martin, S. L., & Kupper, L. L. (2009). Patterns of intimate partner violence victimization from adolescence to young adulthood in a nationally representative sample. *Journal of Adolescent Health, 45,* 508–516. doi:10.1016/j.jadohealth.2009.03.011

Harris, K. M., Halpem, C. T., Entzel, P., Tabor, J., Bearman, P. S., & Udry, J. R. (2008). The National Longitudinal Study of Adolescent Health [research design]. Retrieved from http://www.cpc.unc.edu/projects/addhealth/design

Heyman, R. E., & Slep, A. M. S. (2002). Do child abuse and interparental violence lead to adulthood family violence? *Journal of Marriage and Family, 64,* 864–870. doi:10.1111/j.1741-3737.2002.00864.x

Holt, M., & Espelage, D. (2005). Social support as a moderator between dating violence victimization and well-being among African American and Caucasian adolescents. *School Psychology Review, 34,* 309–328.

Johnson, M. P., & Ferraro, K. J. (2000). Research on domestic violence in the 1990s: Making distinctions. *Journal of Marriage and the Family, 62,* 948–963. doi:10.1111/j.1741-3737.2000.00948.X

Kimmel, M. (2002). "Gender symmetry" in domestic violence: A substantive and methodological research review. *Violence Against Women, 8,* 1332–1363. doi:10.1177/107780102762478037.

Kurdek, L. A. (1998). Relationship outcomes and their predictors: Longitudinal evidence from heterosexual married, gay cohabiting, and lesbian cohabiting couples. *Journal of Marriage and the Family, 60,* 553–568. doi: 10.2307/353528.

Makepeace, J. M. (1983). Life events stress and courtship violence. *Family Relations, 32,* 101–109. doi:10.2307/583984.

Meier, A., & Allen, G. (2009). Romantic relationships from adolescence to young adulthood: Evidence from the National Longitudinal Study of Adolescent Health. *Sociological Quarterly, 50,* 308–335. doi: 10.1111/j.1533-8525.2009.01142.x

Morgan, S. L. & Harding, D. J. (2006). Matching estimators of causal effects: Prospects and pitfalls in theory and practice. *Sociological Methods and Research, 35,* 3–60. doi: 10.1177/0049124106289164.

O'Leary, K. D., Barling, J., Arias, I., Rosenbaum, A., Malone, J., & Tyree, A. (1989). Prevalence and stability of physical aggression between spouses: A longitudinal study. *Journal of Consulting and Clinical Psychology, 57,* 263–268. doi:10.1037//0022-006X.57.2.263

O'Leary, K. D., & Slep, A. M. S. (2003). A dyadic longitudinal model of adolescent dating aggression. *Journal of Clinical Child and Adolescent Psychology, 32,* 314–327. doi: 10.1207/S15374424JCCP3203_01

Roscoe, B. & Benaske, N. (1985). Courtship violence experienced by abused wives: Similarities in patterns of abuse. *Family Relations, 34,* 419–424. doi: 10.2307/583582.

Rusbult, C. E. (1980). Commitment and satisfaction in romantic associations: A test of the investment model. *Journal of Experimental Social Psychology, 16,* 172–186. doi: 10.1016/0022-1031(80)90007-4.

Silverman, J. G., Raj, A., Mucci, L. A., & Hathaway, J. E. (2001). Dating violence against adolescent girls and associated substance use, unhealthy weight control, sexual risk behavior, pregnancy, and suicidality. *JAMA; Journal of the American Medical Association, 286,* 572–579. doi:10.1001/jama.286.5.572.

Simons, R. L., Lin, K., & Gordon, L. C. (1998). Socialization in the family of origin and male dating violence: A prospective study. *Journal of Marriage and the Family, 60,* 467–478. doi: 10.2307/353862.

Smith, P. H., White, J. W., & Holland, L. J. (2003). A longitudinal perspective on dating violence among adolescent and college-age women. *Journal of American Public Health Association, 93,* 1104–1109. doi: 10.2105/AJPH.93.7.1104.

Spriggs, A. L., Halpem, C. T., & Martin, S. L. (2009). Continuity of adolescent and early adult partner violence victimization: Association with witnessing violent crime in adolescence. *Journal of Epidemiology and Community Health, 63,* 741–748.

Stark, E. (2007). *Coercive control; How men entrap women in personal life.* Oxford, UK: Oxford University Press.

Straus, M. A. (2009). Why the overwhelming evidence on partner physical violence by women has not been perceived and is often denied. *Journal of Aggression, Maltreatment and Trauma, 18,* 552–571. doi:10.1080/10926770903103081.

Straus, M. A., Hamby, S. L., Boney-McCoy, S., & Sugarman, D. B. (1996). The revised Conflict Tactics Scales (CTS2): Development and preliminary psychometric data. *Journal of Family Issues, 17,* 283–316. doi:10.1177/019251396017003001.

Tjaden, P., & Thoennes, N. (2000). Prevalence and consequences of male-to-female and female-to-male intimate partner violence as measured by the National Violence Against Women Survey. *Violence Against Women, 6*, 142–161. doi:10.1177/10778010022181769.

Tumey, K. (2012). Pathways of disadvantage: Explaining the relationship between maternal depression and children's problem behaviors. *Social Science Research, 41*, 1546–1564. doi: 10.1016/j/bbr.2011.03.031.

Whitaker, D. J., Haileyesus, T., Swahn, M., & Saltzman, L. S. (2007). Differences in frequency of violence and reported injury between relationships with reciprocal and nonreciprocal intimate partner violence. *American Journal of Public Health, 97*, 941–947. doi:10.2105/AJPH.2005.079020

White, J. W. (2009). A gendered approach to adolescent dating violence: Conceptual and methodological issues. *Psychology of Women Quarterly, 33*, 1–15. doi:10.1111/j.l471-6402.2008.01467.x

White, J. W., Smith, P. H., Koss, M. P., & Figueredo, A. J. (2000). Intimate partner aggression—What have we learned? Comment on Archer. *Psychological Bulletin, 126*, 690–696. doi:10.1037//0033-2909.126.5.690

Williams, T. S., Craig, W., Connolly, J., Pepler, D., & Laporte, L. (2008). Risk models of dating aggression across different adolescent relationships: A developmental psychopathology approach. *Journal of Consulting and Clinical Psychology, 76*, 622–632. doi:10.1037/0022-006X.76.4.622

Chapter 7: Concluding Remarks

This chapter introduced us to the study of crime victimization from the perspective of social learning and life course theories, underscoring the importance of understanding the traumatic effects of experiencing violence and how that experience can shape the course of future behavior. The research study provided us with compelling evidence that the experience of violence during adolescence can mediate the perpetration of violence in inmate relationships during adulthood. This generational continuity of behavior was found to exist even after controlling for various personal traits and social characteristics. This predictive consistency paints a clear picture of the need to address crime victimization as it impacts one's perception of the world, how to respond to conflict and aggression, and the normalization of violence in order to experience a healing that will impact their future choice of responding in like manner.

Victimization, Distress, and Recurrent Patterns of Behavior

Introduction

The concept of recurrent victimization has been studied and analyzed to better inform crime prevention techniques and strategies that identify crime targets and recognize risk factors. From a practical standpoint, this study has contributed to the plethora of knowledge and understanding of crime control practices such as target hardening, crime prevention by environmental design, and other applications stemming from the paradigm of routine activity and rational choice theories. Another application of recurrent victimization that has received attention in recent literature is the psychological effect of victimization on individuals on their personal identity and perception of self and how this affects their future interactions and acceptance of abuse and victimization.

The vast discipline of victimology has dedicated a significant portion of theoretical and conceptual analysis to the crimes of child abuse, child neglect, and maltreatment of children. Perhaps this is one area of study requiring the utmost of attention and dedication to be able to grasp the true extent of the problem, address its underlying causes, and intervene to prevent it recurrence. Researchers have described this type of crime as a "bundling" of various behaviors that encompass forms of physical violence, verbal abuse, emotional cruelty, and other sources of trauma. These collective actions require the study of each behavioral component individually to unravel their unique effects on the future outcome of experiences for child victims. The current study in this chapter focus on just that, drawing on differential oppression theory to explore the impact that child verbal and emotional abuse by parents has on their likelihood of victimization in later adolescent years.

Guiding Questions

As you read, consider the following questions:

1   What effect does parental maltreatment have on the psychological well-being of children and their ability to develop healthy relationships?

2   Do adverse experiences in childhood lead to problematic behaviors in children as adolescents?

3   Is there a correlation between child abuse and neglect and the development of emotional disorders such as anxiety and depression?

Key Terms

child maltreatment   Refers to actions that are intentional or negligent that result in harm or potential of harm to a child, including physical, sexual, and emotional abuse and child neglect.

differential oppression theory   A theoretical understanding of experiencing oppression and its impact on the development of maladaptive behaviors such as passive acceptance of abuse, the exercise of illegitimate coercion, and retaliation.

recurrent victimization   When the victim of a crime experiences more than one incident of victimization.

Sticks and Stones and Broken Bones

The Influence of Parental Verbal Abuse on Peer Related Victimization

Lisa Hutchinson and David Mueller

Introduction

Despite growing social prohibitions against cruelty to children, child maltreatment continues to be a serious, albeit low profile, problem in the United States. Child maltreatment can take various forms including neglect, physical and sexual abuse, and lower-level forms of aggression such as verbal and emotional abuse. Because acts of maltreatment typically take place indoors, away from the prying eyes of neighbors and public officials, measuring the true extent of the problem is difficult at best. While many studies have examined the effect of physical abuse, sexual abuse, and neglect, very few studies have investigated the impact of psychological maltreatment, such as verbal and emotional abuse on children. In fact, the true extent of this type of maltreatment is more difficult to document than physical and sexual abuse (Hussey, Chang, and Kotch 2006). However, a study by Straus and Field (2000) found that 10 to 20 percent of toddlers and 50 percent of teenagers have experienced severe psychological aggression by parents, which included acts such as cursing, threatening to send the child away, calling the child dumb, or otherwise belittling them. Given these numbers, it is disturbing that this type of maltreatment is understudied.

Historically, when measures of verbal and/or emotional abuse have been examined, they commonly get lumped into a battery of independent variables rather than isolated as specific topics of interest (see Loos and Alexander, 1997; Finkelhor et al., 2005). Because different types of maltreatments tend to occur simultaneously, that is, they are bundled together as a package, it becomes important for researchers to unravel the specific effects of verbal abuse from other sources of trauma (Browne and

Finkelhor, 1986; Finkelhor et al., 2005). It is this type of research that will help to unravel the true effects of verbal and emotional abuse on children, and upon which this study focuses.

The present study is designed to build on current knowledge about child maltreatment by exploring the impact that emotional/verbal abuse has on childhood experiences. Drawing on differential oppression theory (Regoli and Hewitt, 2003), the study seeks to understand whether children who are victims of emotional and/or verbal abuse by their parents are more likely to adapt to the oppression through the use of internalization. The study examines whether these children passively accept their inferior status, suppress their hatred for the abuser, and internalize the hatred. Specifically, the study focuses on examining the common internalizing disorder of low self-esteem to determine the impact of the emotional and verbal abuse; the impact being measured by whether these children are more likely to be victimized by their peers.

Previous Research

A review of the extant literature indicates that a linkage between parental maltreatment and the development of emotional and behavioral problems among children has been established (Brown, 1984; Duncan, 1999; Gross and Keller 1992; Hart, Binggeli and Brassard, 1998; Heck and Walsh, 2000). For example, Felitti et al. (1998) and Dube et al. (2003) found that adverse experiences during childhood increase the risk for depressed affect, suicide attempts, multiple sexual partners, sexually transmitted diseases, smoking, and alcoholism. Burgess, Hartman, and McCormack (1987) found that maltreated children often exhibit psychosocial ailments such as bed-wetting, stomachaches, fear of being alone, sleep problems, poor self-concept ratings, distrust of others, and psychological withdrawal (Kaufman and Ciccheti, 1989). Hart et al. (1998) found that maltreated children often experienced anxiety, low self-esteem, suicidal thoughts, emotional disorders, antisocial disorders, learning impairments, and poor physical health. In addition to internalizing disorders such as these, child maltreatment has also been associated with delinquent behavior. Trickett and Kuczynski (1986) as well as Paperny and Deisher (1983) found that maltreated children were more likely than non-maltreated children to exhibit higher levels of aggression towards both persons and property.

While there is a documented link between parental verbal abuse and a negative impact on children, identifying this abuse and its impact on children is a daunting task for several reasons. Though many people assume that they "know it when they see (or rather, hear) it," researchers have been unable to reach an agreed upon definition of what constitutes verbal abuse. In the absence of precise definitions, it is difficult to isolate the detrimental effects of this specific type of abuse (Vissing et al., 1991). Second, bystanders often dismiss incidents of verbal abuse as a private matter or as normal parental discipline (Davis, 1996).[1] Third, given its low-profile nature, existing data on parental verbal abuse is often limited to the most egregious cases.

Fourth, due to problems of under-reporting, official estimates of the extent of verbal abuse are widely assumed to be speculative and unreliable (Straus and Gelles, 1986). Additionally, Zingraff et al. (1993) noted that prior research has also been confounded by methodological limitations (particularly the use of cross-sectional data), which may help to over-exaggerate the maltreatment-delinquency relationship (see Heck and Walsh, 2000).

One of the few rigorous studies that sought to isolate the main effects of parental verbal abuse on delinquency was a study conducted by Vissing et al. (1991). These authors defined parental verbal/symbolic aggression as "communication intended to cause psychological pain to another person, or a communication perceived as having that intent" (Vissing et al., 1991:224). The communicative act may be active or passive, and verbal or nonverbal. Examples include name-calling or nasty remarks (active, verbal), slamming a door or smashing something (active, nonverbal), and stony silence or sulking (passive, nonverbal; Vissing et al., 1991).

Vissing et al.'s (1991) data showed that nearly two-thirds of maltreated children experienced some form of verbal aggression, with an average of 12.6 verbal attacks occurring across the 12-month study period.[2] Results also indicate that verbal aggression by parents was significantly related to childhood problems with aggression, delinquency, and interpersonal relationships even after controlling for gender, age, and socioeconomic status. More importantly, Vissing and her colleagues found that parental verbal abuse was most strongly related to higher levels of childhood aggression irrespective of whether parents themselves were physically aggressive.

Further research suggests that children who are verbally abused by parents also tend to experience negative outcomes such as academic failure (Hart et al., 1998; Kinard, 2001; Wodarski et al., 1990), early experimentation with drugs and alcohol (Perez, 2000), low self-esteem (Briere and Runtz, 1988; Hart et al., 1998), and loneliness and social isolation (Loos and Alexander, 1997). If these studies are indeed correct, then it is safe to assume that the popular childhood saying, "sticks and stones may break my bones, but words will never hurt me," is largely incorrect.

Differential Oppression

The detrimental effect of verbal and emotional abuse is deeply rooted in the theoretical literature. Specifically, Regoli and Hewitt (2000) offer a relatively new theory, differential oppression theory, which provides an appropriate explanation for the various pathways that such abuse may have on children. These theorists suggest that acts of delinquency and self-defeating behaviors often arise out of power struggles between children and adults (e.g., parents, teachers).

According to these theorists, compared to adults, children have little power in today's society and few resources with which to exercise control over their social environments. Kids who perceive themselves as constantly "under the thumb" of adults often become resentful, particularly when they are made to submit to the will of adults in social settings. While power differentials between parents and children are common in many households, Regoli and Hewitt (2000:157) feel that parental authority is oppressive, particularly when parents exercise their power in ways that "prevent children from developing a sense of self as a subject rather than an object," which is often the case in verbal and emotional abuse situations.

Clearly, some degree of parental controls, particularly at an early age, is necessary in order for children to develop self-control. Gottfredson and Hirschi (1990:97), for example, have argued that in order for children to develop self-control, parents must "(1) monitor the child's behavior; (2) recognize deviant behavior when it occurs; and (3) punish such behavior." Monitoring and oversight of children's behaviors are considered critical parental functions insofar as they help children to understand when they have crossed the boundaries of acceptable behavior. However, Regoli and Hewitt (1994) argue that some parents have a tendency to accomplish these tasks in a demeaning manner and under the guise of "knowing and doing what is good for them" (Miller, 1984). While some degree of parental oversight and guidance is necessary, even beneficial for conventional socialization, Gottfredson and Hirschi's own theory implies that parents must, at some point, relax these controls. Yet, Regoli and Hewitt's differential oppression theory suggests that some parents never treat their children as individuals, but rather as objects to be controlled. Further, such parents rarely learn to "lighten up."

The theory of differential oppression is organized around four guiding principles (Regoli and Hewitt, 2006). First, children are easy targets for adult oppression because of their lack of power. Second, oppression of children by adults occurs in various contexts and the degree of oppression to which a child is exposed occurs along a continuum. Third, oppression can lead to various childhood adaptations, including passive acceptance, exercise of illegitimate coercive power, manipulation of one's peers, and retaliation. Fourth, the use of adaptive reactions by children reinforces adults' views that they are "inferior, subordinate beings and as troublemakers" (Ferguson, 2001).

Oppression can occur at both the macro and micro levels, yet it is the oppression that occurs within the micro levels, especially the family, that has the greatest effect on the child's use of delinquent adaptations. As previously mentioned, the theory identified four specific ways in which children adapt to oppression. The first adaptation is passive acceptance of one's status as inferior. According to Regoli and Hewitt (2006), passive acceptance is a form of obedience that is grounded in fear. Although children "learn to hate" their oppressors, they remain fearful of them and thus suppress the hatred. This adaptation, according to the authors, typically leads to internalizing disorders such as alcoholism, drug addiction, and low self-esteem. Passive acceptance is the most common adaptation to oppression and is more common in females.

A second adaptation to oppressive parenting is the exercise of illegitimate coercive power. By participating in delinquent activities, children are able to establish a sense of control or power over their own lives. These acts are simply maladaptive expressions of a desire for autonomy and control. Low-level adaptations may include challenges to parental authority (e.g., sassing, back-talking), defiant body language, sexual misbehavior, illicit drug use, and criminal acts (Ferguson, 2001; Regoli and Hewitt, 2006).

A third adaptation is manipulation of one's peers or siblings in an attempt to enhance social power. To some extent, this adaptation can be seen as a natural extension of deviant role-playing learned from one's own parents (e.g., might makes right). That is, oppressed children may feel the need to manipulate others, such as bullying weaker children, in an attempt to regain a sense of empowerment or control over their own lives (Regoli and Hewitt, 2006).

A fourth adaptation (e.g., retaliation) suggests that some children react to their oppressive environments by lashing out either directly at one's own parents or indirectly at other symbols of their oppression (e.g., school vandalism). While this adaptation may be manifested in outward acts of aggression such as assaulting or even killing one's own parents, anger and resentment may also be directed inwards through acts of self-mutilation, depression, or suicide (Regoli and Hewitt, 2006).

The use of retaliation seems highly plausible since so much of the prior research on child maltreatment suggests that oppression leads to violence. But is it possible that the opposite reaction is just as valid? Clearly, children react to stress in a variety of different ways. Some 70 years ago, Robert Merton (1938) argued that some individuals adapt to stressful situations (e.g., strain) by withdrawing or "retreating" into a world of drugs, alcohol, and low self-esteem. In a similar manner, Regoli and Hewitt (1994) note that the first reaction, passive acceptance, involves identifying with the oppressor. "Oppressed people frequently internalize the image of their oppressors and adapt their guidelines: they become fearful of freedom" (Regoli and Hewitt, 1994:210). In extreme cases, it may be possible for some individuals to develop an acute sense of self-hatred, leading them to engage in behaviors that enhance the odds of further victimization, or as Regoli and Hewitt suggest, to simply become fearful of a world in which they are not oppressed. If these possibilities exist, then parental verbal abuse is not as benign as it first appears. In fact, it suggests that verbal and emotional abuse may increase the odds that a child will be picked on throughout adolescence and perhaps even into early adulthood.

The Current Study

The broad research question addressed in this study is whether there is a relationship between parental emotional and/or verbal abuse, self-esteem, and victimization by peers. The first research question asks whether children who are victims of emotional and/or verbal abuse are more likely to adapt to oppression through the use of passive acceptance as evidenced by low self-esteem. The second research question asks whether those individuals with low self-esteem resulting from parental emotional and/or verbal abuse are more likely to be victimized by their peers.

It is important to note that because different types of maltreatments tend to occur simultaneously, that is, they are bundled together as a package, the use of multivariate analysis can help to obscure important relationships. Thus, unraveling the specific effects of verbal abuse requires researchers to treat this category of maltreatment separately in order to disentangle the various sources of trauma (Browne and Finkelhor, 1986; Finkelhor et al., 2005). It is this type of research that will help to unravel the true effects of verbal and emotional abuse on children and upon which this study focuses.

The study contributes to the literature in a number of ways. First, the study furthers the work of Vissing et al. (1991) in examining the effect of parental emotional abuse on children. Specifically, it is the first study to examine the effects of such abuse on both verbal and physical victimization by peers. Second, much of the current literature has lumped measures of verbal and/or emotional abuse into a battery of independent variables. The current study seeks to unravel the specific effects of verbal abuse by examining its effect separately in order to disentangle the various sources of trauma. Third, the study provides an empirical examination of differential oppression theory. Although first offered in 1991, this theory has not been subjected to many empirical examinations (Regoli and Hewitt, 2006).

Methods

Data for this study were taken from a needs assessment administered to 6th, 8th, 10th, and 12th grade students at four public school districts in a rural southern county during the 2001–2002 school year. All students enrolled in these grades during the specified time period were invited to participate; students were not randomly selected to participate in the study. While the sample may appear to be somewhat of a convenience sample, it should be noted that all students in the designated grades were given equal opportunity to participate in this study and as such it can be described as a purposive sample. Further, after obtaining Human Subjects approval and school board consent in each of the four school districts, passive consent forms were utilized. Therefore, only those students whose parents returned a consent form indicating they did not want their children to participate in the study were excluded; students who did not return a consent form were allowed to participate in the study.[3] A total of 3,654 surveys were administered to students.

However, not all students who participated in the survey were included in the sample. Validity in self-report measures relies on respondents' honesty and candor (Hagan, 1993). Therefore, attempts were made to eliminate from the sample those individuals who did not tell the truth when answering the survey. The current study employed a method of eliminating cases based on invalid data that is consistent with the suggestions of Brown and Zimmerman (2004), who found that youth who indicated they were not honest were more likely to provide inconsistent responses than those who indicated they had been honest. Through the use of an honesty question, as suggested by Brown and Zimmerman (2004), the decision was made to eliminate the responses of those students who indicated they did not tell the truth on the survey. Specifically, students were eliminated from the sample if they responded that they "never" told the truth or told the truth only "once in awhile" or "sometimes." While this may seem a drastic step, if students' self-reported delinquency is to be believed, then their self-reported dishonesty should also be believed (see Brown and Zimmerman, 2004, for a complete discussion of the use of honesty questions as a method of eliminating inaccurate self-report responses).[4]

Another significant source of missing data can be attributed to the instrument design. Questions assessing demographic information were included at the end of the survey instrument. As a number of students did not complete the entire survey and, as a result, failed to complete any item on the last page, this created a large amount of missing demographic data. Because race and gender are two of the most influential predictors of juvenile delinquency, all respondents who did not indicate their race or gender were excluded from the analysis. To determine whether the missing data affected the findings, respondents in the sample were compared to district representations of gender and race. Relative to the district, the sample was disproportionately female and white.[5] Further, the model under study was estimated after excluding gender and race and the results indicated that neither the strength nor the direction of associations changed.

After accounting for missing data on the dependent variables, the final sample consisted of 2,126 respondents with the following demographic characteristics. Fifty-eight percent of the respondents were female and twenty-seven percent were nonwhite. Sixth graders accounted for 26 percent of the sample; eighth graders accounted for 32 percent; tenth graders for 19 percent; and twelfth graders for 23 percent.

Measures

The reliability of the constructs and measures utilized in this study has been well established in previous studies. In addition, a pilot test of the survey was conducted with seventh graders in a local after school program.[6] Prior to analyses, students' responses to index items were summed to create indices. Additionally, principal component analyses were run for each of the indices and the results were analyzed. The range of factor loadings for the study indices was 0.67 to 0.89. In each of the indices, all of the inter-item correlations were statistically significant. Reliability measures, specifically Cronbach's alpha, were then calculated for each index (See Appendix A for item constructs, reliability measures, and factor loadings).

Independent Variables

This study used two independent variables (parental punitiveness and self-esteem). Students' levels of self-esteem were measured using an index originally developed by Rosenberg (1965). This ten-item index sought information regarding students' feelings of self-worth, perceptions regarding their ability to achieve, and satisfaction with themselves. Two dimensions surfaced from the factor analysis of these ten items: positive self-worth and ability to succeed. Positive self-worth consisted of five items and ranged from 0 to 20 with a mean of 13.70 and a standard

Table 9.1   Inter-Correlation Matrix and Descriptive Statistics.

VARIABLES	PEER VICTIMIZATION	ABILITY TO SUCCEED	PARENTAL EMOTIONAL ABUSE	POSITIVE SELF-WORTH	GRADE	RACE
Ability to succeed	−.284 **					
Parental punitiveness	.275 **	−.302 **				
Positive self–worth	−.210 **	.099 **	−.198 **			
Grade	−.153 **	.083 **	.107 **	.090 **		
Race	−.049 **	.042	−.055 **	.014	.017	
Gender	.133 **	−.039	−.032	.002	−.006	.005
Mean	5.35	15.93	6.17	13.70		
SD	7.13	5.31	5.76	5.40		
Range	0–40	0–20	0–24	0–0		
Cronbach's α	.74	.87	.88	.89		

* $p < 0.01$. ** $p < 0.001$ (two tailed).

deviation of 5.40. High scores were indicative of increased self-esteem. Ability to succeed consisted of five items and ranged from 0 to 20 with a mean of 15.93 and a standard deviation of 5.31. Responses for these five items were recoded in reverse numerical order to reflect a positive image of ability to succeed. High scores were indicative of increased perceptions of ability to succeed. Students' experiences with parental emotional abuse were measured along a five item index and ranged from 0 to 24 with a mean of 6.17 and a standard deviation of 5.76. High scores were indicative of high levels of parental punitiveness (see Table 9.1 for descriptive statistics).

To determine the extent to which students had experienced parental emotional abuse, frequencies were run. Table 9.2 shows the results of the specific types of parental emotional abuse experienced by students. The most reported type of parental maltreatment was yelling

Table 9.2   Student Experiences with Parental Emotional Abuse.

FREQUENCY OF EXPERIENCE(S)	TYPE OF EMOTIONAL ABUSE				
	IGNORE	BLAME	YELL	NAG	THREATEN TO SLAP
Never	49 %	36 %	27 %	45 %	66 %
Seldom	24 %	22 %	24 %	18 %	15 %
Sometimes	18 %	21 %	27 %	16 %	9 %
Often	5 %	11 %	12 %	11 %	5 %
Almost always	4 %	10 %	11 %	10 %	6 %

(73 percent), followed by being blamed by their parents when the student was not at fault (64 percent). Over half of the students also indicated that their parents yelled at them or ignored them.

Dependent Variable

Students' experiences with peer victimization within the last year were measured along five items taken from Kaufman et al. (1999) and ranged from 0 to 40 with a mean of 5.35 and a standard deviation of 7.13. A high score on this index was indicative of an increased level of victimization by peers. Dependent variable frequencies were initially run to determine the extent to which students experienced victimization by their peers at school. Table 9.3 shows the extent to which students experienced such behaviors.

Table 9.3   Student Experiences with Peer Victimization at School During the Last Year

FREQUENCY OF EXPERIENCE(S)	TYPE OF VICTIMIZATION				
	VERBAL VICTIMIZATION	PHYSICAL VICTIMIZATION	VICTIMIZATION BY THEFT	VICTIMIZATION BY FORCE	THREATENED WITHOUT WEAPON
Never	41 %	61 %	50 %	90 %	77 %
At least once during last year	25 %	18 %	32 %	5 %	13 %
Once every 3 months	5 %	4 %	4 %	1 %	2 %
Once every 2 months	2 %	2 %	2 %	1 %	1 %
Once a month	3 %	2 %	3 %	1 %	1 %
Two or more times a month	3 %	2 %	2 %	1 %	1 %
Once a week	4 %	2 %	2 %	1 %	1 %
Twice a week	5 %	2 %	1 %	0 %	1 %
Once a day	11 %	6 %	3 %	1 %	2 %

Data reveal that a majority of students had been yelled at, cursed, insulted, or teased by another student at least once during the last year. The majority of students had also been the victim of theft at least once during the last year. Approximately 40 percent of students indicated that they have been hit, kicked, pushed, or shoved at least once during the last year. Almost 60 percent of the students indicated that they had been the victims of verbal abuse by their peers at least once during the last year. About one-quarter of the students indicated that they had been threatened (without a weapon) by another student during the last school year. One-tenth of the students indicated that they had been the victims of a forceful theft attempt during the last year.

Control Variables

In an effort to account for social inequality, three socio-demographic control measures were utilized: race, gender, and grade level. Responses to the question concerning race and gender were originally coded as string values. The answers were converted to numeric values and dummy coded. Race was defined as 0 for non-white and 1 for white. Gender was defined as 0 for female and 1 for male. Responses for grade level were coded as 1 for 6th grade, 2 for 8th grade, 3 for 10th grade, and 4 for 12th grade.

Results

To examine the relationship among study variables, bivariate and diagnostic analyses were run. All of the study variables, except grade level, were significantly correlated with the dependant measure (peer victimization). Inter-item correlations among the independent variables ranged from 0.00 to 0.30, which suggests that multicollinearity did not present a significant problem (see Grimm and Yarnold, 2000). The highest correlation existed between ability to succeed and parental maltreatment ($r = 0.30$, $p < 0.001$). Further, the highest variance inflation factor in the regression models was 1.25 and the lowest tolerance figure was 0.79, which also indicates few problems with multicollinearity (Fox, 1991).

Regression Models

To examine the central tenets of differential oppression theory, a series of step-wise regression analyses were conducted, which focus on assessing four relationships: (1) the relationship between parental emotional abuse and self-esteem; (2) the relationship between self-esteem and peer victimization; (3) the relationship between parental emotional abuse and peer victimization; and (4) the relationship between parental emotional abuse and peer victimization, controlling for self-esteem. In all models significance was measured at the 0.05 level.

The purpose of this study was to determine the effect of oppression, specifically emotional and verbal abuse by parents, and self-esteem on peer-related student victimization. The effects of abuse were examined regarding both verbal and delinquent victimization by peers.

Model 1 examines the relationship between self-reported levels of parental emotional abuse and self-esteem. The two self-esteem indices were regressed on the parental emotional abuse index and the socio-demographic variables. The results (see Table 9.4) indicate that the socio-demographic variables and parental verbal and emotional abuse account for seven percent of the variation in students' levels of positive self-worth ($F = 38.97$, $p < 0.001$). Model 2 results (also in Table 9.4) indicate that the socio-demographic variables and parental and verbal emotional abuse account for 10 percent of the variation in students' feelings regarding their ability to succeed in life ($F = 31.30$, $p < 0.001$).

Table 9.4   OLS Regression: Positive Self-Worth and Ability to Succeed Regressed on Parental Emotional Abuse and Demographic Controls.

	MODEL 1: EXPERIENCE WITH PARENTAL EMOTIONAL ABUSE AND POSITIVE SELF-WORTH		MODEL 2: EXPERIENCE WITH PARENTAL EMOTIONAL ABUSE AND ABILITY TO SUCCEED	
	B (SE)	BETA	B (SE)	BETA
Constant	13.627 *** (.496)		14.575 *** (.662)	
Male	−.050 (.218)	−0.005	−.502 (.296)	−.048
White	−.153 (.240)	−0.013	.499 (.324)	1.538
Grade	.224 *** (.050)	0.095	.316 (.067)	.133
Parental emotional and verbal abuse	−.231 *** (.019)	−0.255	−.285 (.027)	−10.390
F (df)	38.977 (4) ***		31.302 (4) ***	
R^2 (adjusted R^2)	.068 (.067)		.099 (.095)	

*$p < .05.$ **$p < .01.$ ***$p < .001$ (two tailed).

Prior to examining the effect of self-worth and ability to succeed on peer victimization, the first model includes only the demographic variables. The results of this analysis are presented in Table 9.5 (Model 3). Results show that demographic variables account for four percent of the variation in peer victimization ($F = 33.23$, $p < 0.001$). The second research question examined the significance of the relationship between self-esteem and peer victimization. To answer this question, the peer victimization index was regressed on the two self-esteem indices, as well as the socio-demographic variables. The results are also shown in Table 9.5 (Models 4 and 5). After accounting for the socio-demographic indicators, positive self-worth explained an additional six percent of the variation in students' victimization by peers ($F = 60.61$, $p < 0.001$). Males, younger students, and those students who had a negative perception of their self-worth were more likely to be victimized at the hands of their peers. The ability to succeed explained an additional eight percent of the variation, after accounting for the socio-demographic indicators ($F = 39.70$, $p < 0.001$). Similar to previous results, males, younger students, and those who had a negative perception of their ability to succeed were more likely to be the victims of verbal or delinquent activities by their peers.

The third research question examined whether there is a relationship between parental emotional abuse and peer victimization. To answer this question, the peer victimization index was regressed on the parental emotional abuse index. The results are shown in Table 9.6 (Model 6). After accounting for the socio-demographic indicators, this model explained an additional ten

Table 9.5   OLS Regression: Peer Victimization Regressed on Positive Self-Worth and Ability to Succeed

	MODEL 3: CONTROLS		MODEL 4: POSITIVE SELF-WORTH		MODEL 5: ABILITY TO SUCCEED	
	B (SE)	BETA	B (SE)	BETA	B (SE)	BETA
Constant			12.415 *** (.734)		12.231 *** (1.001)	
Male	1.320 *** (.190)	.140	1.929 *** (.289)	.137	1.767 *** (.388)	.126
White	−.040 (.210)	.000	−.571 (.318)	−.037	−.641 (.425)	−.042
Grade	−.390 *** (.040)	−.150	−.342 *** (.065)	−.107	−.199 * (.088)	−.063
Positive self-worth			−.346 *** (.028)	−.256		
Ability to succeed					−.401 *** (.037)	−.301
F (df)	33.23 (3) ***		60.607 (4) ***		39.702 (4) ***	
R² (Adjusted R2)	.04 (.04)		.102 (.100)		.121 (.118)	

$*p < .05.$ $**p < .01.$ $***p < .001$ (two tailed).

percent of the variation ($F = 90.39$, $p < 0.001$). Males, younger students, and those who had experienced emotional and/verbal abuse by their parents were more likely to be emotionally and/or verbally abused by their peers.

The final research question examined whether there is a relationship between parental emotional abuse and peer victimization, controlling for self-esteem. To answer this question, the peer victimization index was regressed on the parental emotional abuse index, the positive self-worth index, and the ability to succeed index. The results are shown in Table 9.6 (Models 7 and 8). In Model 7, parental emotional and verbal abuse and positive self-worth accounted for an additional 13 percent of the variation in peer victimization, after controlling for the socio-demographic indicators ($F = 87.45$, $p < 0.001$). Males, younger students, those who had low levels of self-esteem, and those who experienced high levels of parental emotional and verbal abuse were more likely to be victimized by their peers. The full model (Model 8) explained an additional 23 percent of the variation in peer victimization (after accounting for demographics), indicating that gender, grade level, positive self-worth, ability to succeed, and parental abuse were all important correlates ($F = 68.83$, $p < 0.001$). Parental emotional and verbal abuse demonstrated the strongest association with peer victimization ($\beta = 0.31$, $p < 0.001$), followed by low levels of positive self-worth ($\beta = -0.19$, $p < 0.001$), perceived inability to succeed ($\beta = -0.19$, $p < 0.001$), gender ($\beta = 0.14$, $p < 0.001$), and grade level ($\beta = -0.09$, $p < 0.01$).

Table 9.6 OLS Regression: Peer Victimization Regressed on Parental Emotional Abuse, Positive Self-Worth, Ability to Succeed, and Controls.

	MODEL 6: PARENTAL EMOTIONAL ABUSE		MODEL 7: PARENTAL EMOTIONAL ABUSE AND POSITIVE SELF-WORTH		MODEL 8: PARENTAL EMOTIONAL ABUSE, POSITIVE SELF-WORTH, AND ABILITY TO SUCCEED	
	B (SE)	BETA	B (SE)	BETA	B (SE)	BETA
Constant	6.728 *** (.629)		9.548 *** (.741)		11.779 *** (1.021)	
Male	1.946 *** (.278)	.138	1.969 *** (.278)	.141	1.896 *** (.358)	.136
White	−.320 (.306)	−.021	−.277 (.308)	−.018	−.447 (.393)	−.029
Grade	−.548 *** (.063)	−.172	−463.000 *** (.064)	−.146	−.282 ** (.082)	−.090
Positive self-worth			−.238 *** (.028)	−.176	−.230 *** (.032)	−.193
Ability to succeed					−.253 *** (.036)	−.189
Parental emotional and verbal abuse	.400 *** (.024)	.327	.349 *** (.025)	.286	.399 *** (.035)	.310
F (df)	90.386 (4) ***		87.453 (5) ***		68.831 (6) ***	
R^2 (Adjusted R^2)	.141 (.140)		.173 (.171)		.269 (.265)	

$^*p < .05.$ $^{**}p < .01.$ $^{***}p < .001$ (two tailed).

To test for robustness, the final model was regressed only on the predictor variables found to be significant in Model 8 of Table 9.6. All variables that were significant in the full model were also significant in the trimmed model.

Discussion

To date, only a handful of rigorous studies have been designed specifically to explore the empirical effects of parental verbal/emotional abuse on children. The few studies that do exist have typically found that children who are physically and emotionally abused by their parents are likely to grow up to become physically and emotionally abusive adults (Dube et al., 2003; Felitti et al., 1998; Paperny and Deisher, 1983; Trickett and Kuczynski, 1986; Vissing et al., 1991). Other studies have found that maltreated children also suffer high levels of emotional and behavioral problems that enhance their likelihood of engaging in delinquent behaviors (Brown, 1984;

Gross and Keller, 1992; Heck and Walsh, 2000). However, no study has ever attempted to explore the opposite relationship—the possibility that verbal and emotional abuse by parents leads to similar kinds of victimizations by one's own peers. Findings reported in this study investigate this possibility and reveal that, rather than becoming physically aggressive, some verbally abused children may grow up to become perennial victims who suffer repeated attacks at the hands of their peers.

Data analyzed in this study suggest that parental emotional and verbal abuse, as measured by acts of rejection, condemnation, yelling, nagging, threats of violence, and slapping significantly increases the odds that a child will become the victim of similar abuse at the hands of his/her peers, both in terms of verbal victimization and physical victimization. Conversely, it appears that children, who develop higher levels of self-esteem, as measured by positive self-worth and a perceived ability to succeed, experience fewer acts of victimization by peers.

Though the data cannot speak to causality, the analysis indicates that a possible pathway leading from abuse in the home to later victimization by peers has its roots in the development of self-concept ratings. From the data, it can be posited that children who are emotionally and verbally abused by their parents develop low levels of self-esteem, which, in turn, undermines perceptions of self-worth and perceived ability to succeed in life. As suggested by differential oppression theory, children who suffer parental psychological maltreatment often identify with their adult oppressors and "become fearful of freedom" (Regoli and Hewitt, 1994:210). The effect of this identification often results in low self-worth. Children become accustomed to oppression, believe that they do not deserve anything better, and feel powerless to change their situation. As such, they become prime targets for peer victimization. Children who suffer from a perceived lack of ability to succeed may, in turn, avoid certain kinds of activities that pose a risk of additional failure and/or rejection by others. For instance, boys who avoid certain types of activities, particularly those that involve demonstrations of masculinity and physical prowess, may become targets of further ridicule, bullying, and related forms of delinquent victimization by peers.

With this said, it is important to note that gender appears to be an important determinate in the kinds of peer victimization children experience. For example, Olweus (1994) has noted that boys tend to experience more physical forms of bullying (e.g., unprovoked attacks, acts of intimidation, and threats of violence), whereas girls tend to experience more subtle forms of bullying (e.g., slandering, rumor-mongering, social exclusion, and manipulation of friendship relationships). Though boys are not exempt from psychological attacks by their peers, the aim of such attacks is often intended to raise questions about the victims' masculinity and/or their gender orientation.

Control variables employed in this study suggest that younger boys tend to suffer the highest rates of bullying and peer victimization. Similar research reported by DeVoe et al. (2004) supports this conclusion. Their study, like the current one, also concluded that race is not a significant factor in predicting peer-related victimization.

Limitations of Data

Although the present study contributes to the literature, it is not without limitations. First, the study relies on cross-sectional data collected from students in a rural Southern state. Further, because of various issues, original data collection efforts were unable to elicit a systematic random sample and were forced to include all willing students in the study. While it may appear to some to be a convenience sample, it should be noted that all students in the designated grades were given equal opportunity to participate in this study and as such it can be described as a purposive sample. However, the method in which the data were collected does limit the findings.[7] As such, caution should be taken since the findings in the current study are not offered as ones upon which broad generalizations may be made, but rather as an exploratory study that may help guide future researchers in their attempts to examine this issue more closely.

Another important limitation in the current study is that the temporal ordering of victimization and offending could not be established (a common weakness with cross sectional designs). Future studies, however, should seek to clarify the developmental ordering of parental abuse and peer victimization.

Conclusion

The findings seem to support the tenets of differential oppression theory, especially the utilization of the passive acceptance adaptation. Specifically, the study supports the assertion that passive acceptance of oneself as inferior often leads to internalized manifestations such as low self-esteem or perceived inability to succeed. In the current study, children who experienced lower levels of self-esteem as a result of emotional and verbal abuse were more likely to be victimized by their peers. Again, although the findings do not indicate causality, they do provide an indication that self-concept is an important determinant in how children deal with parental abuse.

Findings in the current study differ from those set forth in previous studies that suggest children who experience verbal abuse by their parents are more likely to become violent or aggressive. While the results do not speak to the aggressive or violent behaviors of psychologically maltreated children, they do demonstrate that psychological maltreatment increases the risk of peer victimization, at least within the study sample. These findings indicate that more exploration into the effects of parental verbal and emotional abuse on future peer-related victimization is needed. Of importance is an examination of the perpetrators of the peer-related victimization. Are these children also the victims of emotional and verbal abuse by adults? If so, why do some externalize the abuse, while others internalize it? Children with high levels of self-esteem were less likely to be victimized by their peers. With this in mind, the role of self-esteem should be more closely examined. Specifically, what is the effect of emotional and verbal abuse on self-esteem and how does that translate into the utilization of the various adaptive reactions by children? Also, do anger and resentment, as speculated by differential oppression theory, affect the utilization of particular adaptive reactions? Finally, given the literature that suggests different victimization patterns based on gender, further examinations should also pay close attention to the role of gender.

In conclusion, the findings reported in this study suggest several policy implications that may be helpful for parents, teachers, and school administrators to consider in their daily interactions with children.

Policy Implications

Parents should be made more aware of the harmful effects of verbal and emotional abuse. As recommended by the American Academy of Pediatrics (AAP), pediatricians are in an optimal position to impart such knowledge, through brochures, verbal guidance, and even home visitation (Kairys, Johnson, and the Committee on Child Abuse and Neglect, 2002). Parents should also be encouraged to engage in more positive means of discipline such as redirection and rewarding children's successes, rather than punishing their failures and/or shortcomings. In this way, self-esteem can be built in children. Safety, acceptance, and praise are also likely to reinforce children's positive self-concept. They will learn to see themselves as capable and valued. By monitoring behavior, yet allowing children to make their own decisions when appropriate, parents can teach responsibility and help raise self-confidence.

Teachers, school counselors, and social workers who work with children are also encouraged by this study to focus on building positive feelings of self-worth in children and cautioned against using unnecessary verbal and emotional abuse as a control device. Moreover, they are encouraged to expand conventional understandings of child maltreatment to include not only incidences of physical/sexual abuse and neglect but also acts of verbal and emotional cruelty against children. Finally, witnessing acts of verbal and emotional abuse should be grounds for reporting and/or preventing so-called "normal" acts of aggression against children by adults.

Finally, school administrators are in a powerful position to help establish a school climate or culture that is focused both on learning and community well-being. A positive school climate can extend beyond the classroom when school personnel are willing to reinforce the importance of positive, pro-social values such as tolerance, harmony, violence prevention, and the need for basic civility in everyday life. Nel Noddings (1992) of Stanford University has an entire curriculum for schools built around an ethic of care (see also Katz, Noddings, and Strike, 1999). Even without embracing Noddings' philosophy of education, administrators are cautioned through this study to attend to the issue of how adults (e.g., teachers, parents, counselors) relate to children, and the negative effects of any abuse of their relationship with children—even at the seemingly harmless level of verbal and emotional abuse.

Endnotes

1 Davis (1996) found that parental threats of corporal punishment are fairly common occurrences in public places (e.g., malls, restaurants, zoos). Given the prevalence of threats made in public places, Davis believes that similar threats of violence against children are even more common in private places, particularly in a child's own home. Yet, because verbal abuse, especially incidents such as threats and intimidation, are so pervasive, witnesses tend to ignore them as "normal" (e.g., typical, unimportant) occurrences.

2 Vissing et al. (1991) are careful to point out that estimates of both the incidence and "chronicity" of these acts are likely to be lower bound estimates given parents' reluctance to candidly divulge known instances of verbal attacks, or because some may truly have forgotten.

3 Only students whose parents signed the consent forms specifying that their children were *not* allowed to participate in the study were excluded from the survey. Thirty-two such forms were received.

4 A total of 579 surveys were excluded as a result of reporting dishonesty on the survey. In results not presented here, we examined the responses of the students who were eliminated from the sample for dishonesty against those who indicated they were honest. Our findings were consistent with those of Brown and Zimmerman (2004). Those students who reported being dishonest did, in fact, provide more inconsistent answers than those who reported being honest.

5 Males made up 51% of the students in the four school districts and 65% of the students in the four districts were White. Furthermore, in results not presented here, we utilized independent sample t-tests to estimate the difference in mean scores for the indices. There was no significant difference for the mean scores on the index between the two groups. For each index, those who did not indicate their race and/or gender scored significantly higher on the index than those who did (and were thus included in the sample). Additionally, we estimated Model 8 using all cases but excluding race and gender as control variables. The associations among positive self-worth, ability to succeed, emotional/verbal abuse, and peer victimization remained statistically significant and in the same direction as the associations with the sample under study here. As such, we argue that the relationships presented here are conservative estimates of the actual relationships that would have been demonstrated had we been able to include all respondents instead of only those who completed the race and gender measures.

6 A variety of issues, such as tracking, conflicts in schedules, constraints placed by school administrators prohibited a representative sample from being selected.

7 The pilot test was administered to this group for several reasons: (1) they approximated the lowest targeted grade level to be included in the study, (2) they would not be unduly biased by participating in the pilot study, as they were 7th graders who were not intended to be included in the study sample, and (3) the program specifically targeted educationally disadvantaged students. Therefore, they were the most appropriate group to provide practical and logistical information such as the determination of total time needed for the administration, the comprehension level of the intended subjects, and the appropriateness of question wording.

References

Briere, J. & Runtz, M. (1988). Multivariate correlates of childhood psychological and physical maltreatment among university women. *Child Abuse and Neglect, 12,* 331–341.

Brown, S. (1984). Social class, child maltreatment, and delinquent behavior. *Criminology, 22,* 259–278.

Brown, T. and Zimmerman, R. (2004). Are adolescents accurate reporters of their alcohol use? *Individual Differences Research, 2,* 17–25.

Browne, A., & Finkelhor, D. (1986). Impact of child sexual abuse: A review of the research. *Psychological Bulletin, 99,* 66–77.

Burgess, A., Hartman, C., & McCormack, A. (1987). Abused to abuser: antecedents of socially deviant behaviors. *American Journal of Psychiatry, 144,* 1431–1436.

Davis, P. (1996). Threats of corporal punishment as verbal aggression: a naturalistic study. *Child Abuse & Neglect, 20,* 289–304.

DeVoe, J., Katharin, P., Kaufman, P., Miller, A., Noonan, M., Snyder, T., & Baum, K. (2005). *Indicators of school crime and safety: 2004.* Washington, DC: U.S. Departments of Education and Justice.

Dube, S., Felitti, V., Dong, M., Giles, W., & Anda, R. (2003). The impact of adverse childhood experiences on health problems: Evidence from four birth cohorts dating back to 1900. *Preventive Medicine, 37,* 268–277.

Duncan, R. (1999). Maltreatment by parents and peers: The relationship between child abuse, bully victimization, and psychological stress. *Child Maltreatment, 4,* 45–55.

Felitti, V., Anda, R., Nordenberg, D., Williamson, D., Spitz, A., Edwards, V., Koss, M., & Marks, J. (1998). Relationship of childhood abuse and household dysfunction to many of the leading causes of death in adults. *American Journal of Preventive Medicine, 14,* 245–258.

Fergsuon, A. (2001). *Bad boys: Public schools and the making of black masculinity.* Ann Arbor, MI: University of Michigan Press.

Finkelhor, D., Omrod, R., Turner, H., & Hamby, S. (2005). The victimization of children and youth: A comprehensive, national survey. *Child Maltreatment, 10,* 5–25.

Fox, J. (1991). *Regression diagnostics.* Newbury Park, CA: Sage.

Gottfredson, M., & Hirschi, T. (1990). *A general theory of crime.* Stanford, CA: Stanford University Press.

Grimm, L., & Yarnold, P. (2000). *Reading and understanding multivariate statistics* (6th ed.). Washington, DC: American Psychological Association.

Gross, A., & Keller, H. (1992). Long-term consequences of childhood physical and psychological maltreatment. *Aggressive Behavior, 18,* 171–185.

Hagan, F. (1993). *Research methods in criminal justice and criminology.* New York, NY: Macmillan Publishing.

Hart, S., Binggeli, N., & Brassard, M. (1998). Evidence for the effects of psychological maltreatment. *Journal of Emotional Abuse, 1,* 27–58.

Heck, C., & Walsh, A. (2000). The effects of maltreatment and family structure on minor and serious delinquency. *International Journal of Offender Therapy and Comparative Criminology, 44,* 178–193.

Hussey, J., Chang, J., & Kotch, J. (2006). Child maltreatment in the United States: Prevalence, risk factors, and adolescent health consequences. *Pediatrics, 118,* 933–942.

Kairys, S., Johnson, C., & the Committee on Child Abuse and Neglect. (2002). The psychological maltreatment of children—Technical report. *Pediatrics, 109,* 68–70.

Katz, M., Noddings N., & Strike, K. (1999). *Justice and caring for common ground in education: professional ethics in education series.* New York, NY: Teachers College Press.

Kaufman, J., & Cicchetti, D. (1989). Effects of maltreatment on school-age children's socioemotional development: Assessments in a day-camp setting. *Developmental Psychology, 25,* 516–524.

Kaufman, P., Ruddy, S. A., Chandler, K. A., & Rand, M. R. (1999). *Indicators of school crime and safety, 1999.* Washington, DC: US Departments of Education and Justice.

Kinard, E. M. (2001). Characteristics of maltreatment experience and academic functioning among maltreated children. *Violence and Victims, 16,* 323–337.

Loos, M., & Alexander, P. (1997). Differential effects associated with self-reported histories of abuse and neglect in a college sample. *Journal of Interpersonal Violence, 12,* 340–360.

Merton, R. (1938). Social structure and anomie. *American Sociological Review, 3,* 672–682.

Miller, A. (1984). *For your own good.* New York, NY: Farrar, Straus & Giroux.

Noddings, N. (1992). *The challenge to care in schools: An alternative approach to education.* New York, NY: Teachers College Press.

Olweus, D. (1994). Bullying: Too Little love, too much freedom. *School Safety Update,* May:1–4.

Paperny, D., & Deisher, R. (1983). Maltreated adolescents: The relationship to a predisposition toward violent behavior and delinquency. *Adolescence,* 18:499–506.

Perez, D. (2000). The relationship between physical abuse, sexual victimization, and adolescent illicit drug use. *Journal of Drug Issues,* 30:641–662.

Regoli, R., & Hewitt, J. (1994). *Delinquency in society* (2nd ed.). Boston, MA: McGraw Hill.

Regoli, R., & Hewitt, J. (2000). *Delinquency in society* (4th ed.). Boston, MA: McGraw Hill.

Regoli, R., & Hewitt, J. (2003). *Delinquency in society* (5th ed.). Boston, MA: McGraw Hill.

Regoli, R., & Hewitt, J. (2005). *Delinquency in society* (6th ed.). Boston, MA: McGraw Hill.

Rosenberg, M. (1965). *Society and the adolescent self-image.* Princeton, NJ: Princeton University Press.

Straus, M. A., & Gelles, R. J. (1986). Societal change and change in family violence from 1975–1985 as revealed by two national surveys. *Journal of Marriage and the Family,* 48:465–479.

Straus, M. A., & Field, C. J. (2000). *Psychological aggression by american parents: National data on prevalence, chronicity, and severity.* Washington, DC: American Sociological Association.

Trickett, P. K., & Kuczynski, L. (1986). Children's misbehaviors and parental discipline strategies in abusive and nonabusive families. *Developmental Psychology,* 22:115–123.

Vissing, Y., Straus, M. A., Gelles, R. J., & Harrop, J. (1991). Verbal Aggression by parents and psychosocial problems of children. *Child Abuse and Neglect,* 15:223–238.

Wodarski, J., Kurtz, D., Gaudin J., & and Howling, P. (1990). Maltreatment and the school-age child: Major academic, socioemotional, and adaptive outcomes. *Social Work,* 35:506–513.

Zingraff, M., Leiter, J., Myers, K., & Johnsen, M. (1993). Child maltreatment and youthful problem behaviors. *Criminology,* 31:173–202.

Appendix 9A   Index Item, Reliabilities, and Factor Loadings.

VARIABLE	CATEGORIES	RESPONSE FORMAT	FACTOR LOADINGS
Peer victimization (α = .74)	Another student yelled, cursed, insulted, or teased you.	Nine point Likert Scale	.71
	Another student hit, kicked, pushed, or shoved you.	from never (0) to once	.78
	Student has had something stolen at school.	a day (8).	.68
	Student has had money or things taken from them by force.		.67
	Another student has threatened them without a weapon.		.75
Parental emotional and verbal maltreatment (α = .88)	Feels parents ignore them.	Five point Likert Scale	.77
	Feels parents blame them for things not their fault.	from never (0) to	.82
	Parents yell at students.	always (4).	.84
	Parents nag student.		.79
	Parents threaten to slap student.		.81
	Parents actually slap students.		.70
Positive self-worth (α = .89)	I feel that I am as worthy as other people.	Five point Likert Scale	.81
	I feel that I have a number of good qualities	from never (0) to	.88
	I am able to do most things as well as most people.	always (4).	.81
	I have a positive attitude about myself.		.85
	On the whole, I am satisfied with myself.		.84
Ability to succeed (α = .87)	*Responses for these five items were recoded in reverse numerical order to reflect a positive image of ability to succeed.*	Five point Likert Scale from never (0) to always (4).	
	Overall, I feel like a failure.		.84
	I don't feel like I have much to be proud of.		.70
	I wish I could have more respect for myself.		.82
	I certainly feel useless at times.		.88
	At times, I think I am no good at all.		.89
Race	Original response format was: a) white, b) African-American, c) Asian-American, d) Hispanic, and e) other. These answers were then recoded from string to numeric values.	The variables were dummy coded as follows: 0) for nonwhites and 1) for whites.	

VARIABLE	CATEGORIES	RESPONSE FORMAT	FACTOR LOADINGS
Gender	Original response format was a = female, b = male.	The variables were dummy coded as follows: 0) for female and 1) for male.	
Grade Level	Original responses for grade level were coded as numeric values as follows: 1) for 6th grade, 2) for 8th grade, 3) for 10th grade, and 4) for 12th grade.		

Chapter 8: Concluding Remarks

The study in this chapter presented us with a very important research question in the exploration of victim studies in child abuse and neglect. Drawing upon the tenets of differential oppression theory, the authors attempt to establish a correlation between parental emotional and/or verbal abuse and the self-esteem of children subjected to this type of oppression and its outcome on their future experience of victimization by adolescent peers. Their study contributed significantly to our understanding of the mediating effects of low self-esteem resulting from parents subjecting children to emotionally and verbally abusive behaviors. The long-term detrimental effects of persistent yelling, condescending speech, rejection, and threat of violence have an impact on a child's development of low self-esteem and their future passive acceptance of abusive behavior and violent victimization by adolescent peers. This finding has important policy implications for acting to ensure that parents are educated about the harmful effects of emotional and verbal abuse on long-term child development and the child's future risk of victimization. Additionally, the role of psychologists, social workers, counselors, and child advocates in addressing feelings of self-worth when working with child victims of abuse becomes of utmost importance to their growth and healthy mental development.

Evolving Trends in Victimology Studies

Victimization and Vulnerability

Introduction

One aspect of victimization studies that appears to be problematic is the exploration of victim traits and characteristics that might account for variations in the distribution of crime and the selection of victim targets. In this discipline, we tend to shy away from concepts that can be misconstrued as victim blaming or placing any sort of responsibility on the victim for their own experience with crime. While this is important and has been the subject of legislative and policy strides in protecting victims of crime from revictimization by the criminal justice system and society in general, it is nonetheless imperative to explore research aspects of victimization that can expand our knowledge of human physical and psychological vulnerability to certain behaviors.

The very nature of human interaction relies significantly on the ability of individuals to communicate information; rely on factors such as trust and sharing; and exchange goods, services, and knowledge based on the expectation of truth and integrity. Entangled with human error and misperception, these interactions become further strained by various forms of deception and malicious actions that place certain individuals at a greater risk of victimization in different contexts. One area of victimology that has dedicated a significant amount of research to the study of crime victimization in different contexts is cyber deviance. In this chapter, our reading selection focuses on the impact of Internet technology in manipulating human psychological weaknesses such as greed and fear and the response to phishing solicitations through email.

Guiding Questions

As you read, consider the following questions:

1. Are there different aspects of human behavior, thoughts, and vulnerabilities that can impact the chances of becoming the victim of a crime?

2. What benefit is there to studying human psychological traits and how they influence interactions with other individuals who are potentially predatory?

3. Can certain situational characteristics alter the outcome of cyber deviance when it comes to such crimes as phishing?

4. How should programming and policies designed to prevent Internet scams consider variations in human responses?

Key Terms

heuristic-systematic processing model (HSM)   A model of human response to communication as a function of variations in the reception and processing of persuasive messages.

phishing   "Baiting" a potential victim by appearing as a trustworthy entity in some form of electronic communication in order to obtain sensitive data such as credit card or bank account information, usernames, passwords, or other personal information.

social engineering   Within the context of information security, this refers to the manipulation of psychological aspects of human behavior, response, and vulnerability to influence a person's actions to provide confidential or personal information.

Got Phished?

Internet Security and Human Vulnerability

Sanjay Goel, Kevin Williams, and Ersin Dincelli

1 Introduction

Social engineering attacks, largely orchestrated through phishing messages, remain a persistent threat that allows hackers to circumvent security controls (Aaron & Rasmussen, 2015). One can manipulate people into revealing confidential information by exploiting their habits, motives, and cognitive biases (Mitnick & Simon, 2002). Countering these characteristics to prevent users from succumbing to phishing emails remains an important research problem that will have a strong impact on information security.

Early research on phishing focused on users' ability to detect structural and physical cues in malicious emails, such as spelling mistakes and differences between the displayed URL and the URL embedded in the HTML code (Jakobsson & Ratkiewicz, 2006). More recent work has focused on cognitive limitations that prevent users from distinguishing between fraudulent and legitimate messages (Dhamija, Tygar, & Hearst, 2006; Downs, Holbrook, & Cranor, 2006). People often process email messages quickly by using mental models or heuristics and, hence, overlook cues that indicate deception (Luo, Zhang, Burd, & Seazzu, 2013). In addition, people's habits, needs, and desires make them vulnerable to phishing scams (Workman, 2007). Watters (2009) concludes that phishing messages elicit automatic modes of response based on structural cues rather than careful deliberation using cognitive processing. If the message suggests it will fulfill, or threaten, important needs, the reader may overlook cues that indicate deception.

Sanjay Goel, Kevin Williams and Ersin Dincelli, "Got Phished? Internet Security and Human Vulnerability," *Journal of the Association for Information Systems*, vol. 18, no. 1, pp. 22-43. Copyright © 2017 by Association for Information Systems.

Awareness of phishing messages among users has increased, but so has the sophistication of these messages (Jagatic, Johnson, Jacobsson, & Menczer, 2007). Hackers design phishing messages today to affect basic human emotions (e.g., fear, greed, and altruism) and often target specific groups to exploit their specific needs. Hackers sometimes even contextualize the messages to individuals by incorporating their personal information (spear phishing). For instance, a new phishing scam has arisen on dating applications; a user (bot) triggers a conversation with another user (victim) and, after a few exchanges, sends a link (malicious) to the victim ostensibly with a picture in an attempt to get the victim to click on it (Jones, 2015). Research shows that spear phishing is more effective than broad phishing messages, which target a wider population (e.g., Wang, Herath, Chen, Vishwanath & Rao, 2012), but few, if any, studies have compared the relative effectiveness of messages contextualized to elicit different emotions in users. We designed our study to fill this gap in the literature.

In this paper, we consider different cognitive biases that inveigle users to click on phishing messages. We focus on the content and framing of these messages and identify the types of messages most likely to deceive users. Specifically, we examine the effectiveness of different contextualized messages designed to exploit basic human emotions and desires. Research in cognitive neuroscience shows that emotions play an important role in decision making by subconsciously steering people toward gains and away from losses (Damasio, 1994). A carefully constructed phishing email may activate basic emotions that nudge people to comply with the disguised malicious request. For example, fear stems from the perception of threat to one's wellbeing and acts as a warning signal for forthcoming harm (LeDoux, 2003). Fear increases immediate precautionary action to protect oneself and one's possessions (Leventhal, 1970). A typical banking scam exploits fear reactions by suggesting that users will have their account blocked unless they change their credentials by clicking on a Web link. The fear of losing something valuable might result in users divulging their credentials to the hacker (Kim & Kim, 2013). Greed is another emotion that hackers who craft phishing emails often exploit (Hong, 2012). The infamous "Nigerian Prince" scam capitalizes on the allure of easy money to deceive and cheat its victims. Coupling greed with scarcity, such as "only a few laptops left" or "the first two hundred respondents are eligible", may establish a sense of urgency (or a fear of losing out) that increases the perceived value of the object (Cialdini, 1993) and may can cloud rational judgment even more (Hong, 2012).

Of course, phishing attacks can manipulate many other emotions and related psychological traits, such as curiosity, anger, patriotism, friendship, altruism, vanity, authority, community belongingness, and sense of duty. In this study, we examine how the framing of message content affects susceptibility to phishing attempts. We manipulate fraudulent email messages to appeal to different desires or needs and contextualize the messages by framing them as either potential gains or losses. We tested the effectiveness of the different messages in a naturalistic setting using college students. The research design also allowed us to examine differences in susceptibility among different subgroups (e.g., males vs. females; academic major).

This paper proceeds as follows: in Section 2, we discuss the extant literature. In Section 3, we discuss the theoretical basis for our research and our hypotheses. In Section 4, we present the research design and review the experimental methodology. In Section 5, we present the experimental results. In Section 6, we discuss the results in detail and present the study's implications and limitations. Finally, in Section 7, we conclude the paper.

2 Literature Review

Phishing's foundations lie in human decision making where one persuades someone else to make non-rational instinctive and emotional choices rather than more deliberative and logical choices—in this case, on clicking malicious links. Anderson and Moore (2009) emphasize that heuristics and biases drive decision making, especially when the user is emotionally aroused and in unusual conditions. The research on phishing correspondingly focuses on understanding the triggers for non-rational decisions and aims to steer users towards more deliberative and rational choices. A large fraction of phishing research involves testing users' susceptibility to phishing when faced with different scenarios and evaluating the impact of interventions on reducing this susceptibility as we discuss further in the literature review. One can broadly classify phishing research into two categories: 1) susceptibility to phishing, including psychological factors, individual differences (e.g., cognitive limitations, personality traits, identity, and demographics), and structural features of the messages (e.g., presence of misspelling); and 2) solutions to reduce susceptibility to phishing (e.g., toolbars and training). Subsequently, we summarize the literature and lay out the motivation for our research in the following subsections.

2.1 Susceptibility to Phishing

Psychological factors are at the core of human vulnerability to deception, and some exploratory work has focused on ascertaining these factors as they relate to phishing. The factors that this research has examined include cognitive limitations, familiarity, emotional arousal, social psychological factors (e.g., trust, fear, and commitment), personal relationships, personality traits (e.g., neuroticism, extroversion, and openness), and demographic variables. We discuss this research in three segments (i.e., psychological triggers, individual differences, and visual/structural cues).

2.1.1 Psychological Triggers for Phishing

Extant literature has attributed phishing susceptibility to human cognitive limitations and psychological manipulation of victims as we discuss further in this section. Dhamija et al. (2006) discuss human cognitive limitations in being able to detect fraudulent messages. They identify five broad categories of strategies that users employ to identify fraudulent websites based on content, URL analysis, URL protocol (i.e., https), and other visual security cues such as use of

HTTPs, bar padlocks, and security certificates. All of the subjects in the study performed at a 40 percent error rate, and the authors found no statistically significant difference between the methods the participants used to identify fraudulent websites.

Downs et al. (2006) investigated the impact of risk familiarity in informing phishing defense strategies. They provided fake identities to twenty subjects and asked them to roleplay email and Web interactions. They found that, when users were exposed to specific scams and could comprehend their modalities, they could protect themselves. However, participants could not defend themselves when exposed to deception that was sophisticated or novel. These results suggest that heuristics that many increase one's susceptibility to phishing scams guide individuals' responses to email requests (e.g., "Amazon is a reputable company, and I may have already given them the information they are asking for; therefore, I would be comfortable giving the information to them again.").

Workman (2008) investigated whether the factors that result in successful marketing campaigns also affect the success of social engineering attacks such as phishing and pretexting. He reviewed the literature on security, management, and social psychology and highlighted important factors that may impact the success of social engineering attacks: trust, fear, commitment, and reactance. He examined the relation between these factors and employee susceptibility to social engineering attacks and found a strong positive correlation of social engineering with trust, fear, and commitment—both for self-reported and observed behavior.

Some work has focused specifically on spear-phishing attacks; that is, phishing emails customized to a specific individual or organization rather than to a specific demographic (students, elderly, women, etc.) or the general population at large. Jagatic et al. (2007) examined whether email senders' personal relationships altered the recipient's susceptibility to phishing attacks. They sent (benign) phishing messages to university students that appeared to come from friends of the subjects using data mined from their profiles online social networks. The manipulated messages produced an 80 percent susceptibility rate compared to only 16 percent for the control group, suggesting that people are more likely to be deceived if messages appear to come from someone in their social network. The study identified the gender of the user (recipient) from their Facebook profile and found that the sender's gender did not have an independent effect on susceptibility. Halevi, Lewis, and Nov (2015) found that 25 of 40 employees (62.5%) clicked on a link embedded in a fraudulent email purportedly from the company's IT manager and addressed to them individually. Egelman, Cranor, and Hong (2008) tested the effectiveness of security warnings by simulating spear-phishing attacks that exposed users to such warnings. They found out that the participants were susceptible to spear-phishing emails and that active phishing warnings demonstrated greater protection against spear phishing.

Butavicius, Parsons, Pattinson, and McCormac (2015) conducted a phishing experiment to examine how phishing messages created using three social engineering strategies (authority, scarcity, and social proof) influenced users' judgments of how safe a link is in an email.

Their experiment included genuine, phishing, or spear-phishing messages. They found that content based on authority was the most effective strategy in convincing users that the link was safe while social proof was the least effective. Also, 71 percent of participants had difficulty distinguishing between genuine and spear-phishing emails and fell prey to phishing emails. Wright, Jensen, Thatcher, Dinger, and Marett (2014) used principles of persuasion to design emails and test their efficacy in phishing susceptibility. They found that messages designed with principles of persuasion were more effective; however, the efficacy of different principles varied.

2.1.2 Individual Differences in Susceptibility to Phishing

Different individuals have a different propensity to becoming victims of phishing attacks based on behavioral traits, demographic characteristics, personality, and habituation; we discuss these individual differences in this section. Moody, Galletta, Walker, and Dunn (2011) extensively investigated individual differences in susceptibility to phishing. They examined disposition to trust and distrust, curiosity, entertainment drive, boredom proneness, lack of focus, risk propensity, and level of Internet usage, attachment to the Internet, and Internet anxiety as the traits related to susceptibility. They found that several of the traits were good indicators of susceptibility to phishing, most notably trust, curiosity, boredom proneness, and risk propensity.

Sheng, Holbrook, Kumaraguru, Cranor, and Downs (2010) focused on demographic characteristics (gender, age, and education level) as predictors of phishing susceptibility. They found that women were more susceptible to phishing than men and that the 18- to 25-year-old individuals formed the most susceptible age group. Flores, Holm, Nohlberg, and Ekstedt (2015) examined cultural differences and personal determinants (e.g., intention to resist social engineering, security awareness, and training) of phishing. In contrast to Sheng et al. (2010), they did not find a significant correlation between phishing behavior and age or gender in their study. They found significant positive correlations between employees' observed phishing behavior and intention, security awareness, and training; however, the strength of correlations differed across different cultures (i.e., US, India, and Sweden). Correlations of both intention and security awareness to phishing behavior were not significant for American and Indian individuals but were for Swedish individuals. The correlation between training and phishing behavior was stronger for the American individuals compared to Swedish individuals and non-significant for Indian individuals.

Halevi, Lewis, and Memon (2013) used the five-factor model of personality to examine the relation between personality and vulnerability to phishing. The five behavior traits in this model are neuroticism, extroversion, openness, agreeableness, and conscientiousness. The authors sent a sample of 100 college students (83% male; ages 17–21) (benign) phishing emails with a malicious link. Specifically, they sent the sample an email that promised a prize of an Apple product to test the individuals' susceptibility to phishing, and the authors considered that they had phished the participants if they clicked on the embedded link. Results showed that females were significantly more likely to be "phished" than men and that students high in neuroticism were more susceptible to the phishing attacks. While interesting, the research does not delve into the psychological reasons of the susceptibility or compare different motivators in susceptibility to phishing.

Vishwanath (2015) investigated the role of habit and cognitive processing in victimization to phishing. He sent 200 randomly selected students a phishing email with an attached survey. He obtained measures of the subjects' level of heuristic and systematic processing, information sufficiency, and personality traits. He hypothesized that systematic (as opposed to heuristic) processing of data would result in lower incidence of phishing victimization. He found that students with low emotional stability had impulsive email habits such as reactively checking email and responding to email notifications and were more likely to click on phishing email links. We elaborate further on systematic and heuristic processing in our theoretical development in Section 3.

2.1.3 Physical Attributes of Messages in Susceptibility to Phishing

Some research has investigated the impact of phishing emails' physical features on users' susceptibility to phishing. For instance, Jakobsson and Ratkiewicz (2006) sent phishing emails with links crafted to look suspicious (e.g., spelling mistakes, escape characters, and naked IP addresses in the URL) and found that four to 14 percent of users still clicked on those links. In a different study, Jakobsson, Tsow, Shah, Blevis, and Lim (2007) examined the effectiveness of trust indicators in email and webpages wherein they asked users to identify features that provoked trust. Their findings indicated that 1) sophisticated layout and legal disclaimers engender trust (e.g., copyright notices), 2) too much emphasis on security is counterproductive, 3) individuals use URLs extensively to evaluate trust, and 4) the impact of third party endorsement varies by whether one recognizes the party's name.

Wang et al. (2012) studied how users process visual cues and detection indicators of phishing messages and decision making process. They found that attention to visceral triggers and phishing detection indicators and to users' phishing knowledge played a critical role in phishing detection. Harrison, Vishwanath, Ng, and Rao (2015) found that information that alludes to social presence fosters heuristic decision making and increases susceptibility to phishing. The authors manipulated social presence with cues such as the university logo, versing security logo, and click-to-chat icons.

2.2 Countering Phishing Messages

Some research has examined the impact of training users in recognizing features in phishing messages to reduce susceptibility to phishing; however, most research has primarily focused on susceptibility to phishing. We have some evidence that educating individuals about common phishing practices reduces their likelihood of being phished (Kumaraguru, Cranor, & Mather, 2009a; Kumaraguru et al., 2009b; Sheng et al., 2010); however, results regarding the efficacy of training have been generally disappointing (Görling, 2006). Anandpara, Dingman, Jakobsson, Liu, and Roinestad (2007) contend that training individuals with phishing IQ tests is ineffective at improving susceptibility because it simply raises fears related to phishing rather than making users better at discerning whether an email is phishing them or not. Still others believe that the effects of such training are short term (Caputo, Pfleeger, Freeman, & Johnson, 2014). There are, however, innovative ways in which one can make phishing education effective. Kumaraguru et al. (2007) and Sheng et al. (2007) demonstrate the use of innovative learning designs based on learning science principles for anti-phishing education. Mayhorn and Nyeste (2012) show that training through comic strips and video games is very effective at reducing vulnerability to social engineering. Arachchilage and Love (2013) show that a game design framework for avoiding phishing attacks is very effective.

In addition to training, researchers have developed other various anti-phishing solutions to reduce individuals' susceptibility to phishing attacks (Emigh, 2005), such as toolbars, browser add-ons, and indicators (e.g., Netcraft and Web of Trust). Dhamija and Tygar (2005) propose an authentication scheme named Dynamic Security Skins that allows users to distinguish "spoofed" webpages using a unique image for each transaction. The scheme displays the image as a "skin" on the transaction window so that the user can verify that the images match and authenticate the content generated by the server. Wu, Miller, and Garfinkel (2006) evaluate the effectiveness of security toolbars as a deterrent to phishing. They conducted a study in which they required participants to respond to twenty emails, five of which were phishing manipulations. They found 33–45 percent incidence of clicking on phishing emails when toolbars were allowed. They also found that providing pop-up blocking warnings reduced the rates, but 70 percent of participants still succumbed to at least one deceptive email.

2.3 Summary of Prior Research

As we can see, the research suggests that psychological factors such as trust, fear, and obedience to authority may increase susceptibility to phishing. Most published studies have focused on users' susceptibility to generic phishing messages without contextualization. Contextualizing messages may increase the effectiveness of phishing, which the recent studies on spear phishing evidence. However, one may not need to personalize phishing messages to be effective; messages designed for a particular group of people may be effective if they identify group-relevant concerns and elicit specific emotions that trigger the desired response. To date, few studies have experimentally investigated the effects of contextualization or directly compared different contextualized messages. As such, we test the effectiveness of contextualized messages designed to elicit different emotions in a targeted population (students). We also adopt a theoretical framework that explains how contextualized messages may increase users' susceptibility to phishing by causing them to make hasty judgments based on initial impressions of the immediate context but also stand up to scrutiny should the users consider the message more carefully.

3 Theoretical Foundations

The considerable research attention that has focused on phishing susceptibility lately lacks an integrating theory. We draw on theories from social and cognitive psychology to provide the conceptual framework for our research. Our basic premise is that successful phishing attacks take advantage of the human tendency to make quick and intuitive judgments based on initial impressions of the immediate context. Although phishing messages contain false information that one may detect with careful scrutiny or investigation, a well-crafted message activates specific motives that push victims toward accepting the message.

Contemporary theories of information processing propose that two modes of processing exist: one quick and intuitive and one slow and deliberate. For example, Kahneman (2011) distinguishes between 1) an automatic and quick mode of thinking designed to detect simple relationships and to integrate information to maintain and update perceptions of our world (system 1) and 2) a slower, deliberate mode of thinking associated with the subjective experiences of agency, choice, and concentration (system 2). Whereas system 1 is a "machine for jumping to conclusions", system 2 allocates attention to effortful mental activities and can compare objects on several attributes, follow rules, and make choices. Similarly, Petty and Cacciopo's (1986) elaboration likelihood model (ELM) of persuasion identifies two cognitive processing routes to persuasion: a central and a peripheral path. The peripheral path is characterized by limited conscious attention that relies on cues and mental shortcuts that bypass counter-argumentation, whereas the central route relies on rational analysis that involves elaborating on information and arguments. When processing information peripherally, people do not think carefully about the content of the message; instead, they are influenced by superficial factors surrounding the communication. Phishing attempts often capitalize on peripheral routes to persuasion by incorporating cues that provoke action without careful deliberation. Such superficial features that often produce action are cues related to authority, scarcity or urgency, reciprocity, and similarity. In a phishing context, individuals will likely process emails from purported authority figures (e.g., bank officials and school administrators) that stress urgent action or evoke feelings of reciprocity along the peripheral path and, thus, lead to action without the user's carefully considering the request. Both Kahneman's theory and Petty and Cacciopo's ELM predict that successful phishing attempts work by pushing or nudging users to divulge information without provoking excessive thought.

Although quickly or peripherally processing information may increase the likelihood of deception, it does not sufficiently explain victimization. One cannot describe people victimized by the Nigerian Prince scam, for example, as always operating in a peripheral or quick thinking mode. Rather, the two modes of processing may occur simultaneously, and some successful phishing attempts capitalize on both systems. The heuristic-systematic processing model (HSM) (Chaiken, 1987; Chen & Chaiken, 1999) provides a strong conceptual basis for understanding how this processing may occur. According to HSM, people use a combination of heuristic (quick) and systematic (deliberate) processing modes to reach judgments. Heuristic processing refers to relying on judgmental rules and cognitive shortcuts (heuristics). It is associated with rapid decisions that individuals often base on immediate emotion and is subject to cognitive biases. Systematic processing involves carefully scrutinizing information and refers to analytically and comprehensively dealing with messages. HSM invokes the principle of least effort; that is, people tend to choose the course of action that requires the least effort, and, thus, heuristic processing often takes precedence over more effortful systematic processing (Eagly & Chaiken, 1993). But heuristic processing does not mean that people ignore motivational concerns. Rather, people sense motivational concerns in the immediate context and then try to spend minimal cognitive effort meeting those immediate motivational concerns. A critical concept in HSM is the notion of a sufficiency threshold, which refers to a desired level of confidence that people have for their judgments (Eagly & Chaiken, 1993). Confidence in one's decision or judgment must pass this threshold level; according to HSM, people will continue processing the message until they are confident that they have surpassed the sufficiency threshold. If people can reach the sufficiency threshold with heuristic processing, then they stop processing information. Otherwise, they are likely to use systematic processing until they reach the sufficiency threshold. The HSM also proposes that one can adjust the sufficiency threshold up or down depending on contextual factors, such as how important the decision is, or how much time pressure one is under. When pressed to make a decision quickly, for example, people may lower their sufficiency threshold, which makes it easier to reach with heuristic processing alone.

Luo et al. (2013) applied HSM to phishing attacks to outline the anatomy of a successful attack. They argue that successful phishing attacks increase individuals' heuristic processing and suppress their systematic processing. Attackers can do so by luring recipients to quickly but inaccurately assess the validity of the message or by reducing the sufficiency threshold so that recipients do not initiate systematic processing. If, however, the recipient fails to remain in heuristic processing mode, the successful (phishing) message is also one built to "withstand" systematic processing, such that, even if recipients scrutinize the message more carefully, they still make an inaccurate assessment of its validity. As Luo et al. (2013) summarize, heuristic and systematic processing may produce the same conclusion and, thereby, increase one's confidence in the judgment. Heuristic processing may create an initial impression that systematic processing subsequently confirms (i.e., a confirmation bias; Kahneman, 2011).

Luo et al.'s (2013) framework suggests that research should focus on factors that: 1) increase the likelihood that recipients will rely on heuristic processing; 2) lower the sufficiency threshold; and/or 3) increase the chances that a message will stand up to scrutiny. We argue that contextualizing an email message to quickly trigger motivational concerns in a context that appears specific to the recipient lowers the sufficiency threshold and helps the message withstand scrutiny should heuristic processing give way to more systematic processing. For example, course registrations are important to college students, and a message that threatens their continuance is likely to create a sense of urgency and the need for quick action. A strong emotion such as fear of losing something of value may subconsciously predispose or push people toward action (Damasio, 1994). As a result, students may quickly respond to a request for personal information in order to secure their courses. In this sense, contextualization acts like pretexting in social engineering attacks. In pretexting, one invents a scenario and incorporates something of specific relevance or importance to the recipient in the scenario, which acts to legitimize the interaction and can induce the recipient to divulge information (Anderson, 2010; Luo et al., 2013). One can also see contextualization as a form of spear phishing, where the attacker targets specific individuals with personalized messages. Typically, spear-phishing victims receive an email that appears to be from someone they know, which increases their trust in the message. In both pretexting and spear phishing, a carefully manipulated context underscores the importance of immediate action, which may simultaneously encourage heuristic processing, increase trust, and lower the sufficiency threshold and, thereby, obviate the need for careful scrutiny of the message.

> **H1**: Contextualized email messages that relate to a recipient's specific concerns increase susceptibility to phishing compared to non-contextualized emails that relate to general or broad concerns.

Another factor that is likely to influence the sufficiency threshold and susceptibility to deception is whether the message is framed to suggest that the recipient gains or loses something of value. People are motivated to gain things of value, and they may be induced to divulge personal information with the allure of money or material goods. However, research associated with prospect theory (Kahneman & Tversky, 1979) suggests that potential losses exert a stronger influence over people's judgments and actions than potential gains. Prospect theory is a descriptive theory of decision making under uncertainty that explains when people will be seek or avoid risk. A key principle of prospect theory is that the way in which people frame an outcome affects their actions. Two key concepts influence judgments: reference dependence and loss aversion. Reference dependence refers to the fact that individuals evaluate decision outcomes relative to a reference point, often the status quo. Individuals see outcomes above the reference point as gains and outcomes below the reference point are as losses. People attach subjective values to gains and losses, such that gains are associated with positive value and losses with negative value. People are maximally sensitive to change near the reference point (greater value attached to amount of change from status quo), and individuals weigh losses more heavily than gains. That is, the pain of losing $100 is greater than the joy of gaining $100. Prospect theory has two important implications for phishing. First, a phishing message crafted to induce an immediate sense of change from the status quo (either in terms of gaining something desired, such as a free gift card, or in terms of preventing the loss of something desired, such as money) will more likely deceive people. Second, the threat of an immediate loss is particularly likely to spur people to action. The negative value associated with loss may lower the sensitivity threshold and produce the belief that quick compliance with the email request will prevent the loss. Thus, messages that threaten the loss of something valuable may be more effective than messages offering the possibility of gain.

> **H2:** Phishing messages that frame potential outcomes as losses are more effective than messages that frame outcomes as gains.

The types of motives and emotions elicited in the recipient may also influence a phishing message's effectiveness. Few studies have examined the motives that phishing messages elicit despite Downs et al.'s (2006) finding suggesting that emails' content is more likely to influence the judged trustworthiness of an email than peripheral cues in headers and subject lines. Drawing on work in evolutionary and social psychology, Lawrence and Nohria (2002) identified four broad, universal motivational drives or "emotional needs" in humans: 1) the drive to acquire, 2) the drive to defend, 3) the drive to bond, and 4) the drive to learn. The drive to acquire relates to the motivation to secure scarce goods for oneself, including intangibles such as social status. One can see achievement and power motives, along with emotions of greed and envy, as manifestations of the drive to acquire. The drive to defend refers to the motivation to protect oneself, one's family, and one's possessions against external threats (physical and psychological). Fear of losing something of value triggers the drive to defend. The drive to bond relates to the pervasive drive to form and maintain lasting, positive interpersonal relationships. Humans desire social connections and, thus, are motivated to join and remain in groups. The drive to learn refers to the motivation to satisfy our curiosity and master our environments. Deceptive content that activates one of these basic emotional needs or drives will most likely to deceive recipients and convince them to divulge personal or sensitive information. In this study, we manipulate the content of phishing emails to activate the first three drives; that is, to acquire, to defend, and to connect. Although these drives are universal, the context in which they operate may vary. For example, face-to-face interactions with others may activate, for example, the drive to bond more easily than asynchronous email communications. However, email communications that identify a path or mechanism for obtaining valued tangible or intangible outcomes may more easily activate the drive to acquire. Thus, we might expect that the motive to acquire, along with associated emotions such as greed, will lower the sufficiency threshold and make people more susceptible to phishing.

> **H3:** Phishing messages that offer recipients the opportunity to acquire new outcomes (tangible or intangible) are associated with greater susceptibility than messages associated with social outcomes.

4 Research Design

Finn and Jakobsson (2007) discuss ethical and technical issues regarding phishing experiments. They define three principal approaches that researchers have used to quantify responses to phishing attacks: surveys, closed-lab experiments, and imitation studies. Survey studies require participants to report their own behaviors. One serious drawback of survey studies is that participants are apt to underestimate or overestimate the possible damages of phishing attacks; they may not be aware of the phishing attack or may not be willing to disclose that they have fallen prey to a phishing attack. Closed-lab experiments allow researchers to evaluate phishing attacks and their countermeasures in a controlled environment, but, at the same time, the participants of such experiments might be biased because they are aware that they are part of an experiment. The third strategy uses deception and imitates real phishing attacks to measure the actual success rate of these attacks under realistic (albeit ultimately benign) conditions. Although the imitation approach is the most realistic research strategy, it possesses ethical concerns because mimicking a phishing attack involves deception and, hence, poses risk of psychological harm or negative reactions in participants. We used the imitation strategy to measure actual behaviors as realistically as possible. However, we included an informational page in the follow-up survey that explained the purpose of the study and how phishing works and provided participants advice about how to avoid phishing attempts (Appendix 10B).

Phishing involves multiple discrete steps that culminate with the user's revealing confidential information to the hacker. The first step is the deception, whereby the victim receives a phishing email, reads the email, and is motivated to react. The second step involves the user's clicking on the link to the phishing webpage and evaluating the information on the page. The third step involves further deception in that the user is convinced to reveal personal information such as credit card number, social security number, or banking information. The user does not necessarily need to follow through to step 3 for the hacker to breach their security. Step 2, in which a user clicks on the fraudulent link, can result in the user's downloading malware to the user's computer, which can cause damage to the computer or, worse yet, install a backdoor through which the hacker can gain access to it. The key question that we address in this research is: what causes people to be deceived by phishing messages, and what motivates them to click on phishing links?

Specifically, we examine the first and second steps of the phishing process, and then, instead of having users reveal their personal information, we direct participants to a benign website, inform them that they have fallen prey to phishing, provide an educational message, and request that they voluntarily complete a survey that assesses their security perceptions and personality traits.

We designed the emails' content to test the hypothesized effects of gain/loss frame, contextualization, and motive. We used positively and negatively framed messages to portray gains and losses, respectively. Positively framed messages presented recipients with the opportunity to acquire something of value (e.g., gift card, iPad mini, computer virus software, and feelings of altruism). Negatively framed messages threatened recipients with the loss of something of value (course registrations and money in bank accounts) or the loss of a potentially valuable opportunity (opportunity for tuition assistance). We varied contextualization in two ways. First, we varied outcomes so that they pertained specifically to students at the university (e.g., course registrations and tuition assistance) or to any person (e.g., $50 gift card and iPad mini). Second, we portrayed the message sender as being from in the university (e.g., student accounts manager) or external to the university (e.g., the Apple research team). Finally, we intended the messages' content to activate individuals' motives to acquire things, protect assets, or connect to/help others. We created eight messages, four with a "gain" frame and four with a "loss" frame. Table 10.1 summarizes the eight emails.

Table 10.1   Characteristics of Phishing Emails.

CONTENT	GAIN OR LOSS	GENERAL MOTIVE	CONTEXTUALIZATION
Gift Card	Gain	Acquisition	Low
iPad Mini	Gain	Acquisition	Low
Virus & firewall software	Gain	Defense	High
Volunteer	Gain (altruism)	Social	Low
Course registration	Loss	Acquisition	High
Bank card	Loss	Acquisition	High
Tuition assistance	Loss (of opportunity)	Acquisition	High
Alumni social network	Loss (of opportunity)	Social	High

The participants in the study were third- and fourth-year students enrolled at a large research university in Northeastern USA. We used a university setting for this study because students frequently fall victim to similar online threats (Johnston & Warkentin, 2010) and because researchers consider them an appropriate group for such applied behavioral research (Gordon, Slade, & Schmitt, 1986). They also fit in the age bracket most susceptible to phishing. We categorized students into four groups according to their broad academic major: social sciences, STEM (science, technology, engineering and mathematics) fields, humanities, and business. The total dataset included 7,225 students, with 3,513 females and 3,712 males. The breakdown by major was as follows: social sciences: 1,791 females and 1,554 males; business: 340 females and 554 males; humanities: 610 females and 518 males; and STEM: 772 females and 1,086 males.

Working with the information technology services professional staff and with institutional review board approval and oversight, we obtained email addresses for all third- and fourth-year undergraduate students. We divided the student sample based on the four broad academic majors and created male and female subgroups in each category. We then randomized each of the eight subgroups and split them into eight blocks. We gave each block a different treatment (email message) based on the framework we define in Table 10.1. Our factorial design was four

Table 10.2   Breakdown of Recipients Based on Eight Different Phishing Email (7,225 in total)

	Field	Gift card	Tuition assist.	iPad	Registration	Firewall	Bank card	Volunteer	Social network
Female	Social science	224	224	224	224	224	224	223	223
	Business	43	43	43	43	42	42	42	42
	Humanities	77	76	76	77	76	76	76	76
	STEM	97	97	97	97	96	96	96	96
Male	Social science	195	194	195	195	194	194	194	194
	Business	70	69	69	70	69	69	69	69
	Humanities	65	65	65	65	65	65	64	64
	STEM	136	136	136	136	136	136	135	135

major categories x two genders x eight interventions. Table 10.2 shows the number of recipients for each of the 64 groups.

We used an automated email distribution service to distribute the phishing emails. The service allowed us to track the emails through the entire phishing process; that is, when users received the email, when they read it, and when they clicked on the phishing link. The service allowed us to create accounts (with arbitrary client addresses) from which we distributed the emails. We created email addresses with the university's "edu" domain extension to imply authenticity and increase the users' trust in the email (i.e., if the user hovered the mouse over the sender's name, it would show an email with "albany.edu" extension, such as itm_maillist1@albany.edu). This technique mimics sophisticated phishing strategies currently in use. To comply with the service's usage policy, we added an unsubscribe message to the bottom of the email, which constituted a single line of text with a link to the email address of the account from which the email was sent. Each email contained a fake phishing link, which was actually a link to the participant survey. Each link uniquely corresponded to a different email so that we could aggregate the responses to specific email accounts. We masked the survey links using a different service to hide the true identity of the link. To make the links more convincing, we used a link that included both the word "ualbany" and a word related to the specific phishing email (e.g., "giftcardsurvey") (e.g., http://ualbany.9nl.com/giftcardsurvey/).

We considered the timing for the experiment carefully because we needed to choose a time that students would most likely check and read their emails. We collected data for 15 days, starting from the last week of classes to end of final examinations to make sure that most of the students saw the emails (Ferguson, 2005). We tracked the number of recipients who opened the phishing emails and the number of users out of the ones who opened the email who actually clicked on the phishing link embedded in the email. Once a user clicked the phishing link, the link directed the user to the survey website. This website contained an informational page that informed the user of the phishing experiment and provided tips for good practices to avoid phishing (Appendix 10B).

4.1 Participant Survey

Via the survey website, we asked participants who clicked on the link to complete a survey at the end of the informational message to obtain data on users' perceptions and individual differences. Only a small fraction of students actually completed the survey, so we treated these data as exploratory. The survey questionnaire assessed users' computer security, their perceptions and scrutiny of the email, and personality traits. We asked participants whether they had a firewall and/or a virus protection program running on their computer (response options were "yes", "no", and "I don't know"). We also asked them how many times their computer had been infected with a virus or malware in the past. Four questions assessed security and anti-phishing behaviors related to the phishing email. We asked participants if they scrolled over the link in the email before clicking on it and whether they searched for information on the topic before responding (response options were "yes" and "no"). We also asked them how suspicious they were of the email on a four-point Likert scale (1 = not at all suspicious, 2 = a little suspicious, 3 = fairly suspicious, 4 = very suspicious). We also asked them if they read the email carefully on a four-point Likert scale (1 = not very carefully at all, 2 = somewhat carefully, 3 = carefully, 4 = very carefully). We measured the personality traits conscientiousness, neuroticism (emotional stability), extraversion, ambition, and achievement drive using a self-report, commercial personality inventory. We assessed the reliability for these scales using Cronbach's alpha and found them to be acceptable for each scale: .79 for conscientiousness, .96 for extraversion, .91 for neuroticism, .72 for ambition, and .73 for achievement drive.

5 Results

A total of 7,225 phishing emails were sent to students and registered as received. Records showed that 1,975 students opened the email that they received, resulting in an "open" rate of 27.3 percent. Further, 964 students clicked on the link embedded in the phishing message, resulting in a "click" rate of 13.3 percent. Thus, over a quarter of those students who received a phishing message opened it, and nearly a half (48.8 percent) of those who opened the email went further and clicked on the link embedded in the phishing message.

5.1 Comparisons Between Message Conditions

5.1.1 Manipulation Checks

We could not test the effectiveness of our manipulation in the study sample because we only had access to participants who we deceived and who volunteered to complete the survey after following the email links. Thus, we conducted a post-hoc manipulation check study using a separate sample of students from the same university. We gave 238 students one of the eight email scenarios and asked them to rate the outcome described in the scenario on the extent to which it described an outcome that was positive or negative as they assessed it and whether it presented the opportunity to gain or lose something. Participants responded on nine-point semantic differential scales, with the poles of the scales anchored at negative (1) vs. positive (9) outcome and opportunity to lose (1) vs. opportunity to gain (9) something. Table 10.3 presents the results. Overall, the participants rated the gain conditions as more positive (Ms = 6.06 vs. 4.64), $t(236) = 4.39, p < .01$) and as having a greater opportunity for gain (Ms = 6.13 vs. 4.8), $t(236) = 3.82$, $p < .01$) than the loss conditions. However, we did not successfully manipulate all of the specific loss conditions. The participants clearly saw the bank card and course registrations as losses and negatively framed, but they did not see the tuition and alumni network conditions as losses and negatively framed. We negatively framed the latter two conditions as presenting the loss of an opportunity, but students did not interpret this frame as a loss. Rather, students interpreted the tuition assistance condition and alumni network conditions as more of a gain than loss opportunity. We also asked participants how motivated they would be to receive the outcome depicted in the email and how much they valued the outcome. A one-way analysis of variance (ANOVA) revealed no significant difference in motivation between the email conditions ($F(7,230) = 2.0$, $p > .05$). This finding suggests that any differences in susceptibility were not due to differences in motivation to pursue the outcome. The results of our manipulation checks suggest that the most appropriate statistical design was to compare the eight email conditions in a single-factor design.

Table 10.3   Results of Post-hoc Manipulation Checks.

CONDITION	POSITIVE (9) VS. NEGATIVE (1) OUTCOME	GAIN (9) VS. LOSS (1)	MOTIVATIONAL VALUE
Gift card	7.28	7.41	4.47
iPad Mini	6.37	6.20	3.87
Virus & firewall software	5.18	5.11	3.79
Volunteer	5.24	5.62	3.59
Course registration	2.64	2.82	4.67
Bank card	3.89	4.07	4.44
Tuition assistance	6.47	6.25	4.14
Alumni social network	5.77	6.23	3.84

5.1.2 Test of Hypotheses

Analyses examined differences in recipients' responses to the phishing messages. Table 10.4 presents the frequency with which recipients opened the different emails and clicked on the link embedded in the phishing messages. We found vast differences between message conditions for both open and click rates. The percent of recipients opening the email message ranged from a low of 1.9 percent for the bank card fraud email to a high of 54.4 percent for the course registration message. A chi-square test revealed significant differences between the eight email conditions ($\chi^2(8) = 617.0$, $p < .001$). Post-hoc comparisons revealed the following pattern for frequency of opening the email: course registration message > tuition assistance and free gift card > free iPad and free computer fire wall > volunteer opportunity > alumni network and bank card fraud (all $ps < .05$). The finding that over half of recipients (54 percent) opened the course registration message supports Hypothesis 1, which suggests that highly contextualized emails capture recipients' attention. In fact, the two messages that produced the highest number of email openings related to salient concerns for most students: keeping course registrations open and tuition assistance. We also contextualized the firewall, alumni network, and bank card conditions in that they were ostensibly sent from university officials and related to student concerns. These messages, however, did not lead to high open rates. Course registrations and tuition are likely to be more salient and important to college students and, hence, more likely to draw their attention. The high open rate for the course registration condition is also consistent with Hypothesis 2 (loss frames result in higher susceptibility than gain frames), but the open rate in the bank card condition, the only other loss condition identified by the manipulation check analysis, was very low. Overall, the average open rate in loss frames did not differ from that in gain frames.

Consistent with Hypothesis 3, messages that related to protecting assets (registrations and computer) or acquiring valued things or resources (iPad, gift card, and money for tuition) were likely to induce recipients to open the email messages. Messages related to social motives (volunteering and networking) were less effective. For the most part, recipients ignored the bank card protection message because, perhaps, they were familiar with similar messages and recognized them as fraudulent.

Table 10.4   Frequency of Opening Email and Clicking on Link by Message Condition.

	Gift card	Tuition assist.	iPad	Registration	Firewall	Bank card	Volunteer	Social network
N	907	907	905	904	902	902	899	899
# open	345_d	357_d	291_c	492_e	269_c	17_a	185_b	19_a
% open	38%	39%	32.1%	54.4%	29.8%	1.9%	20.6%	2.1%
# click	194_b	187_b	178_b	338_c	40_a	3_a	20_a	4_a
% click	21.4%	20.6%	19.7%	37.3%	4.4%	< 1%	2.2%	< 1%

Note: Means with different subscripts in rows are significantly different ($p < .05$).

Results for the frequency with which recipients clicked on the embedded link in the email messages mirrored the results for opening the email. The chi-square analysis revealed significant differences between the eight conditions ($\chi^2(5) = 560.8$, $p < .001$), with the highest click rate (37.3 percent) found for the course registration message, and the lowest rate (< 1 percent) found for the bank card and social network messages. Post hoc comparisons found that the course registration message produced higher click rates than the iPad, gift card, and tuition assistance messages, which did not differ from each other but produced significantly more clicks than did the other four conditions (*ps* < .01).

5.2 Individual Differences: Gender and Major

Additional analyses examined open and click rates by major and gender across the eight message conditions. We found a main effect for gender: collapsing across all eight message conditions, females were more likely to open the email message than males; 29.9 percent of females (n = 1,051) opened their message compared to 24.4 percent of males ((n = 924), $\chi^2(1) = 22.95$, $p < .01$). However, the difference in click rates between males and females was not statistically significant ($p < .05$), with 14.1 percent of females (n = 495) clicking on the link versus 12.6 percent of males ((n = 469), $\chi^2(1) = 3.36$, $p = .067$). We conducted post hoc analyses to examine gender differences in open rates in each message condition. Using a Bonferonni adjusted p-value of .006 (for eight post-hoc tests), we found significant gender differences in open rates for the gift card and course registration conditions. As Table 10.5 shows, women were significantly more likely than men to open the gift card (44 percent vs. 32 percent; $\chi^2(1) = 13.5$, $p < .01$) and course registration (60 percent vs. 49 percent; $\chi^2(1) = 11.6$, $p < .01$) emails. Gender differences in the other conditions were not significant. Thus, the effect of gender on open rates was restricted to the iPad and course registration conditions.

Table 10.5   Open Rates by Message Condition and Participant Gender.

	Gift card	Tuition assist.	iPad	Registration	Firewall	Bank card	Volunteer	Social network
Female	44.1%	41.7%	33.4%	60.2%	32.6%	1.8%	23.3%	1.8%
Male	32.3%	37.1%	31.2%	48.9%	27.2%	1.9%	18.0%	2.4%

Chi square tests also revealed a significant main effect of academic major on the frequency of opening the email ($\chi^2(3) = 12.40$, $p < .01$). Table 10.6 presents the frequency of openings and link clicks by student major, collapsed across all message conditions. Post-hoc comparisons revealed that business and social science majors were more likely to open the email than humanities majors. No other comparisons were statistically significant ($p < .05$). Analyses revealed no significant differences between majors in terms of click rate ($\chi^2(3) = 5.42$, $p = .14$).

Table 10.6   Frequency of Opening Email and Clicking on Link by Major, Collapsed Across Message Conditions.

	SOCIAL SCIENCE	BUSINESS	HUMANITIES	STEM
# open	931	274	269	501
% open	27.8%	30.6%	23.8%	27.0%
# click	466	112	130	256
% click	13.9%	12.5%	11.5%	13.8%

We conducted log-linear analyses to test for higher-order interactions between condition, gender, major, and click and open rates. Results showed no significant gender x condition, major x condition, or gender x major x condition interaction terms for either click or open rates.

5.3 Survey Responses

Of the 964 students who clicked on the link in the email, 206 (21.4 percent) completed the survey on the landing webpage. There were not enough responses in each experimental condition to conduct comprehensive analyses, but we present the following results for informational purposes. Respondents reported being moderately suspicious of the email that they received (mean rating = 2.4 on a 1–4 scale) and being moderately careful in reading the email (mean rating = 2.6 on a 1–4 scale). There were no gender differences in reported suspicion or care, and having a firewall or virus protection did not affect suspicion or carefulness. A majority (59.2 percent) of respondents reported scrolling over the link before clicking on it, and 22.4 percent reported that they searched for information on sender before clicking.

We analyzed suspicion ratings for experimental conditions with more than 10 respondents. ANOVA revealed main effects of condition for suspicion and carefulness in reading email (Fs (3,187) = 8.02 and 5.77, respectively, ps < .01). Post-hoc tests revealed that respondents in the gift card and tuition assistance conditions were less suspicious and read the email less carefully than those in the free iPad condition (ps < .05), while those in the course registration condition fell between these two groups. The only other significant effect was a main effect of condition on conscientiousness (F(3, 133) = 2.68, p = .05). Respondents in the registration and tuition assistance conditions were higher in conscientiousness than respondents in the iPad and gift card conditions, but post-hoc tests between conditions failed to reach statistical significance (p < .05) when we used the Tukey correction for the number of post-hoc comparisons.

The trait of conscientiousness was positively correlated with being suspicious (r = .25) and carefully reading the message (r = .21, ps < .05). These findings are consistent with the behavioral tendencies of conscientious people to pay close attention to details and to be planful, although the findings could also reflect a response bias. Finally, individuals reporting themselves to be high in ambition and achievement striving also reported being more suspicious of the emails (rs = .22 and .23, respectively, p < .05).

6 Discussion

In this study, we examine the impact of the content and framing of phishing emails on user vulnerability. Results suggest that the desire to protect things of value and the opportunity to obtain valued objects are motives that make people susceptible to phishing scams. Further, messages that targeted issues and concerns relevant to the student sample (e.g., course registration and tuition assistance) were most successful (i.e., in convincing the participants to click the link in the email).

6.1 Analysis of Hypotheses

In partial support of Hypothesis 1, student participants were more susceptible to a highly contextualized message pertaining to course registrations than to other generic messages. The threat of losing course registrations spurred over half of recipients to open a fraudulent email message, and over one-third of them to follow the link embedded in the fraudulent message. Of participants who opened the registration email, over two-thirds (68.7 percent) clicked on the phishing link. Thus, the contextualized message channeled recipients through the first two steps of the phishing process and lead them to read the email and click on the embedded link. This "channeling" of behavior is consistent with the heuristic-systematic model (Eagly & Chaiken, 1993) in that message cues (e.g., an important matter and a credible sender) can propel people to act without (or even despite) carefully deliberating on the consequences of their actions. We conducted this study after the advanced registration period for the upcoming semester had closed, a time when students are likely to be highly motivated to protect their course registrations. The saliency and importance of course registrations may have lowered the recipients' sufficiency threshold and caused them to respond to the link quickly without carefully considering the email's legitimacy. Additionally, the strongly contextualized message may have withstood initial scrutiny or skepticism from the individuals' systematic processing system. The survey responses suggest that this may have been the case because respondents receiving the course registration email indicated they were moderately suspicious of the email but still clicked on the link. Luo et al. (2013) suggest that the most effective phishing messages would be those that can operate on both the heuristic and systematic processing systems. The threat of losing course registrations may have lowered the sufficiency threshold in students and pushed them toward quick action, while the rich context cues may have convinced those scrutinizing the message that it was authentic. The second most clicked link (tuition assistance) was also high in contextualization, which further suggests that a personalized context increases susceptibility to phishing. The extreme version of contextualization is a spear-phishing attack that appears to come from someone known to the victim and that addresses the victim by name. The results of spear-phishing studies are similar to ours. Halevi et al. (2015) found that 25 of 40 employees (62.5%) clicked on a link embedded in a fraudulent email purportedly from the company's IT manager and addressed to them individually. Our results suggest that phishing messages need not be personalized to that extent in order to be effective.

Hypothesis 2 states that loss frames increase susceptibility compared to gain frames. The results suggest that this effect may only be true for highly contextualized messages, such as the course registration email. The manipulation check analysis indicated that the only other condition that the participants interpreted as a loss frame was the bank card condition, which resulted in low open and click rates. Although the second most successful message threatened students with the loss of an opportunity for tuition assistance, the manipulation check analyses indicated that students were more likely to adopt a gain frame than a loss frame for this message.

The results also showed that the chance to acquire free goods (an iPad or gift card) increased vulnerability to phishing attacks. One in five students who received a message promising a gift card or an iPad visited the phishing website and, thus, put themselves at risk for being scammed or having the security of their computer and data compromised. This finding is consistent with the drive to acquire that Lawrence and Nohria (2002) identify as a universal emotional need in humans. The lure of "free" goods may lower the sufficiency threshold in recipients and cause them to respond in heuristic processing mode and overlook the risks associated with phishing emails. Some evidence from the post-study survey supports this explanation; respondents reported being least careful when reading the gift card message.

Participants were less susceptible to the phishing messages geared toward social outcomes (altruism and social networks) than for material outcomes. Perhaps these messages were not as believable, or participants were not highly motivated to pursue the social outcomes offered by the phishing message. University students have numerous opportunities to assist others and participate in social activities and networks, which may have reduced the attractiveness of this opportunity.

6.2 Individual Differences

We also examined how vulnerabilities change across different student populations based on academic major and gender. Previous research suggests that women are more susceptible to phishing than men (e.g., Halevi et al., 2013; 2015; Jagatic et al., 2007). We found that women were more likely than men to open phishing messages but not necessarily more likely to click on the embedded links. Perhaps women are more easily enticed to look at phishing emails (step 1 of the phishing process) but are as adept as men at detecting deceptive messaging (step 2). Likewise, business majors were more likely than humanities majors to open emails, although we found no differences in click rates by type of major. A possible explanation for this finding is that the business major at the university is very competitive and attracts highly motivated and engaged students, who may also be more diligent in monitoring and responding to emails linked to the university.

6.3 New Contributions

This study provides several important contributions to information security research. It clearly demonstrates that situational or contextual factors alter the effectiveness of phishing attempts. Users' or recipients' responses are rooted in their perceptions of risk and reward when confronted with a decision choice. Cognitive biases and heuristics, however, may reduce rational logic and increase vulnerability to fraudulent messages. Contextualized social engineering attacks, such as emails to students that threaten the loss of academic registrations, may cause them to overlook cues of deception that they might normally catch. The findings also lend support to the heuristic-systematic processing model (HSM). A contextualized message that threatens the loss of something valuable may be especially likely to prompt people to act quickly without carefully considering the potential consequences of the action. The fear associated with the anticipated loss of something valuable may increase reliance on heuristics and automatic responses (Damasio, 1984; LeDoux, 2003). However, should initial suspicion cause recipients to more systematically process a message, the rich context of the message may convince them that the message is legitimate. The survey results support this assertion by showing that respondents who clicked on the embedded link were moderately suspicious of the email but clicked on the link nonetheless. Perhaps the emotion elicited by the message—the anticipation of gaining or losing something valuable—lowered the user's sufficiency threshold for responding or influenced their appraisal of the legitimacy of the message.

The survey results also suggest that students may be aware of common phishing detection methods. Nearly 60 percent of those who completed the survey reported that they scrolled over the link in the email, and 22 percent reported that they searched for information on the Internet before clicking the link. It is difficult to draw firm conclusions from these findings because of the low response rate and because we cannot determine the veracity of responses, but the findings may indicate that young adults are aware of techniques to detect and protect against phishing. However, the study also shows that contextualized messages that mask URLs and other cues can still channel users toward fraudulent websites.

The vast difference we found in open and click rates is also noteworthy. Although the most influential email threatened the loss of something (course registration), so too did the least influential message (bank card fraud). Perhaps the latter email was less believable to students because it resembled common or known phishing attempts. The university's website, for example, presents an example of a phishing email that asks for bank information. Thus, the bank card message was similar to common phishing attempts; students may have rejected it as a common scam.

6.4 Training Implications

As the literature illustrates, past training has not been very effective, which we posit may be due to the vast array of techniques of deception (in phishing) and human cognitive limitation to process and absorb them. Creating highly focused and contextualized awareness campaigns targeted to different audiences based on their cognitive biases may improve the impact of the training provided. Given that students take emails from university administration (e.g., accounts, scholarships, etc.) and instructors (e.g., grades, assignments, and plagiarism etc.) seriously, such interventions would help provide students with ways to distinguish legitimate from illegitimate emails. Many methods exist to do so, such as: 1) ensuring that all emails come from university email addresses and that all of the links in the email start with the university domain, 2) providing a procedure for students to verify the authenticity of the email either by phone or the Web, and 3) educating students on the importance of verifying emails, especially those that request sensitive information. Additionally, given that financial incentives, even if relatively small (e.g., gift card), strongly motivate students to respond, we could educate students on ways to determine the legitimacy of offers. To create contextualized strategies, we need to understand the psychological traits of specific demographics and create appropriate messages to neutralize individual vulnerabilities.

Phishing is fundamentally a human problem, and education is a critical tool to reduce susceptibility (Jagatic et al., 2007). Anti-phishing training has been ineffective, and poor training results have led some researchers to go so far as to claim that users cannot be trusted to make rational security decisions and that those decisions should be taken out of their hands and made automatically for effective security (Görling, 2006). The conjecture that we draw from our research is that targeted training based on specific biases that increase phishing susceptibility would be effective. For example, to guard against biases that stem from heuristic processing, training might seek ways to raise the sufficiency threshold in recipients and, thereby, increase the chances that users will systematically process messages. Training also needs to counter the effects of pretexting and contextualization. It may be difficult to prevent pretexting, but users can be provided with techniques for verifying authenticity of internal communications, and organizations should develop clear policies about the types of information that might be requested of its members (e.g., "We will never ask for your password, ever"). Our future research will entail incorporating good practices based on learning science principles that are contextualized according to user motivation and psychological biases.

6.5 Limitations and Future Research

This study has several limitations. We did not ask students for personal information or data and, thus, do not know if students would have been deceived into divulging sensitive or confidential information. This is the critical third step of the phishing sequence, where users provide personal information after opening and reading the email and clicking on an embedded link. We need more research to examine vulnerability at this third stage. Nonetheless, clicking on links in emails (step 2) increases vulnerability because doing so may automatically download and install malware on the user's computer. Links can be associated with downloads of executable files that can install trojans on the user's computer without their knowledge. The participants in this study were students enrolled in a U.S. university, and users in different countries and from different cultures may behave differently in regards to phishing (Flores et al., 2015; Tembe, et al., 2014). The study focuses on general phishing attacks via emails and does not address spear phishing or phishing through different channels such as online social media platforms. Further research should investigate whether the effects of contextualized messages generalize to these other forms of phishing.

Finally, we did not have a fully balanced experimental design and our manipulation of gain/loss frame was only partly successful. However, comparisons between the eight scenarios provide insights into the effects of contextualization and framing. Future research should expand on our findings and test the effects of different scenarios in experimental settings.

7 Conclusions

We tested the premise that successful phishing attacks take advantage of the human tendency to make quick intuitive judgments based on initial impressions of the immediate context. We tested the assertion that susceptibility to phishing is strongly associated with the contextual setting of a phishing email via an experiment with emails framed based on our hypotheses to elicit user reaction. We found that the context of the email was strongly related to susceptibility to phishing and that different demographics were associated with susceptibility. The research implies the need for developing context-based education to help users detect phishing emails as an effective counter to the increasing design sophistication of phishing attacks. It also illustrates, based on rate of email opening, differences in susceptibility of different users for specific demographics features (e.g., major and gender). This finding suggests the need to identify the precise vulnerabilities based on demographic groups and provide targeted education designed for each group. In the future, we would like to examine the impact of such targeted education on reducing users' susceptibility to phishing.

References

Aaron G., & Rasmussen, R. (2015). Global phishing survey: Trends and domain name use in 2H2014. *Antiphishing Working Group*. Retrieved February 22, 2016, from http://www.antiphishing.org/download/document/245/APWG_Global_Phishing_Re port_2H_2014.pdf

Anandpara, V., Dingman, A., Jakobsson, M., Liu, D., & Roinestad, H. (2007). Phishing IQ tests measure fear, not ability. In S. Dietrich & R. Dhamija (Eds.), *Financial cryptography and data security* (pp. 362–366). Berlin: Springer.

Anderson, R., & Moore, T. (2009). Information security: Where computer science, economics and psychology meet. *Philosophical Transactions of the Royal Society A, 367*(1898), 2717–2727.

Anderson, T. (2010). Pretexting: What you need to know. *Security Management, 54*(6), 64–70.

Arachchilage, N. A. G., & Love, S. (2013). A game design framework for avoiding phishing attacks. *Computers in Human Behavior, 29*(3), 706–714.

Butavicius, M., Parsons, K., Pattinson, M., & McCormac, A. (2015). *Breaching the human firewall: Social engineering in phishing and spear-phishing emails*. Paper presented at the 26th Australasian Conference on Information Systems, Adelaide, Australia.

Caputo, D. D., Pfleeger, S. L., Freeman, J. D., & Johnson, M. E. (2014). Going spear phishing: Exploring embedded training and awareness. *Security & Privacy, 12*(1), 28–38.

Chaiken, S. (1987). The heuristic model of persuasion. In M. P. Zanna, J. M. Olson, & C. P. Herman (Eds.), *Social influence: The Ontario symposium* (vol. 5, pp. 3–39). Hillsdale, NJ: Lawrance Erlbaum Associates.

Chen, S., & Chaiken, S. (1999). The heuristic-systematic model in its broader context. In S. Chaiken & Y. Trope (Eds.), *Dual-process theories in social and cognitive psychology* (pp. 73–96). New York: Guilford.

Cialdini, R. B. (1993) *Influence: Science and practice*. New York: Harper Collins.

Damasio, A. (1994). *Descartes' error: Emotion, reason, and the human brain*. New York: Penguin Books.

Dhamija, R., & Tygar, J. D. (2005). The battle against phishing: Dynamic security skins. In *Proceedings of the First Symposium on Usable Privacy and Security* (pp. 77–88).

Dhamija, R., Tygar, J. D., & Hearst, M. (2006). Why phishing works. In *Proceedings of the SIGCHI Conference on Human Factors in Computing Systems* (pp. 581–590).

Downs, J. S., Holbrook, M. B., & Cranor, L. F. (2006). Decision strategies and susceptibility to phishing. In *Proceedings of the Second Symposium on Usable Privacy and* Security (pp. 79–90).

Eagly, A. H., & Chaiken, S. (1993). *The psychology of attitudes*. Fort Worth, TX: Harcourt.

Egelman, S., Cranor, L. F., & Hong, J. (2008). You've been warned: An empirical study of the effectiveness of web browser phishing warnings. In *Proceedings of the SIGCHI Conference on Human Factors in Computing Systems* (pp. 1065–1074).

Emigh, A. (2005). *Online identity theft: Phishing technology, chokepoints and countermeasures*. Retrieved from http://www.passfaces.com/published/Phishing-dhs-report.pdf

Ferguson, A. J. (2005). Fostering e-mail security awareness: The West Point carronade. *EDUCAUSE Quarterly, 28*(1), 54–57.

Finn, P., & Jakobsson, M. (2007). Designing ethical phishing experiments. *IEEE Technology and Society Magazine, 26*(1), 46–58.

Flores, W. R., Holm, H., Nohlberg, M., & Ekstedt, M. (2015). Investigating personal determinants of phishing and the effect of national culture. *Information & Computer Security, 23*(2), 178–199.

Gordon, M. E., Slade, L. A., & Schmitt, N. (1986). The "science of the sophomore" revisited: From conjecture to empiricism. *The Academy of Management Review, 11*(1), 191–207.

Görling, S. (2006). The myth of user education. In *Proceedings of the 16th Virus Bulletin International Conference.*

Halevi, T., Lewis, J., & Memon, N. (2013). *Phishing, personality traits and Facebook*. arXiv preprint arXiv:1301.7643v2.

Halevi, T., Memon, N., & Nov, O. (2015). *Spear-phishing in the wild: A real-world study of personality, phishing self-efficacy and vulnerability to spear-phishing attacks.*

Harrison, B., Vishwanath, A., Ng, Y. J., & Rao, R. (2015). Examining the impact of presence on individual phishing victimization. In *Proceedings of the 48th Hawaii International Conference on System Sciences* (pp. 3483–3489).

Hong, J. (2012). The state of phishing attacks. *Communications of the ACM, 55*(1), 74–81.

Jagatic, T. N., Johnson, N. A., Jakobsson, M., & Menczer, F. (2007). Social Phishing. *Communications of the ACM, 50*(10), 94–100.

Jakobsson, M., & Ratkiewicz, J. (2006). Designing ethical phishing experiments: A study of (ROT13) rOnl query features. In *Proceedings of the 15th International Conference on World Wide Web* (pp. 513–522).

Jakobsson, M., Tsow, A., Shah, A., Blevis, E., & Lim, Y.-K. (2007). What instills trust? A qualitative study of phishing. In *Proceedings of the 11th International Conference on Financial Cryptography* (pp. 356–361).

Johnston, A. C., & Warkentin, M. (2010). Fear appeals and information security behaviors: An emprical study. *MIS Quarterly, 34*(3), 549–566.

Jones, N. (2015). A perfect match: Uniting mobile security with your employees' use of online dating apps. *SecurityIntelligence*. Retrieved from https://securityintelligence.com/datingapps

Kahneman, D. (2011). *Thinking, fast and slow*. New York: Farrar, Straus and Giroux.

Kahneman, D., & Tversky, A. (1979). Prospect theory: An analysis of decision under risk. *Econometrica, 47*(2), 263–291.

Kim, D., & Kim, J. H. (2013). Understanding persuasive elements in phishing e-mails: A categorical content and semantic network analysis. *Online Information Review, 37*(6), 835–850.

Kumaraguru, P., Rhee, Y., Sheng, S., Hasan, S., Acquisti, A., Cranor, L. F., & Hong, J. (2007). Getting users to pay attention to anti-phishing education: Evaluation of retention and transfer. In *Proceedings of the Anti-phishing Working Groups 2nd Annual eCrime Researchers Summit* (pp. 70–81).

Kumaraguru, P., Cranor, L. F., & Mather, L. (2009a). *Anti-phishing landing page: Turning a 404 into a teachable moment for end users.* Paper presented at the 6th Conference on Email and Anti-Spam. Mountain View, CA, USA.

Kumaraguru, P., Cranshaw, J., Acquisti, A., Cranor, L., Hong, J., Blair, M. A., & Pham, T. (2009b). School of phish: A real-world evaluation of anti-phishing training. In *Proceedings of the 5th Symposium on Usable Privacy and Security.*

Lawrence, P. R., & Nohria, N. (2002). *Driven: How human nature shapes our choices.* San Francisco: Joseey-Bass.

LeDoux, J. (2003). The emotional brain, fear, and the amygdala. *Cellular and Molecular Neurobiology, 23*(4–5), 727–738.

Leventhal, H. (1970). Findings and theory in the study of fear communications. In L. Berkowitz (Ed.), *Advances in experimental social psychology* (vol. 5, pp. 119–187). New York: Academic Press.

Luo, X., Zhang, W., Burd, S., & Seazzu, A. (2013). Investigating phishing victimization with the heuristic-systematic model: A theoretical framework and an exploration. *Computers & Security, 38*, 28–38.

Mayhorn, C. B., & Nyeste, P. G. (2012). Training users to counteract phishing. *Work, 41*(1), 3549–3552.

Mitnick, K. D., & Simon, W. L. (2002). *The art of deception: Controlling the human element of security.* New York: John Wiley & Sons.

Moody, G., Galletta, D. F., Walker, J., & Dunn, B. K. (2011). Which phish get caught? An exploratory study of individual susceptibility to phishing. In *Proceedings of the International Conference on Information Systems.*

Petty, R. E., & Cacioppo, J. T., (1986). The elaboration likelihood model of persuasion. In L. Berkowitz (Ed.), *Advances in experimental social psychology* (vol. 19, pp. 123–205). San Diego: Academic Press.

Sheng, S., Magnien, B., Kumaraguru, P., Acquisti, A., Cranor, L. F., Hong, J., & Nunge, E. (2007). Anti-Phishing Phil: The design and evaluation of a game that teaches people not to fall for phish. In *Proceedings of the 3rd Symposium on Usable Privacy and Security* (pp. 88–99).

Sheng, S., Holbrook, M., Kumaraguru, P., Cranor, L. F., & Downs, J. (2010). Who falls for phish? A demographic analysis of phishing susceptibility and effectiveness of Interventions. In *Proceedings of the SIGCHI Conference on Human Factors in Computing Systems* (pp. 373–382).

Vishwanath, A. (2015). Examining the distinct antecedents of e-mail habits and its influence on the outcomes of a phishing attack. *Journal of Computer-Mediated Communication, 20*(5), 570–584.

Wang, J., Herath, T., Chen, R., Vishwanath, A., & Rao, H. R. (2012). Phishing susceptibility: An investigation into the processing of a targeted spear phishing email. *IEEE Transactions on Professional Communication, 55*(4), 345–362.

Watters, P. A. (2009). Why do users trust the wrong messages? A behavioural model of phishing. In *Proceedings of the eCrime Researchers Summit* (pp. 1–7).

Workman, M. (2007). Gaining access with social engineering: An empirical study of the threat. *Information Systems Security, 16*(6), 315–331.

Workman, M. (2008). Wisecrackers: A theory-grounded investigation of phishing and pretext social engineering threats to information security. *Journal of the American Society for Information Science and Technology, 59*(4), 662–674.

Wu, M., Miller, R. C., & Garfinkel, S. L. (2006). Do security toolbars actually prevent phishing attacks? In *Proceedings of the SIGCHI Conference on Human Factors in Computing Systems* (pp. 601–610).

Wright, R. T., Jensen, M. L., Thatcher, J. B., Dinger, M., & Marett, K. (2014). Influence techniques in phishing attacks: An examination of vulnerability and resistance. *Information Systems Research, 25*(2), 385–400.

Tembe, R., Zielinska, O., Liu, Y., Hong, K. W., Murphy-Hill, E., Mayhorn, C., & Ge, X. (2014). Phishing in international waters: Exploring cross-national differences in phishing conceptualizations between Chinese, Indian and American samples. In *Proceedings of the 2014 Symposium and Bootcamp on the Science of Security*.

Appendix 10A Email Messages Used in the Experiment

Table 10A.1   Financial Acquisition.

GAIN	LOSS
From: Student Research	**From:** Financial Management
Subject: $50 gift card to fill survey	**Subject:** RIAA Tuition Assistance
Dear Student:	Dear Student:
Receive $50 for completing a short survey! Ludlow Corporation has been measuring consumers' attitudes for three decades, and companies rely on our results to develop and market their products. If you complete our new survey by MIDNIGHT TONIGHT, you will receive your choice of a $50 gift card to Amazon.com or Barnesandnoble.com. Just click on the link below to complete the survey and tell us which gift you want and where to send it.	Recording Association of America has provided 2000 tuition relief vouchers of $300 for students who sign a pledge to not download music illegally from the Internet. This has been provided since your University was able to successfully implement a program to curb illegal download of music from the web. The vouchers are first come first serve until they last. You must act quickly before they run out. Please click on the link below and provide your personal information.
http://ualbany.9nl.com/giftcardsurvey/	http://ualbany.9nl.com/tuitionrelief/
Best Regards, Kevin Peterson	Best Regards,
Ludlow Corporation	Kevin Peterson
	Asst VP, Financial Management

Table 10A.2 Non-Financial Acquisition/Goods

GAIN	LOSS
From: Apple Research Team	**From:** Legal Affairs
Subject: Get a free iPad mini for giving it a test drive	**Subject:** Action Needed to Keep your Registration Open
Dear Student:	Dear student:
You've won an iPad mini! Apple is distributing its new mini tablet to select university students who are willing to help evaluate it. The tablet has the same capabilities as an iPad with a smaller screen. In return for the free tablet all we will request is for you to provide us feedback on the product every two weeks. You will be provided a template to fill out your experiences with the tablet. Apple is an equal opportunity company and you were randomly selected without any cultural or racial bias. Please register at the following link and make sure that you accept the terms and conditions at the end of the form.	The University takes its legal responsibility seriously and is very concerned about illegal download of music on campus. We have been singled out by RIAA as one of the most prolific abusers of illegal music downloads. You have yet to complete the illegal downloading pledge, which the University requires. If you do not complete the form, you will have a block on your registration and will not be able to sign up for courses during the pre-registration period. Please click on the link below to complete the form.
http://ualbany.9nl.com/ipadmini/	http://ualbany.9nl.com/registration/
Best Wishes,	Sincerely,
Apple Research Team	Kevin Peterson
	Legal Affairs

Table 10A.3 Security

GAIN	LOSS
From: Admin	**From:** Student Accounts
Subject: Students—protect your computer with a free firewall	**Subject:** Student Bank Card Fraud Prevention
Dear Student:	Dear Student:
The University takes its information security very seriously and is concerned about the recent spate of cyber attacks on computers within the University. We would like to ensure that all student computers are secure. Any virus infection on your computer can get transmitted to the University network. We have decided to provide students with a firewall program to install on your computers. Please download the firewall on your computer. It is a simple one step process that will add to your security as well as that of the University. Please download the firewall software as soon as you can. This service will not cost you anything.	There have been cyber attacks at several banks that manage visa, master and debit card transactions for online purchases. The attacks have been going on since March of this year but were discovered earlier this month. We suspect that several million bank or credit card numbers have been compromised. If you have used your card for online purchases in the U.S. this year your account may have been compromised. The easiest way to see if your account has been compromised is to click the following link. If your card has been compromised you should call your bank and request a new one immediately.
http://ualbany.9nl.com/studentsoftware/	http://ualbany.9nl.com/FraudPrevention/
Best regards,	Sincerely,
The Information Security Office	The Student Support Office

Table 10A.4   Social

GAIN (REWARDS OF ALTRUISM)	LOSS (POTENTIAL NETWORKS)
From: USA Aid Rescue Organization	**From:** Name: Alumni Network
Subject: Volunteers needed!	**Subject:** UAlbany Friends Network
Hi!	Dear User:
Hurricanes Isaac and Sandy have caused significant devastation in the Gulf Coast and Atlantic Coast regions. Thousands of people have lost everything and have become homeless. The initial response by Americans was outstanding, but these people still need help. Efforts by Red Cross are limited to emergency help. Please make a donation of time or money at the following link. People need our help!	Don't be left friend-less—act now to maintain membership in alumni networks. Your alumni network has established an account for you in their rapidly growing social connections with influential alumni. This network will provide access to internships in all fields of study, as well as to high paying jobs. You must confirm your account or it will be deleted. Click the following link to confirm your personal information and to retain your membership account.
http://ualbany.9nl.com/volunteer/	http://ualbany.9nl.com/UaNetwork/
Kindly,	Sincerely,
USA Aid Rescue Organization	Kevin Peterson
	Alumni Network Coordinator

Appendix 10B Informational Message

You've Been Phished!

Dear Student:

This was an email to test whether or not you would click on a Phishing link. Fortunately, this is only a test and no harm was done to your computer or you. If this had been a real email, you could have become a victim of Phishing. Our goal is to educate students on the dangers of Phishing such that do not become victims of identity theft.

This study is completely anonymous and we do not know who you are. Even some of the most technologically savvy people become victims of such phishing attacks. We will invite you to participate in a short survey study that asks your perceptions of phishing messages. But first, we want to give you some tips to avoid getting phished. Even if you decide not to take our survey, please pay attention to these tips:

1. No legitimate firm is going to ask you for account information, passwords, verification of security questions or other sensitive information.
2. Even if the email address seems to be from a legitimate company you conduct business with it could still be a phishing email with the real address camouflaged. If the email seems suspicious, instead of replying to the email, call the customer service
3. Be especially wary of emails warning you about security breaches and account compromises asking you to provide detailed account information–these are phishing scams
4. Be extra careful of misspelled names e.g., allbany.edu instead of albany.edu or R0gers.com instead of Rogers.com. Check for the name of the company on the Internet.

If you do get phished the hacker may attempt to commit credit card fraud, bank fraud or identity theft. For such scenarios you need to take the following steps:

I. CREDIT/ATM CARD FRAUD

a) Report the theft of information to the credit card company and cancel your current card
b) Check your credit card statement to see if there are transactions you do not recognize
c) Report any unauthorized transactions to the credit card company (your liability is limited to $50)
d) Report any unauthorized transactions on your debit/ATM card within 60 days of receiving the statement (if you report within 60 days your liability is zero else it is unlimited)

II. BANK ACCOUNT THEFT

a) Call your affected financial institution to report the loss right away.
b) Cancel your account and open a new one.

III. IDENTITY THEFT

a) Request credit reports from the three agencies to see if any fake accounts have been opened on your behalf. If true request the malicious activity be removed from your records and a victim's statement be placed on record
b) File criminal report with your local police
c) Report theft to the Social Security Administration's Fraud Hotline
d) Alert passport office to ensure that a passport is not ordered in your name
e) File a complaint to the Internet Fraud Office

To help us improve the security at the University we will appreciate if you could take a short anonymous survey that pertains to your perceptions about risk.

Chapter 9: Concluding Remarks

Developing an understanding of the dynamics involved in crime victimization and criminal offending can produce insightful observations that add to a comprehensive approach in combating crimes involving Internet communication and technology. In this chapter, we see the importance of studying the psychological aspects of human behavior that are involved in the response to malicious solicitations. The research presented to us in this chapter reveals that a major source of breaches in security is basic human susceptibility to deception. Notably, email messages designed to "phish" personal and sensitive information from individuals impact potential victims differently based on the content of the solicitation and aspects of psychological vulnerability such as the fear of losing something of value, the desire for gaining something of value, or just simple weakness and human proneness to greed or get-rich-quick schemes. Offenders can target certain populations and manipulate their weaknesses to increase their likelihood of successfully perpetrating their malicious activities. These findings have strong implications for the development of information security research, policy, and practices that are driven by a theoretical framework of understanding based on the heuristic model of human behavior presented in this chapter.

CHAPTER 10

Crime Victimization in Various Contexts

Introduction

The study of crime victimization encompasses a variety of dimensions that incorporate trends in victimization, the interpretation of causal variables, contextual elements that drive the motive for offending, and the long-term impact of experiencing crime and violence on victims. These aspects drive the theoretical and research components of victimology and determine the course of policy and program development that guides intervention strategies addressing the needs of victims of crime. Imperative to this study is the deconstruction of a range of issues where the intersection of crime and victimization are often misunderstood or neglected due to erroneous judgement, the influence of sociocultural myths, and the lack of proper theoretical conceptualization.

This chapter dedicates three reading selections that address relevant and timely topics within the study of victimology. The first selection considers the problem of drug addiction and the isolated attention to this behavior from an offending perspective without the proper knowledge base of the association between drug use, drug abuse, and the experience of victimization. The second reading explores behavioral elements of adolescent vulnerability to victimization by peers, focusing on the often-negligible attention to individual traits and personal qualities that can influence encounters between teenagers and serve as predictors of violence between them. The third reading presented in this chapter presents a case study on the experiences of intimate partner violence by a male victim at the hands of a female, examining the specific context of these experiences and how they better inform the response to male victimization.

Guiding Questions

As you read, consider the following questions:

1. How can the conditions and lifestyles of drug addicts contribute to their violent victimization?

2. Why is it important to study criminal offenses such as illicit drug use from the perspective of victimology?

3. Are there certain personality traits or social characteristics that influence the selection of victims as crime targets in cases involving bullying?

4. How do we as a society perceive the violent victimization of males at the hands of female perpetrators?

5. Does our response to intimate partner violence sufficiently address the needs of male victims?

Key Terms

Behavior Assessment System for Children (BASC)   A self-report personality assessment test for children that measures behavioral and emotional traits such as anxiety, hyperactivity, and aggression.

Bullying Victimization Scale (BVS)   A self-report survey of school experiences designed to measure aspects of bullying, including extent of the problem at school, personal victimization, and the formal and informal control of bullying.

existential phenomenology   A philosophical approach to understanding whereby we are better informed about a phenomenon based on the lived experiences and meanings of and for others.

routine activity theory   A theory of criminal behavior and victimization that hinges upon the relationship among a motivated offender, a suitable target, and the lack of capable guardianship.

The Drug Addict as a Victim

A Link to Explore

Laura M. Nunes and Ana Sani

Introduction

Victimization is a phenomenon that appears in different settings and includes several dimensions, which themselves also differ according to the type of victim and their specificities. Certain populations have heightened vulnerability, which increases their exposure to the experience of victimization situations. Among these population types, we can also mention those who tend to engage in criminal behaviors but at the same time present characteristics which render them susceptible to victimization. We are talking here about the drug addict, who often has two roles: on the one hand s/he may commit illegal and violent actions, and on the other, s/he may also be the victim of crime and violence.

Drug addiction is one of those behaviors that is related to crime and can at the same time lead to victimization experiences. Several studies (Brochu 2006; Nunes 2011a; Seddon 2006) have been developed with the purpose of examining the link between drug addiction and criminal behavior. Today this drug-crime link is considered unquestionable, although it is also well known that there is no causal relationship between those two behaviors (Bean 2014).

However, it is also understood that the victimization of drug addicts often occurs, and there are not enough studies dedicated to this different mode of connection between drugs and crime. Following this, some authors (MacCoun, Kilmer and Reuter 2003) have stressed the need to study the drug addict, not just because there is a link with criminal behavior, but also considering the victimization suffered by those individuals. It is important to study the victimization of those who, as drug users, are exposed to the violent drug markets, have a high-risk lifestyle, and are under the psychopharmacological effects of the drugs (Goldstein 1985). It is undeniable that these factors increase the vulnerability of this population. Over the last few years, a number of researchers (Goldstein 1985; MacCoun, Kilmer and Reuter 2003; Nunes 2011a; 2011b) have highlighted the urgency of studying drug addict victimization, but the reality is that this domain has received little attention.

In this chapter, we will present some theoretical models regarding the drug-crime link, and explore some approaches to addiction-related violence, in order to explain why it is important to analyze this phenomenon. We will also highlight how these theoretical models are suitable for the possible explanation of the frequent victimization of the drug addict. We will go on to present briefly an integrated model of the drug addict's victimization (Nunes and Sani 2013), and explain the importance of developing modes of evaluation, through victimization surveys, specially designed for drug addicts (Nunes and Sani 2014).

Broadly, the aim of this chapter is to understand victimization from the drug addict's perspective, and raise awareness of a problem that is rarely investigated and not covered by most drug addict support programs.

Drug Addiction and Violence—A Lifestyle Based in Deviant Routines

There is extensive evidence that drug abuse and violence are linked (Caridade and Nunes 2014), and there are analyses that support empirically the link between drug abuse and criminal practices (Brochu 2006; Nunes 2011a). The relation between violent practices and use of drugs is well known. It is also known that drug consumption can be on the part of the offender, on the victim, or both (Fagan 1993; Kleiman and Heussler 2011). So, there are criminal occurrences in which the victim is an individual under the influence of drugs.

Explanations of this link between drugs and violence have focused on aggression patterns rather than the pattern of victimization. Although it is known that drug consumption increases some violent behaviors (Howard and Wang 2003a, 2003b), the reality is that drug effects/consequences also can lead to victimization vulnerabilities. The drug addict is, in effect, an individual with special characteristics which may render him fragile in the face of victimization situations. Indeed, we know that drug use can potentiate the occurrence of victimization experiences (Whitbeck, Hoyt and Yoder 2001). Moreover, while studies have been conducted on the drug-crime link, possible links between drug consumption and victimization experiences (Stevens et al., 2007) have not been so widely explored, and this constitutes a serious failure in analysis of the phenomenon of drug addiction.

Indeed, there are a considerable number of reasons to believe that the drug addict is particularly vulnerable to victimization, especially when those individuals are under the effects of intoxicating substances. This can be explained by different arguments (MacCoun, Kilmer and Reuter 2003):

1 because the person under the intoxicating effects of drugs is an easy target for actions such as robbery, rape, and other crimes;

2 because intoxicated individuals often take on an unsettling demeanor, for example in terms of their appearance, behavior, and speech;

3 because the state of intoxication leads to unpredictable and ambiguous behavior manifestations;

4 because the abovementioned conditions weaken the perception of signals and stimuli, and diminish the capacity of transmission signals to others (i.e., the intoxicated state leads to poor communication);

5 finally, because it is not uncommon in the illegal drug market to find that the individual selling the product, being in possession of large sums of money, is also intoxicated.

These elements make the addict a fragile and desirable target. Indeed, the very lifestyle of these individuals makes them vulnerable to victimization, and the environment they frequent is also frequented by those who may commit crimes against them.

Routine Activities Theory and Drug Addicted Vulnerability

According to Wolfgang (1957), certain crime situations are precipitated by the victim. We can therefore inquire as to whether the drug addict, with all the characteristics mentioned above, is not one of those individuals who create situations which may precipitate their own victimization. As noted, some of these characteristics can indeed enhance such individuals' own victimization, and thus we often find that victims of murder and assault, for example, show signs of having used drugs and having previously been involved in conflicts leading to a physical attack.

Fagan and Chin (1990), in their studies, affirm the vulnerability to victimization situations of those who take drugs. The authors argue that some substances induce behavioral changes that may result in situations with characteristics that potentiate victimization by aggression, for example, carried out by those who are free of the effects of substances. Other authors (Stevens et al., 2007) have found elevated levels of violent victimization among drug users. In order to better analyze this phenomenon, it is necessary to look at the routines of the drug users, in places where there are drugs to buy and sell, with illegal transactions conducted in a highly conflictive context. Indeed, we must take into consideration the fact that the drug user and the criminal exist in the same illicit markets, and that they both have an interest in one product: the drug. So, these two deviant figures turn out to cross each other's paths in the same contexts and confront the same interests.

The theory of routine activities developed by Cohen and Felson (1979) provides an explanation for the occurrence of crime centered in criminal circumstances and contexts. According to this approach, there are three important elements which take place at the same time promoting the criminal occurrence. Those three factors are (i) a motivated offender, (ii) a vulnerable target or possible victim, and (iii) the absence of guardians able to prevent the occurrence. Those three factors work together to create the opportunity for crime.

This theoretical perspective argues that the choices of an individual can influence the possibility of becoming a desirable target (Doerner and Lab, 2012) for a motivated offender who is ready to commit a crime, and is waiting for the most favorable criminal opportunities in a context with no-one to prevent the crime being committed. Thus, an addict may be an appropriate target because of his or her vulnerable state, arising either from being under the influence of drugs or in a state of abstinence. In fact, given the elements explained earlier there are many factors which put the drug addict at high risk of being deceived or attacked (Wilcox 2010).

All of this is also related to the individual's lifestyle, which, in the case of the addict, is highly risky. According to Hindelang, Gottfredson, and Garofalo (1972), the risk of victimization is very much associated with the lifestyle of the people who, in fact, can influence/affect the opportunities for crime, by creating favorable criminal conditions. A drug addict, by virtue of his lifestyle at the margins of society, is generally represented as a deviant individual and therefore at greater risk of being subjected to violent reactions from others. There is an increased likelihood of the addict being involved in crime, either as victim or offender, or even as a witness, because of the places that this population frequent, especially at night, and because of the relationships that these individuals establish with people closely linked to drug misuse and criminal contexts (Kennedy and Forde 1990; Nofziger 2009; Nofziger and Stein 2006).

Thus, direct and/or indirect victimization eventually integrate the everyday life and routines of the drug addict, who has regular contact with deviant and criminal individuals. Also, by dint of their lifestyle the drug addict will tend to have much less protection, especially in the form of formal protection from the social control system, for fear that their deviant activity is discovered by the authorities (Wilcox 2010).

Taken together, this lack of protection, the perceived vulnerability, the motivation of others to engage in criminal practices, and the other factors discussed above, can all explain why someone with a lifestyle linked to drug dependence can be seen as very easily engaged in victimization situations.

Approaches to the Drug-Crime Link and Drug-Victimization Connection

Some theoretical models explain the drug-crime link and drug-related violence from a deterministic point of view, based on the powerful effects of the substances on behaviors.

One such approach is the *Chronic Effects Model*, which suggests that drug addiction becomes chronic and causes neuropsychological functioning changes, developing pathological conditions that contribute to the adoption of violent actions (Rothman, Reyes, Johnson and LaValley 2012). This model focuses mainly on violence developed in the context of intimate relationships. We can look at this theoretical approach as a possible explanation for the violent acts of the drug addict, in the context of close relationships—even though this model can also be applied to violence in other relational contexts. There are models which focus on the generic relation between drugs and crime. Thus, another explanation, the so-called *Psychopharmacological Model*, tries to explain criminal behavior due to the pharmacological effects of the substances (White and Gorman 2000). In this point of view, the intoxicated state can cause behavioral changes and lead to violent actions, and the toxic effects can also lead to criminal behaviors. This is true, but intoxication also tends to leave individuals prostrate, and therefore in a situation of greater vulnerability to victimization (Nunes and Sani 2013). We can therefore say that this model, which explains the link between drugs and crime and violent behaviors, can also support an explanation of the link between drugs and victimization.

Another approach attempts to explain how violence in intimate relationships may be associated with drug use. The *Model of Proximal Effects* refers to the psychopharmacological power of substances, which gradually leads to a reduction of cognitive functioning capacities, and increases impulsivity, which tends to mediate the aggressive behavior (Shorey, Stuart and Cornelius 2011). It seems that some of the factors used to explain this problem are indirectly linked to drugs, but we also can say that the reduction of cognitive capacities can lead to more risky behaviors, and can be exploited by others who would victimize the drug user.

Another model, very close to the one just presented, is the *Economic-Compulsive Model*, which points to drug dependence as a cause of acquisitive crime. This model suggests that crime related to drug addiction occurs because the drug user needs money to buy drugs. However, this argument may be a form of rationalization often presented by addicts about their own criminal behaviors (MacCoun, Kilmer and Reuter 2003). On the other hand, the economic situation of the drug addict, together with the need to maintain the addiction, and abstinence syndrome, may lead individuals to situations that weaken them in a deviant world where they can easily become a victim. Because of this fragility, we can conclude that the reasons behind the criminal practices developed by drug users are the same factors that can expose them to a victimization experience.

Related to the lifestyle perspective, and considering the places where those individuals develop their routine activities, the *Systemic Model* refers to the violence associated with illegal drug markets. This model can help to explain both the criminal behavior and the victimization of the drug addict. This theoretical point of view explores the violence of the drug markets that can potentially lead addicts to violent behaviors in order to protect themselves, as well as to situations in which they are the victims of violent actions (Goldstein 1985). Thus, the study of those violent behaviors, in systemic terms, should emerge as a priority for analysis of the drug-crime phenomenon (Goldstein, Brownstein and Bellucci 1989). However, it is also important to study the victimization of drug users who are exposed to these violent markets (Goldstein 1985). From a systemic and environmental perspective, we can say that the places the drug addict visits frequently are the same places where s/he can commit or become a victim of crime.

Another model presents an integrated perspective. This is the *Tripartite Model* proposed by Goldstein (1985), which points to the combined influence of the factors mentioned earlier. This theory tries to explain the drug-crime link, but it also provides an explanation for the frequent victimization of the drug addict. The author combines three reasons for such linkage: (i) the psychopharmacological effects of the product; (ii) the high costs of certain illegal substances; and (iii) the violence in illegal drug markets. According to the author, those factors could affect the individual's behaviors. So, this could contribute to crime, committed by different types of offender, with different types of victim (Goldstein, Bellucci, Spunt and Miller 1991). As we can see, the reasons that the literature points to for the drug-crime link can also explain the vulnerability of the drug addict to victimization.

Other authors have presented theoretical approaches that take a different, less deterministic perspective, instead taking a processual point of view centered on the lifestyle of the drug addict. From this perspective, we can say that lifestyle, as presented by Faupel (1987; 1981), can relate to the issues associated with the individual's routines that have already been pointed out in this chapter as something to consider.

Faupel presented a model based on analysis of the life structure and career of the individual who uses drugs, and specifically heroin. Faupel (1987) emphasized the link between drug abuse and criminal practices as a process through four stages affected by different variables, such as availability of the substances, the individual's motivations, and their deviant skills. According to the author, the structure of life is related to the standard daily occurrences associated with areas such as labor, domestic and private life, etc. Then, Faupel (1987) argued, there would be four stages: (i) the *casual user*, with low availability of substances and a high life structure; (ii) the *stabilized junkie*, with high availability of substances and a high life structure; (iii) the *free-wheeling junkie*, with high availability of substances but a low life structure; and, at last, (iv) the state of the *street junkie*, with no life structure and no access to substances. This individual is an outsider both in the normative society and in the deviant subculture. He has no place in any social group.

The *street junkie* is lonely and fragile, and exceptionally vulnerable to victimization situations. Indeed, this individual is completely alone, without support or group belonging. At the *free-wheeling junkie* stage the individual has access to drugs but not to a life structure. So, this will be a state in which the addict is at the mercy of illicit drugs markets. In such markets there are high probabilities of being a victim of crime, as we have already seen. These individuals will be subjected to illegal drug market fluctuations, and will obviously be vulnerable to victimization situations in this particularly dangerous environment.

Following what has been said above, we draw attention to an integrated model, proposed by Nunes and Sani (2013). This theoretical approach tries to consider most of the factors that have already been highlighted by the conceptualizations previously developed.

This integrated model argues that it is possible to adopt the Goldstein idea, and take into consideration the fact that drug addicts have constraints related to substances' costs. Because of this, addicts can more easily succumb to forms of criminal or deviant behaviors, such as participation in drug trafficking, and other criminal actions. Furthermore, it is not uncommon for those individuals to have no ways to pay their accounts with their drug suppliers. In those cases, the addict is at the mercy of violent methods used to settle the accounts and resolve conflict. In the illegal context of drug markets these kinds of problems are resolved by violent and unlawful methods.

Considering Faupel's stages, and looking to the problems present in the drug addict's life, including lifestyle and routines in dangerous and illegal business as well as in violent places, it is clear that it only makes sense to think about the problem of drug addiction by integrating these models into a global perspective which integrates all of these described factors (Nunes and Sani 2013).

Reasons to Evaluate the Victimization of the Drug Addict

There are several factors that make it important to evaluate the victimization experiences of the drug addict population, and the violence of illegal drug markets is one of them, since it exposes the addict to numerous risks. This violence relates to the following aspects (MacCoun, Kilmer and Reuter 2003):

1   First, the youth of the participants involved in those transactions (approximately 18–22), can lead to easier involvement in violent actions, and certain markets of some drugs have very young sellers;

2   Second, the price of the drugs, which can be so high as to create competition situations which lead easily to violent occurrences;

3   Third, these illegal transactions are conducted under conditions of pressure and uncertainty, and regulation of the conduct and protection of the business are carried out by violence;

4   Fourth, some drugs turn their users more violent and ready for precipitated behaviors in a conflict situation. It is important to note that, according to some delinquency studies, drug user on drug user crime is very frequent.

On the other hand, and according to Goldstein (1985), it is very difficult to access information about the victimization of drug addicts because these kinds of victims are not interested in talking about it with the police; they do not remember details of the crime or the offender; most victimization questionnaires only ask about drug consumption in general, and not about the role of drugs in the specific offense; in this context, the victim may have instigated some kind of provocation that might have precipitated the crime. So, emphasizes Goldstein (1985), in the face of all this, we cannot overestimate the importance of the drug addict's victimization.

Alcohol-related crime and violence and the victimization associated with alcohol abuse are topics that have been widely studied. However, the relation between illegal drugs consumption and victimization experiences has not had much attention. According to various authors (e.g., MacCoun, Kilmer and Reuter 2003; Nunes 2011b), these are some of the reasons why it is urgent to study drug addict victimization.

Final Notes

As we said at the beginning of this chapter, over the last few decades science has tried to explain the idea that the victim of ongoing violence can sometimes develop a drug abuse problem, in order to develop better methods of support for individuals in such situations. The social sciences have also studied the use of drugs by the offender, as well as the phenomenon of the link between drug abuse and crime. But very few studies have focused on the drug addict as a victim of crime and violence, considering the conditions and lifestyle of those individuals.

Having presented some of the theoretical models relating to the drug-crime link and attending to evidence already revealed in studies pertaining to the victimization of the drug addict, it seems urgent to start studying the experience of victimization situations among drug users. The urgency of such investigation lies in the fact that these individuals not only have potential for delinquent actions, but are also exposed to very difficult situations that can lead to victimization experiences.

In effect, the drug addict is a kind of victim who, for obvious reasons, has no interest in reporting the crime they have suffered to the authorities. However, they are victims of severe situations, and rehabilitation programs should take this into account. For this reason, this is a phenomenon which should be studied with great attention.

To do so, we need to develop victimization surveys specially designed for this very specific population, such as the questionnaire developed by Nunes and Sani (2014) for the Portuguese drug addict population. On the other hand, the general drug addict evaluation should include an analysis of possible situations of victimization so that intervention can be designed to take into account the specificities of these cumulative experiences. It is also imperative to know the role of drugs in the occurrence of crime and to ascertain the influence of substances on the offender's behavior, and also the potential vulnerability of this kind of person to be a victim.

This association between substance abuse and victimization is noteworthy. Investigation of this association is the study of the potential risk of a victimization experience leading to involvement in consumption behaviors, often at early stages of the development of the individual. Drug use can be preceded and contributed to by victimization experiences, and can be a factor which exposes the individual to risks of becoming a victim of violence and crime. Thus, evaluation must consider the register of the consumption, and the consumption history of each individual. It is also very important to analyze the situations of victimization that could have arisen prior to the drug abuse period, as well as after the addiction problem. Only with this kind of information can we design proper intervention programs that consider all of the various dimensions of the drug-violence link. It is imperative to treat this population by acknowledging that most of their problems and victimization experiences are too severe and cause too much damage to be ignored in the treatment processes.

It is impossible to understand those individuals and provide appropriate support without looking at all of the dimensions involved, and victimization risks are one of those factors. The prevention of this population's victimization also necessitates that attention be paid to the routines and lifestyles of the drug addict, and that these persons are able to report these criminal situations to the relevant assistance institutions without fear.

References

Andrews, D., & Bonta, J. (2010). *The psychology of criminal conduct* (5th Ed.). New Jersey: Matthew Bender, & Company.

Bean, P. (2014). *Drugs and crime*. New York: Routledge.

Brochu, S. (2006). *Drogue et criminalité. Une relation complexe* (2ª Ed.). Montréal: Les Presses de l'Université de Montréal.

Caridade, S., & Nunes, L. (2014). Violência nas relações íntimas juvenis e abuso de substâncias: vitimação, agressão e género. *Psiquiatria, Psicologia e Justiça, 6*, 167–189.

Cohen, L., & Felson, M. (1979). Social change and crime rate trends: A routine activity approach. *American Sociological Review, 44*, 588–608.

Doerner, W., & Lab, S. (2012). *Victimology*. 6ª edição Cincinnati: Anderson Publishing.

Fagan, J. (1993). Interactions among drugs, alcohol, and violence. *Health Affairs, 12*(4), 65–79.

Fagan, J., & Chin, K.-L. (1990). Violence as regulation and social control in the distribution of crack. In M. De La Rosa, E. Lambert, & B. Gropper (Eds.). *Drugs and violence: causes, correlates, and consequences* (pp. 8–43). Rockville: U.S. Department of Health and Human Services. National Institute on Drug Abuse.

Faupel C. (1987). Drug availability, life structure, and situational ethics of heroin addicts. *Journal of Contemporary Ethnography, 15*(3/4), 395–419.

Faupel C. (1991). *Shooting dope: career patterns of hard-core heroin users*. Gainesville: University of Florida Press.

Goldstein P. (1985). The drugs/violence nexus: A tripartite conceptual framework. *Journal of Drug Issues, 39*, 143–174.

Goldstein P., Brownstein H., & Bellucci A. (1989). Crack and homicide in New York city, 1988: A conceptual based event analysis. *Contemporary Drug Problems, 16*(4), 651–687.

Hindelang, M., Gottfredson, M., & Garofalo, J. (1978). *Victims of personal crime: An empirical foundation for a theory of personal victimization*. Cambridge, MA: Ballinger.

Howard, D., & Wang, M. Q. (2003a). Risk profiles of adolescent girls who were victims of dating violence. *Adolescence, 38*, 1–14.

Howard, D., & Wang, M. Q. (2003b). Psychosocial factors associated with adolescents boys' reports of dating violence. *Adolescence, 38*, 519–533.

Kennedy, L. W., & Forde, D. R. (1990). Risky lifestyles and dangerous results: Routine activities and exposure to crime. *Sociology and Social Research, 74*, 208–228.

Kleiman, M., & Heussler, L. (2011). Crime-minimizing drug policy. *Journal of Criminal Justice, 39*, 286–288.

MacCoun R., Kilmer B., & Reuter P. (2003). Research on drugs-crime linkage: the next generation. In J. Ashcroft, D. Daniels & S. Hart (Eds.). *Toward a Drugs and Crime Research Agenda for the 21st Century: Special Report* (pp. 65–90). Washington: U.S. Department of Justice Office of Justice Programs.

Nofziger, S., & Stein, R. (2006). To tell or not to tell: Lifestyle impacts on whether adolescents tell about violent victimization. *Violence and Victims, 21*, 371–382.

Nofziger, S. (2009). Deviant lifestyles and violent victimization at school. *Journal of Interpersonal Violence, 24*(9), 1494–1517.

Nunes, L. (2011a). *Droga-crime: (des)construções*. Porto: Edições UFP.

Nunes, L. (2011b). O toxicodependente sob a perspectiva da vitimação. In A. Sani (Ed.), *Temas da vitimologia: realidades emergentes e respostas sociais* (pp. 241–266). Coimbra: Almedina.

Nunes, L., & Sani, A. (2013). Victimization of the drug addict. *Journal of Modern Education Review, 3*(9), 243–250.

Nunes, L., & Sani, A. (2014). Toxicodependência e vitimação: inquérito dirigido a indivíduos dependentes de drogas. *Análise Psicológica, 1*(32), 79–90.

Rothman, E., Reyes, L., Johnson, R., & LaValley, M. (2012). Does the alcohol make them do it? Dating violence perpetration and drinking among youth, *Epidemiologic Reviews, 34*(1), 103–119.

Seddon, T. (2006). Drugs, crime and social exclusion: social context and social theory in British drugs-crime research. *British Journal of Criminology, 46*(4), 680–703.

Shorey, R., Stuart, G., & Cornelius, T. (2011), Dating violence and substance use in college students: A review of the literature. *Aggression and Violent Behavior, 16*, 541–550.

Stevens, A., Berto, D., Frick, U., Kerschl, V., McSweeney, T., Schaaf, S., Tartari, M., Turnbull, P., Trinkle, B., Uchtenhagen, A., Waidner, G., & Werdenish, W. (2007). The victimization of dependent drug users. Findings from a European study, UK. *European Journal of Criminology, 4*(4), 385–408.

Whitbeck, B., Hoyt, R., Yoder, K., Cauce, A., & Paradise, M. (2001). Deviant behaviour and victimization among homeless and runaway adolescents, *Journal of Interpersonal Violence, 16*(11), 1175–1204.

White H., & Gorman D. (2000). Dynamics of the drug-crime relationship. *Criminal Justice, 1*, 151–218.

Wilcox, P. (2010). Victimization, theories of. In B. Fisher, & S. Lab (Eds.), *Encyclopedia of victimology and crime prevention* (pp. 978–986). Thousand Oaks: SAGE Publications.

Wolfgang, M. (1957). Victim precipitated criminal homicide. *The Journal of Criminal Law, Criminology, and Police Science, 48*(1), 1–11.

Adolescents' Vulnerability to Peer Victimization

Interpersonal and Intrapersonal Predictors

Susan E. D'Esposito, Jamilia Blake, and Cynthia A. Riccio

This study explored how certain personality traits, behaviors, and social status may be associated with who is targeted as a victim of peer aggression. The sample consisted of 233 students in sixth through eighth grades from rural communities. Results indicate that symptoms of anxiety, a high sense of inadequacy, and elevated social stress are associated with victimization. The article discusses implications for prevention and intervention.

P eer victimization is a serious problem affecting our nation's schools, with nearly 36% of secondary students experiencing victimization at some point during their school career (Wang, Iannotti, & Nansel, 2009). Nansel and colleagues (2001) found that approximately one in three sixth- through 10th-grade students reported moderate or frequent involvement in bullying behavior, which includes being victimized by peers or bullying others. Peer victimization may take many forms, but is most commonly characterized by being the target of physically (e.g., being hit, pushed, or kicked), relationally (e.g., attempting to damage one's interpersonal relations and social status through social exclusion and rumor-mongering), verbally (e.g., name calling or mean teasing), or cyber (e.g., character defamation through technological means) aggressive acts conducted over time that are intended to cause physical harm, psychological distress, or humiliation.

Considerable research suggests that the consequences of victimization extend beyond embarrassment and may result in psychological and physical distress for some victims (Carney, 2008; Klomek, Marrocco, Kleinman, Schonfeld, & Gould, 2008). Whereas much of the research has explored the consequences of peer victimization, few studies have examined which factors may make some children more vulnerable to victimization than others (Hanish & Guerra, 2000; Hodges & Perry, 1999). Thus, the purpose of this study was to examine the intra- and interpersonal characteristics that are most associated with victimization for adolescent youth. Knowing the characteristics that are most related to victimization may provide school counselors the opportunity to engage those students at risk for victimization in counseling efforts, which might prevent future victimization or significant psychological distress.

Available research provides some information on the outcomes associated with peer victimization. Peer victimization affects a student's sense of security such that victims of peer aggression may suffer psychological harm long after the bullying stops (Farrington, 1993; Gladstone, Parker, & Malhi, 2006; Smokowski & Kopasz, 2005). For example, victimization is associated with greater health problems (e.g., somatization; Nishina, Juvonen, & Witkow, 2005), suicidal ideation, symptoms of depression and anxiety, and low self-esteem (Graham, Bellmore, & Mize, 2006; Peskin, Tortolero, Markham, Addy, & Baumler, 2006). In addition to affecting psychological adjustment, being a victim may have a detrimental effect on an adolescent's social status and interpersonal relationships with peers. Research indicates that adolescents who are chronically victimized also may be rejected by peers (Lopez & Dubois, 2005). At the same time, it is possible that the relationship between victimization and peer rejection is reciprocal, with children who are rejected by peers more likely to be victimized than their accepted peers (Buhs, Ladd, & Herald, 2006).

In addition to the impact on social and psychological adjustment, victimization also has been found to negatively affect students' achievement (Erath, Flanagan, Bierman, 2008); this is particularly likely when victimization is associated with a higher rate of absenteeism from school (Ladd & Ladd, 2001; Nishina et al., 2005) and lower academic achievement (Schwartz, Gorman, Nakamoto, & Toblin, 2005). Ultimately, the interaction of victimization, poor social status, academic difficulties, and increased school absence potentially can affect the development of appropriate support systems and coping skills. The same effects may not be present for all individuals who are subject to peer victimization. The combination of context and individual differences leads to increased vulnerability to victimization (Schwartz, Kelly, Cuong, & Badaly, 2010).

Vulnerability to Victimization

Although extensive research exists about the social and psychological consequences of victimization and the contexts in which victimization is likely to occur, less is known about the intraindividual factors that are associated with or may predict adolescents' risk for victimization. Some studies have suggested that bullies distribute their aggression in a selective process, thus suggesting that factors proprietary to the victim may play a role in attracting their perpetrators (Crick & Bigbee, 1998; Stoody, 2000). Horowitz et al. (2004) suggested that being different from what peers expect and value could target an adolescent for victimization and peer rejection. Further, it is possible that victims have some traits that make them more vulnerable to being bullied than others (Dodge, Bates, & Pettit, 1990; Hodges & Perry, 1999).

Hodges and Perry (1999) found that, in addition to peer rejection, the display of internalizing symptoms and physical weakness significantly predicted victimization in a sample of seventh-grade students. For the children in their study, risk of victimization seemed to be greatest for adolescents who were disliked by peers, perceived as anxious or depressed, and were physically weaker than peers. Physical weakness appears to consistently contribute to victimization, particularly among boys; however, other physical characteristics do not (Hodges & Perry, 1999; Card & Hodges, 2008). That is, studies have found that children who possess physical attributes such as obesity, wearing corrective lenses, speech problems, or exhibiting some form of physical disability are no more likely to be victims of aggression than their peers who do not possess these characteristics (Card & Hodges, 2008). Olweus (1993), however, suggested that these physical characteristics may cause children to have low self-esteem and possess a demeanor that invites harassment. Thus, internal characteristics (e.g., low self-esteem) rather than physical characteristics appear to be a possible predictor of victimization (Perry, Hodges, & Egan, 2001).

Children who appear socially inept have an increased likelihood of being victimized (Ladd & Kochenderfer-Ladd, 2002; Schwartz, Dodge, & Coie, 1993). For example, Bernan (2009) found that children who display inattentive and hyperactive behaviors are more likely to be victimized by peers, perhaps because their impulsive behaviors annoy aggressors, making them easy targets. In addition to exhibiting inattentive and hyperactive behaviors, children who evidenced disruptive behaviors were also more likely to be victimized. Little agreement exists as to whether some victims have poor social skills or are using poor coping strategies that include aggressively reacting to bullying (e.g., bully-victims; Farrington, 1993; Hanish & Guerra, 2000; Olweus, 1993). Hanish and Guerra found aggression and withdrawal to be predictive of victimization in the upper elementary grades. In sum, the current research suggests that children who are physically weaker and who exhibit internalizing symptoms, inattentive and hyperactive behavior, and aggression are at greater risk for victimization than their peers who do not possess these qualities.

On the positive side, research indicates that having friends, especially ones who will help protect against peer aggression, may reduce the chances of victimization and buffer the negative consequences of victimization (Erath et al., 2008; Schmidt & Bagwell, 2007). Thus, support from peers may be an important interpersonal indicator that reduces children's risk for experiencing victimization. For example, Junger-Tas and Van Kesteren (1999) found that only 11% of children who have five or more friends are victimized in school, yet 51% of children who are victims of peer aggression say they have no friends. The importance of peers in shielding children from experiencing victimization may be less salient to girls. Besag (2006) found that many girls' friendships were characterized by bullying behaviors, particularly when girls' friendships involved three or more girls.

Purpose of the Study

Only limited research has examined how behavioral traits and personality factors contribute to an individual's vulnerability to be the target of victimization, particularly in rural communities.

Internal psychological characteristics and external behavioral characteristics need to be considered, yet researchers have integrated few of these factors into recent empirical investigations (Hodge & Perry, 1999; Hanish & Guerra, 2000; Ladd & Ladd, 2001). In the context of universal screening for early intervention and prevention programming, identifying those personality and behavioral characteristics that may be markers of at-risk status for victimization is needed. The purpose of this study was to explore what factors, intrapersonal (e.g., personality traits such as display of internalizing symptoms, behaviors) or interpersonal characteristics (e.g., social status and interpersonal relationships with peers), are associated with victimization. Specifically, the authors were interested in whether intrapersonal characteristics such as internalizing symptoms of depression, anxiety, and secondary symptoms (e.g., sense of inadequacy, locus of control, feelings of independence, and low self-esteem) would be related to victimization.

The authors also sought to examine whether interpersonal characteristics such as social support from peers, perceived social skills, and feelings of stress surrounding interpersonal relationships would be associated with the likelihood that a child is a target for victimization. Given research suggesting that girls are more vulnerable to depression and stress than boys (Leadbeater, Blatt, & Quinlan, 1995) and gender differences in the association between victimization and social status (Berger & Rodkin, 2009), this study also examined whether the relation between intra- and interpersonal characteristics differed for boys and girls.

Students in middle school and junior high school were chosen for this study because adolescence is a period of transitional stress resulting in impulsive behaviors and rapid fluctuations in emotions, which in turn result in the possibility of repeated insults and rejection by peers (Marsh, Parada, Craven, & Finger, 2004; Seals & Young, 2003). Moreover, this specific age group was selected because research indicates that peer victimization occurs most frequently within this age group (Kokkinos & Panayiotou, 2004). The authors selected children from rural communities given the limited research on victimization within that type of community setting. Although students' risk for experiencing violence is generally lower in rural communities (Foster et al., 2005; Hope & Bierman, 1998), students in rural communities might be as likely to experience victimization as children from other settings due to the small and closely knit community context which characterize most rural settings (Beggs, Haines, & Hurlbert, 1996). In many rural schools, the peer network or peer dynamics is unlikely to change, with the same cohort of students being maintained from elementary through high school. Thus, the possibility exists that children from rural communities present the same likelihood of experiencing victimization as adolescents from non-rural settings because they are subject to the same group of aggressors year after year (Beggs et al. 1996).

Method

Participants were recruited from three middle schools and one junior high school in rural communities in the southwestern United States. The sample consisted of 243 students in sixth

(1.7%), seventh (45.1%), and eighth grade (53.2%), aged 12 to 15 years. Due to incomplete assessments, 10 cases were eliminated from the study, leaving 233 valid cases for analyses. Of the participating students, 45% were drawn from school one; 34% from school two; 12% from school three; and 3% from school four. With respect to student's racial/ethnic background and gender, 55.8% of participating students were female and 63.9% of students self-identified as Caucasian (n = 149), 14.6% as African American (n = 34), 11.2% as Hispanic (n = 26), 4.7% as Asian/Pacific Islander (n = 11), and 5.6% as Biracial or other (n = 13). Information on individual student's socioeconomic status was not collected; however, the 2004 United States census data indicated that the median household income for the communities in which the four schools were located ranged from $21,180 to $39,404 (United States Census Bureau, 2004). Additionally, school records indicated that participating school districts were predominantly White; approximately 24 to 55% of the students were economically disadvantaged according to state records.

Procedures

In accordance with IRB approval, parent consent and student assent were obtained. Participating students were administered a battery of instruments. At the request of the principals, these measurements were administered in small groups (between eight and 10 students at a time) to ensure that the students' questions could be easily answered within a reasonable period of time. The students were encouraged to answer each question truthfully, according to their own opinions and not the opinion of their peers. As an incentive to participate in the study, the name of each student who agreed to participate was placed in a drawing to win one of five $20 gift cards to a local store of the student's choice. In order to maintain confidentiality, participating students completed a separate form with their name, mailing address, email address, and phone number to be used for the drawing.

Measures

Behavior Assessment System for Children—Self-Report

The Behavior Assessment System for Children—Self-Report (BASC-SRP; Reynolds & Kamphaus, 1992) was used to assess children's self-reported intra- and interpersonal characteristics that might lead to victimization. The BASC-SRP is a 186-item, true-false measure that assesses clinical and adaptive measures of adjustment. The measure consists of 14 clinical and adaptive scales. Scale scores are reported in t scores with a mean of 50 and standard deviation of 10. The BASC-SRP is an established instrument with acceptable internal consistency reliability and validity (see Reynolds & Kamphaus, 1992). Reliability coefficients from the technical manual for each scale used in the present study are provided; however, a more comprehensive description of the psychometric properties of individual scales as well as the factor analytic structure of the BASC-SRP is available for review in the technical manual (Reynolds & Kamphaus, 1992).

The clinical scales used for this study have adequate reliability as presented in the BASC-SRP manual, and the reliability coefficients from the manual are reported by content area below. The scales provide information on the extent to which the child reports generalized fears, over-sensitivity, and worry (anxiety scale; 17 items; $\alpha = .87$); feelings of loneliness, sadness, and hope-lessness (depression scale; 17 items; $\alpha = .88$); the child's perception as to who has control over his/her life (locus of control scale; 16 items; $\alpha = .87$); the child's belief in the ability to achieve at expected levels (sense of inadequacy scale; 12 items; $\alpha = .77$); and the level of stress children experience when interacting with peers (social stress; 12 items; $\alpha = .81$). Specific adaptive scales were also used to assess students' emphasis on how successful they feel in relating to their peers (interpersonal relations; 10 items; $\alpha = .81$), their self-satisfaction (self-esteem; 6 items; $\alpha = .79$), and their confidence in their own ability to make decisions (self-reliance; 14 items; $\alpha = .71$). Whereas elevated scores on the clinical scales suggest that a child might be experiencing psy-chological maladjustment, elevated scores on BASC-SRP adaptive scales are indicative of positive adjustment and coping. The internal consistency of these scales could not be calculated because access to raw data was unavailable for this sample, but based on other research and replication of internal consistency of the scales (Blake, Lease, Turner, & Outley, in press; Reynolds & Kamphaus, 2004), and the similarity in demographics to the standardization sample, the authors have no reason to believe that the internal consistencies would change for this sample.

Bullying Victimization Scale

The Bullying Victimization Scale (BVS; Reynolds, 2003a) was used to measure adolescents' ex-periences with peer victimization. The BVS is a 46-item, self-report scale designed to assess the bullying behaviors and victimization experiences of children and adolescents in third through 12th grade. Children are asked to report the frequency in which they engaged in bullying or ex-perienced victimization in the past month on a 4-point likert scale (Never to Five or more times). The BVS yields two scales, Bullying and Victimization, that are scored independently since each scale represents distinct dimensions of student involvement in bullying incidents (Reynolds, 2003b). For this study, only the Victimization scale was used. The Victimization scale consists of 23 items measuring physical and relational victimization (e.g., if an adolescent has been physically assaulted, threatened, teased, called names, or intimidated by peers). The items from the Victimization scale were summed to yield a Victimization score and converted to a t score with a mean of 50 and standard deviation of 10. Elevated scores on the BVS victimization scale suggest that a student is the target of bullying and experiencing peer victimization. According to the technical manual, the BVS Victimization scale has adequate psychometric properties. The internal consistency for the Victimization Scale is .93 and the test–retest reliability for the Victimization scale was .80 as reported in the technical manual (Reynolds, 2003b). Consistent with the manual, the Cronbach coefficient alpha of the Victimization scale for the present sample was .93. The BVS Victimization scale evidences adequate construct and content validity. The manual indicates that the Victimization scale correlates moderately with well-validated measures of victimization and established measures of psychological adjustment and distress. Specifically, the BVS Victimization scale correlates with teacher ratings of victimization and various scales within the Beck Youth Inventories of Emotional and Social Impairment (Beck, Beck, & Jolly, 2001) and the Reynolds Adolescent Adjustment Screening Inventory (RAASI; Reynolds, 2001).

Harter Social Support Scale for Children and Adolescents

The Harter Social Support Scale for Children and Adolescents (Harter, 1985) was used to assess adolescent perceptions of the degree of social support they received from close friends and peers. This scale is a 24-item measure that yields four subscales: classmates, friend, parent, and teacher; however, for the purpose of this article, the authors used the classmates and friend subscales. Each sub-scale has six items. Students were asked to rate the extent to which they experienced support from their peers, friends, teachers, and parents on a 4-point likert scale (Never true to Always true). Whereas elevated scores on the friendship and classmate subscales are indicative of a student experiencing positive levels of support from peers and classmates, low scores suggest that a student feels unsupported by friends and classmates and may not be accepted by peers.

The Harter classmate support subscale evidences adequate validity and reliability as reported in the manual (Harter, 1985). Specifically, the classmate support subscale is significantly correlated with children's self-report ratings of global self-worth as well as children's social acceptance and popularity. Reliability estimates for the subscale for middle school students reported in the technical manual range from .74 to .79. The reliability indicated by the test developer was confirmed with the present sample, with a Cronbach's coefficient alpha of .80 noted for the friend subscale and .75 for the classmate subscale.

Demographic Survey

Children's self-reports from a demographic questionnaire was used to identify the gender of students participating in our study. Dummy coding was used to create the gender variable (1 = Girls).

Results

Preliminary Analyses

Pearson correlations between student's Victimization score, Intrapersonal Characteristics (Anxiety, Depression, Self-Esteem, Sense of Inadequacy, Locus of Control, and Self-Reliance), and Interpersonal Characteristics (Interpersonal Relations, Social Stress, Social Support Among Classmates, and Social Support Among Friends) were in the expected direction. Correlations and descriptive statistics are presented in Table 12.1.

Of the intrapersonal characteristics, higher levels of victimization were associated with higher levels of anxiety, more depressive symptoms, feelings of inadequacy, and an external locus of control. Additionally, victimization had a negative correlation with self-esteem and self-reliance, indicating that higher victimization was associated with lower self-esteem and children's difficulty with making decisions. For interpersonal characteristics, victimization was

Table 12.1 Correlation Coefficients and Descriptive Statistics of Study Variables.

	1	2	3	4	5	6	7	8	9	10	M	SD
1. Victimization											51.69	11.03
2. Anxiety	.30										50.86	9.49
3. Interpersonal Relations	−.31	−.33									51.97	7.68
4. Self-reliance	−.08	−.25	.43								51.34	9.07
5. Social Stress	.44	.67	−.53	−.38							51.14	10.31
6. Locus of Control	.34	.49	−.38	−.39	.69						50.73	10.60
7. Sense of Inadequacy	.33	.39	−.41	−.44	.59	.63					48.67	9.23
8. Self-esteem	−.24	−.58	.45	.30	−.68	−.51	−.45				48.54	10.08
9. Depression	.30	.52	−.48	−.44	.73	.70	.67	−.64			50.59	9.48
10. Classmate Support	−.33	−.36	.62	.32	−.57	−.39	−.39	.44	−.48		3.19	0.59
11. Friend Support	−.15	−.17	.42	.17	−.27	−.30	−.24	.15	−.23	.49	3.49	0.59

Note. All correlations are significant at the $p < .001$ level; variables are reported in t scores with a mean of 50 and standard deviation of 10.

associated with poorer interpersonal relations, stress surrounding relationships with peers, and less social support among classmates and friends.

Regression Analyses

To examine whether students' intrapersonal or interpersonal characteristics contributed to peer victimization, the authors conducted hierarchical regression analyses. Prior to conducting these analyses, gender interactions were tested to assess whether the relationship between victimization and intrapersonal and intepersonal charactisitcs differed for boys and girls. A two-step procedure was employed to test interaction effects in which the predictor and moderator variable (e.g., gender) were entered first in the models, followed by the product term of the moderator and predictor variable. All predictor variables included in the interaction models were mean centered (Aiken & West, 1991). Gender interaction effects were nonsiginificant for all the intrapersonal charactersitics, but were significant for the interpersonal variables. Thus, interaction effects were added to subsequent hiearchical regression models for the interpersonal charactersitics. Intrapersonal characteristics was entered into the model first (e.g., Block 1), followed by the addition of gender, main effects, and interaction effects for interpersonal charactersitics (e.g., Block 2).

Results revealed that intrapersonal characteristics explained 17% of the variance in peer victimization. Anxiety and sense of inadequacy contributed significantly to peer victimization; that is, children who were anxious and reported feeling inadequate endorsed greater levels of peer victimization.

Interpersonal characteristics explained an additional 12% of the variance in victimization above and beyond intrapersonal characteristics, $F_{inc}(8,217) = 4.85, p = .000$. Of the interpersonal

Table 12.2   Summary of Hierarchical Regression Analyses Predicting Victimization from Intra- and Interpersonal behaviors.

PREDICTOR	β	95%	CI	TOTAL R^2	ADJ R^2
		VICTIMIZATION			
Block 1: Intrapersonal Characteristics				.17	.12
Anxiety	.16*	.00	.36		
Depression	.04	−.20	.29		
Self-esteem	.00	−.18	.19		
Sense of Inadequacy	.20*	.03	.44		
Locus of Control	.16	−.02	.36		
Self-Reliance	.12	−.02	.31		
Block 2: Interpersonal Characteristics				.30	.23
Gender	−.01	−31.85	39.15		
Social Stress	.36*	.12	.67		
Gender X Social Stress	−.01	−.33	.31		
Interpersonal Relations	−.01	−.33	.32		
Gender X Interpersonal Relations	−.40*	−.85	.04		
Classmate support	−.44**	−13.21	−3.49		
Gender X Classmate support	.43**	3.76	16.46		
Friend Support	.18	−.25	7.10		
Gender X Friend support	−.15	−9.55	1.10		
ΔR^2				.12	

Note. Adj R^2 = Adjusted R^2, ΔR^2 = R^2 change, β = standardized regression coefficient;*p <.05; **p <.001

characteristics, social stress and the interaction effects for classmate support and interpersonal relations were significantly related to victimization. Children who reported experiencing more stress surrounding their interpersonal relations endorsed greater victimization. Whereas having low support from classmates contributed to victimization ($\beta = -.40, t = -3.41, p = .001$) for boys, classmate support was not as related to girls' victimization experiences ($\beta = .84, t = .69, p = .490$). Although poor interpersonal relations did not contribute to victimization for boys ($\beta = -.02$; $t = -.201, p = .804$), for girls, poor intepersonal relations was associated with elevated peer victmization ($\beta = -.28, t = -2.40, p = .018$).

Discussion

The present study was designed to explore how personality traits and behaviors were associated with who is targeted as a victim of peer aggression. The authors found that both intra- and interpersonal characteristics were significant contributors to victimization in adolescents. In particular, these results support the findings of others that anxiety and feelings of inadequacy contribute to whether a child is victimized by his or her peers (Bernstein & Watson, 1997; Horowitz et al., 2004). Also consistent with this is the finding that children who appear socially incompetent and are not assertive have an increased likelihood of being victimized (Ladd & Kochenderfer Ladd, 2002; Schwartz et al., 1993). Thus, children who exhibit feelings of inadequacy, oversensitivity, and worry may be providing a signal to aggressors that they are unable to defend themselves (Bernstein & Watson, 1997; Horowitz et al., 2004), thus increasing the likelihood that they are seen as easy, but not justifiable, targets for bullying.

In contrast to prior research (Craig, 1998; Hanish & Guerra, 2002; Hodges & Perry, 1999; Kochenderfer-Ladd & Skinner, 2002), self-esteem and depression were not significant contributors to victimization in this study. The authors' failure to find a significant relation between victimization and self-esteem is curious, but consistent with the work of Seals and Young (2003). Given that self-esteem was moderately correlated with other intrapersonal variables in the present study, it is possible that the order in which the self-esteem variable was entered into the aggression model might have impacted the degree to which self-esteem explained the variance in victimization; however, the order used was most supported by the existing research. A reanalysis of the model with self-esteem entered first did not alter the findings. These results indicate that self-esteem does not make an important contribution to explaining the variance in victimization for the present sample.

The authors found only partial support for the role of internalizing symptoms in predicting victimization as noted by Hodges and Perry (1999); although anxiety contributed to victimization in the present study, depression did not. The authors attribute this discrepancy to the manner in which they assessed depressive symptoms. Whereas Hodges and Perry (1999) used peer nominations to assess whether children displayed excessive worry (e.g., anxiety) and cried often (e.g., depressed symptoms), the present study used a broad band, self-report measure of psychological functioning to assess whether children experienced symptoms of anxiety or depression. Thus, the peer nomination method employed by Hodges and Perry (1999) may have highlighted the depressive component in a different way (i.e., their peers are interpreting their behaviors as depressive) than the self-report measure used here (i.e., individuals are interpreting their own behaviors as low self-esteem).

Outside of intrapersonal characteristics, the present study identified a number of interpersonal characteristics that were associated with victimization. Children who experienced greater social stress surrounding their relationships with peers endorsed greater victimization. Social stress may be associated with victimization because it serves as a proxy for social support or as an indicator of peer relations. Specifically, children who experience elevated social stress are less likely to have close friends who can assist them in coping with difficult situations and these children may feel anxiety as a result (Reynolds & Kamphaus, 1992). Support from classmates and interpersonal relations were found to be significantly associated with victimization; however, this relationship differed for boys and girls. Low social support among classmates emerged as a significant factor for victimization for males, but not females. The gender difference in the relation between victimization and social support from classmates may be attributed to the differing structure and nature of girls' and boys' friendships and social networks in schools. Research suggests that girls' social networks are more cohesive than boys, allowing for increased intimacy and greater disclosure (Crick & Grotpeter, 1995). Given the cohesiveness of girls' social networks and the relational nature in which girls are more likely to victimize peers (i.e., relational victimization; Crick, Grotpeter, & Bigbee, 1998; Felix & McMahon, 2007; Paquette & Underwood, 1999) it is possible that girls are more likely to experience victimization within their friendships, as opposed to boys. Thus, support from peers may be less important to victimization for girls, because girls are more likely to experience victimization in their friendships as opposed to in the larger peer network (Besag, 2006).

Poor peer relations also were associated with victimization, but this relation was more pronounced for girls than boys. That is, whereas poor interpersonal relations with peers was a significant factor in victimization for girls, having negative peer relations was not as great a factor in boys' risk for victimization. Given the importance girls place on relationships, girls who are unable to relate positively to same gender peers may be at greater risk for exclusion and, consequently, victimization than more socially savvy girls who better understand the inner workings of the peer network (Adler & Adler, 1995).

Limitations of the Study and Directions for Future Research

Several caveats should be considered when interpreting the findings of the current study. Due to the concurrent design of the study, it is not clear whether the significant behavioral difficulties reported by adolescents existed prior to their experiences of victimization or were the result of being victimized by peers. Given the lack of temporal ordering of the variables, causality cannot be inferred. In order to accurately identify the role of interpersonal and intrapersonal behaviors in predicting victimization, the authors recommend that short-term and long-term longitudinal studies be conducted in which intra- and interpersonal characteristics and data on victimization experiences are collected over time. Investigators may consider examining children's social and emotional adjustment and experiences with victimization in late elementary school and compare how these experiences change as the children transition and progress through middle school, when peer aggression and victimization is believed to peak (Seals & Young, 2003). Such information would be particularly useful in determining whether children who exhibit specific psychological and behavior profiles characterized by anxiety, feelings of inadequacy, poor interpersonal relations, and who do not feel supported by their social network are at greater risk of becoming victims of peer aggression.

A second limitation was that the sample used in this study was primarily Caucasian, recruited from three middle schools and one junior high school in rural communities. The inclusion of students from non-urban areas is a strength of this study, as few victimization studies have focused specifically on students from rural communities. However, future studies should include a more ethnically diverse sample of adolescents from rural communities and conduct comparisons between victimization experiences of children from rural and urban community settings. Despite these limitations, this study contributes to the current literature on victimization by identifying the factors that make some children, particularly those in rural communities, vulnerable for being the target of peer aggression, and suggests that, similar to students in other settings, rural middle school students might also pose risks for experiencing victimization.

Implications for School Counselors

School counselors play a vital role in the development and implementation of prevention and intervention efforts to address peer victimization in schools (Blake, 2010). Much of the literature on strategies to reduce peer victimization has focused on school counselors' involvement in program implementation to foster positive school climate (Wigfield, Lutz, & Wagner, 2005) or counseling interventions to reduce bullying once a child has been identified as being victimized (Jacobson & Bauman, 2007). Less discussion has centered on the role of school counselors in implementing early intervention services to prevent peer victimization. Given preliminary evidence that some children may exhibit intrapersonal (e.g., anxiety and feelings of inadequacy) and interpersonal characteristics (e.g., poor social skills, lack of social support from peers) that place them at elevated risk for being victimized and that this relation might vary by a child's gender, school counselors might elect to increase their victimization prevention strategies for certain types of students. For example, school counselors might recommend that girls who appear socially awkward or display interpersonal difficulties participate in counseling groups that emphasize the development of social skills in order to prevent victimization. For boys believed to be at risk for experiencing peer victimization, school counselors might consider inviting participation in counseling groups that focus on fostering alliances and creating friendships, which buffer them against aggressive acts. School counselors can also consult with teachers on how to develop strategies to increase peer support and inclusion in their classrooms (Song & Stoiber, 2008). School counselors can recommend that middle school teachers create inclusive cooperative learning groups by basing group formation on student interests that in turn might foster friendship formation (e.g., "Please gather into groups based on your interests").

School counselors can lead guidance lessons that provide activities for students to learn about moral inclusion and exclusion, which parallels major tenants of peer intolerance for bullying advocated in many anti-bullying prevention programs (Leets & Sunwolf, 2005; Opotow, Gerson, & Woodside, 2005). School counselors can collaborate with history teachers to engage middle school students in discussions on blatant forms of moral exclusion, such as hate crimes, sweatshops, ethnic cleansing, etc., and history teachers can develop lesson plans in which students have to identify when moral exclusion has occurred in history. Then, counselors can collaborate with classroom history teachers by relating historical lessons on moral exclusion to less severe and perhaps more subtle forms moral exclusion within students' immediate social context. School counselors can then help students make conceptual links between moral exclusion and victimization and assist students in identifying what their role is to address or intervene when they observe these acts.

Alternatively, school counselors might consider implementing universal screenings for mental health as a method to identify children at risk for experiencing peer victimization. The identification of such children could be considered a method of early intervention or, if detected early enough, a form of prevention, as it might place school counselors in a unique position to disrupt the cycle of victimization before it starts. In general, universal mental health screening provides a means for early identification of mental health problems through the administration of a screening instrument that is designed to assess psychological or behavioral adjustment difficulties or high-risk symptoms of psychological disorders that students may exhibit (e.g., anxiety; Levitt, Saka, Romanelli, & Hoagwood, 2007). Current data suggests that universal mental health screenings in schools in general leads to improved outcomes for students and a decrease in emotional and behavioral problems (Weist, Rubin, Moore, Adelsheim, & Wrobel, 2007). However, given that mental health problems could be a both a cause and consequence of victimization (Card & Hodges, 2008; Cook, Williams, Guerra, & Sadek, 2010), school counselors might want to administer screening instruments that assess not only student's social and emotional functioning but also their experiences with victimization.

Universal screenings, in the form of brief rating scales that can be administered school-wide, could be used as one tool by school counselors to identify students who display characteristics that place them at risk for victimization. Such screenings could also provide a method to identify children with general psychological adjustment difficulties who are in need of counseling (e.g., children who are experiencing grief after loss of loved one; Dowdy, Ritchey, & Kamphaus, 2010). One example of a screening measure is the BASC-2 Behavioral and Emotional Screening System (Kamphaus & Reynolds, 2007). This is a brief measure, with parent, teacher, and child forms, for use with grades preschool through 12. It takes approximately 5–10 minutes to administer, is available in Spanish, and can be hand scored, computer scored, or scored via scantron. Once students are identified as being at risk for exhibiting mental health problems or experiencing victimization, the school counselor could interview these students to determine whether additional counseling services are needed, such as group or individual counseling, or general social skills training is required. Through the use of universal mental health screening and early intervention, school counselors can be actively involved at the school and individual level in effecting changes that affect the likelihood of victimization for these children. Moreover, the early identification of children with risk factors associated with victimization may provide school counselors with baseline data for monitoring change over time as a result of interventions at the system and individual level.

Conclusion

Evidence is increasing that victimization and bullying are serious problems in schools (Bradshaw et al., 2007; Nansel et al., 2001). The most dramatic findings to date indicate that up to one third of students in middle to high school report either being bullied, being a bully, or both (Nansel et al., 2001). The purpose of this study was to identify critical intra- and interpersonal characteristics that predict victimization, or at least vulnerability to being a victim. Results indicate that factors such as anxiety and feelings of inadequacy are highly associated with a child being victimized. Additional factors, including social stress, peer relations, and level of social support, also were associated with victimization. The students in this study were in sixth through eighth grade, and, in some cases, already may have been victims of bullying at the time of the study. With identification of key characteristics of vulnerability, school counselors may easily implement preventive activities and sup ports as part of school activities. School counselors can take the lead by providing supports and educational programming school-wide, and by providing individual programming to address not only the bullies, but the potential victims. Clearly, additional research is needed in this area as bullying remains a serious issue.

References

Adler, P. A., & Adler, P. (1995). Dynamics of inclusion and exclusion in preadolescent cliques. *Social Psychology Quarterly, 58,* 145–162. doi:10.2307/2787039

Aiken, L. S., & West, S. G. (1991). *Multiple regression: Testing and interpreting interactions.* Thousand Oaks, CA: Sage.

Beck, J. S., Beck, A. T., & Jolly, J. (2001). *Manual for the Beck Youth Inventories of Emotional and Social Impairment.* San Antonio, TX: The Psychological Corporation.

Beggs, J. J., Haines, V. A., & Hurlbert, J. S. (1996). Revisiting the rural-urban contrast: Personal networks in nonmetropolitan and metropolitan settings. *Rural Sociology, 61,* 306–325.

Beran, T. (2009). Correlates of peer victimization and achievement: An exploratory model. *Psychology in the Schools, 46,* 348–361. doi:10.1002/pits.20380

Berger, C., & Rodkin, P. (2009). Male and female victims of male bullies: Social status differences by gender and informant source. *Sex Roles, 61,* 72–84. doi:10.1007/s11199-009-9605-9

Bernstein, J., & Watson M. (1997). Children who are targets of bullying: A victim pattern. *Journal of Interpersonal Violence 12,* 483–498. doi:10.1177/088626097012004001

Besag, V. E. (2006). Bullying among girls: Friends or foes? *School Psychology International, 27,* 535–551. doi:10.1177/0143034306073401

Blake, J. J. (2010). Professional practices related to bullying: Technical report. Texas A&M University.

Blake, J. J., Lease, A. M., Turner, T., & Outley, C. W. (in press). Exploring ethnic variation in the adjustment patterns of aggressive girls. *Journal of Black Psychology.*

Buhs, E. S., Ladd, G. W., & Herlad, S. L. (2006). Peer exclusion and victimization: Processes that mediate the relation between peer group rejection and children's classroom engagement and achievement. *Journal of Educational Psychology, 98,* 1–13. doi:10.1037/0022-0663.98.1.1

Card, N. A., & Hodges, E. V. E. (2008). Peer victimization among schoolchildren: Correlations, causes, consequences and considerations in assessments and interventions. *School Psychology Quarterly, 23,* 451–461. doi:10.1037/a0012769

Carney, J. V. (2008). Perceptions of bullying and associated trauma during adolescence. *Professional School Counseling, 11,* 179–188.

Craig, W. M. (1998). The relationship among bullying, victimization, depression, anxiety, and aggression in elementary school children. *Personality & Individual Differences, 24,* 123–130. doi:10.1016/S0191-8869(97)00145-1

Crick, N. R., & Bigbee, M. A. (1998). Relational and overt forms of peer victimization: A multi-informant approach. *Journal of Consulting and Clinical Psychology, 66,* 337–347. doi:10.1037/0022-006X.66.2.337

Crick, N. R., Grotpeter, J. K., & Bigbee, M. A. (2002). Relationally and physically aggressive children's intent attributions and feelings of distress for relational and instrumental peer provocations. *Child Development, 73,* 1134–1142. doi:10.1111/1467-8624.00462.

Cook, C. R., Williams, K., Guerra, N. G., Kim, T., & Sadek, S. (2010). Predictors of bullying and victimization in childhood and adolescence: A meta-analytic investigation. *School Psychology Quarterly, 25,* 65–83. doi:10.1037/a0020149

Courville, T., & Thompson, B. (2001). Use of structure coefficients in published multiple regression articles: β is not enough. *Educational and Psychological Measurement, 61,* 229–248.

Dodge, K. A., Bates, J. E., & Pettit, G. S. (1990). Mechanisms in the cycle of violence. *Science, 250,* 1678–1683. doi:10.1126/science.2270481

Dowdy, E., Ritchey, K, & Kamphaus, R. W. (2010). School-based screening: A population-based approach to inform and monitor children's mental health needs. *School Mental Health, 2,* 166–176. doi:10.1007/s12310-010-9036-3

Erath, S. A., Flanagan, K. S., & Bierman, K. L. (2008). Early adolescents school adjustment: Associations with friendship and peer victimization. *Social Development, 17,* 853–870. doi:10.1111/j.1467-9507.2008.00458.x

Farrington, D. (1993). Understanding and preventing bullying. In M. Tonry (Ed.), *Crime and justice: A review of research, Vol. 17.* (pp. 381–458). Chicago: University of Chicago.

Foster, S., Rollefson, M., Doksum, T., Noonan, D., Robinson, G., & Teich, J. (2005). *School Mental Health Services in the United States, 2002–2003.* Rockville, MD: Center for Mental Health Services, Substance Abuse and Mental Health Service Administration.

Felix, E. D., & McMahon, S. D. (2007). The role of gender in peer victimization among youth. *Journal of School Violence, 6,* 27–44. doi:10.1300/J202v06n03_03

Gladstone, G., Parker, G., & Malhi. G. (2006). Do bullied children become anxious and depressed adults? A cross-sectional investigation of the correlates of bullying and anxious depression. *Journal of Nervous and Mental Disease, 194,* 201–208.

Graham, S., Bellmore, A. D., & Mize, J. (2006). Peer victimization, aggression, and their co-occurrence in middle school: Pathways to adjustment problems. *Journal of Abnormal Child Psychology, 34,* 363–378. doi:10.1007/s10802-006-9030-2

Hanish, L. D. (2000). Children who get victimized at school: What is known? What can be done? *Professional School Counseling, 4,* 113–120.

Hanish, L. D., & Guerra, N. G. (2000). Predictors of victimization among urban youth. *Social Development, 9,* 521–543. doi:10.1111/1467-9507.00141

Harter, S. (1985). *Manual for the social support scale for children.* Denver, CO: University of Denver.

Hodges, E. V. E., & Perry, D. G. (1999). Personal and interpersonal antecedents and consequences of victimization by peers. *Journal of Personality and Social Psychology, 76,* 677–685. doi:10.1037/0022-3514.76.4.677

Hope, T. L., & Bierman, K. L. (1998). Patterns of home and school behavior problems in rural and urban settings. *Journal of School Psychology, 36,* 45–58. doi:10.1016/S0022-4405(97)00049-6

Horowitz, J. A., Vessey, J. A., Carlson, K. L., Bradley, J. F., Montoya, C., & McCullough, B. (2004). Teasing and bullying experiences of middle school students. *Journal of the American Psychiatric Nurses Association, 10*(4), 165–172. doi:10.1177/1078390304267862

Jacobsen, K. E., & Bauman, S. (2007). Bullying in schools: School counselors' responses to three types of bullying incidents. *Professional School Counseling, 11*, 1–9.

Junger-Tas, J., & Van Kesteren, J. (1999). *Bullying and delinquency in a Dutch school population.* The Hague, Netherlands: Kugler.

Kamphaus, R. W., & Reynolds, C. R. (2007). *BASC-2 Behavioral and emotional screening system.* San Antonio, TX: Pearson.

Klomek, A. B., Marrocco, F., Kleinman, M., Schonfeld, I. S., & Gould, M. S. (2008). Peer victimization, depression, and suicidality in adolescents. *Suicide and Life-Threatening Behavior, 38*, 166–180. doi:10.1521/suli.2008.38.2.166

Kochenderfer-Ladd, B., & Skinner, K. (2002). Children's coping strategies: Moderators of the effects of peer victimization? *Developmental Psychology, 38*, 267–278. doi:10.1037/0012-1649.38.2.267

Kokkinos, C. M., & Panayiotou, G. (2004). Predicting bullying and victimization among early adolescents: Associations with disruptive behavior disorders. *Aggressive Behavior, 30*, 520–533. doi:10.1002/ab.20055

Ladd, B., & Ladd, G. W. (2001). Variations in peer victimization: Relations to children's maladjustment. In J. Juvonen & S. Graham (Eds.), *Peer harassment in school: The plight of the vulnerable and victimized* (pp. 25–48). New York: Guilford.

Ladd, G. W., & Kochenderfer-Ladd, B. (2002). Identifying victims of peer aggression for early to middle childhood: Analysis of cross-informant data for concordance, estimation of relational adjustment, prevalence of victimization, and characteristics of identified victims. *Psychological Assessment, 14*, 74–96. doi:10.1037/1040-3590.14.1.74

Leets, L., & Sunwolf (2005). Adolescent rules for social exclusion: When is it fair to exclude someone else? *Journal of Moral Education, 34*, 343–362. doi: 05/030343-20.

Levitt, J. M., Saka, N., Romanelli, L. H., & Hoagwood, K. (2007). Early identification of mental health problems in schools: The status of instrumentation. *Journal of School Psychology, 45*, 163–191. doi:10.1016/j.jsp.2006.11.005.

Leadbeater, B. J., Blatt, S. J., & Quinlan, D. M. (1995). Gender-linked vulnerabilities to depressive symptoms, stress, and problem behaviors in adolescents. *Journal of Research on Adolescence, 5*, 1–29. doi:10.1207/s15327795jra0501_1

Lopez, C., & DuBois, D. L. (2005). Peer victimization and rejection: Investigation of an integrative model of effects on emotional, behavioral, and academic adjustment in early adolescence. *Journal of Clinical and Adolescent Psychology, 34*, 25–36. doi:10.1207/s15374424jccp3401_3

Marsh, H. W., Parada, R. H., Craven, R. G., & Finger, L. (2004). In the looking glass: A reciprocal effect model elucidating the complex nature of bullying, psychological determinants, and the central role of self-concept. In C. E. Sanders, & G. D. Phye (Eds.), *Bullying: Implications for the classroom* (pp. 63–109). San Diego, CA: Elsevier Academic.

Nansel, T., Overpeck, M., Pilla, R., Ruan, W., Simons-Morton, B., & Scheidt, P. (2001). Bullying behaviors among US youth: Prevalence and association with psychosocial adjustment. *Journal of the American Medical Association, 285*, 2094–2100. doi:10.1001/jama.285.16.2094

Nishina, A., Juvonen, J., & Witkow, M. R. (2005). Sticks and stones may break my bones, but names will make me feel sick: The psychosocial, somatic, and scholastic consequences of peer harassment. *Journal of Clinical and Child Adolescent Psychology, 34*, 37–48. doi:10.1207/s15374424jccp3401_4

Olweus, D. (1993). *Bullying at school: What we know and what we can do.* Cambridge, MA: Blackwell.

Opotow, S., Gerson, J., & Woodside, S. (2005). From moral exclusion to moral inclusion: Theory for teaching peace. *Theory into Practice, 44*, 303–318. doi:10.1207/s15430421tip4404_4

Paquette, J. A., & Underwood, M. K. (1999). Gender differences in young adolescents' experiences of peer victimization: Social and physical aggression. *Merrill-Palmer Quarterly, 45*, 242–266.

Peskin, M. F., Tortolero, S. R., Markham, C. M., Addy, R. C., & Baumler, E. R. (2006). Bullying and victimization and internalizing symptoms among low-income Black and Hispanic students. *Journal of Adolescent Health, 40*, 372–375. doi:10.1016/j.jadohealth.2006.10.010

Perry, D. G., Hodges, E. V. E., & Egan, S. K. (2001). Determinants of chronic victimization by peers: A review and a new model of family influence. In J. Juvonen & S. Graham (Eds.), *Peer harassment in school: The plight of the vulnerable and victimized* (pp. 73–104). New York, Guilford Press.

Reynolds, C. R., & Kamphaus, R. W. (1992). *Behavior assessment system for children: Manual.* Circle Pines, MN: American Guidance.

Reynolds, C. R., & Kamphaus, R. W. (2004). *Behavior assessment system for children* (2nd. ed.): Manual. Circle Pines, MN: American Guidance.

Reynolds, W. M. (2001). *Reynolds adolescent adjustment screening inventory.* Psychological Assessment Resources, Inc., Odessa, FL.

Reynolds, W. M. (2003a). *Bully victimization scale, bully-victimization distress scale, and school violence anxiety scale.* San Antonio: The Psychological Corporation.

Reynolds, W. M. (2003b). *Reynolds bully victimization scales for schools: Manual.* San Antonio: The Psychological Corporation.

Schmidt, M. E. & Bagwell, C. L. (2007). The protective role of friendships in overtly and relationally victimized boys and girls. *Merrill-Palmer Quarterly, 53*, 439–460. doi:10.1353/mpq.2007.0021

Schwartz, D., Dodge, K. A., & Coie, J. D. (1993). The emergence of chronic peer victimization in boys' play groups. *Child Development, 64*, 1755–1772. doi:10.2307/1131467

Schwartz, D., Kelly, B. M., Duong, M. T., & Badaly, D. (2010). A contextual perspective on intervention and prevention efforts for bully-victim problems. In E. M. Vernberg & B. K. Biggs (Eds.), *Preventing and treating bullying and victimization* (pp. 17–44). New York: Oxford University Press.

Seals, D., & Young, J. (2003). Bullying and victimization: Prevalence and relationship to gender, grade level, ethnicity, self-esteem, and depression. *Adolescence, 38*, 735–747.

Song, S. Y., & Stoiber, K. C. (2008). Children exposed to violence at school: An evidence-based intervention agenda for the "real" bullying problem. *Journal of Emotional Abuse, 8*, 235–253. doi:10.1080/10926790801986205

Smokowski, P., & Holland Kopasz, K. (2005). Bullying in school: An overview of types, effects, family characteristics, and intervention strategies. *Children & Schools, 27*(2), 101–109.

Stoody, M. A. (2000). How bullies pick their victims: A systems approach. *Dissertation Abstracts International Section A: Humanities & Social Sciences, 61*(12-A), 4675.

U.S. Census Bureau (2004). State and county quick facts. Retrieved from http://quickfacts.census.gov/qfd/states/48000.html

Wang, J., Iannotti, R. J., & Nansel, T. R. (2009). School bullying among adolescents in the United States: Physical, verbal, social, and cyber. *Journal of Adolescent Health, 45*, 368–375. doi:10.1016/j.jadohealth.2009.03.021

Weist, M. D., Rubin, M., Moore, E., Adelsheim, S., & Wrobel, G. (2007). Mental health screening in schools. *Journal of School Health, 77*, 53–58. doi:10.1111/j.1746-1561.2007.00167.x

Wigfield, A., Lutz, S. L., & Wagner, A. L. (2005). Early adolescents' development across the middle school years: Implications for school counselors. *Professional School Counseling, 9*, 112–119.

The Lived Experiences of a Male Survivor of Intimate Partner Violence

A Qualitative Case Study

Ann Marie Nayback-Beebe and Linda H. Yoder

Domestic violence, or intimate partner violence (IPV) as it has been identified more recently in the literature, has emerged as a significant public health crisis within the United States that affects millions of individuals and families each year. According to the Centers for Disease Control and Prevention (CDC, 2011), IPV exists along a continuum from a single occurrence of violence to continued battering. It is defined as physical or sexual violence, threats of physical or sexual violence, and emotional abuse that occur between two people in a close relationship. In a report by the Department of Justice (DOJ) summarizing the results of The National Violence against Women Survey, Tjaden and Thoennes (2000) estimated the annual incidence of male-to-female perpetrated rape and physical assaults at approximately 4.8 million, and the incidence of female-to-male perpetrated physical assaults at approximately 2.9 million. The National Center for Injury Prevention and Control (2003) cited the annual cost of IPV for direct medical and mental health care costs and lost productivity at approximately $5.8 billion.

Although rates of male-to-female physical IPV have been declining over the past 30 years, the rates of female-to-male physical IPV have remained constant (Douglas & Hines, 2011). From 1994 to 2004, the percentage of males reporting victimization from IPV grew from 48% to 64%; however, men reported they remained more reticent to report IPV than women due to privacy concerns (DOJ, 2007). Furthermore, of the CDC's estimated 24% of dating and marital relationships with acknowledged IPV, nearly half involved reciprocal violence in which both partners were perpetrators of violence (Whitaker, Haileyesus, Swahn, & Saltzman, 2007). Of the intimate relationships reporting only one perpetrator of violence in this same study, women were identi-fied as the physical aggressors 71% of the time.

Purpose

With the increased reporting of female-to-male perpetrated IPV, nurses and other health care providers must appreciate the personal experiences of male survivors of IPV as they cope with, and attempt to leave, an abusive intimate relationship. Therefore, the purpose of this phenom-enological qualitative case study was to explicate the lived experience of a male survivor of IPV and the real-life context in which the violence emerged. By doing so, nurses can more fully empathize with their male patients who report IPV, and provide them with appropriate, supportive care.

The purpose of this phenomenological qualitative case study, analyzed using Colaizzi's (1978) method, was to gain a holistic understanding of the lived-experience of a male victim of intimate partner violence and the real-life context in which the violence emerged.

Relevant Literature

Moderate-intensity female-to-male perpetrated IPV, which typically involves slapping, grab-bing, or pushing, is not a rare occurrence among males in the United States (Caetano, Vaeth, & Ramisetty-Mickler, 2008; Whittaker et al., 2007). In spite of this, the majority of public attention and funding for research, prevention efforts, and intervention programs for IPV has centered on male-to-female perpetrated violence because of obvious sex disparities in rates of victimization (CDC, 2011; World Health Organization, 2005). Research over the last 30 years has focused on exploring why men are most often perpetrators of IPV, why women remain in abusive relation-ships, and how the public health sector can develop effective programs to intervene and protect women from further violence (Gbenekama, 2008). While these research endeavors are critical to explaining IPV from the perspective of female survivors and male perpetrators, they may not be applicable in heterosexual intimate relationships in which the violence is perpetrated unilaterally against the man.

A study of 1,656 male victims of IPV (Coker et al., 2002) found the lifetime prevalence of physical IPV was 5.8%; sexual IPV was 0.2%; and psychological IPV was 17.3%. For the men in this study, the strongest lifetime risk factor for becoming a victim of IPV was a childhood history of physical or sexual abuse by a relative. The strongest risk factor identified for men in a current abusive intimate relationship was a female partner who engaged in heavy alcohol use. The latter finding mirrors findings by Caetano, Vaeth, and Ramisetty-Mikler (2005a), who found heavier drinking among females was associated with recurrent female-to-male perpetrated violence. This study also concluded unidirectional female perpetration and male victimization were highest among couples of mixed ethnicity; however, for male perpetrated violence, these rates were highest among African American and Hispanic couples (Caetano et al., 2005b).

Furthermore, IPV can produce significant short-term and long-term physical and mental health sequelae for its victims. Among possible health consequences of IPV are physical injuries that can lead to disability and death, post-traumatic stress disorder, depression and anxiety, substance use disorders, insomnia, and chronic pain (Caetano et al., 2005a; CDC, 2011; Coker et al., 2002). A U.S. population-based study demonstrated both male and female victims of physical IPV have an increased risk of current poor health, depression symptoms, substance misuse, injury, and development of a chronic medical or mental illness (Coker et al., 2002). When both psychological and physical IPV victimization scores were included in the analysis, these negative health outcomes were associated more highly with psychological, rather than physical, IPV scores. This is of critical importance given the fact men are more likely to report psychological abuse in their intimate relationships, and almost half the women and more than 78% of men in this sample reported being victims of psychological partner violence.

Help-seeking behaviors and experiences of male and female victims of IPV differ as well. In general, studies of help-seeking behaviors in response to IPV demonstrate women are more likely than men to seek help, and for men who do seek help, several barriers must be overcome (Galdas, Cheater, & Marshall, 2005). Barriers explicated in prior qualitative studies of male victims of IPV include community domestic violence (DV) services that do not assist men; accusations by DV hotline personnel that men callers were the actual perpetrators of the violence; police who failed to respond; and a higher burden of proof required within the judicial system to demonstrate male victims were not the perpetrators (Cook, 2009; Hines, Brown, & Dunning, 2007). Results of a study by Douglas and Hines (2011) found men who seek help for IPV victimization have the most positive experiences when seeking help from family, friends, and mental and medical health care providers. Because of identified differences in the prevalence rates of IPV by sex, race, and help-seeking behaviors; a dearth of research on female-to-male perpetrated IPV; and a generalized lack of knowledge and experience by health care providers in recognizing male victims of IPV, gaps exist in the literature. This case study will explicate the lived-experience of a White male victim of physical and psychological IPV.

Method

Study Design
This interpretive, qualitative case study was informed by existential phenomenology for data analysis (Denzin & Lincoln, 1998). This approach was chosen to facilitate an understanding

of the life experiences that radically alter and shape the meanings people give to themselves and their experiences (Denzin, 1989). Three in-depth, semi-structured interviews were conducted over several weeks to answer the following research question: *What is the lived experience of living in and leaving an abusive intimate relationship for a White middle class male?* The in-depth interview has been deemed the most useful means for accessing marginalized individuals within a society, capturing their subjugated voices, and understanding their social reality (Hesse-Biber & Leavy, 2006). According to Munhall (2007), *meaning*, within the context of phenomenology, is the "transaction between an individual and a situation so that the individual both constitutes and is constituted by the situation" (p. 162). Ultimately, meaning is shaped by the individual's *experience* and *perception*. Existential interpretive phenomenology was chosen to facilitate understanding by acknowledging and valuing the meanings a male survivor of IPV ascribed to the experience of living in, and leaving, his abusive relationship. Yin (2003) recommended the qualitative case study design when the researcher wishes to uncover the contextual conditions relevant to the phenomenon under study and as a preliminary step in guiding future research. By employing this method, the researcher can better explore contextual conditions experienced by the participant related to female-to-male unilaterally perpetrated IPV.

Sample

Prior to data collection, institutional review board (IRB) approval was obtained from a large Midwestern state university. The participant for this study met the following inclusion criteria: (a) he self-reported that he was a survivor of physical abuse, emotional abuse, verbal abuse, harassment, and/or humiliation by a current or former intimate partner; (b) the violence he experienced occurred in the context of a heterosexual relationship; and (c) he was either in the process of leaving, or had left, the relationship in which the violence occurred. Initial contact with the participant was gained through a mutual acquaintance. The participant was a 44-year-old male who self-identified his race as "Caucasian" and his socioeconomic status as "middle class." He had been divorced for 2 years after an 18-year marriage to the alleged female perpetrator of the violence. There were no reports of reciprocal violence, and the last episode of abuse occurred 1 year after his divorce was finalized. He has subsequently remarried.

Study Procedure

The purpose of the study was explained to the participant and he was given an opportunity to ask questions prior to the formal interview. Although the need for formal written consent was waived by the IRB, the purpose, risks, benefits, and confidentiality of the study were explained and verbal consent for participation was obtained at the beginning of the audio-recorded interview. Given the social stigma experienced by male victims of IPV, careful steps were taken to ensure participant confidentiality, and these steps were shared with the study participant prior to data collection. Data were collected in a private location of the participant's choosing, and limited demographic information about the participant and perpetrators involved in the alleged violence was collected. Involved persons were assigned a pseudonym within the transcripts to protect their identity.

The interview began with the researcher addressing the participant as follows: *Tell me how this all began for you ... when you identified that you were in a relationship involving violence ... when you decided to leave ... and what that experience of living in and leaving the relationship was like.* The semi-structured interview relied on a set of questions to guide the conversation while also allowing the interviewee the latitude of exploring topics relevant to the phenomenon of interest. Prior research involving male participants in verbal discourse revealed that, unless participants are solving a specific problem, they often find it difficult to engage in discourse about their personal feelings (Shaw & Beauchamp, 2000). Maintaining this awareness, additional probing questions ("Can you explain that further?" and "Do you remember how that made you feel at the time?") were used to engage the respondent in a continued reflective discussion.

Three 1-hour, semi-structured, in-depth interviews were conducted over a 1-month period. Each interview, which lasted approximately 1 hour, was recorded and transcribed verbatim. The researcher compared the interview transcripts word for word against the recorded interviews to ensure accuracy of the data before destroying the interview tapes.

Data Analysis

As the transcribed interviews were verified to ensure accuracy, the researcher made memos in the margins to capture the emotion behind the participant's words as well as any initial gestalt identified by the researcher. Transcripts were analyzed using Colaizzi's (1978) phenomenologic technique for data analysis. Initially the transcripts were read and reread to gain an overall impression of the data. Immersion within the transcripts and phenomenological reflection allowed the researcher to develop a sense of the whole of the interview as a context for the experience. Significant words, phrases, and sentences were extracted in relation to the phenomenon and grouped into clusters. Subsequently, clustered statements were read alongside the transcript for the next level of abstraction: delineation into themes to illuminate meanings that reflected the experience of the male survivor of IPV as he was living in and leaving the abusive relationship. To ensure trustworthiness of the data and achieve rigor, the investigator's research peers revalidated theme clusters. The participant then reviewed the identified themes and was able to validate the findings as a reflection of his own experience.

Findings

Interviews revealed three separate themes and one overarching theme related to the lived experience of a male survivor of IPV as he was living in and leaving an abusive intimate relationship. The two identified themes related directly to the experience of living within the abusive relationship are *confrontation from within* and *confrontation from without.* The identified theme related to the experience of leaving the abusive relationship was *realization and relinquishment.* Finally, the overarching theme of living within and leaving the abusive relationship was *living with a knot in your stomach.*

Theme 1: Living in the Relationship—Confrontation from Within

The survivor described his *confrontation from within* as his experience of continually having to define and redefine his values and beliefs according to the actions of the perpetrator. He described setting boundaries according to his value system for what he considered acceptable and moral behavior within an intimate relationship. Then, subsequently he would move or ignore those boundaries once the abuser violated the boundary or "crossed the line." This constant process of confronting his value system, and redefining or denying it, produced a state of internal turmoil.

> I was starting to think what is it that I have done to cause her to act the way she does. What could I have done differently that would have changed it? Should I not have confronted her on the boyfriend, you start to question your own beliefs and values. And then you get to the point where you play the scenario in your head, over and over and over again. Trying to figure out … to make some sense of it … and there is no sense to be made.

The survivor described a time when he defined his value by "drawing the line," the perpetrator "crossed the line," and the survivor redefined his value by "moving the line." Initially, the survivor did not believe in divorce and admitted:

> *Drawing the Line:* I was raised to believe that marriage is sacred and sanctified by God as an institution between a man and a woman that, um, fidelity is one of the requirements for that … to be faithful and monogamous. That while you had problems, you never went across that line … So I was quite in a conundrum where I don't believe in divorce, but yet my wife either has cheated or was in the process of cheating … Even in that, I never had any inkling that I was going to leave her, um, I said this is something that can be solved with counseling. We are just not communicating. We are not getting it. She's at a point in her life where she's, we got married young, and she's sowing some wild oats …

> *Crossing the Line:* I said, "Well, Joan, we've been married almost 18 years now, what's his name?" She said, "What do you mean?" I said, "You don't just walk

away from an 18-year marriage, a brand new house, and four kids for nothing. What's his name? I deserve to know his name." And she said, "His name is Tom."

Moving the Line: We can get divorced, and we can do this the easy way, or the hard way. I said for the kid's sake, I'd rather do it the easy way. But you know, there is no easy way to get divorced.

A second example was the survivor's initial belief that IPV was a private family issue. As the level of violence escalated, this belief changed.

Drawing the Line: She went screaming around to the front yard, and the girls got all upset. They all started running around crazy, too. I just wanted to get the whole thing diffused and get in the house. The neighbors were out there, and I just didn't want to make a scene in front of the others. I just wanted to get inside and just deal with it as a family.

Crossing the Line: And, uh, then she hauled off and slapped me right there in front of the bank, on the side of the face. Then I reached out to deflect, and she came around and hammer-fisted me on the side of the face again.

Moving the Line: So I called the police thinking, there would be some security cameras outside that had probably caught it on tape. But there weren't. So the police officer came and took my report.

Theme 2: Living in the Relationship—Confrontation from Without

The second theme identified by the co-creator as part of the experience of living in an abusive relationship was *confrontation from without*. For the survivor, it began with those outward actions or experiences that precipitated the abusive behavior in the relationship.

So it was generally those sorts of things that precipitated it. Whenever I confronted her on something she was doing that I didn't agree with.

So I confronted her with that (phone calls from men at the house, men showing up at the house with flowers) and it became verbally abusive. And then I confronted her with our phone bill with the phone number of the guy that had been calling the house with all the phone calls ... And she came up from behind and grabbed my arm, scratched it and twisted it, and grabbed the phone out and said, "This is my damn phone and you can't have it." Made this big scene in the front yard ...

These actions led to excusing, discounting, ignoring, or diminishing the abuse by the abuser, the survivor, or witnesses to the abuse. These things combined to produce a state of constant external turmoil in the survivor's life.

Then I reached out to deflect and she came around and hammer-fisted me on the side of the face again. Again ... shock. It hurt but it wasn't like, I'm gonna go unconscious type of hurt, so you know ...

Oftentimes she would use the same terminology with the kids, calling them idiots, and I would tell her it was inappropriate to call the kids idiots because it would affect their self-esteem. She would say, "They know I am just kidding."

And while that was pending, we were in a phone conversation discussing transferring the kids during Christmas ... She got upset with me and she said, "You know, I'd like to just shoot you in the face." I said, "Is that a threat? Did you just threaten to kill me?" She said, "No, that's a promise." And, uh, I said, "Holy cow." And so after we had been talking, our youngest daughter Mallory had been standing right beside her. I got on the phone to talk to her and said "Mallory, did you hear what mom just said?" She said, "Yeah, Dad, what did you do to make her so mad?"

She got up, came across the table, grabbed my face with her fingernails, and rammed my head up against the brick wall that I was sitting up against. It just stunned me. I mean, it wasn't like a I'm going to crush your head into the wall type hit, it was more like a dismissive, grab my face, and push it up against the wall.

Theme 3: Leaving the Relationship—Realization and Relinquishment

The identified theme related to the experience of leaving the abusive relationship was *realization and relinquishment*. It identified the point when the survivor of IPV realized his value boundaries had been nullified repeatedly and he lived in a state of constant internal and external turmoil.

For this survivor, alienation from the children by the abuser was the singular defining value that had been violated and could not be tolerated. This led to the realization that there were only two choices: to live within the relationship with acceptance of the violence, or to change his own behavior and leave the abusive relationship. *Realization* describes when the process of leaving began from within the survivor.

> I bear hugged her. Restrained her and said, "I've had enough of it, and I'm not going to take it anymore."

> No, um, it wasn't just violence; it was also alienation from the children. Now the children hated me ... and every chance she got to use profane language in front of me and the children ... calling me a (expletive) in front of the children ... I've been referred to as the sperm donor, the biological father, every name that you can imagine ... um, have been used by both my ex-wife and my children.

> There is nothing you can do...you are hopeless in this situation. There are no good options. Literally, every decision you make is a bad one. You're left with, which one is the least bad decision to make. Because every one of them is going to hurt and is going to have a profound impact on your life and the lives of the people that you love.

> It just floors me ... just cause you're a man doesn't mean you need to get beat on ... any more than a woman should get beat on. It's just not right.

Relinquishment occurred once the survivor had accepted his choice, the confrontation from within ceased, and he had begun to advance emotionally. As he was leaving the relationship, he described the male perspective of attempting to make sense of the violence and experiencing a tremendous sense of loss.

> And then you get to the point where you play the scenario in your head, over and over and over again. Trying to figure out ... to make some sense of it ... and there is no sense to be made. It's not a logical thing. It doesn't make any sense.

> ... the fact that how, as a man that has been through physical abuse, and verbal, and mental ... um, it's very ... it makes you ... it takes something away from you. It's a violation that is hard to describe. It's a sense of loss, a sense of lack of control over your own circumstances.

So there was an immense sense of loss, fear, and I really felt bad for our children. Because they are really the ones that got the short end of the stick.

These three themes (*confrontation from within*; *confrontation from without*; and *realization and relinquishment*) illustrated the experience of living in and leaving an abusive intimate relationship for a White, middle-class male. From these themes, an overarching theme emerged that summarized the entire experience.

Living with a Knot in Your Stomach

Throughout the interview, the co-creator often spoke of a visceral response to the confrontation from within and without, as well as when he realized he had to leave the relationship:

> That knot in your stomach, again, it's like panic. You don't know why or what or what you've done. You just know that something in the back of your mind is going, "What in the world is going on?" I'm in this story that it's, like, I'm outside looking in. I don't believe what is happening. You know, it's so surreal.

When the investigator revalidated the themes with the co-creator, his final remark was how the knot only subsided once he had finally relinquished any control over the relationship and responsibility for the abuse that transpired.

Discussion

In this study, the researchers explored the experience of a White male survivor of IPV while he was living in and leaving an abusive relationship. The experience expressed by this person was one of continual confrontation within and surrounding him. The confrontation from within involved a repeated process of defining boundaries for his personal value and belief systems regarding appropriate behavior within an intimate relationship. This was followed by redefining or negating these boundaries once they were violated by the individual perpetrating the abuse. The confrontation from without involved a continued pattern of verbal, emotional, and physical abuse that was diminished, denied, or dismissed by him or others. This is consistent with research that showed IPV is a gradual process that involves a slow disintegration of a victim's sense of self (Alabama Coalition Against Domestic Violence ([ACADV], 2008). Ultimately, the environment became so stressful and chaotic that the person began to doubt himself, and lose his sense of reality and self-esteem (Cook, 2009).

For this co-creator, the experience of leaving an abusive relationship was a journey that encompassed both realization and relinquishment. As he noted as a male survivor of IPV, "... it takes something away from you. It's a violation that is hard to describe." A number of factors have been identified within the literature that makes leaving an abusive relationship difficult. Some of these include the demasculinization that occurs as a result of being a male survivor of domestic violence and, for the participant, the shame of divorce (Cook, 2009; Hines et al., 2007). Moreover, survivors often believe it is in the children's best interest to keep the family together. Leaving is a process that may take seven or more attempts to complete (ACADV, 2008). For this individual, the marital relationship ended before there was a formal realization and acceptance of the abuse. The abuse continued for over a year after his divorce. After the divorce, only the validation of witnessed emotional, verbal, and physical abuse by friends and family allowed entrance of the survivor into other healthy, intimate relationships. Then he was able to come to full realization and relinquishment.

This qualitative study shared the silenced voice of a White middle class male survivor of IPV as he was living in and leaving an abusive relationship. After the investigator completed data analysis, theories were reviewed for applicability to this middle-class male survivor of IPV. Of the seven explanatory theories for victimization cited in the literature (Brewster, 2002), only the Psychological Theory resonated with this co-creator's experience. The Psychological Theory suggested self-blame, denial, loyalty to the sanctity of marriage, and feelings of responsibility for helping the perpetrator contribute to the ongoing cycle of victimization for him.

Finally, the confrontation from both within and without, as well as the overarching theme of *living with a knot in your stomach,* explicated the body's physical response to stress and violence that has been cited within the stress and coping literature (Lazarus & Folkman, 1984). For example, chronic stress has been implicated in the development and exacerbation of multiple diseases, such as major depression, cardiovascular disease, HIV/AIDS, and cancer (Cohen, Janicki-Deverts, & Miller, 2007). Additionally, this supports findings by Coker and colleagues (2002) that for men and women, higher psychological IPV scores were associated more strongly with poorer physical and mental health.

Future Research

The use of the qualitative case study method was appropriate for gaining insight into the experience of a male survivor of unilateral IPV and elucidating areas for further research. Further qualitative studies using a larger sample size would enable a richer, more inclusive description of the experience of living in and leaving an abusive relationship for male victims. A larger sample should include heterosexual men across the spectrum of age, socioeconomic status, and race to shed light on the differences of experience in living in and leaving relationships involving abuse for men.

Nursing Implications

Medical-surgical nurses work in a variety of patient care settings where they observe the interpersonal dynamics between patients and their family members. The additional stress of illness and/or hospitalization can precipitate further strain on intimate relationships and expose signs of intimate violence between patients and their family members. Based on the positive help-seeking experiences of male victims of IPV in the medical and mental health care environment (Douglas & Hines, 2011), nurses should be involved actively in identification of and screening for the presence of IPV in the lives of male and female patients. Intimate partner violence screening of all patients for abusive experiences, regardless of sex, should be in place. Nurses must realize both men and women can be victims of IPV. A perceptive understanding of IPV, empathy for victims, and knowledge of local resources are essential for nurses to function as advocates in the medical-surgical arena.

Conclusion

Use of an interpretive qualitative paradigm allowed the experience of a White male middle class survivor of IPV to be revealed. The experience was filled with an overwhelming accumulation of confrontation that emanated from within the survivor of violence and surrounding him. To leave the relationship, the survivor moved from a realization that the abuse was happening on multiple levels and was not going to change, to relinquishment of control over the circumstances of the relationship. Based on the thematic findings of this qualitative research study, further research is needed to reflect theories of victimization as they pertain to males across race and socioeconomic status and to identify risk factors for male survivors of IPV that would make identification easier and interventions more salient for nurses in both inpatient and outpatient settings. Nurses must understand that IPV occurs in the lives of both men and women.

References

Alabama Coalition Against Domestic Violence (ACADV). (2008). *Barriers to leaving.* Retrieved from http://www.acadv.org/barriers.html

Brewster, M. P. (2002). Domestic violence theories, research, and practice implications. In L. R. Roberts (Ed.), *Handbook of domestic violence intervention strategies* (pp. 23–48). New York, NY: Oxford University Press.

Caetano, R., Vaeth, P. A., & Ramisetty-Mikler, S. (2005a). Drinking, alcohol problems and the five-year recurrence and incidence of male to female and female to male partner violence. *Alcoholism: Clinical and Experimental Research, 29,* 98–106.

Caetano, R., Vaeth, P. A., & Ramisetty-Mikler, S. (2005b). Unidirectional and bidirectional intimate partner violence among White, Black, and Hispanic couples in the United States. *Violence and Victims, 20,* 393–406.

Caetano, R., Vaeth, P. A., & Ramisetty-Mikler, S. (2008). Intimate partner violence victim and perpetrator characteristics among couples in the United States. *Journal of Family Violence, 23,* 507–518.

Centers for Disease Control and Prevention (CDC). (2011). *Understanding intimate partner violence: Fact sheet.* Retrieved from http://www.cdc.gov/ViolencePrevention/pdf/IPV_factsheet-a.pdf

Cohen, S., Janicki-Deverts, D., & Miller, G. E. (2007). Psychological stress and disease. *Journal of the American Medical Association, 298,* 1686–1687.

Coker, A. L., Davis, K. E., Arias, I., Desai, S., Sanderson, M., Brandt, H. M., & Smith, P. H. (2002). Physical and mental health effects of intimate partner violence for men and women. *American Journal of Preventative Medicine, 23,* 260–268.

Colaizzi, P. (1978). Psychological research as the phenomenologist views it. In R. Valle, and M. King, (Eds.), *Existential phenomenological alternatives for psychology.* New York, NY: Oxford University Press.

Cook, P. W. (2009). *Abused men: The hidden side of domestic violence* (2nd ed.). Westport, CT: Praeger.

Denzin, N. (1989). *Interpretive interactionism.* Newbury Park, CA: Sage.

Denzin, N., & Lincoln, Y. S. (1998). *Strategies of qualitative inquiry.* Newbury Park, CA: Sage.

Douglas, E. M., & Hines, D. A. (2011). The help-seeking experiences of men who sustain intimate partner violence: An overlooked population and implications for practice. *Journal of Family Violence, 26,* 473–485.

Gbenekama, D. G. (2008). Male reports of abuse in domestic violence on the rise. *Proquest Dissertations and Theses, 0208*(0391). (AAT No. 1454090)

Galdas, P. M., Cheater, F., & Marshall, P. (2005). Men and health help-seeking behavior: Literature review. *Journal of Advanced Nursing, 49,* 616–622.

Hines, D. A., Brown, J., & Dunning, E. (2007) Characteristics of callers to the domestic abuse helpline for men. *Journal of Family Violence, 22,* 63–72. doi:10.1007/s10896-006-9052-0

Hesse-Biber, S. N., & Leavy, P. (2006). *The practice of qualitative research.* London, England: Sage.

Lazarus, R. S., & Folkman, S. (1984). *Stress, appraisal, and coping.* New York, NY: Springer.

Munhall, P. (2007). *Nursing research: A qualitative perspective* (4th ed.). Sudbury, MA: Jones and Bartlett.

National Center for Injury Prevention and Control. (2003). *Costs of intimate partner violence: Against women in the United States.* Atlanta, GA: Centers for Disease Control and Prevention.

Shaw, E., & Beauchamp, J. (2000). Engaging men in counseling: Issues for female therapists. *Psychology in Australia, 6,* 26–34.

Tjaden, P., & Theonnes, N. (2000). *Full report of the prevalence, incidence, and consequences of violence against women.* Research Report. Washington, DC: National Institute of Justice and the Centers for Disease Control and Prevention.

U.S. Department of Justice (DOJ). (2007). *Intimate partner violence in the U.S.* Retrieved from http://www.nij.gov/topics/crime/intimate-partner-violence/

Whitaker, D.J., Haileyesus, T., Swahn, M., & Saltzman, L. S. (2007). Differences in frequency of violence and reported injury between relationships with reciprocal and nonreciprocal intimate partner violence. *American Journal of Public Health, 97,* 941–947.

World Health Organization. (2005). *Multi-country study on women's health and domestic violence against women.* Geneva, Switzerland: World Health Organization.

Yin, R. K. (2003). *Case study research: Design and methods* (3rd ed., Vol. 5). Thousand Oaks, CA: Sage.

Chapter 10: Concluding Remarks

This chapter has brought us full circle to some of the most timely and relevant issues and concepts within the field of victimology studies. We have seen here the importance of examining the concept of crime victimization from multiple perspectives that account for the interplay between personal traits and vulnerabilities, contextual elements of individual routine and social environment, and various cultural constraints and biases. The theoretical constructs and research studies presented have provided a heuristic understanding of the need to build sound criminal justice policies and practices that account for an integrated arrange of responses that address the varied and diverse needs of victims of crime. Criminal offending does not occur in a vacuum without consideration of the context of the crime, offender traits and personality, and the various sociocultural influences on human behavior. Likewise, the experience of victimization is a paradox of circumstances, situational variations, and individual vulnerabilities that all must be studied and analyzed in order to develop a more comprehensive approach in the development of victim services that shape and direct the course of future research development.

CONCLUSION

The collection of readings we have examined throughout this book have brought us to a closer, more introspective understanding of the terminologies and dimensions associated with victimology studies. We have seen that although the term "victim" has many different aspects and meaning in our society, the field of victimology has advanced a more comprehensive, scientific approach in studying the relationships among victims of crime, criminal offenders, and agents of the criminal justice system. These dynamics also do not exist in a vacuum but rather, are shaped by the larger sociocultural context and meanings attached to the definition of crime and crime victims.

Our navigation through this series of readings included a look at the global complexity of crime victimization from an international perspective, as we took on a comparative approach in the analysis of the many facets of the field of victimology. From this foundation, the policy challenges in defining victimization as well as developing interventions for the restoration of victims of crime are properly addressed from a philosophical and practical standpoint. This level of analysis also finds its way in the clarification of the myriad of issues pertaining to the intricate connections between the micro- and macro-level considerations in explaining crime victimization when seeking to integrate the theoretical literature in constructing a dynamic connection between criminal offending and crime victimization, and the relationship between both.

The field of victimology reveals to us an empirical dedication to addressing questions concerning the treatment of crime victims in various social contexts. From this study, we have become better informed of the roles of police officers, prosecutors, judges, and other agents of criminal justice in providing a wide-ranging response to victims of crime that restores to them a sense of control over their lives, in a manner that is emotionally sensitive to their social, psychological, physical, and emotional needs. This, in turn, has impacted decades of social activism in the advancement of victims' rights dedicated to advancing laws and protections to ensure that victims of crime are treated fairly and with dignity and the evolution of practices such as restorative justice designed to heal, empower. and restore victims of crime in a manner that accounts for their unique traits and experiences with crime.

Finally, we have seen the pivotal role that victimology as a discipline has played in creating a knowledge base that supports a multidimensional approach when addressing the various needs of individuals impacted by crime as well as advocating for changes that can reduce the risk of criminal offending and victimization. Moving forward, our goal is to continue to apply the concepts and models developed form this field of expertise, in order to integrate various paradigms of theory and practice that can serve as the momentum for years to come in expanding our study of crime victimization and adequately addressing victims' needs.